TOURING IN
South Africa

To Charlene, with my love

To Dad, Have a lovely birthday 1992,
Lots of love from
Jenny, George & Kim xxx.

TOURING IN
South Africa

MAXWELL LEIGH

STRUIKHOF PUBLISHERS

Struikhof Publishers (Pty) Ltd

An operating division of The Struik Group (Pty) Ltd,
Struik House, Oswald Pirow Street,
Foreshore, Cape Town, 8001

Registration no: 71/09721/07

First published by C. Struik (Pty) Ltd 1986
First published by Struikhof Publishers (Pty) Ltd 1989
Second impression 1990
Third impression 1991

The following photographers kindly provided material for this
book:
B Breakey (© Struikhof) – 50, 51, 68
J R Dickson – pages 4-5; 54, 56, 103, 113, 184, 192, 240, 243
Durban Publicity Association (Gonsul Pillay) – 183
A Elliott – pages 68-69
Frontline Features – pages 118-119
K Gerhardt – 16, 18, 20, 73, 82, 102, 175, 185
R Johannesson – 13, 28, 67
P John (© Struikhof) – page 1; 53, 58, 60, 61, 62, 66, 69, 74,
76, 83, 86, 87, 91, 92, 93, 100, 101, 108, 109, 110, 115, 116, 119,
120, 122, 133, 136, 137, 138, 139, 140, 142, 143, 149, 150, 151,
152, 153, 155, 156, 157, 160, 161, 162, 163, 164, 165, 166, 167,
174, 177, 178, 181, 182
M Leigh (© Struikhof) – 19, 21, 23, 24, 26, 32, 34, 42, 43, 44,
48, 52, 55, 70, 71, 75, 79, 81, 89, 95, 96, 99, 104, 105, 106,
111, 114, 117, 118, 123, 128, 129, 130, 131, 134, 135, 141, 144,
146, 147, 154, 171, 172, 173, 180, 186, 189, 195, 200, 203, 207,
209, 216, 220, 233, 235, 236

Dr H F le Roux – 63, 77
J Levy – 98, 107
National Parks Board – 90, 221, 223, 225, 226, 227
H Potgieter – pages 2-3; page 8; pages 10-11; 1, 2, 3, 4, 5, 6,
7, 8, 9, 10, 11, 12, 14, 15, 17, 25, 27, 29, 30, 31, 35, 36, 37, 38,
39, 40; pages 40-41; 41, 45, 46, 47, 49, 57, 65, 72, 78, 80, 94,
97, 112; pages 98-99; 124, 125, 126, 127, 132, 159, 168, 169,
176; pages 146-147; 187, 188, 190, 191, 193, 194, 196, 197,
198, 199, 202, 204, 205, 206, 208, 210, 211, 212, 213, 214;
pages 168-169; 215, 217, 218, 219, 222, 224, 228, 229, 230,
231, 232, 234, 237, 238, 239, 241, 242, 244
S Robertson, FIP – 121, 158, 170, 201
L W Smuts – 64, 85
South African Tourism Board – 22, 59, 84, 88, 145, 148, 179
Stellenbosch Farmers' Winery – 33
Copyright remains with the above photographers unless stated
otherwise.

Designed by Abdul Latief Gallie
Maps by Institute of Cartographic Analysis, Stellenbosch
University
Photoset by McManus Bros (Pty) Ltd, Cape Town
Reproduction by Unifoto (Pty) Ltd, Cape Town
Printed and bound in Singapore

ISBN 0 947458 19 0

ACKNOWLEDGEMENTS

Writers whose works have been consulted either as sources of information or of leads in the search for information in the compilation of *Touring in South Africa* include many of the contributors to the *Standard Encyclopaedia of Southern Africa*; John Bond *(They were South Africans)*; L E O Braack *(The Kruger National Park)*; T V Bulpin *(Discovering Southern Africa)*; Jose Burman *(Waters of the Western Cape, The Little Karoo, The False Bay Story, The Cape of Good Intent, Wine of Constantia, Coastal Holiday)*; A P Cartwright *(Valley of Gold)*; David Coulson and James Clarke *(Mountain Odyssey in Southern Africa)*; I D du Plessis *(The Cape Malays)*; Aubrey Elliott *(The Magic World of the Xhosa)*; Basil Holt *(They Came our Way)*; W P U Jackson *(Wild Flowers of the Western Cape, Wild Flowers of Table Mountain)*; Graham Knox *(Estate Wines of South Africa)*; Cecily Niven *(Jock and Fitz)*; J J Oberholster *(Die Historiese Monumente van Suid-Afrika)*; Thomas Pakenham *(The Boer War)*; Brian Rycroft and Ray Ryan *(Kirstenbosch)*; Patricia Storrar *(Portrait of Plettenberg Bay)*; Molly D'Arcy Thompson *(Forgotten Corners of the Cape)*; Eric Turpin *(Basket Work Harbour)*; and Eric Vertue *(Travels with Eric Vertue)*.

Gratitude is expressed to them all as well as to the many who in other ways have helped or encouraged me, particularly my wife who, with her almost infallible 'bump' of locality, acted as my chauffeur for most of the 50 000 km that had to be travelled and assumed the role of secretary, arranging schedules, booking accommodation, managing the exchequer and checking every distance and turn in the route directions as each of the 83 tours was completed.

And, if the decision had been mine, I could not have chosen a more patient, generous and meticulous editor than Leni Martin. To her and to Peter Borchert, Editorial Director of Struik, who gave me this absorbing assignment, my thanks are unbounded.

SYMBOLS & ABBREVIATIONS

N1	National road		Road with tunnel		Alternative tour route
R40	Major provincial road		Bridge		Route direction
	Minor provincial road		Gate	✳	Place of interest
	Untarred road	△ 2675	Spot height in metres	🏛	Historical place of interest
●●●●●●	Walking trail		River with waterfall	✕	Battlefield
	Cableway		River with dam or lake	Ⓥ	Viewing point
	Railway with tunnel		Non-perennial watercourse	✈	Airport or airfield
	Railway with station or siding		Dry pan		Border control post
	International boundary		Lighthouse		
	Independent state boundary		Nature reserve or park	Abbreviations in the text:	
	Provincial boundary		Scenic part of the route	SP – signpost	
	Urban area		Tour route	NM – National monument	

The seven regions into which South Africa has been divided for the purposes of this book are shown on the map below and can be colour-matched with the chapter headings on the page opposite. Towns indicated on the map are the starting points of tours in the relevant chapters. The contents list opposite gives the tour number, the name of the tour, its starting point and the number of the page on which it can be found.

The distance given at the beginning of each tour is the approximate length of the tour, to the nearest 10 km.

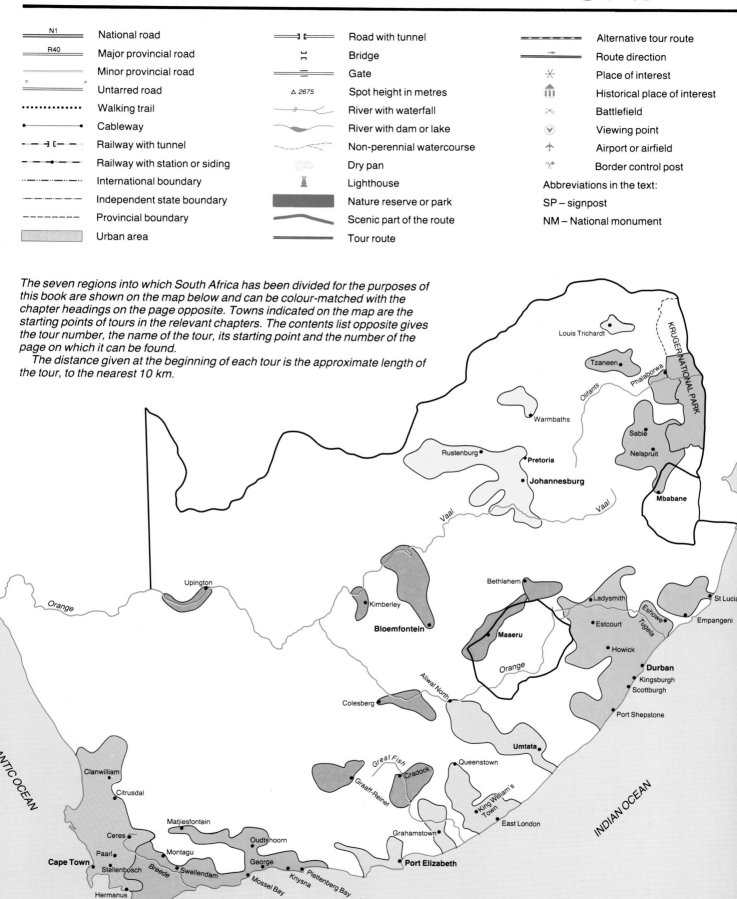

CONTENTS

INTRODUCTION

Luxuriant tropical forests and waterless wastes, mountains of breathtaking grandeur and savanna plains reaching from one horizon to the other, long golden beaches and wave-pounded rocky coastlines – all combine to form the scenic kaleidoscope that is South Africa. And a miscellany of cultures, from the earliest history of man, have made their marks upon the landscape, have erected simple dwellings or stately buildings representative of a gracious age, have carved ways through the mountains and tamed the land with agriculture. Wherever the wanderer roams in this land of vast and seemingly empty spaces, there is something of unique interest or incomparable beauty.

The carefully planned routes in *Touring in South Africa* are intended to help the traveller find and appreciate some of the areas of fascination often missed in a country of such great distances that there is usually a tendency to speed from point of departure to destination. There are times, too, when holiday-makers and business visitors, feeling that all sources of interest and appeal in a centre have been exhausted, wish to explore the surrounding countryside but hesitate about which direction to take. It is hoped that this book will assist their explorations and facilitate the discovery of much that is unknown, even to many of those who have lived in the region all their lives.

All of the 83 self-contained tours in the book can be completed in a day, although some, inevitably, involve more travelling than others. All, too, are 'circular' in that they start and end in the same town, but in a few instances it has proved impossible to avoid retracing the route to a certain extent. Each tour is accompanied by an easily-read map, detailed route directions, descriptions of the most interesting aspects of the region and full-colour photographs of some of the features to look out for.

Preparation of the book entailed about 50 000 km of motoring, during which every relevant distance and route direction was logged as meticulously as possible. But roads are constantly being reconstructed, sometimes even rerouted, and cartographers readily acknowledge that a map is out of date the day it is published. Where a change has occurred in a road included in any of these tours it is hoped that new direction signs along the way will enable the traveller to make the necessary adjustments to the route and still find his course without difficulty. It is also true that the odometers of different cars frequently vary from one to another, and this may manifest apparent discrepancies in the distances given in the route directions. The differences will be insignificant over one or two kilometres, but over long distances the odometer factor should be borne in mind.

Every tour has been tested in an ordinary sedan car of 1,6-litre engine capacity or less, and no roads included have been found too rough for safe travel, although it may be inadvisable to use some after heavy rain. Where a detour to a feature of special interest or beauty entails a really rough ride, some comment on the condition of the road is included.

Ensuring that all tours start and finish in the same town has resulted in some being longer than might otherwise have been planned. For this reason an early start will give maximum time for relaxed enjoyment, avoid a rush towards the end of a long tour, and minimise the possibility of having to miss out what, because it is perhaps the best, has been saved for last. Taking to the road in good time is also advisable for tours that include long stretches of untarred road or routes through mountainous regions with winding passes that merit concentration and demand careful driving. A preliminary perusal of a tour before setting out will, therefore, be worth the trouble.

Approaching the popular resort at the mouth of the Mtata River

CHAPTER ONE
The Western Cape

CITY VIEWS

Short though it may be, a tour from Cape Town to Camps Bay – via Tafelberg Road and Signal Hill – affords captivating views of the city and allows for a cableway trip up Table Mountain.

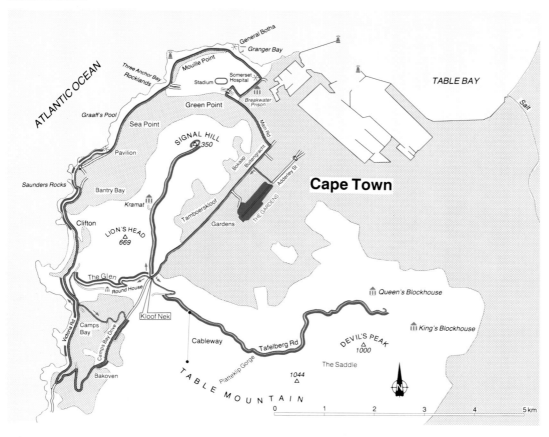

CAPE TOWN The materialistic Dutch East India Company, at whose behest Jan van Riebeeck established a replenishment depot on the shore of Table Bay in 1652, cared not that Sir Francis Drake had proclaimed the Cape of Good Hope the fairest seen in the whole circumference of the earth. The location of the victualling station halfway between the Netherlands and the company's interests in Asia was purely functional, its beauty incidental. And yet for 250 years Cape Town was no more of a blemish on the landscape than was necessary and indeed one of the loveliest cities in the world. Sadly, twentieth century 'progress' has destroyed much of the Mother City's charm, although in more recent years people who care have been heeded and much that is of historical and architectural worth is now being preserved.

From the foot of Government Avenue (NM) at the mountain end of Adderley Street drive north-westward up Wale Street and after 500 m turn left (SP Cableway) into the Buitengracht (the 'outer canal', once the north-western limit of Cape Town). The Buitengracht is also the south-eastern limit of the

exclusively Muslim area of Bokaap, which extends up the slopes of Signal Hill between Strand and Carisbrook streets.

BOKAAP (NM) – or the Malay Quarter – is an area once occupied by white craftsmen to which many Muslim slaves gravitated after the

emancipation in 1834. It has, as well as several mosques, the greatest concentration of pre-1840 architecture in South Africa and many of the buildings have been carefully restored in recent years.

1. Table Mountain with its 'cloth' of cloud dominates Cape Town

Follow the Buitengracht into New Church Street (SP Kloof Nek) which after another 600 m runs into Kloof Nek Road. At the Kloof Nek traffic island 3,5 km from Adderley Street take the first exit to the left (SP Tafelberg Road) and reach the lower cableway station 1,5 km further on.

TABLE MOUNTAIN CABLEWAY The 1 244 m-long cableway, which lifts passengers from 366 m to 1 067 m above sea level in five minutes, was opened in 1929 and since then has conveyed more than 5 million trippers safely up the mountain. The cars operate half-hourly between 08h30 and 18h00 in the winter months and between 08h30 and 22h30 during the summer season, wind permitting.

TABLE MOUNTAIN (NM), the best-known of South Africa's mountains, is 1 086 m above sea level at its highest point, Maclear's Beacon, which is a 50-minute easy walk from the upper cableway station. The first recorded ascent was in 1503 by the Portuguese navigator Admiral Antonio de Saldanha, who named the mountain 'Taboa do Cabo', 'the Table Head'. As recently as 400 years after the admiral's climb there were only six known routes up the mountain, but today there are more than 300. From Table Mountain a 50-km range reaches southward to Cape Point, forming the backbone of the Cape Peninsula. This mountain chain is a botanist's paradise, with roughly 2 250 plant species, some of which are found nowhere else in the world. And, although hunters have exterminated all the big game from the mountain, there are still dozens of species of small fauna. There is even a patch of land, about the size of a soccer field and known only to a handful of lepidopterists, on which the world's only colony of a certain species of butterfly exists.

Continue south-eastward along Tafelberg Road, originally the Contour Path, reaching Platteklip Gorge – the most direct and one of the easiest rambles up Table Mountain – 1,5 km from the lower cableway station, and the path up to The Saddle between Table Mountain and Devil's Peak 900 m further on. There are viewpoints all along Tafelberg Road, which is open to private vehicles as far as the turning circle 5,5 km from the lower cableway station. From the circle one may walk further along the Contour Path, taking routes down from it to the Queen's Blockhouse or up to the King's Blockhouse.

BLOCKHOUSES The King's Blockhouse (NM) and what remains of the Queen's Blockhouse were components of the fortifications built

2. From Signal Hill Robben Island is seen beyond Sea Point

by General Sir James Craig at the start of the first British occupation of the Cape in 1795.

Return to the Kloof Nek traffic island, take the third exit to the left (SP Signal Hill Road) and drive 1,5 km to the path (left) to one of six kramats of great significance to Cape Muslims.

KRAMATS The western Cape's 'sacred circle' of six kramats – tombs of pioneer holy men – are at Constantia, Oudekraal near Hout Bay, Signal Hill where there are two, Robben Island and Faure. Muslims living within the 'circle' believe it protects them from fire, famine, plague, earthquake and tidal waves. Devout adherents of Islam keep the graves at the kramats covered with many sheets of expensive, brightly coloured material, and Muslims about to start the *hadj*, or pilgrimage to Mecca, regard a visit to each shrine in turn an act of special merit.

Drive 2 km further to the Signal Hill parking area for wonderful views over Sea Point of the Atlantic Ocean, Robben Island and Blouberg beyond.

SIGNAL HILL This fell – the 'rump' stretching away from Lion's Head – was once the vantage point used for the exchange of messages between the city and approaching or departing ships. A shot is still fired from a signal gun on the hill to mark noon every day except Sunday.

LION'S HEAD The summit of this striking 669-m sugarloaf mountain, which from some angles can be said to resemble the head of a lion, was in days long past the station of a signalman who fired a cannon to herald the approach of ships so that

farmers could have wagons of victuals standing by when anchor was dropped in Table Bay. For those energetic enough to take the relatively easy walk to the top, Lion's Head affords an incomparable 360° panorama of sea, mountain and city.

Return to the Kloof Nek traffic island, turn sharp right (SP Round House) and drive down Kloof Road through The Glen to reach the left turn to the Round House after 1,2 km.

ROUND HOUSE The Round House, once used by Governor Lord Charles Somerset as a shooting lodge, occupies a site on which a circular building of some sort has stood since before 1813. In the nineteenth century the Round House became an hotel and amusement resort and since 1904, when it was acquired by the Cape Town Municipality, a succession of lessees have maintained its reputation for refreshment.

Continue down The Glen and make a U-turn left into Lower Kloof Road at the stop street 900 m from the Round House. Run into Victoria Road (M6) in Camps Bay 600 m from the stop street.

CAMPS BAY When his ship left Table Bay in 1779 young Friedrich von Kamptz of Mecklenburg remained behind and married the widowed owner of the farm Ravensteyn on which this delightful maritime suburb has since developed. By the time Von Kamptz sold the farm to the Dutch East India Company in 1781 Ravensteyn was known as the Baai van Von Kamptz and the name, albeit corrupted, has survived.

Bear left into Strathmore Road 100 m after joining Victoria Road, turn left into Sedgemoor Road after another 100 m and left again (SP

Kloof Nek) into Geneva Drive 700 m further on to drive through the prime residential area of Camps Bay. After 900 m turn right into Camps Bay Drive, left into Houghton Road 2,3 km further on and right into Victoria Road in Bakoven – probably named because of an oven-shaped boulder at the water's edge – after another 500 m. Curve northward round the cove at Bakoven, run back into Camps Bay 900 m after rejoining Victoria Road and into Clifton 1,8 km further on.

CLIFTON Originally emergency housing after World War I, the earliest bungalows on the hillside at Clifton were regarded as 'movable summer cottages'. Although they are on municipal land which may not be bought, these attractive homes have now virtually become 'fixed' property. The four Clifton beaches far below Victoria Road are famous for their sunbathing bikini belles.

Continue into Bantry Bay and 4,7 km after rejoining Victoria Road turn left into Sea Cliff Road to run steeply down to the popular tidal pool at Saunders Rocks. At the traffic island 600 m from Saunders Rocks take the first exit left into Beach Road at Sea Point.

SEA POINT The 4-km Sea Point beachfront of promenade, lawns, playgrounds, rock gardens and tidal pools was once the 'front garden' of a pleasant stretch of homes and a few hotels but is now dominated by high-rise blocks of expensive apartments. The area has been called Sea Point ever since Captain Sam Wallis, master of one of Captain James Cook's vessels, quartered his men here to escape a smallpox epidemic which afflicted Cape Town when the explorer's flotilla spent some time in Table Bay in 1776.

Continuing along Beach Road, pass the Sea Point Pavilion with its swimming pool and restaurant 600 m from the traffic island; Graaff's Pool, a spot for sunbathing in the buff behind a concrete wall – but for men only – 800 m from the Pavilion; the Cape Town studios of the SABC (right) 600 m from the pool; and the cove at Rocklands after another 100 m. Turn left at the traffic lights 500 m further on to remain in Beach Road at Three Anchor Bay. Pass the Green Point lighthouse (NM), the country's first lighthouse when it was built in 1824, 500 m from the traffic lights and reach the *General Botha*, South Africa's Merchant Navy Academy, at Granger Bay 1,2 km further on.

GENERAL BOTHA This training establishment was originally accommodated in the former Royal Navy cruiser HMS *Thames* at moorings in Simon's Bay. It moved ashore, first to Simon's Town and then to Gordon's Bay before being transferred to Granger Bay in 1963.

Continue 800 m along Beach Road and turn right into Portswood Road at the west gate of the docks (left) and the crenellated Somerset Hospital (NM) on the right. Built in 1862, this was the country's first doctor-training hospital. After 200 m pass the high wall around the old Breakwater Prison (NM) where up to a thousand convict labourers employed on the Table Bay breakwater were accommodated. Turn left (SP City) to the traffic circle 800 m from the Somerset Hospital, take the second exit and turn left into Main Road (M61) at the traffic lights 200 m from the circle. Turn right into the Buitengracht at the traffic lights 1,4 km further on, after 600 m turn left into Wale Street and drive 500 m back to the starting point at the top of Adderley Street.

3. Blocks of flats overlooking Clifton beaches

ROUND THE CAPE PENINSULA

When winter gales buffet this southern extremity of Africa the name 'Cabo de Tormentoso' given it by early European explorers is totally descriptive. But in balmy weather the Cape Peninsula is truly beautiful.

4. Chapman's Peak drive

CAPE TOWN See Tour 1.

Leave central Cape Town from the intersection of Adderley and Strand streets, driving south-eastward on Eastern Boulevard and passing the Castle after 400 m. After another 500 m fork left (SP Muizenberg, Southern Suburbs, Airport, N2) and 2,6 km further on pass the Queen's Blockhouse (see Tour 1) on the slopes of Devil's Peak. Continue on Eastern Boulevard as it becomes Rhodes Drive at Groote Schuur Hospital 4,4 km from the tour start.

GROOTE SCHUUR HOSPITAL
Groote Schuur, the teaching hospital of the University of Cape Town's Medical School, had a high reputation in many countries even before it captured public imagination all over the world with

the first transplant of the human heart in 1967. The hospital has frequently been enlarged since it was opened in 1938.

Fork right (SP Muizenberg, M3, M4) 4,7 km from the tour start to reach Mostert's Mill 400 m further on.

MOSTERT'S MILL See Tour 3.

Continue southward, passing on the right the memorial to Cecil Rhodes on the slopes of Devil's Peak and reaching the University of Cape Town 6,6 km from the start of the tour.

UNIVERSITY OF CAPE TOWN
The South African College – out of which UCT, the country's first teaching university, developed – was founded as a private venture by churches and citizens in 1829. After occupying rented premises in the

city the college acquired its first building in 1841 and its first residence and women students in 1887. University status was granted in 1918, and in 1928 most of the faculties moved from the city to the present campus, one of the most beautiful university sites in the world. With 10 faculties, the university now has some 12 000 students and a teaching staff of over a thousand.

Fork right (SP Muizenberg, M3) into Edinburgh Drive 10,4 km from the tour start, follow the M3 signs and at the T-junction after another 12,4 km turn left (SP Muizenberg). After 900 m turn right (same SP) at the traffic lights on to Main Road, and 500 m further on right again (SP Kalk Bay via Boyes Drive) off Main Road.

BOYES DRIVE runs parallel to the main through-route from Lakeside to Kalk Bay but, being at far greater elevation, affords fine views of the popular yachting lake Sandvlei with the Marina da Gama on its eastern shore, of Muizenberg, Kalk Bay and the only two independent municipalities on the Cape Peninsula, Fish Hoek and Simon's Town.

MUIZENBERG was originally a Dutch East India Company cattle post established about 20 years after Jan van Riebeeck founded the first white settlement at the Cape in 1652. It later became a military post whose commander, Sergeant Willem Muijs, gave his name to the place ('Muijs se berg', or 'Muijs's mountain'). After the Battle of Muizenberg, the *coup de grâce* in the British capture of the Cape in 1795, the settlement became a

5. Noordhoek beach curves round towards Kommetjie

staging post between Cape Town and Simon's Town. With its long, safe bathing beach Muizenberg developed into South Africa's premier holiday resort and retained this status for many years.

KALK BAY The fishing harbour of Kalk Bay was named by virtue of the lime ('kalk') obtained by burning seashells in a kiln at this spot for the thick whitewash which not only enhanced the appearance of the early Cape buildings, but also protected their primitive bricks against weathering. A whaling station at Kalk Bay lasted only a short time, but the fishing conducted from the little harbour has survived for more than two centuries.

Fork left (no SP) 7 km after turning on to Boyes Drive to descend steeply to Kalk Bay. At the traffic lights turn right (SP M4, Cape Point) back into Main Road, pass the right turn to Clovelly 1,4 km further on and run into Fish Hoek.

FISH HOEK A bay where the Dutch East India Company maintained a fishing station, Fish Hoek was permanently settled only in 1818 when Governor Lord Charles Somerset granted land on condition that the right to fish remain free, that no winehouse be opened and that only white people be entitled to live, trade and own land here. These conditions have been diligently observed throughout the residential municipality's development. In 1927 scientific attention focused on Fish Hoek when the remains of a Pleistocene or Holocene human who lived about 10 000 years ago were found in Peers Cave behind the town.

Fork left (SP Simon's Town, Cape Point) on to the M4 at the traffic circle 2,8 km from the Kalk Bay traffic lights, pass Glencairn and after curving round Simon's Bay reach Admiralty House on the left 6,7 km from the circle.

SIMON'S TOWN For almost 200 years Simon's Town has been a naval base, although its history as an anchorage goes back to 1743 when it was made the winter roadstead of the Dutch East India Company. The British used it as a bridgehead when they occupied the Cape in 1795, and in 1814 made it the South Atlantic Station of the Royal Navy, which it remained until the port was taken over by the South African Navy in 1957.

Turn left 1,7 km from Admiralty House to the Martello Tower.

MARTELLO TOWER This martello tower, which houses exhibits of the South African Naval Museum, was built by the British the year after

6. Kalk Bay harbour lies between St James, in the foreground, and Fish Hoek

they occupied the Cape in 1795 and it is thought by some authorities to be the oldest British fort of its kind in the world.

Continue on the M4, swinging inland at Smitswinkel Bay, and after 10,7 km turn left (SP Cape Point) to drive 13,9 km through the Cape of Good Hope Nature Reserve to Cape Point.

CAPE OF GOOD HOPE NATURE RESERVE
This reserve was started in 1936 to preserve the indigenous flora and fauna of the Cape Peninsula. Though exposed, often windswept and less verdant than the rest of the Peninsula, the 7 750-ha reserve has as many plant varieties as there are in the whole of Britain. In addition to the predominating protea and heath varieties there are numerous endangered species and a few that are found nowhere else. The fauna includes eland, bontebok, rhebok, grysbok, springbok, baboons, porcupine, ostrich and zebra.

CAPE POINT
The principal road through the reserve ends near the summit of Cape Point in a parking area, whence visitors may walk or take a bus up the steep slope to the highest point. From this position the panorama is breathtaking, encompassing the whole of False Bay and the Hottentots Holland Mountains beyond. By far the most dramatic view, however, is downward, for the vantage point is 209 m above the rocks on to which the Atlantic Ocean crashes. The southernmost spot of the Peninsula is not, as many believe, Cape Point but the Cape of Good Hope, 2,3 km to the west and about 200 m further south, to which there is an access road 2,7 km from the parking area.

Return from Cape Point to the T-junction north of the entrance to the reserve, turn left (SP Cape Town via M65, Scarborough, Kommetjie, Chapman's Peak), after 8,7 km fork left (same SP) on to the M65 and drive through the seaside hamlet of Scarborough. Pass Witsand and carry straight on at the crossroads 9,5 km from the last fork

to come abreast of Slangkop lighthouse. Look northward to see the Sentinel guarding the entrance to Hout Bay and to the west of the Sentinel the 653-m Karbonkelberg. Turn left (SP City via Chapman's Peak, Ou Kaapse Weg) 12,1 km from the last crossroads and 1 km further on left again (SP Noordhoek, City via Chapman's Peak) on to the M6.

CHAPMAN'S PEAK
Between 1915 and 1922 the dream of the Administrator of the Cape, Sir Frederick de Waal, to have a road from Hout Bay to Noordhoek was put into effect by the engineering genius of Robert Glenday. The road ascends from Noordhoek and curls round two-thirds of Chapman's Peak, clinging in innumerable curves to the steep slopes of the mountain until it reaches its highest point 160 m almost sheer above the sea. From the railed observation stage at this point the drive descends gradually as it traverses the seaward slopes of Noordhoek Peak and drops to below the 100-m contour after winding along the foot of Constantiaberg, ensuring a splendid, ever-changing vista of sea and mountains as it snakes along the rocky coast to Hout Bay.

From the observation stage at the summit of Chapman's Peak drive 4,3 km before turning right to the ruins of East Battery, just off the road.

EAST BATTERY
These Dutch East India Company fortifications (NM) – built between 1781 and 1784 under the supervision of the French garrison sent to the Cape after France, supporting the American colonies, declared war against Britain – were strengthened in 1794 and had the blockhouse added by the British after they occupied the Cape in 1795.

From East Battery drive into Hout Bay, turn left (SP Harbour, Boat Trips) 2 km from the battery into Princess Street and then right (SP City) into Victoria Avenue 900 m further on, or left to visit the harbour.

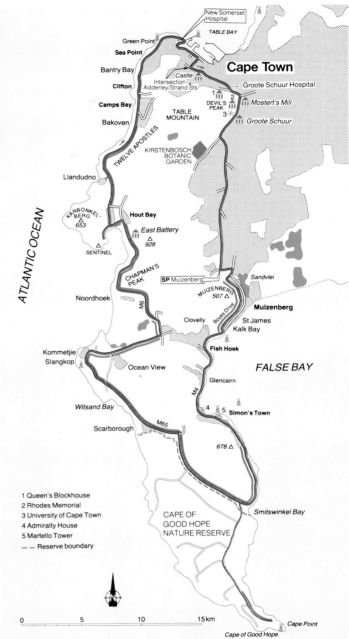

1 Queen's Blockhouse
2 Rhodes Memorial
3 University of Cape Town
4 Admiralty House
5 Martello Tower
– – – Reserve boundary

0   5   10   15km

HOUT BAY,
where there is a thriving fish and rock lobster processing industry supported by a substantial fleet of trawlers and other craft, was named in 1652 by Jan van Riebeeck, whose men had found the area round the bay heavily wooded ('hout' meaning 'wood'). The bay is a popular yachting, boardsailing and powerboating resort, and a converted naval launch, hugging the spectacular coastline, carries trippers between the harbour and Table Bay docks.

Return to Victoria Avenue, drive northward on to the M6 to climb Hout Bay Nek and reach the left turn to the well-to-do residential resort of Llandudno after 4,7 km. Continue 6,9 km to Bakoven and

1,5 km further on enter the maritime suburb of Camps Bay at the foot of the Twelve Apostles, the western buttresses of Table Mountain. Fork left 9,3 km from the turn-off to Llandudno to drive along Victoria Road above the famous bathing beaches of Clifton, reach fashionable Bantry Bay 2,2 km from the fork and 800 m further on turn left into Sea Cliff Road. Follow this road into Sea Point's Beach Road and continue along it as it hugs the coast. At the Somerset Hospital 6,1 km after turning into Sea Cliff Road, turn right into Portswood Road. Turn left (SP City) 800 m further on, take the first turn left out of the traffic circle reached after another 100 m and follow the M6 signs back to the city.

3
70 km

HISTORIC BUILDINGS AND STATELY HOMES

Along tree-lined roads that wind through attractive suburbs the traveller comes across some of the Cape Peninsula's most historic buildings and stately homes of the early Cape Dutch period.

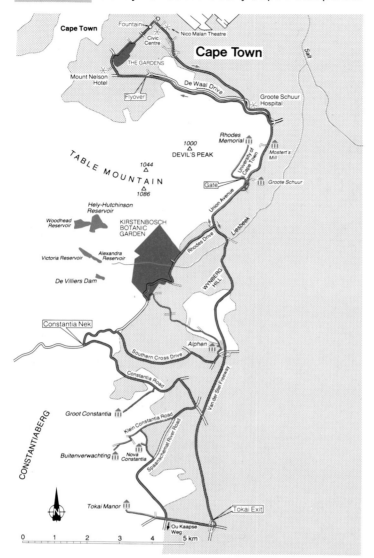

CAPE TOWN See Tour 1.

Drive 200 m towards the sea from the fountain in the Heerengracht, turn right (SP S Suburbs via Eastern Boulevard) into Hertzog Boulevard and, after passing the Nico Malan Theatre (left) and the Cape Town Civic Centre (right) 300 m further on, join the Eastern Boulevard (SP N2, Airport, M3 Muizenberg) 900 m from the Heerengracht. Pass the Good Hope Centre on the right 1,1 km from the Heerengracht and Groote Schuur Hospital (see Tour 2) 4,2 km from the same point. Fork right (SP M3, M4, Muizenberg) on to Rhodes Drive 4,9 km from the Heerengracht and reach Mostert's Mill 900 m further on.

MOSTERT'S MILL In about 1796 Gysbert van Reenen built the mill (NM) which is known by the name of his son-in-law, Sybrandt Mostert. Van Reenen sold Mostert the farm Welgelegen with the mill, which the Netherlands Government helped restore to working order in 1936.

Continuing southward along Rhodes Drive, pass the memorial to Cecil Rhodes on the slopes of Devil's Peak after 200 m and the University of Cape Town (see Tour 2) 300 m further on. Pass the western entrance to Groote Schuur (left), once the home of South Africa's Prime Ministers and soon to become a museum, 1,5 km from Mostert's Mill.

GROOTE SCHUUR The Groote Schuur estate took its name from the barn ('schuur') built for storage during Jan van Riebeeck's regime at the Cape and subsequently

converted into a house. It was bought in 1891 by Cecil Rhodes who bequeathed part of it to the nation and part to the University of Cape Town. The part left to the nation includes the stately home, Groote Schuur, recreated for Rhodes by Sir Herbert Baker out of the fire-ruined converted barn; Westbrooke, the mansion which became the official residence of successive Governors General and State Presidents; and the land on which Mostert's Mill stands. Paddocks in other parts of the estate not occupied by the university are grazed by herds of antelope and wildebeest. And brooding over all from the imposing memorial on the slopes of Devil's Peak is the bronze statue of Rhodes.

Bear left (SP Hoofweg, Rhodes Memorial) immediately after passing the entrance to Groote Schuur, turn right (SP Rhodes Memorial) under the bridge at the traffic lights and left (no SP) after another 200 m. Drive 1,8 km through parkland to the memorial, from which there is a panoramic view over the Southern Suburbs and the Cape Flats to the Hottentots Holland Mountains. Return to Rhodes Drive, which now becomes Union Avenue. Fork right (SP Muizenberg, Bishopscourt, M3) at the traffic lights 2,1 km further on and cross the Liesbeek River immediately afterwards into Edinburgh Drive. Follow the M3 signs, the route continuing as the Van der Stel Freeway, take the Tokai exit 9,5 km from the right fork and turn right (SP Tokai) into Tokai Road at the stop street 500 m further on. At the intersection after another 1,5 km, where the SP to the left indicates Ou Kaapse Weg, cross straight over and drive another 1,5 km to Tokai Manor.

TOKAI MANOR There are those who claim to have seen the ghost of a horseman riding up the steep, curved steps of the unusually high stoep and in through the imposing front door of gracious Tokai Manor (NM). Legend has it that the rider is the shade of a youth who, for a bet one night, undertook the ride, circling guests seated at the table in the dining room and meeting his death when his horse stumbled on the way down the steps. The 1796 U-shaped manor, the facade of which is believed to have been designed by the distinguished architect Louis Thibault, has two gables at either side and two at the back as well as the main one in front. It is privately occupied and therefore not open to the public, but

7. Rhodes Memorial, designed by Sir Herbert Baker

the sight of its attractive proportions from the entrance gate is worth the deviation. The estate was probably named after Tokaj in Hungary where the famous Tokay (Tokaji) wine is produced.

Return to the last intersection, turn left into Orpen Street (M42), left into Nova Constantia Road 2,5 km further on and, after another 500 m, left again through white gateposts into Nova Constantia.

NOVA CONSTANTIA This homestead, which was dilapidated when the Tupperware Company bought it in 1972 and restored it to use as its South African headquarters, was completed, probably also to Thibault's design, in 1808 for Lambertus Colijn on land that had once been part of the great Bergvliet estate.

Turn left into Nova Constantia Road, left again into Klein Constantia Road after 600 m, left yet again (SP Buitenverwachting) after another 300 m and then right into the avenue of oaks leading to Buitenverwachting another 200 m ahead.

BUITENVERWACHTING For Arend Brink the property he bought here in 1794, another part of the original Bergvliet estate, must have been 'beyond expectations', for that is what 'Buitenverwachting' means. The beautiful manor house in its spacious, oak-dotted surroundings of vineyards, forest and hillsides retains much of the rural charm it had when it was completed in 1796. While the homestead is privately occupied, the public is welcomed to other parts of this reminder of an age of gracious living, particularly the restaurant on the estate.

Return to Klein Constantia Road and turn right. After 1,5 km turn left into Spanschemat River Road and, at the traffic lights 800 m further on, left again (SP Hout Bay, Groot Constantia) into Ladies Mile Road. Turn left into Constantia Road 1 km from the traffic lights, left again (SP Groot Constantia) after another 1 km, reach the first gate to Groot Constantia 600 m further on and pass through the second 400 m still further.

GROOT CONSTANTIA (NM) is one of the three parts into which the original Constantia estate, granted to Simon van der Stel by the Dutch East India Company in 1685, was divided in 1712. The other parts were Klein Constantia and Bergvliet, both of which were subsequently subdivided. Thus Hoop op Constantia, Nova Constantia, Buitenverwachting and the land on which the privately-owned Klein Constantia homestead stands were all once part of Van der

Stel's domain. Groot Constantia was acquired in 1778 by Hendrik Cloete who made the estate famous for its wine and employed Thibault and the sculptor Anton Anreith to build the wine cellar, the pediment of which is regarded as one of the country's great art works. The same team is also believed to have converted Van der Stel's modest homestead into a manor house of distinction. This building was destroyed by fire 40 years after the government bought the estate in 1885, but it was recreated by the architect F K Kendall and the result is acknowledged as the finest of all old Cape houses.

Return to Constantia Road, turn left and drive 3,2 km to the traffic circle at Constantia Nek. Take the exit SP M63 via Rhodes Drive, turn right into Southern Cross Drive 1,7 km from the circle, and right again (no SP) into Brommersvlei Road at the stop street 2,9 km further on. Turn left (no SP) into Constantia Main Road after another 800 m, left (SP Hohenhort, Alphen) 200 m from the last turn and left again into Alphen Drive 300 m still further to reach Alphen (left) after 100 m.

ALPHEN An estate once noted for its Burgundy, Sauvignon Blanc and Claret, Alphen was first granted in 1714 to Theunis Dirk van Schalkwyk and he was followed by a succession of owners until in 1854 it was bought by Dirk Cloete, a descendant of whom still owns it. By 1965 the encroachment of spreading Cape Town had whittled away so much of the estate that it was unable to grow enough grapes to remain viable. Happily, though, the remaining 5,4 ha of Alphen together with its H-shaped 1753 manor house were declared a national monument in 1973. In its delightfully rustic setting the homestead, one of the few double-storeyed houses of its type that have been preserved, is now a top-class hotel, and those who visit it are able to indulge briefly in the standard of gracious living its owners have maintained for more than two centuries.

Turn left out of Alphen into Alphen Drive, fork left into Hohenhort Avenue at the traffic island 1,2 km from Alphen and carry straight on (SP Cape Town via Kirstenbosch) 800 m from Alphen Drive. Turn left (SP City via Rhodes Drive) 1 km further on, right (SP Kirstenbosch) into Rhodes Drive at the stop street after 400 m, left (SP Kirstenbosch) 1,3 km from the stop street and finally left into Kirstenbosch 700 m further on.

KIRSTENBOSCH, headquarters of the National Botanic Gardens of South Africa, was owned by the Dutch East India Company in the

8. Mostert's Mill

early days of the Cape settlement and remained government property until 1811 when it passed into private ownership. It was bought by Cecil Rhodes in 1895 to further his desire to preserve the eastern slopes of Table Mountain and bequeathed by him to the nation. The National Botanic Gardens took it over in 1913 and, dedicated as its staff is to the cultivation and study of indigenous South African flora, it has become one of the world's major botanic gardens. Although the floral displays are most spectacular between August and November, there is infinite delight to be experienced in following its many pathways at any time of the year.

Turn left out of Kirstenbosch back on to Rhodes Drive and left again (SP City) into Union Avenue 1,8 km further on. Bear left (SP Stad, M3) on to De Waal Drive 5,1 km after turning into Union Avenue and, after another 3,2 km, turn left into Jutland Avenue immediately before the road ahead passes under a flyover. Bear right (SP City via Orange Street, Sea Point) at the traffic lights 1 km further on, pass the Mount Nelson Hotel on the left after 400 m and turn right after another 400 m into Grey's Pass which curves into Queen Victoria Street. Turn right into Wale Street (with St George's Cathedral on the right) 700 m from the last turn and then left into Adderley Street 100 m further on.

9. Tokai Manor

4
280 km

IN AND OUT OF THE SWARTLAND

Anything but black nowadays, the Swartland has lost much of the renoster bush which seasonally turns blackish and so gave the name to this sometimes green, sometimes golden region of wheatlands.

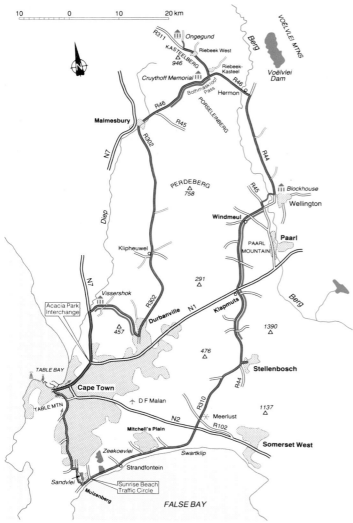

CAPE TOWN See Tour 1.

Leave Cape Town south-eastward on Table Bay Boulevard (N1) from the seaward end of the Heerengracht and after 11,5 km take the exit SP Goodwood West, Acacia Park, Malmesbury. Veer left (SP N7, Malmesbury) 100 m further on and turn right (SP Durbanville) off the N7 on to the Vissershok Road after another 11,2 km.

VISSERSHOK ROAD This road from the N7 to Durbanville takes its name from the farm Vissershok on the southern bank of the Diep River 1,3 km from the N7. The farm, once owned by Hendrik Visser, has a 1768 gabled homestead surrounded by white walls with a huge gate in each of them, and was originally a Dutch East India Company post where stock was kept and wheat was grown. The Diep River, which rises near Riebeek-Kasteel and runs into the sea through the wide, shallow lagoon called Rietvlei, used to be deep enough for fishing boats to be rowed from the mouth to the company's post at Vissershok.

Drive 12,9 km through a beautiful undulating area of dairy farms and wheatlands to the traffic circle at the municipal offices in Durbanville.

DURBANVILLE, once an outspan inelegantly named Pampoenkraal but renamed in 1836 in honour of Sir Benjamin D'Urban, is a dormitory town which has retained much of its rural character and boasts a fine racecourse run by the Durbanville Turf Club.

At the traffic circle at the Durbanville Municipal Offices take the second exit into High Street, turn left into Wellington Road at the traffic lights at the second intersection 400 m further on and drive through Durbanville on the R302. Cross the railway at Klipheuwel after 18,4 km and turn left (SP Malmesbury) to remain on the R302 400 m further on.

KLIPHEUWEL, which takes its name from the stony hill nearby, is the site of a Department of Telecommunications ship-link radio installation established by the Marconi company in 1924.

Pass the Klipheuwel ship-link radio installation (right) 2 km from the last turn and drive 27 km before

10. The farmhouse near Riebeek West in which Jan Smuts was born

crossing the Diep River into Voortrekker Road in Malmesbury.

MALMESBURY, originally Swartlandskerk but renamed in 1829 by Governor Sir Lowry Cole in honour of his father-in-law, the Earl of Malmesbury, is the heart of the wheat-producing Swartland. Not surprisingly, therefore, it has one of the biggest flour mills in the country, and the farmers' cooperative based in the town is South Africa's largest wheat distributor. A mineral spring near the municipal swimming pool used to be valued for its therapeutic qualities but is no longer exploited. Of historic interest in Malmesbury are the Nagmaalput ('communion well') in a corner of Lewis Stores in Piet Retief Street, the old church building of the Swartland congregation, a Victorian home at 14 Faure Street and the New Apostolic church in Voortrekker Road.

Turn right (SP Paarl, Riebeek-Kasteel, Wellington) into Rainier Street 150 m north of the Diep River, turn right (SP Paarl, Riebeek-Kasteel) into Piet Retief Street 250 m further on, turn left (SP Riebeek-Kasteel, Hermon) on to the R46 after another 3,9 km and drive towards the south-eastern end of Kasteelberg. Continue for 11,3 km to reach the top of Bothmaskloof Pass – between Kasteelberg in the north and Porseleinberg in the south – overlooking Riebeek-Kasteel and one of Cape Town's major water storage dams, Voëlvlei, at the western foot of the Voëlvlei Mountains. Beyond these mountains can be seen the Witsenberg range, often snow-capped in winter. Turn left to the Cruythoff Memorial 700 m beyond the top of the Bothmaskloof Pass.

PIETER CRUYTHOFF, Corporal of Midshipmen and Superintendent of Agriculture at the Cape settlement, whom Commander Jan van Riebeeck sent north with an expedition of 15 men to make contact with the Namaqua Hottentots in 1661, passed this way and gave Kasteelberg its original name, Riebeek-Kasteel. This memorial in his honour records that his party observed 13 'horses', which were probably zebra, five rhinoceros and thousands of hartebeest grazing in the beautiful valley to the east.

Continue 2,7 km north-eastward on the R46, turn left (SP Riebeek-Kasteel, Riebeek West, Moorreesburg) on to the R311 and pass the right turn into the village of Riebeek-Kasteel 1 km further on. Drive 4,5 km north-westward to the Dutch Reformed church in Riebeek West.

RIEBEEK WEST In a lovely setting among vineyards in the eastern shadow of the Kasteelberg, Riebeek West is distinguished by having produced two South African Prime Ministers: General Jan Christiaan Smuts, who was born on the farm Ongegund (NM) 3 km north-west of the village, and Dr Daniël Francois Malan, whose birthplace was the farm Allesverloren. They attended the same school and Smuts was at one time the Sunday School teacher of the boy from Allesverloren who was to become his arch-rival in politics.

Continue 3 km north-westward on the R311 from the Riebeek West Dutch Reformed church, turn right on to PPC (Pretoria Portland Cement) property and obtain a permit from the company's office to visit Ongegund at the edge of a quarry. The unpretentious yet appealing white-walled and thatched farmstead in which Smuts was born is reached by turning left off the road to the cement works 1,6 km from the R311 and left again 300 m further on. Return from Ongegund to the R311, turn left and drive 8,5 km through Riebeek West and past Riebeek-Kasteel to the R46 before turning left again (SP Hermon, Gouda, Wellington). After 8,5 km pass the left turn into the rural village of Hermon – named after Mount Hermon which is alluded to in Deuteronomy – and after another 1 km turn right (SP Wellington) on to the R44. Pass the Wellington Blockhouse (see Tour 11) after 22,5 km and reach the traffic circle at the north-western end of Main Street in Wellington 400 m further on.

WELLINGTON See Tour 11.

From the traffic circle take the R44 (SP Malmesbury), cross the Berg River after 1,6 km and fork left 100 m from the river. Turn left (SP Paarl) on to the R44/R45 3 km further on, turn right (SP, Cape Town) on to the R44 1,1 km still further and reach Windmeul 5,6 km from the last turn. The R44 now runs southward through the delightful vineyards and dairy farms of Agter Paarl below the western slopes of Paarl Mountain and underpasses the N1 22,4 km from the last turn. At the stop street at Klapmuts 600 m from the N1 carry straight on and reach the traffic lights on the outskirts of Stellenbosch 15,6 km further on. Cross straight over and run 1,1 km along the eastern side of the railway before turning left into Merriman Avenue.

STELLENBOSCH See Tour 12.

Return along Merriman Avenue from the centre of Stellenbosch to the R44 and turn left. Turn right off the R44 at the station 600 m further on and after 4 km turn left (SP Faure, N2) on to the R310. Pass the

11. Wheatlands near Malmesbury

historic wine farm Meerlust (left) with its stately home – not open to the public – after 10 km and 200 m further on a wind pump in the middle of a farm dam (left).

WIND PUMP IN A DAM The wind pump whose vanes project above the surface of the water is in a surprisingly good state of repair in spite of the dam having been constructed many years ago. When the pump that originally stood on ground now flooded eventually disintegrated, its suppliers were granted permission by the owner of Meerlust to replace it with a new one – not to pump water, of course, but as a product-promotion ploy that passers-by certainly do notice.

Continue south-westward on the R310, crossing the R102 700 m from the wind pump and passing over the N2 (SP Muizenberg) 2,6 km further on. After about 2,5 km breast a line of sand dunes to come within view of the sea and, where the R310 becomes Baden Powell Drive 4,4 km from the N2, reach the extensive beach along the northern shore of False Bay. Pass the left turn to Swartklip Cove after 900 m.

SWARTKLIP West of Swartklip, for more than a century one of the most popular surf-angling spots on the Cape coast, the wide beach suddenly narrows between the surf and a stretch of weathering sandstone cliff, along the face of which there is a constant wheeling of innumerable seagulls. The spectacle is worth a stop.

Continue some 20 km westward round the False Bay seafront to the

end of Baden Powell Drive at the traffic circle at Sunrise Beach. Take the second exit into Muizenberg's Royal Road, after 600 m cross the outlet from Sandvlei and immediately afterwards turn left into Vlei Road, which runs round to the right into Beach Road.

MUIZENBERG See Tour 2.

Continue along the R310 as Beach Road runs into Atlantic Road, pass the Muizenberg Pavilion (left) 300 m from the turn into Beach Road, pass under the Southern Suburbs railway line after another 300 m and turn right into Main Road (SP Lakeside, M4) at the traffic lights 100 m further on. Turn left

12. All but the top of a wind pump is submerged in a dam on the farm Meerlust

(SP Boyes Drive) 800 m after joining Main Road, turn right (SP Wynberg, City) at the stop street 700 m further on and continue northward along Boyes Drive, overlooking Sandvlei, where the Imperial Yacht Club is based. Turn left back into Main Road at the end of Boyes Drive 2,7 km from the last stop street, left again (SP Ou Kaapse Weg, City) into Steenberg Road (M64) after another 450 m and turn right (SP City) on to the Simon van der Stel Freeway (M3) 1 km further on. Follow the M3 signs to the city, passing the right turn to D F Malan Airport and Groote Schuur Hospital after 15,9 km. At the fork 1 km further on choose between veering to the left (SP City via De Waal Drive) on to the M3 or to the right (SP City, Foreshore, Sea Point via Eastern Boulevard).

5

390 km

FLORAL KALEIDOSCOPE

In spring the western Cape explodes into tracts of wild flowers and one may drive from patches near the coast to kaleidoscopes in the Swartland, passing towns whose history dates from the earliest Dutch settlement.

13. Visitors drive among the spring flowers on the farm Waylands

CAPE TOWN See Tour 1.

Leave Cape Town from the seaward end of the Heerengracht, driving south-eastward along Table Bay Boulevard (N1). After 2,3 km take Exit 2 (SP Paarden Eiland, Milnerton, Atlantis, Velddrif) on to the Marine Drive (R27) and reach the traffic lights at the entrance to Milnerton 4,6 km further on. Turn left (SP Blouberg) on to the R305 7,5 km from the traffic lights to drive along the beachfront at Table View. Take another left turn (SP Blouberg) 3,5 km further on into Sir David Baird Drive and after 300 m turn left yet again into Stadler Road, from where there is one of the most painted and photographed views of Table Mountain. Drive 500 m to a parking area on the beachfront at Ons Huisie.

BLOUBERGSTRAND The seaside village of Bloubergstrand developed near the cove chosen by Major-General Sir David Baird in 1806 to land his 6 654-strong army when he was sent to take the Cape from the Batavian Republic, an ally of France with whom Britain was at war. The invaders were resisted by a motley multinational force of about two thousand commanded by the Governor, Lieutenant-General Jan Janssens, but the outnumbered and outgunned defenders retreated after a skirmish, and the Cape capitulated. Had Janssens stayed to fight it out against the exhausted and parched British troops, the second British occupation of the Cape might not have eventuated. In springtime masses of yellow daisy-like 'perdeblom' and 'vygies' of many shades present an eye-catching foreground to views of Table Mountain. Ons Huisie (NM), one of the oldest cottages once

occupied by fisherfolk at the Cape, is now a restaurant.

Drive round Ons Huisie to return to Sir David Baird Drive. After 500 m turn left at a T-junction into what at this stage has become the Otto du Plessis Marine Drive (R305), pass the 231-m Blouberg (right) after 3,5 km and reach the left turn (Sixth Avenue) to the beach at Melkbosstrand.

MELKBOSSTRAND Another seaside village, Melkbosstrand is popular with farmers of the western Cape who for generations have vied with each other here in traditional 'boeresports' (farmers' contests) during the summer holiday season.

Return to the Otto du Plessis Drive, turn left and veer inland, carrying straight on across the R27 at the stop street 1,4 km from Sixth Avenue. Cross the Atlantis railway line after 5,1 km, turn left at the crossroads 400 m further on and 2 km from the crossroads run into a famous old eucalyptus avenue, on either side of which are some of the biggest dairy farms supplying the Cape Peninsula. Pass a left turn to Atlantis 14,6 km from the last crossroads and after another 1,7 km emerge from the eucalyptus avenue into Reygersdal Drive through the industrial and coloured residential settlement of Atlantis. At the crossroads 1,6 km after leaving the eucalyptus avenue, turn right (no SP) into Charel Uys Drive and leave Atlantis on the R307, re-entering the avenue of gum trees 2,6 km from the crossroads. Pass the right turn to the Pela Mission Station after another 500 m and leave the avenue of trees for the last time 1,1 km further on. After 1,8 km turn left (SP Mamre) off the R307 on to a badly corrugated gravel road, veer right and cross a brook at the Mamre Clinic (left) 1,3 km from the R307. Fork left into Church Street to reach a thicket of oaks and pine trees in which nestle the oldest buildings of this historic mission station.

MAMRE In 1808, at the request of the Governor of the Cape, the Earl of Caledon, Mamre was founded on the farms De Kleine Post and Cruywagenskraal in the Groene Kloof by the Moravian missionaries J P Kohrhammer and J H Schmidt. Interest in the area, however, dates back to 1700, when the meat

contractor Henning Hüsing was granted grazing rights in the Groene Kloof. The following year Governor Willem Adriaan van der Stel established the military encampment De Kleine Post to protect the local farmers from marauding Bushmen, and this later became a Dutch East India Company cattle post which existed until 1791. The Hottentots who congregated at the Moravian mission after 1808 built long neat rows of whitewashed, thatched cottages with half-hipped roofs, some of which are still intact and lend Mamre a quality of unique architectural charm. The double-ended church, whose original simplicity was somewhat marred by the addition of baroque gables, was dedicated in 1818 and, like several other buildings, is a national monument.

Return along Church Street to the fork at the clinic and turn sharp left to drive uphill through a fir plantation. Turn left (no SP) back on to the tarred R307 and drive through the rest of what is now called Groenkloof. Reach the entrance (right) to Waylands farm 11 km after rejoining the R307 and, during the season, take a circular drive among the flowers, returning to the R307 600 m further on. Reach the Oudepost farmstead (left) 2,1 km from the Waylands exit.

WAYLANDS AND OUDEPOST are two farms in the Darling district whose owners open parts of their property to visitors during the wildflower season. Almost every square metre of veld has something of wonder and beauty to see, but maximum pleasure can be derived from a visit only by those who stop their vehicles and walk through the veld.

From Oudepost continue 2 km northward on the R307 to Darling.

DARLING Formerly Groene Kloof, but renamed in 1853 in honour of the Lieutenant-Governor of the Cape, Sir Charles Darling, this town is the hub of a wheat, wool, pea, wine, lupin and dairy farming district. However, it is best known for the abundance and variety of the wild flowers that bloom in the surrounding countryside. In springtime when the veld is at its gayest a garden laid out at the southern entrance of the town is a blaze of variegated colour.

Continue north-westward up Darling's Main Street, turn right (SP Yzerfontein, Langebaan, Saldanha, Vredendal) into Da Gama Road which swings away to the north-west and drive 11 km out of Darling on the R315 to the stile (left) which gives access to the Tienie Versveld Flora Reserve.

14. Blouberg Strand glows in the rays of the afternoon sun

TIENIE VERSVELD FLORA RESERVE
This 20-ha reserve in the gently-rolling landscape of a southward projection of the Sandveld was part of the farm that Martin (Tienie) Versveld presented to the nation through the National Botanic Gardens of South Africa. While there are many wildflower annuals in the reserve, it is particularly noted for its bulbous plants of the *Gladiolus* (kalkoentjies and pypies), *Babiana* (bobbejaantjies), *Lachenalia* (klossies), *Geissorhiza* (syblom and sysies) and *Spiloxene* (sterretjies) genera. There is also a profusion of chincherinchees and the insectivorous sundew.

Continue 3 km westward on the R315, cross the R27 and after 3 km turn right (SP Langebaan) on to gravel. Drive 11,8 km before turning left (SP Churchhaven) at a T-junction and reach Churchhaven 10,2 km further on.

CHURCHHAVEN
lies on the lagoon side of the spit that separates the Langebaan Lagoon from the sea. Strange names on the headstones in its graveyard suggest that the fishing village became the home of sailors from all parts of Europe who either jumped ship or were wrecked near here and settled down with amenable local women to raise large families of fisherfolk.

Continue 4,4 km past Churchhaven to the entrance to the Postberg Nature Reserve at Kraalbaai.

POSTBERG
Only when the wild flowers are at their best – in August and the first half of September – is the Postberg Private Nature Reserve open to the public. Said to have the widest variety of birds, game and Sandveld flowers in the western Cape, the reserve has a population of about 10 species of antelope as well as zebra, wildebeest, black-backed jackal, bat-eared fox, Cape wild cat and many smaller mammals. There are superb views of Langebaan Lagoon from Vlaeberg in the reserve, and at the summit of Constable Hill there is an old cannon which recalls the days when the Dutch maintained a fort here.

Return past Churchhaven and 14,6 km from Kraalbaai turn left (SP Langebaan) round the lagoon to reach the Langebaan village 17,4 km further on.

LANGEBAAN
which in spring is also surrounded by thousands of veld blooms, is a resort from which fishing boats, waterskiiers and South African Air Force crash boats set out.

Drive 9,1 km north-eastward from the village to the R27, turn left (SP

Velddrif) and after 10,1 km left again (SP Vredenburg) on to the R45. Reach the Dutch Reformed church in Vredenburg after another 9,7 km.

VREDENBURG
It was only after the Dutch Reformed Church established a congregation here in 1875 that peace came to Procesfontein (meaning 'lawsuit spring') – so named because of a prolonged bitter dispute between two farmers over a water source – and the settlement was called Vredenburg ('town of peace'). It is now an important commercial centre of the west coast.

Continue westward from Vredenburg on to the R399, reach the end of the tar after 1,3 km, turn left (SP Paternoster) 600 m further on and reach Paternoster after another 8 km.

PATERNOSTER
noted for the rock lobster its fishermen land, is a picturesque village of whitewashed cottages, which appears on some old maps as St Martin's Paternoster. A 3-km drive south-westward along the coast to the Columbine Nature Reserve is rewarding in the flower season.

Return 600 m south-eastward from the Paternoster Hotel, turn left (no SP) and after 7,7 km left again (SP Stompneus Bay, St Helena Bay). Drive 5,7 km to a T-junction, the left arm of which runs into the fishing village of Stompneus Bay. Turn right (SP St Helena Bay, Velddrif) and 600 m further on reach the left turn to the Da Gama Monument commemorating the landing of the Portuguese navigator here in 1497. Continue 5,2 km south-eastward along the coast to the fishing harbour at St Helena Bay.

ST HELENA BAY
has the greatest concentration of fishing industry activity in South Africa. In the town 11 factories process 60 percent of the country's 500 000-ton annual haul from the sea.

Continue 10,6 km south-eastward from St Helena Bay before turning left (SP Velddrif) on to the R399. Turn left (SP Velddrif) 10,2 km further on and left again (SP Laaiplek, Berg River Mouth, Dwarskersbos) in Velddrif after another 1,4 km.

VELDDRIF AND LAAIPLEK
The 'West Coast Twins' on the estuary of the Berg River together comprise a single municipality which thrives on the catching and processing of fish, with trawlers of considerable

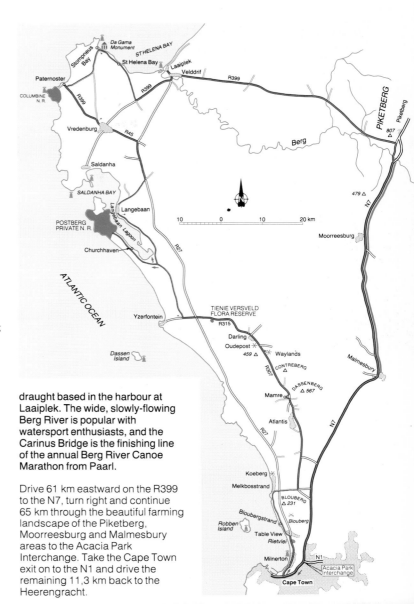

draught based in the harbour at Laaiplek. The wide, slowly-flowing Berg River is popular with watersport enthusiasts, and the Carinus Bridge is the finishing line of the annual Berg River Canoe Marathon from Paarl.

Drive 61 km eastward on the R399 to the N7, turn right and continue 65 km through the beautiful farming landscape of the Piketberg, Moorreesburg and Malmesbury areas to the Acacia Park Interchange. Take the Cape Town exit on to the N1 and drive the remaining 11,3 km back to the Heerengracht.

15. Churchhaven, on the western shore of the Langebaan Lagoon

SOUTHERN SANDVELD

The Sandveld stretches northward from the Piketberg range to the Olifants River and westward to the sea from the mountains behind which the river runs through its beautiful fertile valley.

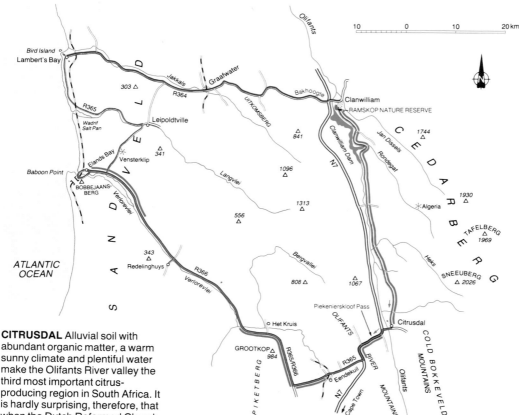

CITRUSDAL Alluvial soil with abundant organic matter, a warm sunny climate and plentiful water make the Olifants River valley the third most important citrus-producing region in South Africa. It is hardly surprising, therefore, that when the Dutch Reformed Church established a congregation and village here to serve the upper part of the valley in 1916 the new community was named Citrusdal. Orange groves from which high-quality fruit is harvested every year stretch along the valley on either side of the town and at blossom time the redolence emanating from them is heavenly. The main industry of the town is the packing of many thousands of tons of the fruit for export every year. With the northward spread of viticulture up the west coast regions of the Cape, Citrusdal also now has a winery.

Head westward (SP Piketberg, Clanwilliam, Cape Town) along Paul de Villiers Street from its intersection with Voortrekker Street on to the R303, cross the Olifants River and turn left (SP Piketberg) on to the N7 1,9 km from the river. Start the ascent of the Piekenierskloof Pass after about 1 km and reach the summit 5 km further on.

PIEKENIERSKLOOF See Tour 9.

Continue south-westward from the top of the pass, a short distance from which there is a viewing point over the beautiful valley between the Olifants River Mountains in the east and the Piketberg in the west.

Turn right (SP Eendekuil) on to the R365 10,2 km after joining the N7 and drive through the valley just viewed from Piekenierskloof. Turn right (SP Piketberg, Cape Town) 7 km further on and pass the left turn into Eendekuil (SP Porterville, Gouda via Eendekuil) after 400 m.

EENDEKUIL, or 'duck pond', is a name which is thought to have

originated in the days when the waters hereabouts abounded with waterfowl. The importance of the village lies in it being the nearest railway station to Citrusdal and therefore the loading point of large quantities of citrus fruit. Eendekuil also has a cooperative cheese factory supplied with milk by dairy farmers in the Piketberg, Porterville and Moorreesburg districts.

Continue 7,9 km towards the Piketberg and under the hang of the mountain turn right (SP Elandsbaai, Lambertsbaai) on to the R365/R366. About 9 km after joining the R365/R366 pass through the gap between the 984-m Grootkop, at the northern end of the Piketberg, and three conical hills at the southern end of the Waterberg. Pass the right turn to Het Kruis, Leipoldtville and Lambert's Bay on the R365 12,5 km from the last turn and continue westward on the R366 which is tarred for another 16 km. After running along the bank of the Verlorevlei River turn left (SP Redelinghuys, Aurora) 26,1 km from the turn-off to Het Kruis and drive 1 km into Redelinghuys.

REDELINGHUYS was founded at the head of Verlorevlei in 1906 when the Dutch Reformed Church started a separate congregation on land given for the purpose by J N Redelinghuys.

Return from Redelinghuys to the R366 and turn left, reaching the marshland at the head of Verlorevlei after 3,5 km. Continue along the north-eastern bank of the vlei as it widens out.

VERLOREVLEI When Simon van der Stel journeyed this way to Namaqualand in 1685 he referred to the river now called Verlorevlei as 'het Cleyne Oliphants Rivier of Zeekoe Vallei'. It was subsequently called the Zand River, but in 1724 Ensign Jan Rhenius gave it the old form of the name it has retained – Verloren Vallei, meaning 'lost valley'. The estuary formed by the river is seasonal, filling up in winter and losing most of its water in summer.

Pass the right turn to Lambert's Bay 22,4 km from the Redelinghuys turn-off and after another 3,7 km fork right (SP Elandsbaai) for a circular drive of the Elands Bay area.

ELANDS BAY is *the* place on the Cape's west coast for surfing and in good conditions offers a nearly perfect wave. The spot draws large crowds of surfers at long weekends, in spite of primitive facilities and barren surroundings. Until the surfers found it, Elands Bay's *raison d'être* was a small fishing harbour at the foot of the Bobbejaansberg just south of the mouth of Verlorevlei. The railway line specifically constructed for the transport of ore from the world's richest iron deposits at Sishen in the northern Cape to Saldanha Bay runs through a tunnel under the Bobbejaansberg.

16. Verlorevlei flows into the sea at Elands Bay

Reach the fishermen's cottages 400 m from the fork at the start of the circular drive, pass under the Sishen railway line 400 m further on and cross Verlorevlei by causeway after another 800 m. Once over the causeway turn left, cross under the Sishen line 400 m further on and after another 1,5 km turn left across another causeway where the birdlife on this tranquil part of the vlei is worth pausing to watch. After 300 m the road returns to the fork at the start of the circular drive. Backtrack 3,7 km before turning left (SP Lambertsbaai) and after another 5 km come abreast of Vensterklip – a rocky knoll with a hole right through it – to the right about 500 m off the road. Reach a T-junction 7,5 km from Vensterklip, the right arm of which leads 1,5 km to Leipoldtville.

LEIPOLDTVILLE The village of Leipoldtville was created in 1905 when the Dutch Reformed congregation at Clanwilliam separated into two independent entities. The new congregation was named after the Reverend Christian Friedrich Leipoldt, their minister who remained at Clanwilliam and the father of the distinguished physician, poet and author, Dr Louis Leipoldt. The village, which consists of little more than a church, a store and a garage, serves the numerous small farms clustered along the valley of the Langvlei River as far as the Wadrif Salt Pan.

At the T-junction turn left (SP Lambert's Bay) on to the R365 and after 10,5 km breast a rise for the first sight of the Wadrif Salt Pan.

WADRIF SALT PAN After a rainy season the Wadrif Salt Pan, formed by the lower reaches of the Langvlei River which has a huge sand dune at its mouth, becomes a beautiful stretch of water frequented by countless aquatic birds, among them thousands of flamingoes. At other times the pan becomes so dry that salt 'farming' has been considered.

17. The fertile Olifants River valley, seen from Piekenierskloof

Cross the bridge over the Sishen line 15,6 km from the Leipoldtville T-junction, reach the seashore 1,8 km further on and drive 8,4 km along it to the Lambert's Bay boundary sign, 400 m beyond which the road becomes tarred. Turn left (SP Lambert's Bay) towards the seafront 600 m from the boundary sign. Turn right at the second stop street 200 m further on and left at the harbour entrance after another 300 m to reach the parking area whence there is walking access to Bird Island.

LAMBERT'S BAY, at the mouth of the Jakkals River, was the last spot on the African coast at which Bartolomeu Dias anchored before

he was blown southward in 1488 and then sailed northward to make a landfall near the mouth of the Gourits River. The bay was named after Rear-Admiral Sir Robert Lambert who, as senior officer of the Royal Navy at the Cape in 1820 and 1821, surveyed this part of the coast. In 1901 what was dubbed at the time the 'only naval battle of the Boer War' was fought at Lambert's Bay, when the commando led by General J B M Hertzog opened fire on the British ship *Sybille*. The nucleus around which this fishing town and holiday resort developed was the lobster-processing factory built by Axel Lindström, a Swede who came from America in the Anglo-Boer War and founded the Lambert's Bay Canning Company. The original fishing harbour, situated in the estuary of the Jakkals River which is now closed, has been replaced with a new one by throwing out two concrete 'arms' from the holm known as Bird Island, just off the coast south of the river mouth. The southern arm which connects the 3-ha island to the mainland has made it possible to walk to this remarkable bird sanctuary where thousands of roosting gannets and cormorants make it one of the attractions of the west coast.

Return to the harbour entrance, turn left 50 m further on and right after another 50 m at the stop street opposite the hotel. At the stop

18. Trawlers at their moorings in Lambert's Bay

street 200 m still further turn left (SP Graafwater, Clanwillliam) on to the R364. Reach the left turn into Graafwater after 30,4 km.

GRAAFWATER See Tour 7.

Continue eastward on the R364, breasting the Uitkomsberg range 10,3 km from the Graafwater turn-off. After another 13 km the town of Clanwilliam and the Clanwilliam Dam come into view from Bakhoogte. Pass under the N7 4 km further on, cross the Olifants River after 100 m and turn right into High Street in Clanwilliam 2,4 km further on.

CLANWILLIAM See Tour 8.

At the Old Jail (NM) at the southern end of Clanwilliam's High Street fork right (SP Ou Kaapse Weg) and 1,2 km further on right again to the Ramskop Nature Reserve.

RAMSKOP The Ramskop Nature Reserve, which incorporates the Clanwilliam Wild Flower Garden, is the natural habitat of a variety of small mammals such as buck, hares and dassies. The 7,5-ha wild flower garden, started in 1967, has about 200 indigenous plant species which present a magnificent display in springtime.

Return to the last fork and turn right to continue south-eastward along the eastern bank of the Clanwilliam Dam on the Ou Kaapse Weg – the original road to Cape Town. After 7,2 km pass the left turn to Algeria Forestry Station at the threshold of the Cedarberg Wilderness Area.

CEDARBERG Climbers, hikers, naturalists, rock-art enthusiasts and others who revel in wilderness experience return again and again to the mighty Cedarberg range, which takes its name from the cedar trees which grow in these mountains at altitudes between 1 000 and 1 400 m. Weird rock formations, waterfalls, crystal streams and pools, winding trails, the rare snow protea and a wealth of other flora, well-preserved Bushman paintings and air like champagne all contribute to the delight derived by aficionados of this vast rugged mountain region. The highest peaks, an even greater spectacle than usual when they are capped with snow, are the 2 026-m Sneeuberg and the 1 969-m Tafelberg.

From the turn-off to Algeria continue southward for 13,3 km to a gate and, after closing it behind you, carry straight on at the crossroads 7,9 km further on. After another 29,1 km reach the intersection between the Ou Kaapse Weg and the R303 in Citrusdal.

7
250 km

NORTHERN SANDVELD

The tranquility of wide, open spaces which must have represented a daunting obstacle to the early Dutch explorers of the Cape, and an unspoilt Atlantic coastline lend appeal to the northern Sandveld.

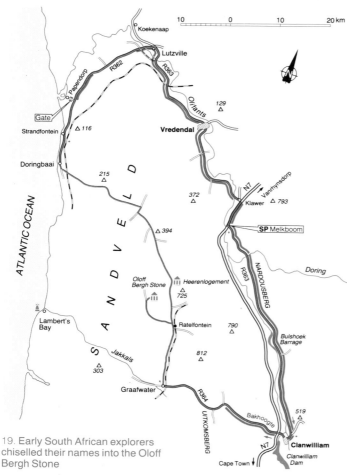

19. Early South African explorers chiselled their names into the Oloff Bergh Stone

CLANWILLIAM See Tour 8.

Leave Clanwilliam heading westward along Graafwater Road, cross the Olifants River and carry straight on (SP Graafwater, Lambert's Bay) at the junction 100 m from the river. Immediately afterwards cross under the N7 and on to the R364 to start the ascent of Bakhoogte, from which, looking back, there is a fine view over Clanwilliam and its dam. From the top of Bakhoogte the road runs through valleys dotted with plantations of rooibos tea and then down the northern edge of the Uitkomsberg range before crossing the railway to the northern Cape 27,1 km from the Olifants River. Turn right (SP Graafwater, Vredendal) into Graafwater 400 m after crossing the railway.

GRAAFWATER Although the railway to the north-western Cape reached Graafwater in 1910 the village did not acquire its own local government until 1953. Its economy is based on agriculture, the main products being grain and wool.

Continue northward through Graafwater and out of the village on to gravel, after 12,9 km reach the Ratelfontein railway station and turn left (SP Olof Bergh Klip, Bergfontein) 800 m further on. Fork right (SP Olof Berghfontein) after 9,1 km, right again through a gate 150 m further on and drive 350 m to another gate just beyond which is a big rock beside a fountain.

OLOFF BERGH STONE A plaque on the rock (NM) records: 'On an expedition to the Copper Mountains in 1682 Oloff [sic] Bergh discovered this fountain and named it Berg Fontein. Simon van der Stel (1685), J Starrenberg (1705), K J Slotsbo (1712) and J T Rhenius (1721) passed here on their journeys to the north.' Bergh, Slotsbo and Rhenius chiselled their names into the rock.

Return from the Oloff Bergh Stone to the turn 800 m from Ratelfontein station, turn left and after 8,5 km reach the gate (right) to the Heerenlogement, a cave in the 725-m Heerenlogementsberg. Turn left through another gate to the farmhouse on the opposite side of the road to collect the key to the Heerenlogement and sign the visitors' book. Follow the left-leading track immediately inside the Heerenlogement gate to the white blockhouse about 200 m away.

HEERENLOGEMENTSBERG BLOCKHOUSE This small corrugated-iron blockhouse (NM) below the Heerenlogement was one of the series constructed between Noupoort and Lambert's Bay by the British in the Anglo-Boer War to cut off a possible invasion of the Cape Colony from the north by Boer forces. It originally stood on a farm between Graafwater and Lambert's Bay, but was bought and moved to its present site shortly after the war for use first as a dwelling and later as a storeroom.

HEERENLOGEMENT The Heerenlogement (NM) (meaning 'gentlemen's lodging') reached by a five-minute walk up the track alongside the fence, is a cave which became celebrated because of the distinguished travellers of long ago who took shelter in it on their way north. The first white explorer known to have overnighted in the cave was Olof Bergh, whom Commander Simon van der Stel sent in 1682 to investigate the possibility of exploiting Namaqualand's copper. Van der Stel himself was to use the Heerenlogement three years later on his way to sink a shaft in the Copper Mountains. Famous pioneers whose names are engraved inside the cave include: Kaje Jesse Slotsbo, a member of the Dutch East India Company's Council of Policy (1712); the expedition leader Ensign J T Rhenius (1721); the botanist C P Thunberg (1721); Governor Hendrik Swellengrebel (1777); the naturalist Francois le Vaillant (1783); the Wesleyan missionary Barnabas Shaw (1816); and the road engineer Andrew Geddes Bain (1854). An old white milkwood tree observed by Swellengrebel still grows in a rock crevice in the wall of the cave.

After returning the key, continue 16,2 km north-westward before turning right (SP Doringbaai, Vredendal) and then left (SP Doringbaai, Strandfontein) 900 m further on. Cross the Sishen railway line after another 16,5 km and turn right (SP Doringbaai, Strandfontein) at the T-junction 1,5 km from the railway to drive 1,3 km to the first stop street in Doringbaai.

DORINGBAAI The pretty cove at Doringbaai, where a few fishing smacks are based, has a factory where lobster, fish and vegetables are canned.

Return to the last-mentioned stop street, turn left and, having run back on to tar after 4,6 km, turn left (SP Strandfontein) 7 km from Doringbaai into Strandfontein.

STRANDFONTEIN An attractive, well-laid-out cluster of seaside homes, an hotel and an amphitheatre-like caravan park on the slope overlooking the sea constitute Strandfontein, a resort on a pleasant little bay popular with many of the farmers of the immediate hinterland. Quiet for most of the year, it becomes remarkably lively during the holiday season. Once a somewhat unsophisticated settlement, Strandfontein has changed beyond all recognition over the past 30 years, with property owners replacing many of its cottages with much more ostentatious dwellings.

Return to the entrance to Strandfontein, turn left on to what from here becomes the R362 and after 6,6 km reach an unmarked gate (left) which gives access to Papendorp 1,5 km from the tarred road.

PAPENDORP, a coloured settlement on the east bank of the Olifants River where a large island splits it into two streams, was pioneered by members of the Fryer family. Descendants of Irish folk among the 1820 Settlers who were allocated land in the Clanwilliam area, the Fryers remained when their compatriots became disaffected with the north-western Cape and settled elsewhere. At low tide what has been a considerable lagoon before the ebb becomes a narrow stretch of water with mudflats on either side where hundreds of wading birds may be seen searching for food. When the tide is in, the river is navigable by shallow-draught craft all the way to Lutzville about 30 km away.

Continue northward from the turn-off to Papendorp and after 16,9 km turn left (SP Lutzville, Nuwerus), remaining on the R362, to drive through vineyards of the lower reaches of the Olifants River. Cross the river by causeway 500 m from the last turn and drive a further 1,7 km to the Dutch Reformed church in Lutzville. If the water is over the causeway, backtrack 400 m, turn left (SP Vredendal, Vanrhynsdorp) and either turn left again over the bridge 3,5 km further on to visit Lutzville or give it a miss and turn right on to the R363 to Vredendal.

LUTZVILLE Once called Vlermuisklip, Lutzville was renamed in 1923 when Johan Lutz was sent by the Department of Lands to lay out a village and prepare land for an agricultural settlement. The area is now irrigated with water conducted by canal from the Clanwilliam Dam and Bulshoek Barrage, making viable the many small farms stretching along the intensively cultivated banks of the Olifants River downstream from Lutzville to Ebenhaeser and upstream to Klawer. About 7 km north of

20. The coast at Papendorp

Lutzville is the village of Koekenaap, of which the name is of more interest than anything else. The most intriguing of the stories about its origin is told by members of the Leipoldt family whose first South African forebear was the Rhenish missionary J G Leipoldt, founder of Wuppertal (see Tour 8). It is said that two German missionaries making their way back from the north reached the Olifants River at this point, coming upon it suddenly as they breasted the high ground on its northern bank. Seeing the grand view of the huge horseshoe bend in the river below, the man ahead excitedly yelled to his companion in Low German: 'Kuk hinab, kuk hinab!' (Look down there!). The local Hottentots acting as guides to the missionaries adopted the cry as a name for the place, corrupting it to Koekenaap.

Drive 400 m eastward from the Lutzville Dutch Reformed church and at the crossroads north of the town turn right (no SP) on to the R363, cross the Olifants River 3,1 km further on and pass a right turn to Lutzville and Nuwerus immediately afterwards (where the detour from the causeway rejoins the route). Pass under the Sishen railway bridge – until recently the highest in the country – 6,5 km from the river, reach the first of two Dutch Reformed churches in Vredendal 12 km further on and the second 400 m still further.

VREDENDAL In 1668 a party of Dutch East India Company servants on a cattle-bartering expedition clashed with Namaqua Hottentots who had stolen some of their cattle at what became known as Bakkeleij Plaatz ('fighting place'). The Dutchmen killed three Hottentots, whose leader subsequently negotiated for accord at a spot which has been known ever since as Vredendal, 'the vale of peace'. The town owes its existence to the

Olifants River irrigation scheme which originally incorporated only the Bulshoek Barrage and a canal system, but now conducts water stored in the Clanwilliam Dam. The ample water supply has led not only to the agricultural prosperity of the area around Vredendal but also to considerable industrial development in the town, where there is a large cooperative winery, a furniture factory, an extension of the South African Dried Fruit Cooperative and two mineral water factories. Vredendal has, indeed, developed to such an extent in recent years that it has usurped the position of Vanrhynsdorp as the major business centre of the region.

Carry straight on (SP Klawer) at the crossroads at the second Dutch Reformed church in Vredendal and leave the town to drive alongside the canal of the Olifants River irrigation scheme. Continue on the R363, crossing the Olifants River 20,1 km from the crossroads and entering Klawer 300 m further on.

21. The main canal in the Olifants River irrigation scheme meanders between Klawer and Clanwilliam

KLAWER, which takes its name from the clover that grows wild in the area, is an important station on the railway to the northern Cape and a business centre for surrounding farms. It is the place at which the Olifants River is bridged for both the road to Vredendal and the railway.

Cross the railway 200 m after entering Klawer, turn right (SP Clanwilliam) on to the N7 at the T-junction 1,2 km further on and after another 6,3 km turn left (SP Melkboom) on to the gravelled R363 immediately before the N7 swings south-westward over a bridge across the Olifants River. Cross the Doring River 8 km further on for a delightful, meandering 18,7-km drive along the lower slopes of the Nardousberg range, which forms the eastern wall of the Olifants River valley, to the Bulshoek Barrage. Pass the conical 519-m Spitskop in the east just before running back on to tar, turn right (SP Clanwilliam) on to the R364 22,5 km from the Bulshoek Barrage and cross the Jan Dissels River into Clanwilliam 1 km further on to drive another 300 m before turning left into High Street.

ACROSS SEMI-DESERT TO A MOUNTAIN SANCTUARY

8
420 km*

When rain does fall in the hard and barren Knersvlakte flowers materialise as if from the droplets. Not far south of this semi-desert lie fertile valleys among the spurs of the majestic Cedarberg.

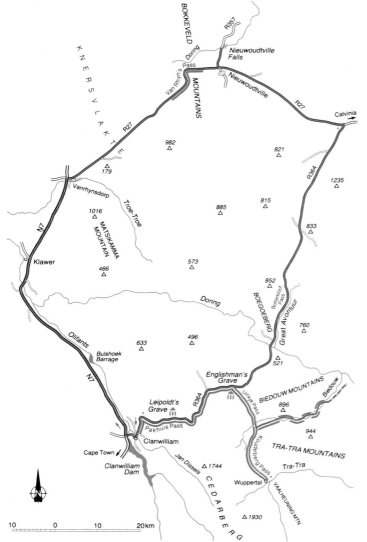

The distance given allows for about 15 km into the Biedouw Valley.

CLANWILLIAM In the western shadow of the Pakhuis Mountains at the northern limit of the Cedarberg range, Clanwilliam was originally called Jan Disselsvlei after the amateur botanist Jan Dissel who fossicked along the valley of the river that was also named after him. A sub-magistracy was established at Jan Disselsvlei in 1808 and six years later Governor Sir John Cradock renamed the place in honour of his father-in-law, the Earl of Clanwilliam. In 1820 an effort was made to settle four parties of Irish immigrants along the Jan Dissels River, but most of them soon sought other pastures among the rest of the 1820 Settlers in the eastern Cape. It was an Irish settler descendant, Charles Fryer, nevertheless, who was elected the first mayor when the village became a municipality in 1901. Clanwilliam is the centre of an agricultural region most widely known for its rooibos tea, although citrus fruit, wool, wheat and beef are equally important products.

Turn left at the stop street 600 m north of the Dutch Reformed church in Main Street, turn left again (SP Klawer, Citrusdal) 2,6 km further on after crossing the Olifants River, and after another 500 m turn right (SP Klawer) on to the N7. Reach the Bulshoek Barrage on the Olifants River 19,3 km after joining the N7.

22. A carpet of wild flowers in the Biedouw Valley

OLIFANTS RIVER Elephant really did inhabit the valley of the Olifants River in days gone by. Indeed, the explorer Jan Danckaert gave the river its name because he spotted a herd of about 300 nearby in 1660. Another fact of zoological interest is that the Olifants is the only water in which the Clanwilliam yellowfish (*Barbus capensis*) occurs. The river provides the water for a major irrigation scheme which was initiated with a diversion weir at Bulshoek and an unlined canal in 1913. Subsequently the weir was converted into a barrage, the canal was extended and concreted and the water stored behind the barrage was supplemented from the Clanwilliam Dam, which had been completed higher up the river. Now the main canal – which at times can be seen snaking alongside the N7 – and its branches irrigate the land of nearly a thousand farmers over a distance of about 100 km. The valley of the Olifants River, from near its source south of Citrusdal to its mouth in the north, constitutes the Clanwilliam Wild Flower Area, where the plants that bloom in mass displays in springtime are similar to those of Namaqualand. *Mesembryanthemum* ('vygie') species predominate in the north of the area, and in the south the commonest varieties are the Clanwilliam daisy (*Euryops speciosissimus*) and the 'skilpadbessie' (*Nylandtia spinosa*).

Continue northward from Bulshoek and 58 km after joining the N7 pass the village of Klawer (see Tour 7). Turn right (SP Vanrhynsdorp, Vredendal, Calvinia) 22,7 km further on and turn left (SP Vanrhynsdorp, Calvinia) into Van Riebeeck Street at Vanrhynsdorp after another 400 m.

VANRHYNSDORP Dominated by the flat-topped Matsikamma Mountain, Vanrhynsdorp was established in 1887 on a farm owned by Petrus van Rhijn, who was later to represent Namaqualand in the old Cape Parliament. Sheep farming is the principal activity of the district and there is also some wheat production, but the 'crop' for which it is most famous is the flora which bursts from the hard sun-baked earth in a blaze of colour in a springtime that has been preceded by good rain. There are years when parts of the countryside are transformed into a spectacle from horizon to horizon, but even in 'poor' seasons there are enough veld flowers to delight visitors, especially those who forsake their cars and walk among the blooms.

Drive 100 m northward along Troe-Troe Street from its intersection with Van Riebeeck Street, turn right (SP Calvinia, Johannesburg, Upington)

into Church Street and left (same SP) into Residential Street 600 m further on to travel north-eastward on the R27 across the Knersvlakte.

KNERSVLAKTE The Knersvlakte is an arid, desolate region between the latitudes of Bitterfontein in the north and Vanrhynsdorp in the south and between the narrow coastal strip of the Sandveld in the west and the Bokkeveld Mountains in the east. In the days when a man who rented land from the state was known as a 'knecht van de staat' the region was called the Knechtsvlakte – 'the plain of the bondsmen' – but this name seems to have been conveniently corrupted to describe the gnashing ('kners') of teeth that accompanied the ox-wagon expeditions of yore across this inhospitable thirstland. The flora of the Knersvlakte Wild Flower Area is dominated by the glowing colours of numerous mesembryanthemum varieties.

Where the R27 converges with the Bokkeveld Mountains 35 km from Vanrhynsdorp, start the ascent of Van Rhyn's Pass.

VAN RHYN'S PASS is one of the 10 major mountain passes constructed by the South African road engineer Thomas Bain. Widened and tarred in 1962, it is a busy gateway, for most of the freight carried between Cape Town and the Namaqualand towns of Loeriesfontein, Brandvlei and Kenhardt is transported by road and has to pass this way. In the relatively short distance of 8 km the pass conveys the traveller across the Bokkeveld escarpment into a startlingly different world – from the semi-desert landscape of the Knersvlakte to a plateau with trees and grassland and water-filled dams. With an annual rainfall of 350 mm – more than twice as much as the erratic precipitation of the rest of the area – the Nieuwoudtville region is known as the 'Boland of the North-west'.

At the crossroads 53 km after joining the R27 turn left (SP Loeriesfontein) on to the R357 Drive 6,4 km to the right turn through a gate and cross the Doring River to reach the Nieuwoudtville Falls about 200 m off the road.

NIEUWOUDTVILLE FALLS This waterfall, over which the Doring River drops some 100 m into a deep rock pool, is a pleasant spot for an alfresco lunch or tea break. Although the falls are at their most spectacular after rain, there is always some water in the river.

Backtrack the 6,4 km to the R27 and turn left at the entrance to Nieuwoudtville, a village at the

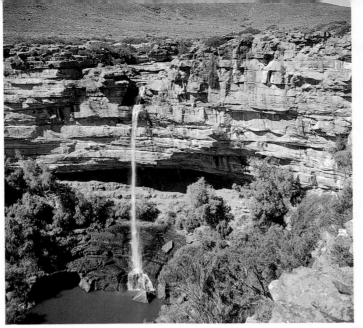

23. The Nieuwoudtville Falls

24. Cottages at Wuppertal

centre of an area producing wool and cereals. Drive 34,5 km before turning right (SP Clanwilliam) on to the R364 to travel across the Bokkeveld plain towards the Cedarberg, seeing veld flowers all along the way in August and September. After 42,6 km on the R364 start descending the Botterkloof Pass which runs down the Great Avontuur River valley in the Boegoeberg range into the valley of another Doring River. After 82,2 km on the R364 turn left (SP Wuppertal, Biedouw Valley), traverse the western end of the Biedouw Mountains by way of the Uitkyk (Hoeksberg) Pass and turn left (SP Uitspankraal) into the Biedouw Valley 14,5 km after leaving the R364.

BIEDOUW VALLEY This fertile valley, through which the Biedouw River flows between the Biedouw Mountains in the north and the Tra-Tra range in the south, can be one of the most spectacular of all the veld flower regions, particularly when in a good year the mesembryanthemums and other varieties of 'vygie' extend from either side of the road right up into the mountains. So aware of their floral treasures are the sheep farmers of the valley that during the height of the flower season they find grazing elsewhere for their flocks, which relish many wildflower species.

After driving as far down the Biedouw Valley as the spirit moves, backtrack to the last turn-off and turn left to drive 18,4 km down the Koudeberg Pass through an eastern spur of the Cedarberg to Wuppertal.

WUPPERTAL Nestling in a deep, secluded dale between the Vaalheuning ('pale honey') Mountain in the east and the northern end of the Cedarberg range in the west Wuppertal is reminiscent of James Hilton's *Shangri-La*, 'the floor of the valley, hazily distant, welcoming the eye with greenness' as one suddenly spots it from the steep, winding road down the Koudeberg Pass. It was here on the northern bank of the Tra-Tra River in 1830 that Johan Gottlieb Leipoldt, grandfather of the renowned poet-physician Dr Louis Leipoldt, and Theobald von Wurmb established the first Rhenish mission farm in South Africa, naming it after the Rhineland valley of the River Wupper. The two Germans ministered temporally as well as spiritually to their flock, which at first comprised only local coloured folk but grew considerably when freed slaves settled in the village after 1838. The missionaries taught the villagers farming techniques and a variety of trades, such as bricklaying, joinery, thatching, millinery, tanning and shoemaking. So skilled did they become at shoemaking that the countrywide reputation of the Wuppertal *velskoen* endures to this day. The community built terraces of neat thatched and whitewashed cottages which are still a visual treat, and the graceful gabled church they erected in 1834 is a tribute to their craftsmanship. Responsibility for Wuppertal was transferred to the Moravian Church in 1965, and the affairs of the community are ordered by a council of 16 led by the incumbent clergyman.

Backtrack 32,9 km to the R364, turn left and drive 100 m to the 'Englishman's Grave'.

'ENGLISHMAN'S GRAVE' Lieutenant Graham Clowes of the Gordon Highlanders, who had left his home in Hertfordshire to fight in the Anglo-Boer War, was killed in action on 30 January 1901 and buried at this spot nearby.

Continue westward and after 14,5 km start the ascent of the Pakhuis Pass to traverse the mountains of the same name.

PAKHUIS PASS The Pakhuis Pass, which was constructed by Thomas Bain in 1887, and the majestic mountains of the area with their weird rock formations were among the favourite haunts of Louis Leipoldt, and when he died his ashes were buried in a simple grave in a Bushman rock shelter 9,3 km from the start of the pass.

Continue 17,1 km westward from Leipoldt's grave to the Dutch Reformed church in Clanwilliam.

WHERE AN EARTHQUAKE WROUGHT HAVOC

Mountain-ringed towns of the western Cape were rocked in 1969 by an earthquake which killed nine people and left buildings in ruins, but prompted restoration which might otherwise never have been contemplated.

CERES See Tour 10.

Drive 200 m south-westward along Voortrekker Street (R46) from its intersection with Vos Street in Ceres, cross the Dwars River and 1,3 km further on start the ascent of Michell's Pass (see Tour 10). Travel 9,8 km from the tour start before forking right (SP Wolseley, Tulbagh) to remain on the R46, and 5,3 km further on pass the left turn to Wolseley as the road runs into the 'Land van Waveren' between the Witsenberg range in the east; the Watervalsberg, Obikwa Mountains and Saronsberg in the west; and the Great Winterhoek Mountains in the north. Fork right (SP Tulbagh) off the R46 11,2 km from the turn-off to Wolseley and drive 4,6 km to the Tulbagh boundary sign. Turn left (SP Museum and Restored Church Street) 500 m further on into Vos Street, which then runs into Church Street.

25. Tulbagh's Church Street has been restored after an earthquake

TULBAGH In spite of the favourable report given by early explorer Pieter Potter to the Dutch East India Company in 1658 on the 'beautiful valley' east of what were to become known as Saronsberg, the Voëlvlei Mountains and the Watervalsberg, it was to be more than 40 years before the Land van Waveren was named and settled. Governor Willem Adriaan van der Stel was the man who instigated settlement. He was enchanted when he visited the valley in 1699, named it after the Amsterdam family of Waveren to whom his wife was related and soon after his return to the Cape sent burghers to establish the first farms in the area. A Dutch Reformed congregation was formed in 1743 and at first called Roodezand, but was renamed in 1804 by Governor Jan Janssens in honour of one of his

predecessors, Ryk Tulbagh. The Roodezand Church, built in the year the congregation was formed, has withstood the wear of more than two centuries, including a period of dereliction after a new church was built and a severe earthquake. Twice restored, it is now the Oude Kerk Volksmuseum (Old Church National Museum). The earthquake (Richter magnitude 6,5) which damaged the Oude Kerk on 29 September 1969 caused havoc over a wide area from Saron in the north to beyond Ceres and Wolseley in the south. Huge dislodged boulders struck sparks as they crashed down the mountain slopes, igniting much of the countryside, while historic buildings, including stately homesteads as old as 200 years, were extensively damaged or reduced to rubble. Modest Tulbagh homes were also devastated and Church Street, whose buildings were the town's first, appeared to be in ruins. But the disaster created a unique opportunity to restore the whole of Church Street and, four years later, the biggest restoration project ever undertaken in South Africa had been completed. With the greatest concentration of historic monuments in the country, Church Street now forms an almost perfect image of an eighteenth-century South African rural village precinct – and a singular tourist attraction.

At the northern end of Church Street turn right into Waveren Street, pass the Pastorie (NM) on the left and turn left out of town immediately afterwards to drive 3,2 km to Tulbagh's Old Drostdy.

DE OUDE DROSTDY Because the water resources of the community were overtaxed when Hendrik Bletterman, the Stellenbosch magistrate, was asked to establish a new magistracy at Tulbagh in 1803, he took the unusual step of choosing a site outside the village. The neo-classic building, designed by Louis Thibault, served as a drostdy from 1806 only until 1822 when it was damaged in a storm and Governor Lord Charles Somerset moved the magisterial seat to Worcester. The building was further damaged by fire in 1934 and it collapsed in the 1969 earthquake. The ruin was then bought and restored by the National Monuments Council. At the re-opening in 1974 De Oude Drostdy (NM) was handed in trust to the

Drostdy Wine Cellars, which uses the building as its head office and maintains it as a museum where, among other items, furniture of the eighteenth and nineteenth centuries is displayed.

Return to Tulbagh and drive to the southern end of Van der Stel Street before turning right into Station Road (SP Cape Town, Gouda). Turn right (SP Gouda, Cape Town) on to the R46 at the junction 3,1 km further on and descend from the Land van Waveren through beautiful Nuwekloof between the Obikwa Mountains in the north and the Voëlvlei Mountains in the south.

NUWEKLOOF Up in the Voëlvlei Mountains on the left of the road through Nuwekloof there is a fastness which in the early days of the settlement at the Cape was the headquarters of a Hottentot chief who wreaked havoc on wagon convoys on their way to Table Bay. His strategically-positioned scouts would pick up the signals from Cape Town notifying outlying farmers of ships approaching the bay, and as the burghers trekked southward with supplies of victuals the Hottentots attacked and plundered them. A punitive expedition finally rounded up the marauders and put an end to their unwelcome exploits.

Turn right (SP Porterville, Piketberg) on to the R44 7,7 km after joining the R46, pass the right turn to the village of Gouda after another 1,6 km, and 14,8 km further on turn right to drive 3,3 km to Saron.

SARON was established by Rhenish missionaries who bought the farm Leeuwenklip at the foot of the Blocxberg [sic] (now Saronsberg) in 1846. The Dutch Reformed Church eventually took over the mission and now it is a village exclusively for coloured people, some of whom still specialise in making the *velskoen* their forefathers were taught to fashion by their German mentors. Saron's handsome whitewashed church dates from 1852, but the parsonage, Leeuwenklip's homestead in the Cape Dutch style, is thought to be 70 years older. Many of the thatched, mud-brick cottages that characterised the village were damaged or destroyed in the 1969 earthquake.

Return from Saron to the R44, turn right and drive 21,1 km to come abreast of the Dutch Reformed church in Porterville.

PORTERVILLE It is fitting that a public figure noted for his kindliness, his impartiality in the administration of justice and his fine oratory should be commemorated as William Porter is in the name of this town. Porter, appointed

26. The Vier-en-twintig Riviere flows westward from the Winterhoek peak

Attorney-General of the Cape in 1839, was so highly regarded that when he resigned from the position in 1865 to enter politics, the Legislative Assembly voted him his full salary for life.

Porterville was laid out by F J Owen, who also named it, on his farm Pomona in 1863. A relic of interest is a Dutch East India Company cannon which stands in front of the police station. Mounted at one time on the farm Dammetjies, it was one in a series stretching from Cape Town which were fired successively to inform farmers whenever a ship to which they could sell provisions had arrived in Table Bay.

Continue northward (SP Citrusdal) out of Porterville on the R365 between the Olifants River Mountains in the east and the Piketberg range in the west. Turn right (SP Citrusdal) on to the N7 35 km from the Porterville Dutch Reformed church and start the ascent of the Piekenierskloof Pass 10 km further on.

PIEKENIERSKLOOF From time immemorial men have made their way from the valley of the Olifants River to the Kruismans River valley through this defile in the Olifants River Mountains. First blazed by indigenous people, the trail was subsequently used by the colonists who eventually settled in the north-western Cape. However, a proper road through the pass – albeit along a different route – was completed only in 1858 by Thomas Bain and named in honour of Governor Sir George Grey. This route has been superseded higher up the defile by a modern tarred road, which has reverted to the old name Piekenierskloof Pass, recalling the days when pikemen ('piekeniers') were stationed in the mountain gap to repulse marauding Hottentots. Grey's Pass was the first of many major constructions directed on his own by Thomas Bain, whose renown and certainly his output was even more prodigious than that of his father, Andrew Geddes Bain (see Ecca Pass, Tour 32). The younger Bain had his basic training from the elder, to whom he had been appointed assistant in the construction of Michell's Pass. As well as being a road engineer, he was a railway engineer, geologist, irrigation surveyor and amateur archaeologist of note.

Turn right (SP Citrusdal) on to the R303 20,7 km after joining the N7 and drive 3 km into Citrusdal.

CITRUSDAL See Tour 6.

Drive eastward along Paul de Villiers Street from its intersection with Voortrekker Street to rejoin the R303. From here the road climbs to the Cold Bokkeveld first by way of the Middelberg Pass and then the Buffelsberg Pass – where there are proteas in profusion – between the Cold Bokkeveld Mountains in the west and the Cedarberg range in the east. Travel 72,9 km after rejoining the R303 to reach the appropriately-named Op die Berg (meaning 'on the mountain'), a hamlet with an incongruously ultra-modern church against the rugged skyline of the Skurweberg. Start the descent of the Gydo Pass 24,4 km further on.

GYDO PASS The Gydo Pass – from the summit of which there are wonderful views of the Warm Bokkeveld and, to the south of it, the Hex River Mountains – links the Cold Bokkeveld with the Warm Bokkeveld. The first road through the gap between the Skurweberg range in the west and the Gydoberg in the east was constructed in 1848 by Andrew Geddes Bain at the same time as he was working on Michell's Pass. It was replaced by a modern tarred road only after World War II.

Drive 12 km from the top of the Gydo Pass to come abreast of the Dutch Reformed church in Prince Alfred Hamlet.

PRINCE ALFRED HAMLET This fruit-despatching centre, which was laid out by Jan Goosen in 1861 on his farm Wagensboomrivier, was named in honour of the first Duke of Edinburgh, Queen Victoria's second son, who had visited South Africa the previous year.

Continue southward to reach the Ceres Vallei Dutch Reformed church 8,9 km from its sister church in Prince Alfred Hamlet.

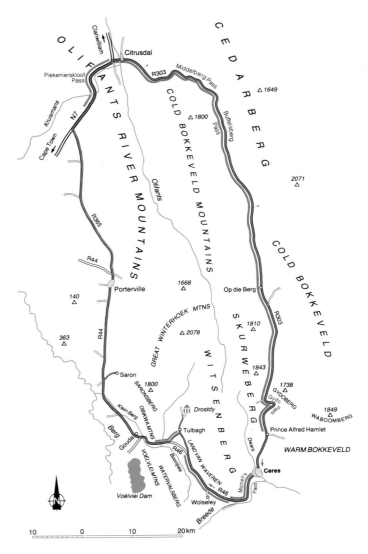

27. The Ceres Valley

10
230 km

VALLEYS OF BEAUTY AND PLENTY

Some of South Africa's most fruitful regions are in the beautiful valleys of the Hex, Breede and Slanghoek rivers, all prolific in the yield of their famous vineyards and orchards.

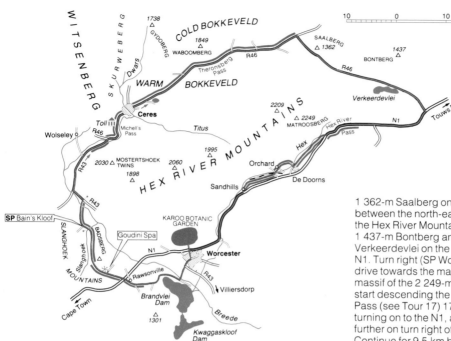

CERES It was the fertility of the soil of the region that prompted those who founded Ceres on the well-wooded banks of the Dwars River to name it after the Roman goddess of agriculture. The completion in 1848 of Michell's Pass through a gap in the Skurweberg range was the spur to the laying out of a town in the south-western corner of the Warm Bokkeveld basin, and the first plots were sold in 1849. Though remote from the diggings and mines, rural Ceres took on a hectic lease of life during the diamond and gold rushes to the north two decades after the town was established. The vast cavalcade of fortune-hunters from all over the world who scampered northwards passed this, the most direct, way – through Michell's Pass, across the Warm Bokkeveld, through Theronsberg Pass and Karoopoort and across the Karoo – to Kimberley and the Transvaal goldfields. The rushes created a huge demand for farm produce, wine and brandy, horses, mules and fodder as well as for temporary accommodation. Ceres became a major staging post on the diggers' road and the last outpost before the long trek through the wilderness. A result was the formation of the town's first big company, the Diamond Fields Transport Company, which ran a weekly service between Cape Town and Dutoitspan, near Kimberley. The days of the northward rush were limited, however, as were those of

transport-riding. But Ceres had other resources to fall back on, not least being the deciduous fruit which has ensured enduring prosperity. In recent years the trout-fishing streams in the vicinity, occasional snow on the Matroosberg which attracts skiiers, and the local authority's conscientious provision of facilities for camping, swimming and other sports have made Ceres a popular holiday resort.

From the police station in Voortrekker Street drive north-eastward out of Ceres on to the R46 across the Warm Bokkeveld.

BOKKEVELD This productive area is divided into the Warm Bokkeveld in the south and the Cold Bokkeveld in the north by the small range composed of the Gydoberg and the Waboomberg, with the Hex River Mountains forming the southern and eastern boundary of the Warm Bokkeveld. The name of the region is thought by some people to have originated because the land was suitable for goat-rearing and by others to refer to the springbok herds once plentiful here.

Ascent of the Theronsberg Pass over the southern foothills of the 1 849-m Waboomberg begins 13,7 km from the tour start. Turn right (SP Touws River) to remain on the R46 28,6 km further on, and drive 33,5 km – at first past the

1 362-m Saalberg on the left, then between the north-eastern limit of the Hex River Mountains and the 1 437-m Bontberg and finally past Verkeerdevlei on the right – to the N1. Turn right (SP Worcester) and drive towards the majestic rock massif of the 2 249-m Matroosberg, start descending the Hex River Pass (see Tour 17) 17 km after turning on to the N1, and 9,1 km further on turn right off the N1. Continue for 9,5 km before turning right into Malherbe Street in De Doorns.

DE DOORNS The farm on which De Doorns developed was called 'De Doorns boven aan de Hexe Rivier' because of the many thorn trees along the upper course of the Hex River. The thorn trees eventually made way for extensive vineyards, many of which produce grapes for the table as well as for wine-making. The town is the business centre of the rich Hex River valley agricultural region.

Drive northward along Malherbe Street out of De Doorns towards the Hex River Mountains and then westward along the foot of them through tracts of vineyard. Fork right at the hamlet of Orchard 6,1 km after turning into Malherbe Street, pass the right turn to Modderdrif 500 m further on and cross the railway line. Turn right (SP Sandhills) after another 500 m and drive past the handsome homesteads with beautiful gardens of numerous well-established wine farms. Pass Sandhills station 8,5 km after crossing the railway and 600 m further on turn right on to the N1. Drive 19,3 km to the right turn to the Karoo Botanic Garden, 1,3 km off the N1.

KAROO BOTANIC GARDEN For climatic reasons, most of the plants indigenous to the arid two-thirds of South Africa cannot be grown at Kirstenbosch, headquarters of the National Botanic Gardens, but they thrive only 100 km away at Worcester. The enchantingly laid-out Karoo Botanic Garden, which has plants typical of Namaqualand and Namibia as well as the Karoo, is affiliated to Kirstenbosch, although it originated as a private venture near Matjiesfontein in 1921. The inaccessibility of the original site led to the garden's transfer to Worcester in 1946. Apart from the veld flowers which contribute to the garden's beautiful spectacle of colour in spring, there are many other fascinating plant species which have evolved various means to withstand long periods of drought.

Return from the Karoo Garden to the N1, cross it into Worcester and at the second traffic lights, 1,6 km from the N1, turn right into High Street.

28. 'Vygies' ablaze in the Karoo Botanic Garden outside Worcester

WORCESTER See Tour 17.

From the Civic Centre in High Street drive 1 km south-westward towards the stately Cape Georgian Old Drostdy (NM – now the Worcester Technical High School), turn left into Somerset Street and 400 m further on turn right (SP Villiersdorp) into Durban Street and out of town on the R43. After 1 km leave the R43 which takes a left turn to Villiersdorp, cross the Breede River 2,7 km further on and turn right (SP Rawsonville) after another 700 m. Drive 12,7 km across the Goudini region of the Breede River valley, passing the northern end of the Brandvlei Dam, to the Dutch Reformed church in Rawsonville.

RAWSONVILLE, centre of another

noted viticultural region, was named after the distinguished scholar and public administrator Sir Rawson Rawson, who was Cape Colonial Secretary when the town was founded in 1858. Some local people prefer to call Rawsonville Goudini, the name of the region in which it is situated as well as the name of the Dutch Reformed congregation.

Continue 100 m past the Rawsonville Dutch Reformed church, turn left (SP Slanghoek) and cross the N1 1,5 km further on. Turn right after another 3,9 km and drive 200 m to the left turn to Goudini Spa.

GOUDINI SPA Slightly radioactive

thermal springs which yield water at 40 °C feed three swimming pools, two of which are enclosed, at the Goudini Spa on the eastern slopes of the 978-m Badsberg. The resort also has holiday flats, rondavels, a licensed restaurant and a variety of sporting facilities.

Backtrack the 200 m to the Rawsonville-Slanghoek road, turn right and drive 11,9 km along the eastern side of the verdant Slanghoek Valley, bounded by the Badsberg in the east and the Slanghoek Mountains in the west and south, before crossing the Slanghoek River. After another 1,7 km turn right (SP Bain's Kloof) and cross the Breede River 4,9 km further on. Turn left on to the R43 1,3 km from the river, after 3,2 km turn right (SP Wolseley, Ceres), thus remaining on the R43, and pass the left turn to Wolseley 7,4 km from the last turn. The road now curves round the two mountains known as the Mostertshoek Twins. Recross the Breede River 14,6 km from the last turn and immediately afterwards turn right (SP Ceres) on to the R46 to wind alongside the river where it has gouged out the narrow defile through which Michell's Pass runs.

MICHELL'S PASS Without a way

through the Skurweberg range Ceres would have been no more than a small market town for the farmers of the Warm Bokkeveld. Millions of years before the village was established, though, the Breede River had cut a natural passage through the mountains and all that was needed was for man to build a road through it. The early Warm Bokkeveld settlers did take farm produce through the natural Skurweberg gateway – known as Mostertshoek because a man named Jan Mostert either found the route or owned a farm at the start of the defile – but they had to transfer everything on to pack animals and leave their wagons on the eastern side of the mountains before they could undertake this arduous part of the journey. A rudimentary road came later but it was difficult and

hazardous, winding back and forth across the boulder-strewn river and ascending steeply up the precipitous slopes. Then, at the behest of Colonial Secretary John Montagu and in cooperation with Surveyor-General Charles Michell, Andrew Geddes Bain (see Ecca Pass, Tour 32) tackled Mostertshoek. He began work in 1846 with 200 convicts as labourers and completed the 9-km road through the Skurweberg range two years later. The pass, named in honour of the Surveyor-General, was opened with pomp and ceremony by Governor Sir Harry Smith in the presence of a multitude of citizens in wagons, traps and coaches as well as on horseback who took part in a procession to the summit. Not only of great importance to Ceres and the rest of the Bokkeveld regions, however, for

29. The Michell's Pass toll house

many years Michell's Pass was part of the highway to the north and therefore of value to the economy of other regions, particularly the Karoo. The pass was widened and in parts straightened in 1946 to accommodate the motorised traffic Bain could not have contemplated when he designed it, but it is still essentially the road he built. The Toll House (NM) he added as a finishing touch has been restored and stands 5,9 km from the bridge over the Breede River at the bottom of the pass.

Continue 4,2 km from the Michell's Pass Toll House back to the tour start in Ceres.

30. Workers' cottages on a Hex River valley wine farm

HEART OF THE BOLAND

For two centuries mountains hampered eastward expansion, until pioneer engineers such as A G Bain forced routes through the highland – the 'Boland', now the tranquil setting for viniculture and fruit-growing.

31. Laborie, a Paarl wine estate owned by the KWV

PAARL When Abraham Gabbema, Jan van Riebeeck's fiscal, in 1657 was exploring the area where Paarl was eventually to develop, he saw three rock massifs – the biggest boulders in South Africa – on the mountain overlooking the Berg River. As they glistened in the sun after rain he thought of jewels and named the mountain 'De Diamandt en de Peerl Bergh' – 'the Diamond and the Pearl Mountain'. The first colonists allocated farms at the foot of the mountain in 1687 called the area De Paarl, and the same name was given to the town established on the banks of the Berg River in 1690. There is now a garden of wild flowers atop Paarl Mountain (NM) and it can be reached by way of the 11-km Jan Phillips Drive leading off Main Street 2 km south of the Strooidak Church. The lofty obelisks on the southern slopes of

the mountain are elements of the Taalmonument, which commemorates the birth in Paarl of the Afrikaans language ('taal') movement in 1875. Now one of the largest towns in the western Cape, Paarl is a major centre of industry that was founded as much on wagon-building as on viniculture. And yet, in spite of industrialisation, Paarl, in its setting of vineyards and with its stately homes, gracious public buildings and oak-lined streets, retains much of its charm. Among the more notable of the town's 30-odd national monuments is the Strooidak (thatched) Church, more properly the Huguenot Church which was completed in 1805, and the Oude Pastorie (old parsonage) which dates from 1787 and is now a museum with displays of furniture, Cape silver, antique glassware, porcelain and copperware. It was at

Paarl that Dr Charles Kohler, through his founding of the Kooperatiewe Wijnbouwers Vereniging (KWV, or Cooperative Wine Farmers' Association) revolutionised the South African wine industry. By achieving the cooperation of all wine farmers, developing export markets, increasing local consumption and controlling quality, the KWV put the country's viniculture on to a stable and prosperous footing. Another national monument to which visitors are welcome is Laborie, an old wine estate owned by the KWV. On the mountain side of Main Street 2,5 km south of the Strooidak Church, the property includes an expertly-restored Cape Dutch homestead and the Laborie taphouse where wines of the Paarl region are served with traditional food.

Drive 3,4 km southward from the Strooidak Church, turn left (SP Worcester) on to the N1 and cross the Berg River 2 km further on. Fork left (SP Wemmershoek, Huguenot, Wellington) after 900 m and 300 m further on turn right (SP Wemmershoek) on to the R303 to drive through the Berg River valley. After 14,4 km on the R303 pass the left turn to Wemmershoek Dam, a visit to which entails obtaining a permit in advance from the Municipality of Cape Town. At the stop street 2,8 km further on turn left (SP Franschhoek) on to the R45 to drive to Franschhoek through the valley between the Wemmershoek

32. Wellington Blockhouse, built by the British in the Anglo-Boer War

Mountains in the north-east and the Groot Drakenstein and Franschhoek mountains in the south-west.

FRANSCHHOEK See Tour 13.

At the Huguenot Monument in Franschhoek turn left (SP Villiersdorp, Caledon) and 800 m further on start the ascent of the Franschhoek Pass (see Tour 13), reaching the top 7,4 km from the monument. Continue to the north-eastern end of the bridge over the Theewaterskloof Dam (see Tour 13) and turn left (SP Villiersdorp), thus remaining on the R45. Reach the Dutch Reformed church in Villiersdorp 9,5 km from the bridge.

VILLIERSDORP A tranquil town graced by oak trees, Villiersdorp is the centre of a prosperous apple-growing region which also produces grapes, onions, peaches and apricots. The original village was established by Field-Cornet Pieter de Villiers, some of whose descendants were to become prominent not only locally but in national affairs. One of them, Sir David de Villiers Graaff, who was elected Mayor of Cape Town in 1891 and served as a Cabinet Minister in both the Cape and Union Parliaments, founded the town's well-known De Villiers Graaff High School in 1907 with a gift of land and £50 000. Sir David's son, De Villiers Graaff, became the Leader of the Opposition in Parliament in 1957. The nature reserve just outside the town is worth a visit, especially in November when the summer annuals are blooming.

From the Dutch Reformed church drive north-eastward on to the R43 and cross the Breede River after 37,4 km. Turn right (SP Worcester) 12,5 km further on, after 1 km turn left into Somerset Street and at the Cape Georgian building (NM) of the Worcester Technical High School (the Old Drostdy) turn right (SP N1, Cape Town) into Worcester's High Street.

WORCESTER See Tour 17.

Drive 200 m north-westward up High Street, turn left (SP N1, Cape Town) into Rabie Avenue, cross the road-over-rail bridge after 1,1 km and join the N1 (SP Cape Town) 1,8 km further on. After 1,1 km turn right (SP Wolseley, Ceres, Bain's Kloof) on to the R43 and continue 17 km to Botha's Halt, a siding created so that the White Train in which King George VI and his family travelled during their 1947 tour of South Africa could be drawn up for a brief spell to enable local farmers to meet the royal visitors. Turn left (SP Bain's Kloof, Wellington) on to the R303 8,9 km further on, cross the Breede River and start the ascent of Bain's Kloof 3,4 km from the river.

BAIN'S KLOOF Until the middle of the nineteenth century the way from Cape Town to the north-east was a tortuous one. Confronted by the great mountain barrier just beyond Paarl, travellers had to trek some 70 km due north to reach the first practicable gap, the Roodezand Pass north of Tulbagh, swing south again for about 40 km through the Tulbagh Valley, then south-east for a comparable distance through the Breede River valley and finally head 70 km north-eastward along the Hex River to the Karoo, from where they could at last head directly for their destination. Then came that energetic Colonial Secretary John Montagu under whose untiring direction more road-building was done at the Cape in a decade than in the previous century. And to implement his programme there was the pioneer of South African mountain-pass engineering, Andrew Geddes Bain. When Bain completed Michell's Pass (see Tour 10) in 1848 the wagon journey from Cape Town to Beaufort West was cut from 20 days to 12, providing as it did direct access to Ceres and thence via the Theronsberg Pass and Karoopoort to the Karoo. But there was still the 70-km northward haul to the Roodezand Pass and then the 40-km southerly leg to Michell's Pass. Montagu dreamed of a direct route from Wellington to Ceres through the Slanghoek Mountains. And Bain found it, reporting that the course of the Wit River could be followed between the Limietberg and the Slanghoek Mountains. He was commissioned to build a road through the defile and completed it in 1853, more than four years after he had started. To this day it is regarded as a masterpiece of engineering. Where latter-day road-builders would have used dynamite Bain was obliged to use gunpowder to blast passages through solid rock, and retaining walls had to be built where the road wound for more than 100 m along the edge of a towering precipice. Those dry-stone retaining walls in Bain's Kloof and other passes have withstood the heavy wear of more than a century, and are admired not only by engineers but by everyone with the imagination to appreciate what they entailed. Apart from having been widened in places and tarred, Bain's Kloof Pass has hardly changed. From its 610-m summit the panoramic views over Wellington and Paarl in the south-west and towards the Swartland in the north-west are unsurpassed.

Drive 15 km from the top of Bain's Kloof Pass into College Road in Wellington. Follow College Road as it runs into Church Street and

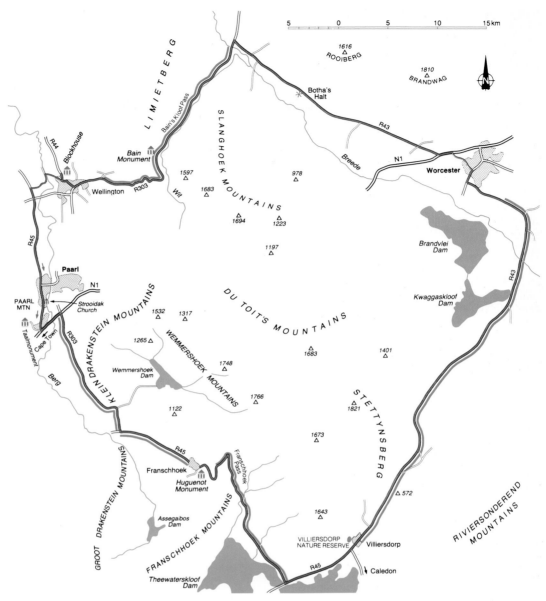

continue to the Dutch Reformed church at the T-junction ahead.

WELLINGTON Because it was the limit of settlement by the early colonists the Wellington area was first called Limiet Vallei, but those of the French Huguenots who in 1668 were allocated farms here preferred the name 'Val du Charron' ('valley of the wagonmaker'). The Dutch version of this, 'Wagenmakers Vallei', lasted until 1840 when Governor Sir George Napier was asked to name the village that had been established round a church built two years earlier on the farm Champagne. Distressed that no town in the colony bore the name of the victor of Waterloo, he called the new place Wellington. The town grew rapidly and prospered after the opening of Bain's Kloof, becoming an important stop on the route to the north. The advent of the railway in 1863 accelerated the process, and although trains and

cars led to the demise of wagon-building – the town's premier industry up to that time – other industries, including piano-making, took its place. Wellington is also noted for its contribution to education. The country's first teacher-training college was established here in 1896, there are numerous schools, and the Huguenot College for training Dutch Reformed mission and social workers is housed in the fine buildings of the defunct Huguenot University College.

From Wellington's Dutch Reformed church proceed 1,7 km north-westward along Main Street, cross the road-over-rail bridge and turn right (SP Hermon) immediately afterwards to drive 650 m to a short path to the Wellington Blockhouse.

WELLINGTON BLOCKHOUSE (NM) Early in 1901 the British introduced a system of thousands

of blockhouses, initially erected 3 000 m and then 1 000 m apart, for the purpose of protecting their lines of communication from the Republican forces in the Anglo-Boer War. Most of these small forts were of corrugated iron and few have survived, but others built of stone are still to be seen in various parts of South Africa. The sturdier blockhouse, a double-storey, loopholed structure to which access could be gained only by ladder, was usually built at a key position such as a bridge or entrance to a town. This is the most southerly of these stone structures.

Backtrack the 650 m to the Main Street, turn right (SP Malmesbury) into Lady Loch Road and cross the Berg River after 1,5 km. Turn left (SP Paarl, Cape Town) 200 m further on and after another 3 km left again (SP Paarl) on to the R45. Continue 6,6 km and turn left into Paarl's Main Street.

THROUGH THE VINEYARDS

Set against a background of surrounding mountain splendour and enhanced by oaks, the many vineyards and stately historic homesteads of the Stellenbosch winelands are a source of infinite delight.

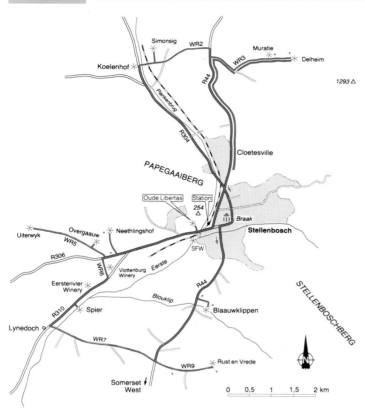

STELLENBOSCH In 1679, the year Simon van der Stel was installed as commander of the settlement at the Cape, he travelled to the interior and, after camping on the bank of the Eerste River in the beautiful countryside where Stellenbosch now stands, allocated land in the area to a number of burghers, naming the place after himself. When the town was established in 1685 Van der Stel initiated the tradition of planting oak trees here, as he did in other parts of the Cape – a tradition that has earned

Stellenbosch the sobriquet Eikestad, or 'town of oaks'. Oaks, jacarandas and other trees indeed make a major contribution to the comeliness of the town, which from its inception has been the administrative and business centre of one of the Cape's most productive wine and fruit regions. The cradle of Afrikaans culture, it has also been in the vanguard of South African education since its earliest days, having numerous state and private teaching institutions. The most notable of

these is the University of Stellenbosch, a development from the Dutch Reformed Theological Seminary, which was founded in 1863. It became the Stellenbosch College in 1881, Victoria College in 1887 and was granted university status in 1918. Stellenbosch has been graced with stately homes and public buildings throughout its existence and, with many of the earliest standing to this day, it has 76 national monuments – more than any other South African centre outside Cape Town. Dorp Street, with its oaks, rows of small whitewashed houses and water furrows, Drostdy Street and the streets round the Braak (Nederlands for 'fallow land'), the town's central 'square', are particularly well endowed with historical and architectural treasures and merit a tour on foot.

From the traffic circle at the Stellenbosch Post Office opposite the Braak drive 200 m southward along Bird Street, turn right (SP Cape Town, Strand) into Dorp Street, left (SP Somerset West, Strand) on to the R44 800 m further on and after another 4 km turn left into Blaauwklippen.

BLAAUWKLIPPEN Lying in the western shadow of Stellenbosch-berg, Blaauwklippen dates back to 1692 when Governor Simon van der Stel granted the land to the skilled artisan Gerrit Visser. The estate, with its fine Cape Dutch H-shaped homestead completed by Wouter Hoffman in 1789, is more than just a wine farm. Cheese – and a unique variety called Blaauwklippen Country Blue – is made and sold with a variety of traditional Cape fare to visitors who come to taste and perhaps buy wine. There is also a museum with an extensive collection of Cape furniture, kitchen utensils and horse-drawn vehicles, some of which are used for trips through the vineyards. As a wine estate, Blaauwklippen was all but derelict when Graham Boonzaier acquired it in 1971 and replanted the vineyards with 11 noble cultivars.

Turn left out of Blaauwklippen back on to the R44, left on to the WR9 3,8 km further on and fork left after another 1,9 km to drive 1,4 km to Rust en Vrede.

RUST EN VREDE Two centuries after the farm Bonte Rivier, now

Rust en Vrede, was granted to Willem van de Wêreld in 1694 the production of wine on the estate was abandoned. It was not until the Springbok rugby three-quarter Jannie Engelbrecht bought the property in the 1970s, restored the beautiful homestead and other buildings and replanted the vineyards with Shiraz, Cabernet Sauvignon, Tinta Barocca, Cinsaut and Chenin Blanc that Rust en Vrede vintages resumed their rightful place in the cellars of the Cape.

Return from Rust en Vrede to the R44, cross straight over (SP Lynedoch) on to the WR7 and drive through fields of strawberry plants, some of which are guarded by the most convincing scarecrows. Turn right (SP Stellenbosch) on to the R310 5,7 km after joining the WR7 and turn right into Spier 1,7 km further on.

SPIER is a combination of five farms, one of which was named Speyer by one of its early owners after his home town in Germany, on land originally granted to Arnout Jansz in 1692. Niel Joubert, descendant of a Huguenot who came from the Loire Valley in 1688, bought Spier in 1965 and restored its historic buildings, including the original cellars, that were built early in the eighteenth century. Both red and white wines are produced and are available on the estate, the attractions of which include the Jonkerhuis Restaurant.

From Spier return to the R310, turn right, and then left into the Eersterivier Winery 2 km further on.

EERSTERIVIER WINERY A visit to the Eersterivier-Valleise Koöp Wynkelder, where cellar tours can be arranged with the manager, gives an idea of the modern wine-making process. The winery, on the farm Vlottenburg allocated to the French Huguenots Pierre Rochefort and Gerard Hanseret in 1657, processes grapes grown on the hillsides within a 15-km radius.

Return from the Eersterivier Winery to the R310, turn left and after 200 m turn left again on to the WR6, passing the Vlottenburg Winery on the right almost immediately afterwards. Turn right on to the R306 1,1 km from the R310 and almost immediately left on to the WR5 to drive 3,4 km to Uiterwyk.

UITERWYK The 1791 homestead (NM) on Uiterwyk, whose history as a farm dates back to 1682, has been excellently preserved and retains its original yellowwood floors and ceilings. A new cellar has superseded the original which was built in 1798 and is now used only for storage and maturation of the

33. Harvesting grapes in a western Cape vineyard

Cabernet Sauvignon, Pinotage, Steen and Colombar wines produced on the estate by Danie de Waal and his son Chris.

Backtrack 2,7 km from Uiterwyk along the WR5 and turn left into Overgaauw.

OVERGAAUW bears the maiden name of the wife of Dirk van Velden, grandfather of Abraham Julius van Velden who acquired the estate, part of the farm By-den-Weg, in 1907. Red wines are now produced by Abraham's son David and grandson Braam from Cabernet Sauvignon, Pinotage, Merlot and varieties of Port grapes; and whites from Sylvaner, Kerner and Steen.

Return from Overgaauw to the R306, turn left and after 600 m left again to drive 1,2 km to Neethlingshof.

NEETHLINGSHOF The well-preserved homestead (NM) on Neethlingshof was built by Charles Marais in 1814, although the farm was first allocated to Willem Barend Lubbe in 1699. Today, thanks to the efforts of Jannie Momberg, who bought the estate in 1963, Neethlingshof has one of the most highly organised cellars in South Africa. The grape varieties on which the estate's wines are based include Chenin Blanc, Clairette Blanche, Colombar, Pinotage, Cinsaut, Cabernet Sauvignon and Tinta Barocca.

Return from Neethlingshof to the R306 (which becomes the R310 after a short distance), turn left and after 3,5 km left again to Oude Libertas.

OUDE LIBERTAS The Oude

Libertas complex, built in 1977 by Stellenbosch Farmers' Winery on part of the farm Libertas once owned by the colourful but recalcitrant Adam Tas, includes a vinotèque where visitors may taste the winery's product and an amphitheatre which from December to March becomes the venue for musical presentations and ballet. As the number of visitors at a tasting is limited, it is advisable to make telephone bookings in advance. The winery was founded in 1935 by a character probably even more colourful and versatile than Tas. Charles Winshaw, a Kentucky adventurer-turned-doctor, first arrived in South Africa to deliver mules for the British Army in 1899, remained to practise medicine and make wine until he became insolvent in 1921 and, after a spell back in America, returned to Stellenbosch to become one of the most prominent and respected figures in the wine industry.

From Oude Libertas continue eastward on the R310, passing the Stellenbosch railway station on the left after 1,2 km. Turn left on to the Koelenhof Road at the traffic lights 1,8 km from the station, right (SP Koelenhof Station, Elsenburg) into the Kromme Rhee Road (WR2) after another 7,3 km, and left into Simonsig 1,1 km further on.

SIMONSIG, comprising the two original land grants Simonsig and De Hoop along the Plankenbrug River, is one of the largest private wine estates. Its owner, Frans Malan, was a founder-promoter of the Stellenbosch Wine Route and the first wine-maker to produce a South African sparkling wine – Kaapse Vonkel – by the *méthode champenoise*, the method used by

the French to make champagne. A greater selection of varietal wines is made in the cellar on De Hoop than by any other producer in the country.

Continue 2,6 km eastward on the Kromme Rhee Road from Simonsig, turn right on to the R44, left on to the Knorhoek Road (WR3) after 400 m and left again after another 1,2 km to drive 1,9 km to Muratie.

MURATIE The early nineteenth-century Muratie homestead, hidden away in a dense thicket of trees in a valley on the Simonsberg, incorporates the ruins ('muratie' in Nederlands) of an earlier farmhouse built on land allocated to

34. The homestead of Blaauw-klippen was completed in 1789

Lorenz Campher in 1685. The farm was almost derelict when the German artist Georg Canitz bought it in 1925 and, guided by the distinguished oenologist Professor A I Perold, pioneered the planting of the Pinot Noir grape. Muratie has since become noted for the fine Pinot Noir wine, among others, produced by Canitz, his daughter Annemarie, who inherited the estate on his death in 1959, and their successive wine-makers, Wynand Viljoen and Ben Prins.

Continue through Muratie to reach Delheim 900 m further on.

DELHEIM De Driesprongh, the property on which Delheim wines are made and part of the land granted to Lorenz Campher, had never been properly farmed until H Hoheisen, a retired builder, bought it in 1938, cleared some of its bush and planted vines with the intention of making wines of quality to compare with those on famous neighbouring estates. It was, however, only after he was joined in 1951 by his wife's nephew, Michael ('Spatz') Sperling, a German-trained farmer who eventually assumed total control, that the quality gradually developed and the wide variety of wines with the Delheim label acquired the reputation for which they have become noted.

From Delheim return to the R44, turn left and after 7,1 km left again into Stellenbosch to reach the post office 1,5 km further on.

35. Dorp Street in Stellenbosch has many treasures of historical value

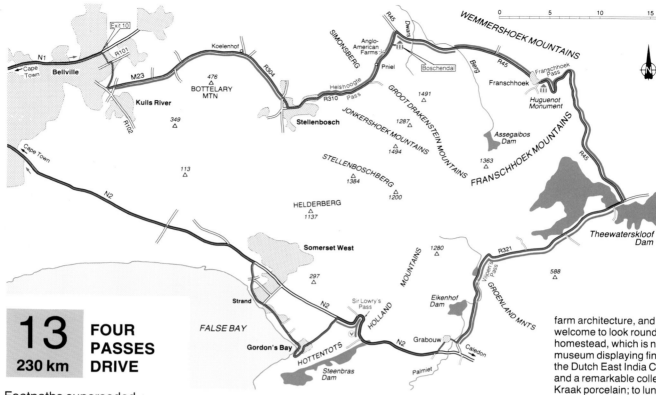

13

230 km

FOUR PASSES DRIVE

Footpaths superseded game trails through the mountains, wagon tracks obliterated footprints and now wide roads make it possible to do a round trip from Cape Town through four of these passes in a single day.

CAPE TOWN See Tour 1.

Leave Cape Town on the N1 from the seaward end of the Heerengracht, following the signs to Paarl. Take Exit 10 (SP Bellville East, Kuils River, Eversdal) 22,5 km from the tour start, 400 m further on turn right (SP Bellville E, Kuils River) on to the Old Oak Road and at the traffic lights 700 m further on cross Suikerbos Street. After 1 km turn left at the traffic lights on to the Old Paarl Road (R101) and 400 m further on turn right (SP Stikland Industrial, Kuils River) into La Belle Road. After another 2,3 km turn left (SP Stellenbosch) on to the Bottelary Road (M23).

BOTTELARY ROAD This pleasant drive between fields and vineyards runs past Bottelary Mountain which takes its name from the farm Bottelary ('bottling plant' or 'butlery') on its slopes. Towards the end of the Bottelary Road the 1 390-m Simonsberg, named after Governor Simon van der Stel, lies ahead. From this angle the mountain resembles the Governor –

or any other man – lying supine, his head to the south and his toes pointing north.

At Koelenhof, 15,6 km after turning on to the Bottelary Road, turn right (SP Stellenbosch) on to the R304 which runs into Bird Street in Stellenbosch (see Tour 12) 6,7 km further on. Drive along Bird Street and at its intersection with Merriman Avenue turn left to travel 1,4 km eastward past many University of Stellenbosch buildings to a traffic circle. Take the second exit out of the traffic circle into Cluver Street (R310) and after 500 m turn right (SP Ida's Valley, Paarl, Franschhoek), so remaining on the R310. Bear right 700 m from the last turn and 1,3 km further on start the ascent of Helshoogte, reaching the top after another 4,9 km.

HELSHOOGTE The pass Helshoogte, literally 'hell's heights', enabled the Huguenots, who in 1688 settled in the valley which was subsequently named Franschhoek, to travel between their farms and Stellenbosch over the saddle between Simonsberg in the north and the Jonkershoek Mountains in the south. In spite of plantations of trees which obscure the view in parts, the pass is a fine scenic drive.

At the fork 10 km from the Merriman Avenue traffic circle bear left and 2 km further on drive through Pniel, a coloured village which was founded in 1843 as a Dutch Reformed mission station. Continue

into the enchanting valleys of Banhoek and Groot Drakenstein to the Rhodes Fruit Farms, 2,1 km from Pniel.

RHODES FRUIT FARMS It was at Groot Drakenstein that the 'father' of the South African deciduous fruit industry, Harry Pickstone, bought numerous farms in the 1890s on behalf of the financier Cecil Rhodes, thus forming the nucleus of the trust company Rhodes Fruit Farms Ltd. Fruit there had certainly been in South Africa since the first settlement at the Cape, but it had been of no commercial significance until Pickstone introduced sound horticultural techniques and marketing practices and started supplying farmers with trees that had been properly cultivated and grafted. The farms are now run by the Anglo American Corporation.

The right turn to Boschendal is 1 km past the Rhodes Fruit Farms.

BOSCHENDAL, a farm with a history dating back to 1865, was among those bought by Pickstone for Rhodes Fruit Farms. The magnificent H-shaped homestead and its extensive outbuildings have been completely restored, particularly careful attention having been paid to the unique acorn-motif friezes discovered under layers of paint and colourwash round the doors and windows and under the cornices of every room. Dominated by the Groot Drakenstein Mountains, Boschendal is one of the finest examples of Cape Dutch

farm architecture, and visitors are welcome to look round the homestead, which is now a museum displaying fine furniture of the Dutch East India Company era and a remarkable collection of Kraak porcelain; to lunch either in the restaurant or under the nearby trees; and to taste and perhaps buy the wines of the estate.

Turn right (SP Franschhoek, Villiersdorp) on to the R45 1,6 km beyond Boschendal and continue 14,4 km to Franschhoek, the R45 running straight into Huguenot Street.

FRANSCHHOEK, embraced in the curve of the imposing Franschhoek Mountains, dates from 1688 when the first of a small band of French Huguenots were allocated farms in this valley. Their farms and the homesteads they built are among the most beautiful in the country and many retain their evocative original names – La Provence, La Terre de Luc, Languedoc, La Motte, Bien Donne . . . The central figure of the imposing Huguenot Monument, erected in Franschhoek in 1938 to mark the 250th anniversary of the French refugees' arrival, stands on the world with her feet on France and bears a Bible in one hand and a broken chain in the other to symbolise freedom from religious persecution. The three arches behind her – the centre one surmounted by the sun of righteousness – represent the Trinity, and the lily pond at her feet the tranquillity that comes after strife. The monument is tastefully flanked by the buildings of the Huguenot Museum.

Turn left (SP Villiersdorp, Caledon) at the monument end of Huguenot Street and start the ascent of the Franschhoek Pass after 800 m.

FRANSCHHOEK PASS Apart from ancient elephant trails and Bushman paths, which were of use to the early colonists only if they travelled on foot or on horseback, Franschhoek was completely isolated by encircling mountains from the country to the east until 1817. In that year the Catspad, a road poorly constructed through the Franschhoek Mountains by S J Cats, was completed. Within five years floods had rendered it impassable and, at the behest of Governor Lord Charles Somerset, Major W C Holloway of the Royal Engineers started work on a new pass which was completed in 1825. A feature of it easily missed by the hasty is the Jan Joubertsgat Bridge 13 km from the Huguenot Monument. Thought to be South Africa's longest used bridge, its 5-m arch bearing a 5,5-m span is one of the most attractive examples of dressed-stone masonry in the country.

About 18 km from the Huguenot Monument the water of the Theewaterskloof Dam can be seen.

THEEWATERSKLOOF DAM In the dry season water from this dam on the Riviersonderend is transferred through a tunnel to the Franschhoek Valley. But when the Berg River on the other side of the mountains is in spate its surplus water is pumped through the same tunnel to the Theewaterskloof Dam, which has become a popular watersport playground.

Turn right (SP Grabouw, Caledon) over the Theewaterskloof Dam bridge on to the R321 26,2 km from the Huguenot Monument. Start the ascent of Viljoen's Pass 16 km further on.

37. Franschhoek in its mountain valley

VILJOEN'S PASS From the summit of this pass over the Groenland Mountains, which follows the gorge of the Palmiet River, there is a superb view of the vast valley of the Riviersonderend. The pass, which was in existence in the early nineteenth century, was renamed in honour of Sir Anthonie Viljoen, who became a pioneer of the Elgin apple industry after the Anglo-Boer War.

Turn right (SP Grabouw, Cape Town) 29,4 km from the Theewaterskloof Dam bridge and after another 500 m cross the Palmiet River into Grabouw.

GRABOUW, in the angle between the Hottentots Holland Mountains and the Groenland range, is the centre of the fertile Elgin region, the second largest apple-producing area in the country. Industries related to the processing and marketing of deciduous fruit make the main contribution to the town's economy.

Turn right (SP Cape Town) on to the N2 2,3 km from the Palmiet River and drive 7,9 km to the left turn to the Steenbras Dam.

STEENBRAS DAM The Steenbras Dam, for many years after it was completed in 1921 the main source of Cape Town's water, is situated in a scenic area with terraced rock gardens along the steep riverbed. Admission is strictly by permit, obtained in advance from the Municipality of Cape Town.

From the dam turn-off drive to the edge of the Hottentots Holland plateau and, at the top of Sir Lowry's Pass 8,7 km after joining the N2, turn left to a viewing site.

SIR LOWRY'S PASS When the Dutch settlers first started travelling eastward from the Cape they

36. The small boat harbour at Gordon's Bay

followed the route that had long been used by Bushmen and Hottentots to the plateau beyond the Hottentots Holland Mountains. And the indigenous people, in their turn, followed a trail blazed for them by migrating animals, which they called Gantouw (meaning 'elands' path'). The trail was arduous, but it held few hazards for men on foot or even on horseback. For ox wagons and carts, however, the gradients were perilous, and many a vehicle was damaged along the way. For a long time the only route from the Cape Flats to the east, it was used until 1828, when Major Charles Michell, the Cape Colony's Superintendent of Works, constructed a road that traversed the face of the mountain and named it in honour of Governor Sir Lowry Cole. Parts of the old Gantouw (NM), with grooves gouged by wagon wheels into the rock in places, can still be seen a half-hour walk from the summit of the pass. Although Sir Lowry's Pass is scenic

over its entire length, the panorama from the summit viewpoint makes a pause worthwhile.

Turn left (SP Gordon's Bay, Kleinmond) 6,5 km from the top of the pass. Drive 4,9 km before turning left at Gordon's Bay and right into Faure Street 2,1 km further on to wind down the hillside past the harbour to the seafront. Continue 1,5 km to the beach.

GORDON'S BAY has had a fishing harbour since the beginning of the eighteenth century when the place was named Fisch Hoek. It was renamed at the end of that century in honour of Colonel Robert Gordon, the last commander of the Dutch East India Company garrison at the Cape. With safe bathing and good water for rock and sea angling, boardsailing, powerboating and other aquatic sports, Gordon's Bay has become a popular holiday and retirement resort.

Continue along the seafront and turn left 5 km from the beach at Gordon's Bay to drive along the beachfront at Strand and reach the traffic circle in the centre of town.

STRAND Like Gordon's Bay, Strand has had a commercial fishing industry since the beginning of the eighteenth century. The town started developing as a resort in the mid-nineteenth century when Daniel van Ryneveld allowed farmers to erect holiday shacks on property he owned beside the sea.

From the traffic circle in Strand continue 3,5 km along the seafront before the road swings towards the Helderberg above Somerset West. Turn left (SP Stellenbosch) 5,3 km from the traffic circle, and left again on to the N2 (SP Cape Town) 1,7 km further on to drive 45 km back to Cape Town.

TO THE EAST OF FALSE BAY

Rugged irregularity characterises the scenic coastline where the Hottentots Holland Mountains, among other ranges, run down to the sea and men have constructed a spectacular marine drive.

38. Seaside homes at Betty's Bay

HERMANUS See Tour 15.

From the war memorial above the Old Harbour in Hermanus drive 300 m north-eastward along Marine Drive before turning right into Main Road. At the traffic circle 3 km further on take the third exit into Main Road, Voëlklip, turn left (SP Stanford, Gansbaai) after 2,8 km and turn right on to the R43 100 m further on to drive some 9 km along the northern shore of Kleinriviers-vlei. Cross the Klein River 23,1 km from the war memorial and at the crossroads 900 m further on reach the right turn into Stanford (see Tour 15) and the left turn to Salmonsdam. Take the left turn on to the R326, turn right (SP Salmonsdam, Elim) on to gravel after 4,3 km and drive along the valley of the Klein River. After 7 km turn left (SP Salmonsdam) to reach the entrance to the Salmonsdam Nature Reserve 5 km further on.

SALMONSDAM NATURE RESERVE Salmonsdam, in the steep valley of the Perdeberg River, is an Eden of magnificent mountain scenery and fynbos. 'Fynbos' is the name for the rich variety of plants characteristic of the Cape Floral Kingdom, one of the world's six recognised botanic regions. The thousands of species of fynbos, with their infinite diversity of form, colour and size, are well represented in this reserve, and in spring the mountain slopes blaze with colour.

Return from the reserve to the R326, turn right (SP Riviersonder-end) and continue further up the Klein River valley, reaching the top of the lovely Akkedisberg Pass 7,9 km further on. Turn left (SP Caledon) on to the R316 18,4 km after rejoining the R326, cross a railway line 27,2 km further on to run into Church Street in Caledon and reach its intersection with Mill Street after another 550 m.

CALEDON See Tour 15.

From the intersection of Church and Mill streets in Caledon follow the SPs to Cape Town on to the N2. Continuing westward, cross the Swart River 8,7 km further on and the Bot River after another 12 km.

BOT RIVER The river we now know as the Bot was known to the Hottentots as the 'Gouga', which means 'an abundance of fat'. The same word 'gou' was used for butter, a commodity produced in abundance by the Hottentots living on the river banks where the pasture was good. Merchants who travelled from the settlement at the Cape to have their butter casks filled in exchange for a variety of wares simply used a translation of 'Gouga' in their naming of the river and records show that as early as 1672 they called it the Botter. The river, which rises south of the Theewaterskloof Dam, forms a marsh near its mouth and then an expansive stretch of water known as Lake Marina.

Pass under the R43 to Hermanus 2,2 km after crossing the Bot River and start the ascent of the Houhoek Pass after another 1,5 km to reach the summit 4,6 km from the under-pass. Turn right (SP Houhoek) off the N2 2,4 km still further. Cross the railway 300 m from the N2 and reach the Houhoek Inn 200 m from the level crossing.

HOUHOEK Less than 25 km from the hazardous route up which they had struggled through the Hottentots Holland Mountains, early travellers on their way eastward were faced by another formidable obstacle in the form of the 896-m

mountain now known as the Houwhoekberg. The Swede Oloff Bergh, who led many early expeditions from the Cape, crossed the mountain in 1682 by way of what came to be variously called the Hout Hoek (because of all the timber around the glen) and Houw Hoek (because of the holding back required of the oxen descending it). Grooves cut into rock by the wheels of wagons mark the earliest track, which was superseded in 1831 by a road laid out by Major Charles Michell, the engineer of Sir Lowry's Pass. Subsequent reconstruction and rerouting culminated in the present fine highway across the mountain. The village of Houhoek, now bypassed by the highway, is famous for its inn, which was established in 1834 to cater for the needs of the wagoners who outspanned at the top of the pass and to serve as a staging post for horse-drawn traffic. The mighty eucalyptus tree growing in front of it was planted by innkeeper Beyers in 1859 to mark the birth of his daughter Gertrude Maria. Modern travellers through the pass rarely miss an opportunity to quaff an ale at the inn, which has retained much of its charm.

Return from the inn to the N2, turn right and travel 21 km before crossing the Steenbras River. Reach the entrance (left) to the Steenbras Dam (see Tour 13) 900 m from the river. Turn left to the viewing site at the top of Sir Lowry's Pass 700 m beyond the entrance to the dam. The start of the Boland Hiking Trail, which gives access to part of the original Gantouw Pass, is opposite the turn-off to the viewing site.

SIR LOWRY'S PASS See Tour 13.

Turn left out of the viewing site on to the N2 for the descent of the pass. After 6,1 km turn left (SP Gordon's Bay, Kleinmond) on to the R44 and right at the stop street at the entrance to Gordon's Bay 4,5 km further on. After another 50 m turn left into Sir Lowry Street to drive 200 m to the beachfront.

GORDON'S BAY See Tour 13.

Turn left out of Sir Lowry Street into Beach Road and drive round the bay, passing the South African Naval College (right) after 1 km and reaching the Gordon's Bay harbour entrance 300 m further on. At the stop street 350 m beyond the harbour entrance turn right on to the R44 for the scenic run along Clarence Drive, from which there are views across False Bay to Table Mountain and the rest of the Cape Peninsula. Cross the Steenbras River by way of the Benning Bridge 4,9 km after joining the R44 and 1,9 km further on reach a

39. Houhoek Inn and the giant eucalyptus planted in 1859

monument (left) commemorating Jack Clarence after whom this marine drive is named. Reach the entrance to the Kogel Bay Resort (right) 4 km from the monument.

KOGEL BAY The appearance of the long, inviting beach at Kogel Bay (Koëlbaai), where there is a resort for use by coloured people, belies its nature. Bathers have to be cautious of currents and a dangerous backwash.

Cross the Rooiels River 8,4 km south of the Kogel Bay resort.

ROOIELS The cluster of holiday homes on what was once a farm granted to Abraham Louw in 1839 is named after the 'rooi-els' (literally, 'red alder') which once thrived here but has now been almost eradicated from the area. The river of the same name runs into what used to be called Waaigat Bay but is now known as Rooiels Bay, a safe and attractive spot for a family day on the beach.

The R44 now swings inland to the east of Hangklip Mountain and reaches a right turn (SP Pringle Bay, Hangklip) 5,8 km from the Rooiels River.

PRINGLE BAY In recent years developers have turned the northern slopes of the striking 454-m peak Hangklip above Pringle Bay – named after Rear-Admiral Thomas Pringle who at one time commanded the Royal Navy's station at the Cape – into a fashionable residential area.

CAPE HANGKLIP Hangklip, or 'hanging rock', was formerly designated Cabo Falso (the 'false cape') because its resemblance to Cape Point occasionally prompted navigators from the east to turn north earlier than they should have done. The mountain was once the refuge of escaped slaves who harried stock farmers driving their herds to the Cape Town market, and an inlet in the northern corner of Pringle Bay is still officially designated Drostersgat ('deserters' cove'). Until 1930 there was a whaling station in Stony Bay on the eastern side of the promontory from which Hangklip rises.

Pass another right turn to Hangklip 4,5 km from the last and reach the post office at Betty's Bay 2,2 km further on.

BETTY'S BAY, around which there are the homes of retired people and the seaside cottages of weekenders, was once the site of a whaling station. Part of the station's jetty as well as the remains of the ramp on which carcases were winched ashore can still be seen in the western part of the bay.

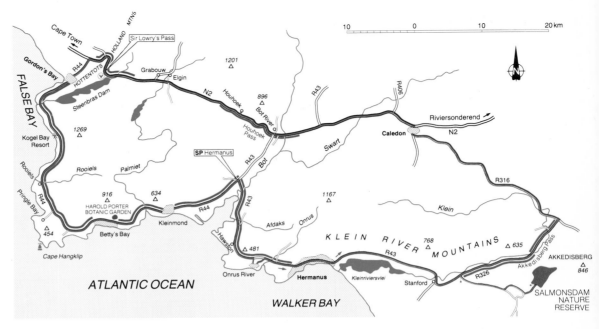

Turn left into the Harold Porter Botanic Garden 2,7 km from the Betty's Bay post office.

HAROLD PORTER BOTANIC GARDEN This reserve – through which there are several enchanting paths – was named after Harold Porter, one of the founders of the company that developed Betty's Bay and donor of the land for this section of the National Botanic Gardens. The area has one of the densest concentrations of fynbos in the western Cape.

Cross the Palmiet River 7,7 km from the Harold Porter Garden, reach the first Kleinmond houses 1,9 km from the river and the main Kleinmond caravan park 4,7 km from the same point.

KLEINMOND, with some luxurious homes, less sophisticated holiday cottages and several caravan and camping sites clustered round Sandown Bay, is a seaside resort at the foot of the Palmietberg that is becoming increasingly popular. The author D F Malherbe based his graphically descriptive novel *Hans-die-Skipper* on the lives of the doughty fishermen who used to set out from the harbour to wrest a living from the sea in the 1920s.

Continue on the R44 to a stop street 10,9 km from the Kleinmond caravan park, turn right (SP Hermanus) on to the R43 and cross the Bot River after 1,6 km. Turn right (SP Onrus River, Vermont) 12,6 km further on and drive straight to the seafront at Vermont. Turn left to drive along the coast, about 300 m of the road being untarred, turn right into Macfarlane Street after 750 m and right again into De Villiers Street at the stop street 350 m further on. Turn right

once more into Atlantic Drive after another 400 m and reach the lagoon at the mouth of the Onrus River 600 m still further. Turn left out of Atlantic Drive back to the De Villiers Street intersection 1 km from the lagoon, thus having completed a circular drive through the resort of Onrus River.

VERMONT AND ONRUS RIVER Though little more than 10 km long, the river which rises in the Babilonstoring Mountains and runs into the sea through a lagoon was regarded by the Dutch settlers who first saw it as restless. So they named it Onrust, the spelling of which has been modernised in spite of opposition from traditionalists. Particularly vociferous defence of the 'T' in the original form of the name came from the colony of

distinguished South African artists who have homes at Onrus and the contiguous resort of Vermont. The colony has included the writers Uys Krige, Jan Rabie, Jack Cope and Elsa Joubert; the sculptor Bill Davis; and the painters Gregoire Boonzaaier, Marjorie Wallace and Cecil Higgs.

From the De Villiers Street intersection drive 600 m northward along Van Blommestein Street, turn right and at the stop street 800 m further on right again back on to the R43. Cross the Onrus River after 600 m and reach the main intersection in Hermanus 4,5 km further on.

40. Hangklip, the dominant feature at Pringle Bay

CHAPTER TWO
The Southern Cape

TIP OF AFRICA

420 km

Attractive seaside resorts, historic villages and mountain scenery are features of a tour which includes a visit to the southernmost cape of Africa where two oceans meet.

HERMANUS Above the cove to the west of the Old Harbour at Hermanus there is a plaque marking the spring which attracted the first permanent resident, Hermanus Pieters, to what is now one of the most fashionable seaside and retirement resorts on the Cape coast. Pieters, a Hollander who came to the Cape early in the nineteenth century, was an itinerant teacher of Caledon farmers' children. He also had sheep and it was in moving them to fresh pastures that he came upon the enchanting bay – subsequently named after a Royal Naval officer called Walker – on which Hermanus was eventually established. The spring came to be known as Hermanuspietersfontein, a name which was also applied to the early settlement but shortened to Hermanus when municipal status was accorded in 1904. For more than a century the Old Harbour (NM) was the heart of a thriving fishing industry based on the large catches in and around Walker Bay. Its exposed position and tricky

entrance held many a peril for the fishing crews, however, and it has long been replaced by a safer, more modern harbour further west. Among the attractions which make Hermanus popular are its fine, safe beaches; the Kleinriviersvlei lagoon, with its opportunities for yachting and other water sports; the Fernkloof Nature Reserve in the saddle between Lemoenkop and Olifantsberg; the extensive cliff-top walk with endlessly unfolding vistas over the rocky coastline; the Rotary Mountain Way which runs along the heights above the town; and the bounty of Walker Bay which anglers share with professional fishermen.

From the main traffic intersection in Hermanus drive north-westward on the R43 and after 2,6 km turn right on to the Rotary Mountain Way, a 7-km drive along the Olifantsberg overlooking the town and bay. Having completed the drive, return to the R43, turn right and drive 1,5 km before turning right again (SP Caledon) on to the R320 through the Hemel en Aarde Valley.

HEMEL EN AARDE This pleasant agricultural valley between the Babilonstoring Mountains in the north and the Kleinriviersberg range in the south was not always the felicitous place it is today. Here in the mountains between 'hemel en aarde' – heaven and earth – South Africa's first leper colony, indeed the country's first specialised public health institution, was established in 1817 and run by Moravian missionaries until 1845, when all lepers were sent to Robben Island.

Turn left into Caledon 35,8 km after joining the R320.

CALEDON The establishment of Caledon stemmed from the mineral springs, one cold and six hot, which generate 2 million litres of chalybeate, radioactive water a day at 49 °C and were at one time highly valued for their curative properties. The land on which they bubble to the surface at the foot of the 1 089-m Swartberg was granted to Ferdinand Appel in 1709 to provide accommodation for the sick and for

visitors, but the first bath house was constructed only in 1797. A church village called Swartberg was established on the farm in 1810, and in 1813 it was renamed by Governor Sir John Cradock in honour of his predecessor, the Earl of Caledon. A spa with a sanatorium and first-class hotel superseded the earlier amenities at the thermal springs early in the twentieth century but was destroyed by fire in 1946 and has not been replaced. However, it is still possible to 'take the waters' in a swimming pool to which a caravan park and camping site are attached. More famous now than the springs is Caledon's Victoria Park, established in 1899 and more popularly referred to as the Caledon Wild Flower Garden. In 1933 Cecil Young, with the generous support of public-spirited citizens of the town, turned the garden into a veritable landscaping masterpiece and a joy to the thousands of visitors who come in spring to see not only the kaleidoscope of colour in the garden, but also the Caledon Wild Flower Show.

From Holy Trinity Church in Prince Alfred Street drive 1,5 km north-westward, turn left (SP Cape Town) on to the N2 and continue 2,4 km before turning right (SP Greyton) on to the R406. Cross the Swart River 3,2 km from the N2 and the Riviersonderend 23,3 km further on. Pass the left turn to Villiersdorp 1,7 km from the Riviersonderend and after another 300 m turn left to drive 1,6 km to Genadendal.

GENADENDAL This charming village in the southern shadow of the Riviersonderend Mountains' developed from the earliest mission station in the country, founded in 1737 by the Moravian Georg Schmidt. The nucleus of the settlement comprises the church, church bell (NM) in a handsome bell 'tower', parsonage, school building, disused water mill and several pretty thatched and limewashed cottages, all structures of cultural and historical significance which have survived from the mission's earliest days.

Return from Genadendal to the R406, turn left (no SP) and drive 3,8 km to Greyton.

GREYTON This tranquil village on the southern slopes of the Riviersonderend range has become a fashionable retreat for city folk who have acquired homes here and spend weekends among more permanently rustic neighbours. The first plots on either side of what is now the pretty oak-lined main street were sold in 1854, and the village was named after Governor Sir George Grey.

Travel 800 m from the boundary sign at the entrance to Greyton and turn right (SP Riviersonderend) out of the main street of the village to remain on the R406. Continue 28,3 km before turning right (SP Riviersonderend), fork left after another 800 m and 6,6 km further on turn left on to the N2 to reach the Dutch Reformed church in Riviersonderend after 2,5 km.

RIVIERSONDEREND The centre of a farming district, Riviersonderend takes its name from the river which at one time was regarded as having no end. A Dutch Reformed congregation was established here in 1922 and the town was laid out three years later.

From the Dutch Reformed church in Riviersonderend continue 20,9 km eastward on the N2 and turn right (SP Bredasdorp, Napier) on to the R317. Drive 52,8 km before turning left (SP Bredasdorp) and 3,1 km further to the first traffic lights in Bredasdorp.

BREDASDORP In 1837 a Dutch Reformed centre was established on the farm Langefontein and named after Michiel van Breda, a local farmer who had promoted the project and was also first mayor of Cape Town and a member of the Cape Legislative Assembly. Bredasdorp is now the hub of a dairy and wheat farming region, and principal town of Africa's southernmost district. The small but fascinating Bredasdorp Maritime Museum features many of the ships that have been wrecked on the region's notorious coast.

From the Dutch Reformed church in Bredasdorp drive south-eastward out of town (SP Waenhuiskrans) on the R316 to reach Waenhuiskrans after 24,3 km. Continue 900 m past the Waenhuiskrans boundary sign and turn left to the beach, harbour and fishing village.

WAENHUISKRANS A picturesque village with thatched, limewashed fishermen's cottages, Waenhuiskrans is so named

because of a huge cavern in a nearby cliff which probably could accommodate several wagons. Its unofficial name, Arniston, derives from the British troopship *Arniston*, wrecked in the vicinity with the loss of 372 lives in 1815. A memorial records that the sons of Lieutenant-Colonel Andrew Giles of the 173rd Regiment perished in the wreck with Lord and Lady Molesworth in whose charge they were for the voyage home to Britain from India.

Return to the R316 and 6,1 km from the Waenhuiskrans boundary sign turn left (SP Struisbaai). Continue 6,9 km and turn left again (SP Struisbaai, Die Mond), after 400 m turn right (SP Struisbaai), and 7,4 km further on turn left (SP Struisbaai, Agulhas) on to the R319. Reach the thatched fishermen's cottages at the outskirts of Struisbaai after 16,1 km.

STRUISBAAI Named 'Aguada de São Jorge' by Bartolomeu Dias in 1488, Struisbaai seems to have acquired the original form, 'Vogel Struys Baay' ('Ostrich Bay'), of its present name in the seventeenth century. For many years it was no more than a rudimentary harbour with a cluster of fishermen's cottages but, with its fine 16-km beach, good surf and rewarding angling, it has become a popular resort of holiday homes, camping and caravan parks and a motel.

Continue 6,1 km on the R319 to reach the sign which adjures: 'Keep our cape the fairest – L'Agulhas, the southernmost town.'

CAPE AGULHAS, which takes it name from the Portuguese word for needles because early Portuguese navigators discovered that their compass needles showed no deviation here, is the southernmost point of the continent and thus demarcates the Atlantic from the Indian Ocean. The country's second oldest lighthouse, dating from 1849, stands idle near the resort, having been replaced by one with a beam of 18 million candle power. East of the cape there are

41. The old harbour at Hermanus

'vywers', fish traps which early men created by building low dams across shallow gullies so that fish would be stranded in them at low tide. Some vywers have been maintained down the centuries and are used even in modern times.

Return to Struisbaai and turn left (SP Elim, Die Dam, Gansbaai) 3,7 km after passing the Struisbaai fishermen's cottages. Drive 36 km to the Elim boundary sign.

ELIM was founded as a mission station in 1824 by Bishop Peter Hallbeck of the Moravian Brethren or Herrnhuters, who named it after the place where the Israelites rested after crossing the Red Sea. The community, still of Moravian persuasion, consists of stock, fruit and vegetable farmers, farmworkers, domestic servants and artisans, among whom the Elim thatchers are renowned for their craftsmanship. The church clock, acquired for Elim in 1914, has been working since 1764 when it was built in Germany for a church in Herrenhut. A memorial giving

thanks to God for the emancipation of slaves in 1838 stands near the Elim church. The village's restored corn mill was built in 1828.

Turn right (SP Gansbaai) 600 m from the last boundary sign and drive 19,6 km to the unaccountably-named community of Baardskeerdersbos ('beard-shaver's bush'). Continue 18,7 km before turning right (no SP) and 8,7 km further on turn left to reach the harbour at Gansbaai.

GANSBAAI Some of the English surnames of Afrikaans-speaking families at Gansbaai are accounted for by the settlement in the area of survivors of the British troopship *Birkenhead*, wrecked at nearby Danger Point in 1852. The heroism of the steamer's military passengers, who stood in order on deck while the women and children were taken off, has become a legend. The harbour at Gansbaai is the centre of the local fishing activity.

From the Gansbaai post office drive 21,3 km north-eastward on the R43 to Stanford, passing after 3,5 km the left turn to Die Kelders, a resort with a large sea cavern which may be visited.

STANFORD Captain Robert Stanford, a retired British Army officer who had bought and settled on the property Kleinrivier, won fame and a knighthood for defying his fellow citizens and supplying the controversial convict ship *Neptune* with provisions when she arrived at the Cape in 1849. The village that came into existence on Kleinrivier was named in his honour.

From Stanford drive 25,3 km round Kleinriviersvlei to the main traffic intersection in Hermanus.

42. Homes in the historic village of Genadendal

16
290 km

THE LAST PONT

South Africa's last vehicle pont affords a unique travelling experience early in a journey to the mouth of the Breede River and thence, by way of two scenic mountain passes, through the Langeberg range.

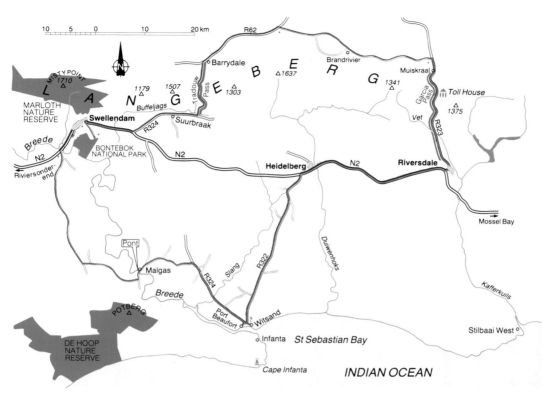

SWELLENDAM Nestling in a valley through which the Koringlands River comes tumbling down from the Langeberg, Swellendam was once the last settlement through which adventurers passed on their way eastward from the Cape. The handful of burghers who settled on the slopes of the Langeberg and along the Breede River and its tributaries undoubtedly found the region as attractive as the Hessekwa Hottentots had done before them – but for different reasons. With its teeming game, it had been a rewarding hunting ground for the Hottentots. To the white men it represented excellent land on which to establish themselves as farmers. Swellendam became a sub-drostdy for the 'outlying districts' of the colony in 1743, and two years later a magisterial district in its own right. The Drostdy was built and in 1747 the district was named in honour of Governor Swellengrebel and his wife Helena van Damme. Although small, the village which sprang up round the Drostdy developed considerable importance as the 'capital' of the Overberg. Its importance may, indeed, have given the local burghers ideas for, aggrieved by the conduct of the Dutch East India Company, in 1795 they dismissed the *landdrost* and proclaimed Swellendam a republic,

with Hermanus Steyn as the somewhat reluctant 'president'. 'Independence' lasted only four and a half months, however, for when the British occupied the Cape Steyn's 'subjects' swore allegiance to King George III and the *landdrost* was reinstated.

For many years Swellendam's prosperity was dependent on cattle, sheep and horse farming. The wheat for which the region is well-known came later, and now dairy farming and fruit are achieving

importance. Prominent among those who contributed through commerce to the town's early prosperity was Joseph Barry, a successful merchant in the Overberg area and founder of the trading firm Barry and Nephews. Of the craftsmen who met the farming community's needs, none became so well known as Barry, but their skills are recalled in the cluster of workshops that have been recreated near the Drostdy and equipped with the tools of their

trades as blacksmiths, charcoal burners, coppersmiths, coopers, shoemakers and millers. Numerous well-preserved buildings reflect Swellendam's past, not least of them the Drostdy (NM), a charming building of great architectural and historical value which is now a museum exhibiting furniture fashioned long ago, old household utensils, some of the early paper money used in the town and old animal-drawn vehicles. Other national monuments are the old jail; the thatched dwelling next door which was once the post office and home of the jailer-cum-postmaster; the burgher Oefeningshuis (meeting house) which was built in 1837 for church services; the Auld House, which once belonged to the Barry family; the old Boys' School; the Heemradenhuis (local council office); and The Cottage, a T-shaped home in typical Cape architectural style that is thought to have been built in 1832. The Marloth Nature Reserve overlooks Swellendam from the slopes of the Langeberg, and south of the town is the Bontebok National Park.

To reach the park, bear right at the eastern end of Voortrek Street into Swellengrebel Street, cross the N2 and then the railway line, and follow the road a short distance beyond the Swellendam airfield on the right.

BONTEBOK NATIONAL PARK

Zoologists assert that the bontebok would by now have been extinct had it not been protected since 1830 on the southern Cape farms of the Van der Byl, Van Breda, Albertyn and Uys families. Even so, by 1927 there were only 121 of the species in the coastal belt south of the Langeberg range, which for centuries had been its natural habitat. With only 22 of the remaining animals as a nucleus, in 1930 the government established the Bontebok National Park on a farm south of Bredasdorp. Although the danger of extinction was averted, the farm was not ideal and the park was relocated to its present position. The bontebok have multiplied and the park has now been stocked with springbok, rhebok, duiker, grysbok and red hartebeest.

Return to Swellendam and from the Dutch Reformed church in Voortrek Street drive 3,1 km south-westward before turning left (SP to R60). After 800 m turn right (SP Riviersonder-end) on to the N2 and 3,3 km further on cross the Breede River. After another 1,5 km turn left (SP Malgas, Infanta) and drive 40,6 km before turning left again. Continue 2,2 km to the pont at Malgas.

43. Oom Moxie Dunn, harnessed to the cable along which he hauled the Malgas pont for more than 25 years

MALGAS In the heyday of Swellendam's prosperity one of the principal modes of freight transport between the district and Cape Town was the coaster, and the main inland port was Malgas, or Malagaskraal as it used to be known. Mariners who had negotiated the shoals at the mouth of the Breede River were able to navigate their vessels some 50 km upstream to Malgas, and most famous of the ships that did so was the trader Joseph Barry's *Kadie*. For six years, until she stranded on rocks in the river in 1865, the 158-ton *Kadie* carried agricultural produce to the Cape and returned with wares for the Barry commercial enterprises. The vehicle pont at Malgas, the last still in use in South Africa, was for many years powered by one man, Oom Moxie Dunn, who harnessed himself to the standing cable and 'walked' his conveyance across the water. Now two assistants provide the power under Oom Moxie's supervision. The tariff ranges from 50c a crossing for a threshing-machine, tractor, lorry, car or any number of small livestock from one to 50 and 25c for a motorcycle, bicycle, wheelbarrow or person on horseback, to 20c a pedestrian and 15c each for a horse, donkey or cow.

Once across the river, drive 2,6 km before forking right (SP Heidelberg) and another 3,9 km before forking right again (SP Witsand). After 7,1 km turn right (no SP) on to the R324, continue 18,5 km and turn right into Port Beaufort.

PORT BEAUFORT Like many another place in South Africa, Port Beaufort is named in honour of a relation of one of the governors, in this instance the Duke of Beaufort, father of Lord Charles Somerset. Now only a seaside and angling resort, it was once a thriving little port pioneered in 1817 by Benjamin Moodie who owned the Swellendam farm Grootvaders-bosch, had shipping interests and built the first stone 'warehouse' at Port Beaufort. Maritime activity increased considerably from 1822 when Joseph Barry became involved, but when the Barry empire, with business undertakings in towns and villages throughout the Overberg, became insolvent in 1866 Port Beaufort ceased to be a port. The old customs house, now an inn, and the thatched church (NM), built in 1849 by Joseph's nephew Thomas Barry, remain to recall the heyday of the village.

Return to the Port Beaufort turn-off, turn right and drive 2,4 km eastward to Witsand.

WITSAND This is a charming resort for fishing, walks among the dunes, photography and water sports.

Return to the Port Beaufort turn-off, turn right (SP Heidelberg) on to the R322 and continue 35 km north-eastward to the N2. Turn right (SP Heidelberg), continue 3,4 km and turn left into Heidelberg.

HEIDELBERG Because the farmers in the area where Heidelberg now stands had to travel so far to either Swellendam or Riversdale to attend church, a new congregation in between was established in 1855, and Doornboom, a property on the Duiwenhoks River, was bought as a church farm. The village that developed was given the name of the German city where the Heidelberg Catechism originated. In place of the original Dutch Reformed church there is now an imposing edifice of distinctive Gothic design which dominates the centre of this little town surrounded by wheatlands. Much smaller but noted for its beautiful rose windows and valuable wood sculptures is the Anglican Church of St Barnabas.

Return from Heidelberg to the N2, turn left and after 31,1 km turn left (SP Riversdale, Ladismith) into Riversdale.

RIVERSDALE Named in 1838 after Harry Rivers, the commissioner and magistrate at Swellendam who eventually became the Cape Colonial Treasurer, Riversdale is a farming centre on the Vet River. Two places of particular interest in the town are Jurisch Park and Versveld House. The park, a proclaimed botanical garden, is divided into one section for exotic plants and another, the Van Riebeeck Garden, for indigenous plants. Versveld House was bequeathed to the community by Theodore Versveld to accommodate the Africana collection presented by Julius Gordon in memory of his parents who had been citizens of Riversdale. Among the treasures housed here are paintings by Volschenk, a native of Riversdale, Bowler, Amshewitz, Irma Stern and Wenning. Books, antique furniture and china are also included in the collection.

Fork left 600 m from the turn-off into Riversdale, turn left (SP Ladismith, Laingsburg, Van Wyksdorp, Barrydale) on to the R323 and after 500 m left again (same SP). Start the ascent of the Garcia Pass 9,2 km from the last turn and reach the old toll house after 10,6 km and the summit after another 1,3 km.

GARCIA PASS This dramatic portal through the Langeberg range to the Little Karoo was discovered by Riversdale's civil commissioner, A H Garcia, who in 1868

44. The Swellendam Drostdy, now a museum

constructed a bridle path through the gorge of the Kafferkuils River. It was left to the civil engineer Thomas Bain, however, to build a proper road and this was completed in 1877.

Turn left (SP Barrydale, Brandrivier) 9,3 km from the old toll house on to a gravel road which runs along the northern side of the Langeberg range. After 19,7 km fork right and 17,3 km further on turn left (SP Barrydale) on to the R62, coming abreast of the Barrydale Dutch Reformed church after 16,9 km.

BARRYDALE This tranquil village of neat homes in expansive gardens developed around the church built by the local farming community at the top of the Tradouw Pass soon after its completion. The village is said to have been named in honour of Joseph Barry, or at least of his family. Barrydale has long been the centre of an area well known for its apples, peaches, apricots and other deciduous fruits, but there was a time when the local farmers were bitten by the ostrich feather bug and some of the grand homes built with feather-boom fortunes are a reminder of more affluent times (see Little Karoo, Tour 21). At the beginning of World War II Barrydale farmers, who had failed in an earlier attempt to produce grapes and wine, formed a wine and brandy cooperative which has met with far greater success.

45. Barrydale, at the northern end of the Tradouw Pass

From the Dutch Reformed church drive 1,5 km westward, turn left (SP Swellendam, Heidelberg via Tradouw Pass) on to the R324 and continue 2,3 km to the start of the Tradouw Pass, reaching the summit 8,9 km further on.

TRADOUW PASS The name is thought to derive from the Hottentot words 'tra' ('woman') and 'dau' ('path' or 'way through'), but why the route should have been regarded as a woman's way is not known. The pass, constructed by convicts under the direction of road-builder Thomas Bain and opened in 1873, follows the ravine of majestic scenery through which the Tradouw River rushes to its confluence with the Buffeljags River. Halfway up the pass may still be seen what was once the toll station and earlier one of the camps in which the convicts were accommodated.

Turn right (SP Swellendam) 18,2 km after joining the R324 and drive 4,8 km to Suurbraak.

SUURBRAAK, a cluster of thatched cottages at the foot of the Tradouw Pass, was founded as a mission station by the London Missionary Society in 1812.

Continue 11 km on the R324 to the N2, turn right and drive the remaining 10 km to Swellendam.

17

290 km

THE BREEDE RIVER VALLEY

Routes through majestic mountain ranges give access to the extensive winelands of the valley of the life-giving Breede River and lead to out-of-the-way places in other beautiful Boland valleys.

MONTAGU This pretty little town, named after John Montagu who was Colonial Secretary when it was founded on the farm Uytvlugt in 1851, nestles in a basin bounded by mountains at the western end of the Little Karoo. Part of its charm lies in the number of houses dating almost from its inception, some of which are national monuments. Thermal springs 3 km from the centre of town first made Montagu a popular

Cogman's Kloof was a hazardous route until 1877 when work which had been started in 1869 on a better road was completed by the road engineer Thomas Bain. Bain took his route over higher ground than had previously been followed and consequently had to blast a great deal of rock, some of it the hardest he had ever encountered. The tunnel, 16 m long and 5 m high, which he constructed through

Kalkoenkrans is a spectacular feature of the pass in its equally spectacular setting of contorted, lichen-covered rock formations of many beautiful hues. During the Anglo-Boer War the British sealed Cogman's Kloof to Boer forces and built a fort atop Kalkoenkrans from which the road on either side of the tunnel could be commanded. The ruins of the fort, which was manned by Gordon Highlanders, can be seen from the road beneath it. The pass served in its original state until 1952 when a new road was constructed, although some of Bain's sections were incorporated in the modernisation.

Turn left (SP Bonnievale, Swellendam) on to the R60 6,4 km from the start of the tour, and right (same SP) off the R60 6 km further on. Drive another 9,9 km to the Bonnievale Dutch Reformed church, which is approached from the north up Church Street.

BONNIEVALE In 1902 the Cape Government Railways opened a siding halfway between Robertson and Swellendam in the fertile valley of the Breede River and called it simply Vale. The appropriate adjectival part of the name Bonnievale was added in 1917. While the Cheddar and Gouda varieties produced by Bonnievale's cheese factory have won distinction, the district is essentially a wine-producing region and, like Montagu, is noted for its muscadel and other sweet varieties.

Drive around the Bonnievale Dutch Reformed church to join the southern section of Church Street, turn left into High Street, 500 m further on turn right on to the R317 and after 900 m cross the Breede River. Turn right (SP Robertson via Langverwag) 1,4 km from the river and left (SP Boesmansrivier, McGregor) 7,7 km further on. Drive another 30,2 km to the left turn into McGregor.

McGREGOR Originally called Lady Grey after the wife of Governor Sir George Grey, this town was renamed in honour of the Reverend Andrew McGregor who came to South Africa from Scotland in 1862 and served the Dutch Reformed Church with distinction in nearby Robertson for 40 years. McGregor, with its blend of Cape Dutch and English architectural styles, has been authoritatively described as the best-preserved and most complete example of mid-nineteenth century townscape in the Cape. The town is the centre of an area which has from its inception depended on fruit and wine production, although there was a time when it was also famous for the long bamboo whipsticks it supplied to the drivers of oxen teams all over South Africa.

Return to the entrance to McGregor and drive 19 km north-eastward to the road-over-rail bridge into Robertson, bearing right immediately after crossing the Breede River at 16,9 km.

ROBERTSON, sometimes called the 'Garden Town of the Boland' because of its charming gardens and jacaranda-lined streets, was named after Dr William Robertson, the Scottish theologian who recruited Andrew McGregor for the Dutch Reformed Church in South Africa and during his own ministry in Swellendam was mainly responsible for the establishment of six new congregations, including the one at the town that bears his name. The first Robertson plots, laid out on the farm Over het Roode Zand ('beyond the red sand') were sold in 1853, and the town that developed is surrounded by some of the country's most valuable land,

centre for holidays, and the spa hotel at which the waters were exploited was instrumental in the town being officially proclaimed a health resort in 1936. The spa complex was, however, destroyed by the wall of water which deluged down the course of the Keisie River and claimed the lives of 13 Montagu people in devastating floods in 1981. Like others of the Little Karoo, the district of Montagu prospered during the ostrich feather boom early in the twentieth century and took a beating when the industry slumped after World War I. The farmers who turned again to their vineyards and orchards have since ensured a name for their region's wines as well as keeping a giant fruit-canning cooperative prosperously busy. Montagu was the place chosen by the English author Francis Brett Young to spend his last years.

From the bridge at the western entrance to Montagu drive through Cogman's Kloof on the R62.

COGMAN'S KLOOF The most westerly pass between the western Cape and the Little Karoo,

46. Above Bain's tunnel in Cogman's Kloof is the ruin of a British fort

he tract along the Breede River having been so highly priced at times that it was called the Goudmyn ('gold mine'). Its fertile, lime-rich soil makes the Robertson district one of the country's major wine-producing regions, although table grapes, dried fruit, lucerne and racehorse breeding also contribute to the local economy. Because of the town's vinicultural importance it is fitting that the KWV should have established in Robertson one of its 'taphouse' restaurants, Brandewynsdraai, where traditional South African dishes may be savoured with wines of the region.

From the road-over-rail bridge into Robertson turn left into Voortrekker Street and 200 m further on left again (SP Worcester) on to the R60. After 1,5 km turn left and drive another 2,1 km to Silver Strand.

SILVER STRAND is an attractive holiday resort with a long sandy beach on a tree-lined stretch of the Breede River. The Robertson municipality has provided accommodation and amenities for watersport and angling enthusiasts.

Return to the R60 and turn left for a drive towards Worcester. To the north there are splendid views of the Langeberg range. After 28,7 km turn right (SP Nuy) to drive towards the 1 664-m Rabiesberg which towers over the vineyards through which this part of the tour runs. Turn left (SP Overhex) 22,8 km after turning off the R60 and 1,7 km further cross the railway and turn right back on to the R60 to drive about 9 km into Worcester.

WORCESTER Now one of the major centres of the Boland, Worcester was named by Lord Charles Somerset in honour of his elder brother, the Marquis of Worcester, when the town was laid out on the farms Roodewal and Langerug in 1820. It has a delightful setting ringed by the imposing ranges of the Waaihoek, Hex River, Dutoits and Slanghoek mountains, the higher peaks of which may be capped with snow in winter. Worcester's economy is based mainly on grapes, the district being the country's biggest producer of not only wine but also table varieties. In addition, it produces South Africa's greatest volume of brandy and other spirits. The community is well served educationally and culturally, with high schools, technical training centres, schools for the blind and deaf, a Little Theatre, the Hugo Naudé Art Centre, and three outstanding museums: the Worcester Museum, the Afrikaner Museum and the Boland Open-Air Farm Museum. Because it tends to be live, the open-air museum is of special interest. A modern display

complex is surrounded by nine replicas of early farm buildings: a tobacco shed, soap kitchen, horse-driven mill, farm dwelling, water mill, wine cellar, coach house, smithy and a 'kapstylhuis' such as shepherds once used. In the seasons when the appropriate products are available there are such demonstrations as wine trampling, distillation of spirits in a traditional still, threshing, shearing, leather preparation and the manufacture of harness. Not far from the museum one of Worcester's oldest dwellings, the homestead of the original farm Kleinplasie has been restored and serves as one of the KWV's 'taphouse' restaurants where wine

may be not only tasted and bought to take away, but also enjoyed with traditional South African meals. Just outside Worcester, the Karoo Botanic Garden (see Tour 10) is worth a visit, especially in springtime.

Leave Worcester by the most easterly of the three exits on to the N1, turn right and drive 43 km through the vineyards and orchards of De Wet, Sandhills, Orchard and De Doorns in the Hex River valley to the start of the Hex River Pass.

48. A donkey stands ready to draw water from the well at Worcester's Open-Air Farm Museum

47. Vineyards beside the road that runs along the Hex River valley

HEX RIVER PASS The Hex River Pass, through which the N1 climbs to the Karoo, pierces the highland where the Hex River Mountains in the north converge with the Kwadouws range in the south. The railway pass, an acclaimed engineering achievement dating from 1875, affords a train ride of singular excitement, descending as the line does by a series of many tight curves on an average gradient of 1:31. The line is being doubled, the extra set of tracks having broader curves on a far easier gradient but with a total of 16 km of tunnels. One of the five tunnels will be 13 km long, the longest in Africa.

At the summit of the Hex River Pass, 53 km after joining the N1, turn right (SP Montagu) on to the R318. Drive 82,6 km back to the Memorial Garden in Montagu, at first across a plateau of wheatlands, then traversing the Waboomberg by way of the Rooihoogte Pass, then through Die Koo and, after the splendid Burger Pass, through Die Keisie.

DIE KOO and DIE KEISIE These two high-lying fertile valleys at the northern foot of the Langeberg range take their names from the rivers which flow through them: the Koo which runs north-westward into the Keerom Dam, and the Keisie running south-eastward to join the Cogman's Kloof River. Both valleys are breathtaking in their beauty, especially in spring when there are wild flowers in profusion and the fruit trees which make the region prosperous are in blossom.

OASIS OF THE KAROO

The impressive scenery of the rugged Cape mountains lends an additional dimension to a visit to Matjiesfontein, where life slows down to the gracious tempo characteristic of the Victorian age.

MATJIESFONTEIN is unique. With the exception of the station and a few other railway buildings, the entire hamlet is a national monument, and not only in the sense of preserving historical and cultural values. It could also be described as a monument to James Douglas Logan who, as an impecunious young Scot on his way to Australia in 1877, elected to remain in South Africa and in time created this oasis in the hard, arid and sparsely vegetated Karoo. As a former North British Railways employee, Logan sought similar work in Cape Town and before long had become district superintendent of the Cape Government Railways line between Touws River and Prince Albert Road. The Karoo captivated him. He resigned from the railways and acquired an hotel in Touws River, but after a time transferred all his effort to the place in the middle of nowhere that takes its name from the 'matjiesgoed' reeds from which mats were made. He bought large tracts of land in the area cheaply, became a model farmer, planted trees, opened up South Africa's first artesian well, sank many boreholes, laid a pipeline to the village he had started to develop and sold water rights to the railways at considerable profit. He also found that his 'weak chest' was cured by the Karoo climate and envisaged his hamlet becoming a great health resort. So, in addition to the stream of celebrities who followed the vogue of making the sea voyage to the Cape and a trip to Matjiesfontein, there came those like George Lohmann, who at the time was described as 'one of the greatest all-round cricketers the world had ever seen'. When Lohmann's health broke down Logan brought him from England to an environment which is said to have prolonged his life for some years. Olive Schreiner, another guest who came for health reasons, chose to live at Matjiesfontein not only because the climate alleviated her asthma, but also because she loved the 'wild exhilaration and freedom' which came to her when she walked over the Karoo. Matjiesfontein bustled at no time more vigorously than during the Anglo-Boer War when it was the Cape Command base of the British forces and at times quartered up to 12 000 Tommies. The light standards which line the main street came from London and were converted for use with incandescent lamps when Logan gave his hamlet the distinction of being the first place in the country lit by electricity. It was also the first South African village to have waterborne sewerage. As the twentieth century advanced, however, the popularity of Matjiesfontein gradually waned, the Lord Milner Hotel, built early in the Anglo-Boer War, was allowed to run down and the village virtually went to sleep. It awoke in the late 1960s when hotelier of note David Rawdon bought Matjiesfontein lock stock and barrel and, with minimal structural alteration, was able to restore it to its former stateliness.

From Matjiesfontein turn left on to the N1 and drive 10,7 km to a left turn through a gate to the private Matjiesfontein cemetery.

MATJIESFONTEIN CEMETERY
In this little graveyard are buried Jimmy Logan with members of his family, including his wife and son, as well as Anglo-Boer War soldiers and other visitors who have died at Matjiesfontein. The imposing monument on the slope overlooking the gravestones commemorates the death in 1899 of Major-General Andy Wauchope of the Black Watch, whose body was interred here although he was killed at the Battle of Magersfontein (see Tour 46). Also in the cemetery is George Lohmann's grave, the headstone topped by a relief representation of the wickets and bails of the sportsman's life being sent flying by the cricket ball of what was presumably tuberculosis.

Turn left back on to the N1, continue 17,3 km and turn left again (SP Witberge) across the railway line for a drive through the valley south of the Witberge range.

WITBERGE DRIVE There are as many as eight gates to open and close, in the first 16 km of this splendid 38-km scenic drive through the valley south of the Witberge range, but its charm makes the trouble worthwhile. The fertility of the narrow strip of land is in marked contrast with the barrenness of the Karoo a bare 10 km away across the mountains to the north. In springtime, where the landscape is not green with wheat, it can be a spectacle of colour – the lilac and white of daisies, the varied, brilliant shades of 'vygies', the pink of fruit blossom and the yellow and blue of lupins.

Turn right (no SP) on to the R323 66,7 km after turning off the N1, pass the left turn to the Floriskraal Dam 7,8 km further on and start the ascent of the Rooinek Pass through the Wit Nekke after another 8,3 km. Turn right (SP Ladismith) 17,4 km after joining the R323.

GROOT RIVER VALLEY After ascending between the Suurkloof se Berg and the western end of the Elandsberg range, the road runs west and then south between the Matjiesgoed Mountains and the Anysberg range in the west and the Klein Swartberg range in the east. It then turns east before entering the valley of the Groot River.

Continue 62,5 km from the last right turn before forking left to drive 15,4 km to Ladismith.

LADISMITH In a splendid setting dominated by the 2 197-m cleft-peaked Toorkop ('magic mount'), Ladismith was founded in 1851 when the Dutch Reformed Church bought part of the farm Elandsvlei to form a new congregation. Originally Lady Smith and then Ladysmith in honour of Lady Juana Smith, wife of Governor Sir Harry Smith, the name of the town was changed to its present form in 1879 to avoid confusion with the Natal Ladysmith. The ostrich feather boom (see Little Karoo, Tour 21) early in the twentieth century brought prosperity to Ladismith and the slump after World War I resulted in bankruptcy for many. Although ostriches have again assumed a role in the economy of the district, apricots, peaches and pears, a winery, cheese factory and wheat cooperative play more important ones. Ladismith also boasts what is probably the smallest hydro-electric plant in South Africa. Two-thirds of the way up the 2 126-m mountain which appears as Toringberg on the official map but is known as Elandsberg to the local people, a tiny light can be seen from the town at night, although it burns 24 hours a day. It was placed there by Ladismith resident Stanley de Witt to mark the first anniversary of South Africa becoming a republic in 1961. In successive climbs he hauled up pockets of cement and sand, a bicycle dynamo fitted with paddles, a length of pipe and a bicycle lamp. He dammed a perennial stream on the mountain, channelled its overflow through the pipe to the paddles of the dynamo placed further down and connected the dynamo to the lamp. However, the bulb of a bicycle lamp will burn continuously for only three months, so at the time of publication this doughty republican had undertaken the arduous climb up the Elandsberg with replacements about a hundred times.

From the Standard Bank at the corner of Van Riebeeck and Church streets drive 400 m southward along Van Riebeeck Street, turn left (SP Calitzdorp,

Oudtshoorn) on to the R62 and after 12,8 km pass the left turn to Hoeko.

HOEKO The bronze plaque of the National Monuments Council marks the home in Hoeko where the politician, man of letters and champion of the Afrikaans language C J Langenhoven was born. Signs point the way to the farmhouse 2,4 km from the R62.

At 7 km and 10 km from the turn-off to Hoeko reach the right turns to Zoar and Amalienstein respectively.

ZOAR AND AMALIENSTEIN The interwoven histories of these two settlements dates from 1817 when the unordained preacher Petrus Jacobus Joubert of the South African Missionary Society (SAMS) founded the mission of Zoar. Unable to replace Joubert when he left Zoar in 1833, the SAMS asked the Berlin Missionary Society (BMS) to run the mission. Expecting their tenure to be temporary, however, the Germans established Amalienstein on an adjacent farm, naming it after a benefactress, Amalie von Stein. The SAMS resumed control of Zoar in 1856 and the German missionaries retired to concentrate on Amalienstein. Zoar continues to be a mission of the Dutch Reformed Church, which took over from the SAMS, but Amalienstein was sold by the BMS after World War I. The economy of both settlements still concentrates heavily on agriculture.

Opposite the turn-off to Amalienstein turn left off the R62 (SP Laingsburg, Seven Weeks Poort) and drive 6,5 km to the start of the Seven Weeks Poort.

SEVEN WEEKS POORT
Magnificent, rugged scenery is the characteristic of this 15-km defile which snakes alongside a river course through the Klein Swartberg range. The road through this mountain gap, completed in 1862, is vulnerable to flood, but the early recommendations of experts that its level be raised were disregarded. So the gravel route is little changed, crossing and recrossing the river between converging vertical rock buttresses that form in places a chasm barely wide enough for both watercourse and road. It is certainly impassable after heavy rain, but when the weather is fine poet Louis Leipoldt's description of the Seven Weeks Poort as 'one of the seven wonders of the Cape Province' is fully justified.

At the end of the Seven Weeks Poort, 21,8 km from the turn-off opposite Amalienstein, turn left (SP right: Gamkaspoort Dam, No through road). Drive through the

Koueveld Pass and then down the valley between the Elandsberg in the north and the Klein Swartberg in the south, crossing the Buffels River 70 km from Amalienstein and ascending through the Wit Nekke to the Rooinek Pass where the road joins the R323 from Ladismith 3,6 km from the river. Continue 23,4 km on the R323 before turning left on to the N1 at Laingsburg. Drive 29 km further to the left turn into Matjiesfontein.

50. Seven Weeks Poort traverses the Klein Swartberg range

51. Zoar, the village founded by Petrus Joubert of the South African Missionary Society in 1817

SOUTHERN FOOTHILLS OF THE SWARTBERG

19
170 km

The old concrete road from Oudtshoorn to Calitzdorp passes through a region where ostrich farming is highly intensive, while the return route along the Nels River valley affords many scenic pleasures.

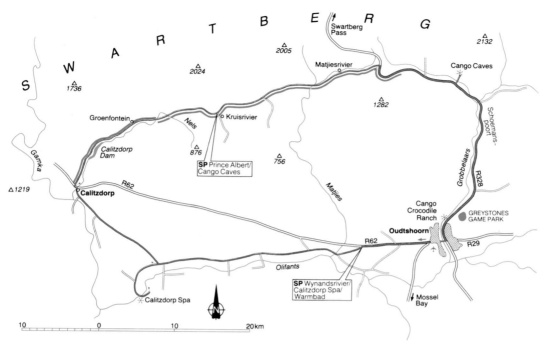

OUDTSHOORN In addition to being the ostrich-feather capital of the world – the only place on earth where the precious feathers are regularly auctioned – Oudtshoorn is an important educational centre, a military training base and the focal point of a region which produces tobacco, dairy products, wheat, mohair and more white honey and lucerne seed than any other district in the country. The settlement came into existence in 1847 on the Grobbelaars River between the Swartberg range in the north and the Outeniquas in the south. It was named by Civil Commissioner Egbertus Bergh, husband of a granddaughter of the Baron Pieter van Rheede van Oudtshoorn who had died in 1773 on his way to take up his appointment as Governor of the Cape. A feature of the town is its stone buildings, in particular the former Boys' High School whose façade is regarded as the finest example of stone masonry in the country. The school now houses a museum which reflects the life of the pioneers of the district and, not surprisingly, has an extensive display devoted to the ostrich and the industry based on it. Among the other imposing stone buildings, both in the town and in the surrounding country, are some of the mansions built for feather barons during the ostrich boom just after the turn of the century (see Little Karoo, Tour 21). Examples are Greystones, Welgeluk, Pinehurst (the only survivor of three

buildings actually known as 'ostrich palaces' and now a residence of the Oudtshoorn Teacher Training College) and the turreted house which was built for J H J le Roux and is now an annex of the C P Nel Museum. Oudtshoorn boasts another museum, Arbeidsgenot, which was the home in High Street

of C J Langenhoven, champion of the Afrikaans language and author of many much-loved works, including the words of South Africa's national anthem, *Die Stem*.

52. Calitzdorp Spa

At Arbeidsgenot has been preserved the atmosphere of the home of a professional man of Langenhoven's time, for he was a lawyer and politician as well as a distinguished man of letters.

From Oudtshoorn's Civic Centre drive 11,5 km westward (SP Calitzdorp), first along Voortrekker Street and then on the R62, before turning left (SP Wynandsrivier, Calitzdorp Spa, Warmbad) on to the old road to Calitzdorp.

OLIFANTS RIVER VALLEY
The concrete road which has been replaced by the more northerly R62 between Oudtshoorn and Calitzdorp enables the traveller to observe from close quarters ostrich farming at its most intensive. On either side of the road 'pairs' of prize birds, often with large broods of young, are enclosed in small lucerne paddocks where they can easily be seen. A 'pair' consists of a male, with his handsome black and white plumage, and either one or two females whose feathers are dull and brownish-grey. One of the members of a broody 'pair' may be seen on a clutch of 12 to 15 eggs laid in a mere scrape in the ground which the farmer will have sheltered from the sun with a simple reed structure. The sitting is done in shifts. During the day, when her drab colour makes her inconspicuous in the veld, the female will be observed on the nest, but those who pass by late in the afternoon will see that the male has started his stint which lasts until about nine o'clock the next morning, his black feathers providing camouflage during the hours of darkness. Unlike the male, whose sitting function serves the usual avian purpose of keeping the eggs warm, the female covers the clutch to protect it from the intense daytime heat of the Karoo. Indeed, between them a 'pair' maintain their prospective offspring at a constant temperature.

Anyone approaching a paddock fence once the chicks have been hatched is met by an angry adult rushing towards him with wings outspread, neck extended and beak open and hissing. The charge ends with a menacing stamp and an extra flap of the wings just short of the enclosure wire. Such an experience is startling, to say the least, and would be dangerous but for the restraining barrier between the bird and what it regards as a threat to its family. The male is also dangerous during the mating season. After working himself up into a frenzy with a war dance, he charges the object of his jealous wrath and kicks downwards at it with his most deadly weapon, the chisel-like nail of the larger of the two toes at the end of his long powerful leg. Serious injury can be inflicted, and an unarmed person's only defence is to lie down flat on the ground where the vicious kick can do minimal harm. With luck the passer-by may also be able to watch a male perform the mating dance, waving his long, sinuous neck in elegant, sensuous circles, gracefully flapping alternate fluffed-out wings and swaying from side to side as he approaches at a crouch the object of his affection. The traveller may see, too, flocks of newly-stripped ostriches being herded along the road, a sorry sight in their near nakedness, although no cruelty is involved in the plucking process.

Turn left (SP Calitzdorp Spa) 29,6 km after turning off the R62 and drive 6,7 km to the spa, keeping left after 4,1 km where the right turn leads to Vanwyksdorp.

CALITZDORP SPA On the south bank of the Olifants River, about 5 km before its confluence with the Gamka to form the Gourits, thermal springs emerge at a temperature of 51 °C. Although the weakly chalybeate waters had been used therapeutically from time to time over a long period, steps to popularise them for the economic benefit of the district were taken by the Calitzdorp Divisonal Council only in 1960. Since then a modern holiday resort has been developed, with a restaurant and entertainment complex, swimming pools with water at 35 °C, sauna baths, a camping area, a caravan park and superbly sited and fully equipped chalets overlooking the spa.

From the spa backtrack 6,7 km before turning left (no SP) to drive 16 km to the Calitzdorp Dutch Reformed church, approaching the town through farmland on which orchards and vineyards are now more in evidence than ostriches.

CALITZDORP Like the farmers of Oudtshoorn, many in the Calitzdorp region concentrated on ostriches during the feather boom and took a tumble when the slump came after World War I. Their plight was severely aggravated by drought and the district became impoverished. After that war, however, the building of the Calitzdorp Dam on the Nels River, the construction of a railway line to Calitzdorp and a return to viticulture and fruit farming enabled the district to survive the further serious setback of the Depression. Since 1933 the economy has steadily improved, although, like many another rural community, the attraction for youth of better opportunities elsewhere has resulted in Calitzdorp's gradual depopulation. While recovery from the feather slump was much slower in Calitzdorp than in Oudtshoorn,

ostrich farming in the district is back on a sound footing, sharing economic prominence with the production of tobacco, lucerne, cereals and deciduous fruit, including grapes. The community that started developing around the church built on the farm Buffelsvlei in 1857 was named originally Calitz Dorp after the many units of the Calitz family on the property. The present church, which is Renaissance-Byzantine in style, has a Marseilles roof and seats 1 500, replaced the 1857 building in 1912.

From the Dutch Reformed church in Calitzdorp drive 200 m up Andries Pretorius Street and turn left (SP Groenfontein) on to a gravel road with a sign warning that the route is impassable for long vehicles.

NELS RIVER VALLEY The warning to drivers of long vehicles may be forbidding, but the drive to the Cango Caves through the beautiful narrow valley of the westward-flowing Nels River and then the Matjies River valley – both in the southern foothills of the majestic Swartberg range – is scenically well worthwhile. The road, a feature of which are long stretches of dry-stone retaining walls, may be narrow and some of its bends are certainly extremely tight, but its surface is good in fine weather. After heavy rain, however, flooding of the numerous causeways by means of which the road crosses and recrosses the river may render the route impassable. While some farms in the Nels River valley are show places and, with their grainlands, orchards and vineyards, emit an aura of prosperity, there are others which in marked contrast appear sadly run down or even abandoned.

53. Male ostriches sprint away into the veld

Bear right 29,7 km after turning out of Andries Pretorius Street in Calitzdorp and, at the Kruis River petrol pump 30,7 km from the same point, turn left (SP Prince Albert, Cango Caves). Pass the right turn to Lategansvlei 8,3 km further on and climb higher into the mountains before the road descends into the valley of the westward-flowing Matjies River to meet the R328 26,2 km from the petrol pump. Turn right (SP Cango Caves,

Oudtshoorn) and drive 12,2 km before turning left to the Cango Caves.

CANGO CAVES See Tour 20.

Return to the R328, turn left and drive the remaining 29,4 km back to the Oudtshoorn Civic Centre, running at first alongside the Grobbelaars River through pretty Schoemanspoort with its numerous willow-shaded picnic spots. The Greystones Game Park and the Cango Crocodile Ranch (see Tour 20) are 25 km and 25,5 km respectively from the turn-off to the caves.

54. Farmlands near the Cango Caves

20 190 km SWARTBERG PASSES AND SUBTERRANEAN FAIRYLAND

Two of the most scenic routes in the country, Meiringspoort and the Swartberg Pass, traverse the majestic Swartberg range, while deep below the same mountains are hidden the wonders of the Cango Caves.

OUDTSHOORN See Tour 19.

From Oudtshoorn's Civic Centre drive eastward (SP Meiringspoort) up Voortrekker Street on to the R29 and reach the post office at De Rust after 36,7 km.

DE RUST The hamlet of De Rust, which provides the local farming community with limited services, has one claim to fame in having been established on the farm De Rust, once owned by the man who showed that there was a way through the Swartberg range and therefore had Meiringspoort named after him.

Continue north-eastward on the R29, passing after 700 m the right turn to Uniondale. Reach the start of Meiringspoort 4,5 km further on.

MEIRINGSPOORT When Thomas Bain and others were searching for a way to cross the barrier of the Swartberg range that divides the Great from the Little Karoo, it was Petrus Johannes Meiring who showed them a possible route from his farm De Rust between the towering walls of rock which form the majestic gorge of the Groot River. Bain's brother-in-law, A G de Smidt, was appointed to construct the road, and it was completed in 1857 and formally opened the following year. Because any alternative was deemed too expensive, the road was routed dangerously near the level of the river and by 1885 had been completely washed away by a series of floods. It was rebuilt in 1886 and, although it is still at the bottom of the gorge, it is now tarred. For 17 km the route follows the river through incomparable scenery between colossal, multicoloured sandstone cliffs which dwarf the traveller below. Meiringspoort was a happy haunt of the writer C J Langenhoven who created Herrie, the much-loved circus elephant of Afrikaans literature which in *Sonde van die Bure* hauled the author in his imagination through this mountain defile in an old tramcar. Langenhoven carved the name 'Herrie' into a rock close to the road where all who are not in a hurry may see it to this day, 10,6 km from the De Rust post office.

After emerging from Meiringspoort 22,2 km from the De Rust post office, continue 1,4 km and pass the left turn into Klaarstroom immediately before the R29 curves round the north of the hamlet. After another 7,5 km turn left (SP Prince Albert) off the R29 on to the R407 to drive through Kredouws Pass, which starts 20 km from the last turn, and the fertile valley between the northern foothills of the Swartberg and the main range. Reach the old water mill at the outskirts of Prince Albert after 46,7 km.

PRINCE ALBERT Nestling among the northern foothills of the Swartberg range, Prince Albert is a charming Karoo town of large irrigated plots on which fruit trees, vegetables and flowers grow so luxuriantly that the place was once known as 'Kweekvallei' ('the valley where things grow'). Sheep and goats graze between homes illustrating a variety of architectural styles, from Cape Dutch and Georgian to Karoo and Victorian.

The water mill (NM), run by generations of the Albert family, ground wheat until the 1970s.

After exploring Prince Albert return to the water mill and backtrack 2,4 km before turning right (SP Oudtshoorn, Calitzdorp, Ladismith via Swartberg Pass) on to the R328 to traverse the Swartberg Pass.

SWARTBERG PASS South Africa's distinguished pass-builder, Thomas Bain, was not exaggerating when he reported that although a more direct route than Meiringspoort could be opened through the Swartberg range from Prince Albert, it would be steep. It took Bain, with hundreds of convicts providing the labour, four years to complete the tremendous project. Clinging at times to the mountainside and following the folds created by the crumpling of the earth's crust, his road, which entailed the building of great retaining walls, snakes upwards in a seemingly endless series of curves, U-turns and zigzags to a height of 1 585 m above sea level. There is no relief in the climb – from whichever side it is undertaken – and, while a well-maintained car makes the ascent without trouble, it must have been a Herculean slog for the draught animals that originally hauled coaches and wagons over the pass. Remnants of the stone buildings in which the convict labourers were once quartered can still be seen in places. Rain, snow and ice, which can at times render the pass unusable, must have made life for those unfortunate workers almost intolerable. For those who care to stop as frequently as the availability of viewing spots permits, the ever-changing vista is magnificent. And, looking back down the lower stretches of the road and its upward meanderings, one is able not only to revel in the scenic splendour, but also appreciate the engineering feat achieved by Bain and his team. The traveller's Swartberg treat is not over when the summit is reached. The great elevation lends majesty to a panorama which encompasses the Cango Valley, the patchwork of the intensively cultivated plain of the Little Karoo, and the distant Outeniqua Mountains in the south. Perspectives may alter, but the view is there at every level, at almost every curve of the 10-km descent into the Cango Valley.

Pass the right turn to Matjiesrivier and Calitzdorp 31,5 km from the water mill in Prince Albert and 12,2 km further on turn left to the Cango Caves.

CANGO CAVES It takes little imagination to realise why so many of the exquisite crystalline forms sculpted by nature in the chambers

55. C J Langenhoven honoured Herrie the elephant by carving its name on a rock in Meiringspoort

of the Cango Caves have been described in such enchanting terms. In this veritable wonderland one can actually *see* organ pipes which seem to have been fashioned out of glass, a fairy fountain, Jack Frost, an angel's wing, a draped shawl, chandeliers, bunches of translucent grapes, a candle, a glass-blower's fantasy. . . The caves take their name from the nearby Cango River, whose designation in turn is thought to be a corruption of the Hottentot words '!a-!kanub', meaning 'valley in the hills'. In 1780, following a shepherd's discovery of a hole in a hillside above the valley, farmer Jacobus van Zyl became the first man to venture any distance into this series of fairyland caverns. Stone-age Bushmen had known of the caves but, judging by the restriction of their rock art and implements to just inside the entrance, they had penetrated only as far as there was enough light. The first vast chamber into which Van Zyl descended by means of a rope bears his name. No doubt he was enthralled by what he could perceive by the light of the flaming torches he and his followers bore. The formations he saw had been formed over many millennia by water laden with calcium carbonate percolating through the earth above and depositing the salt in the form of stalactites hanging from the roof, stalagmites reaching up from the floor, helictites which developed in all directions, the flowstone drapes down the walls, rimstone pools around which calcite accumulates, straws down which water

57. Swartberg Pass

unceasingly drips, and beautiful tiny calcite flowers. After Van Zyl's first steps exploration followed along the 775-m length of what until 1972 was the known limit of the caves, now called Cango I. Then a gap which had been found in the deepest section by a survey party of the South African Spelaeological Society, led by Jose Burman, was widened to permit the exploration of another 270 m of caverns and passages, the Wonder Cave or Cango II. And in 1975 yet another breakthrough was effected into the most extensive section of all, Cango III, a 1 000-m series of chambers of which the biggest is the length of three rugby fields. At present the public is admitted only to Cango I, with its recorded commentaries and electric lighting designed to illuminate, and even enhance, the beauty of nature. This may change, but it will not be entirely for the best. Those who have been privileged to enter the more recently explored sections have been amazed by the comparison between their pristine splendour and the part which for more than 200 years, though still impressive, has been steadily dulled by pollution and despoliated by vandalistic souvenir hunters.

Return to the R328, turn left and after 25 km turn left into the Greystones Game Park.

GREYSTONES GAME PARK
The park is sited on the hills from which the sandstone used in Oudtshoorn's many fine buildings was quarried. Visitors may leave their cars in safety anywhere in the park to get as close as they choose to springbok, zebra, blesbok,

56. Dripstone formations in the Cango Caves are among the most beautiful in the world

wildebeest, gemsbok, cranes, rheas, a camel and even a cross between a donkey and a zebra. Animals which are either too dangerous for human proximity (such as caracal, lynxes and a spotted hyena) or too likely to wander (baboons and bat-eared foxes) are in enclosures. The cheetahs are also in enclosures, but several of them are so tame that visitors are invited into their paddock to pet them and be photographed with them. There is also an aviary in the park.

Drive another 500 m south-westward on the R328 to the Cango Crocodile Ranch on the right.

CANGO CROCODILE RANCH
This ranch, the first crocodile show farm in South Africa, has more than

200 of the reptiles, from hatchlings only 35 cm long to veterans of up to 4 m. The biggest, Zindago, a Shona word meaning 'he who lives by himself', is said to have eaten two people after escaping from an enclosure in which it was kept by the Rhodesian National Parks Department some years ago. Guides conduct visitors on an informative and at times exciting tour of the ranch.

From the crocodile ranch turn right on to the R328 and drive the remaining 3,4 km to Oudtshoorn's Civic Centre.

FEATHERLAND – THE LITTLE KAROO

One of South Africa's shortest-lived booms was that of the ostrich-feather industry. Its heyday may be over, but the ostrich is still a tourist attraction and an important factor in the economy of the Little Karoo.

LITTLE KAROO Nowhere else on earth is the ostrich exploited to the extent that it is in the sunny, relatively dry Little Karoo, a habitat which is superbly suited to this, the largest bird in the world. Although flightless, the ostrich has the ability to run at 48 km/h and can kick like a mule. Its feathers have been coveted from time immemorial, and ostrich farming was conducted in North Africa long before the South African ostrich industry was

58. On the slipway at Mossel Bay

established. It took South African farmers, however, to discover that instead of having to capture wild birds and pen them for regular plucking, ostriches could be domesticated, if not tamed, and exploited to an unprecedented degree by breeding them in captivity. Moreover, these pioneers developed sophisticated farming methods, including the use of specially-designed incubators, which increased the ostrich population enormously and doubled the feather production. The export of feathers began early in the

nineteenth century, although commercial ostrich farming started only in the middle of the century. By 1882 the commercial flock had risen to some 100 000 birds and by 1914 to about 750 000, although the peak of the feather trade was in 1913, a year in which 450 000 kg of plumes fetched nearly £3 million. Just before World War I the foibles of fashion led the trade into a decline and the war turned the decline into a slump. Breeding pairs of birds which might previously have fetched as much as £1 000 became almost valueless, while many a feather baron who had become enormously wealthy during the boom went bankrupt. There were minor revivals between the wars, but only in the 1940s, when a technique for tanning the bird's skin was developed, did ostrich farming come back into its own, though the heyday of the early 1900s has never been matched. Nowadays, while the feathers are still exported to markets all over the world, the skin is turned into a wide variety of popular leatherware and the flesh is made into food, the most popular form of which is biltong.

MOSSEL BAY After Bartolomeu Dias, searching for a sea route to the east in 1488, had been blown far south of what he called the Cape of Storms – now the Cape of Good Hope – he headed northwards and sighted the mouth of the Gourits River. Because it appeared unsafe for landing, he sailed another 30 km to the north-east until he found a more hospitable spot to come ashore. This bay, which they called Aguada de São Bras, became a regular port of call for the Portuguese who came after Dias,

the attraction being the spring he had found conveniently near the beach. It was near the spring that these mariners left letters for other callers to carry forward, the first recorded despatches having been placed in an old boot hung in a milkwood tree in 1500. The 'post office tree' (NM) is still there above Munro Bay, 1 km east of the railway station. Two 'post office stones' under which sailors secluded other letters at the watering place have been preserved, one in the Mossel Bay library and the other in the South African Museum in Cape Town. Visitors nowadays may post letters in an officially recognised mailbox shaped like the boot of a sixteenth-century Portuguese sailor. What is believed to have been the first Christian church in the country was built at Mossel Bay in 1501 by one of the early navigators, João da Nova. After the Portuguese came the Dutch, among them Paulus van Caerden who renamed the watering place Mossel Bay because, it is said, he could find only mussels with which to replenish his lazaret. It was from Mossel Bay that the first consignment of South African wheat was shipped by the Dutch to Batavia in 1788, but a town was established on the shore of the bay only in 1848, after the British had taken over the Cape. The Governor, Sir Harry Smith, called it Aliwal after his victory over the Sikhs at Aliwal in India two years previously, but because the Dutch name was more popular it was subsequently resuscitated. The port, being closer than any other to the Little Karoo, assumed considerable importance at the time of the ostrich-feather boom, only to lose some of it when the slump came. It is, nevertheless, the country's fifth busiest harbour today, although Mossel Bay's economy is now more dependent on other business, important among them being tourism.

From the Mossel Bay library in Marsh Street drive 800 m up the hill, cross the road-over-road bridge and immediately afterwards turn right (SP Oudtshoorn). After 7,3 km turn right over the railway and into Hartenbos.

HARTENBOS is a huge holiday cottage complex which teems during the summer season with vacationers, particularly from the rural areas.

From Hartenbos drive 1 km northward on the R102 before crossing the N2 on to the R328 (SP Oudtshoorn). Continue 28,4 km to the start of the Robinson Pass and to its summit 9,7 km further on.

ROBINSON PASS Early adventurers travelling from the Cape to eastern parts of the country

found their path along the coast blocked by the then much larger fastnesses of the Knysna and Tsitsikamma forests. Compelled to trek inland, if they attempted to do so in the region of what is now Mossel Bay, they were faced with the equally formidable barrier of the Outeniqua Mountains. With the help of local Hottentots, however, they found a way through the range in 1690, and for more than a century Attaqua Kloof was the only route through to the coastal regions of the eastern Cape. And when the Little Karoo and Langkloof became settled it gave the farmers there access to Mossel Bay. As settlement progressed eastward, pioneers of the George, Knysna and Plettenberg Bay areas found the westward trek to Attaqua Kloof too long before they could head inland over what was still a rough and difficult track. So the more direct Cradock's Pass between George and Knysna was constructed and, because it was as arduous as Attaqua Kloof, in due course was replaced by the Montagu Pass (see Tour 25). The people of Mossel Bay could now take either the irksome, degenerating Attaqua Kloof or what was for them, in turn, a long deviation through George and the Montagu Pass. Thomas Bain was therefore commissioned in 1867 to construct a compromise to the east of Attaqua Kloof, the Robinson Pass, which he completed in 1869. It was named after the Commissioner of Roads, M R Robinson, who had been indefatigable in his efforts to persuade the government that a new pass was essential. Since the widening and tarring of the pass in the 1950s it has been possible to speed on easy curves and gradients from Mossel Bay to the

860-m summit and reach Oudtshoorn 87 km from the point of departure in little more than an hour. Those who can afford to travel this road at leisure enjoy pausing wherever there is a lay-by to appreciate the majesty of the 1 363-m Ruitersberg, and of the 1 263-m Skurweberg towering above the valley of the Moeras River. At the pass summit the view to the west over the sharp peaks of the Outeniqua range tailing away into the distance is also splendid.

Turn left (SP Volmoed) 81,7 km from the Mossel Bay library and drive 2,5 km to the Highgate Ostrich Farm. Alternatively, continue 2,9 km on the R328 to the Safari Ostrich Farm on the right.

59. Safari, an ostrich farm near Oudtshoorn, welcomes visitors

HIGHGATE AND SAFARI

Thousands of tourists flock to Oudtshoorn every year to marvel at the gawky, flightless creatures with splendid plumage which made the region prosperous, but there is nowhere that the visitor can learn as much about the ostrich in as short a time as at these show farms. Efficient, knowledgeable guides outline the biology, breeding habits and history of the bird, relate some of the amazing anecdotes told about it, talk about the feather industry and give practical demonstrations of how an ostrich is caught and relieved of some of its

plumage and of how it can ingest the most extraordinary objects. For some tourists, however, the highlight of a visit is a race between these fleet-footed birds ridden by jockeys in the gay colours of the turf. There is little opportunity to study form, though, and there are no bookmakers or tote facilities.

Return from either ostrich farm to the R328 and drive 10 km or 7 km to Oudtshoorn's main traffic intersection.

OUDTSHOORN See Tour 20.

Leave Oudtshoorn's main traffic intersection southward along Langenhoven Road and drive 47 km on the R29 to the top of the Outeniqua Pass.

OUTENIQUA PASS The Outeniqua

Pass is the newest of the routes through the Outeniqua Mountains, providing a route from George to the Little Karoo more suited to speedy modern traffic than the Montagu Pass. It was designed by the wartime Chief Engineer of National Roads, P A de Villiers, and work started in 1943 with Italian prisoners of war providing skills and labour. Rock had to be blasted to create cuttings many metres deep and gorges had to be filled to even greater depths. The result, which was opened in 1951, is a wide highway with gentle curves and gradients which enable the motorist to drive from George to Oudtshoorn at high speed. What applies to other modern South African passes goes particularly for the Outeniqua Pass; it is a pity that the urge to get from one place to another in a hurry is so great that it eclipses enjoyment of the environment. And the environment of this pass is not only a scenic delight but historically evocative. To appreciate some of its history, pause 51 km from Oudtshoorn at the toposcope which directs attention to the remote side of the valley where beacons pick out the route followed by the Voortrekkers up Cradock's Pass; to the Montagu Pass snaking deep down in the Malgas River gorge below; and to the railway hugging the contours near the crest of the mountains high above it.

At the junction 55,5 km from Oudtshoorn turn right (SP Blanco) on to the R404 and drive 2 km to Blanco.

BLANCO See Tour 25.

Leave Blanco south-westward and after 3 km fork left. Continue 6 km — crossing the old main road (R102) — to the N2, turn right and after 33 km take the exit SP Mossel Bay, Hartenbos on to the R102. Drive 8,8 km back to Marsh Street in Mossel Bay.

60. Robinson Pass provides a route between Mossel Bay and Oudtshoorn

MOSSEL BAY'S WESTERN SEABOARD

The coastline between Stilbaai and Mossel Bay was the first land Bartolomeu Dias saw after rounding the Cape in 1488. A scenic road now runs close to this shore, within sound of the crashing breakers.

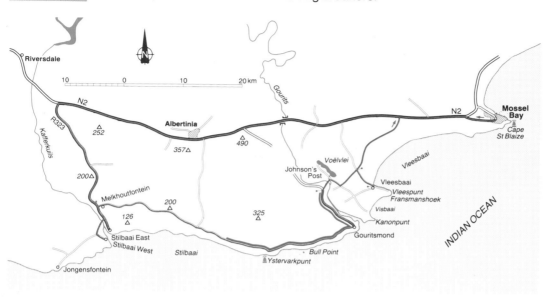

congregation before he left the district in 1882. The settlement on the farm Grootfontein was named after him. Extensive beds of ochre had been discovered in the region almost a century earlier, when explorer John Barrow had passed this way in 1797 on an expedition to the territory ruled by Gaika, paramount chief of the Xhosa. The mineral was first exploited here for use in the South African paint industry in 1925, and extensive mining continues. The tall succulent *Aloe ferox*, which lends a blaze of colour to the region in June and July, also makes a contribution, albeit a modest one, to the economy. The freshly-cut fleshy leaves of the plant are stacked on animal skins or sheets of plastic stretched over hollows in the ground and the juice thus collected is reduced by boiling. The dried concentrate is sold for medicinal purposes, either in the crude state as 'Cape Aloes' or, after being refined to obtain its active principle, as aloin.

MOSSEL BAY See Tour 21.

Leave Mossel Bay westward on the N2 and drive 30 km to the Gourits River.

GOURITS RIVER The great gorge of the Gourits River was a formidable obstacle in the way of those travelling north-eastward from the Cape until it was bridged in 1892 by what for many years was to be the longest, at 219 m, and highest, at 61 m, span in Africa. The line of the New Cape Railway, which reached Mossel Bay in 1906,

shared this steel bridge with road traffic and so subsequently did that of the South African Railways until a separate bridge for trains was constructed in 1931. The imposing modern road bridge was opened in 1977, and like so many other impressive South African bridges, has guard walls so high that it is impossible to see the gorge as one speeds over it. To appreciate the awesome depth of the ravine cut through the landscape by the river, it is necessary to stop and walk to a vantage point away from the bridge. The pause enables the traveller to

understand why it has always been deemed economically impracticable to take water from the Gourits River for irrigation purposes.

Continue 14,5 km westward on the N2 to the right turn into Albertina.

ALBERTINIA, a small town of less than 2 000 inhabitants, was where the Reverend J R Albertyn of the Dutch Reformed Church in Riversdale paved the way for the establishment of a new

Return to the N2 from Albertina and, turning right, continue 26 km westward before turning left (SP Stilbaai, Jongensfontein) on to the R323. Drive 40,3 km to the bridge over the Kafferkuils River 3 km before it flows into Stilbaai. Remain on the eastern bank of the river and continue southward to Stilbaai East. Return to the bridge, cross the river, turn left and drive 4 km to Stilbaai West.

STILBAAI The plots on which the first of the holiday cottages of Stilbaai were built, with scant regard

61. An imposing bridge carries the N2 over the Gourits River

for town planning, were sold towards the end of the nineteenth century. Good boating and fishing water in the estuary of the Kafferkuils River and a fine beach have made the place extremely popular with the farming community of the region, and at Christmas and Easter the small permanent population is swelled by thousands of holiday-makers. An important location in archaeological terms, Stilbaai has given its name to a phase of the Middle Stone Age. It was on a site about 6 km west of the Kafferkuils River that Dr C Heese found implements of what is now known as the Stilbaai, or Still Bay, Culture. Since the discovery of this type of site in the 1920s Stilbaai Culture sites have been found in other parts of southern Africa. Another relic of prehistory to be seen at various spots along this coast is the vywer (originally 'vijwer', meaning 'pond'). Using rocks and stones, primitive man built a number of these low enclosures in tidal gullies into which fish could swim at high tide and be trapped when the sea ran out again. Some of the vywers are still maintained and occasionally used (see Cape Agulhas, Tour 15).

From the bridge over the Kafferkuils River backtrack 3,9 km on the R323, turn right (SP Melkhout-fontein, Gouritsmond) and reach Melkhoutfontein 900 m further on.

MELKHOUTFONTEIN, 5 km upstream from the mouth of the river, is a random settlement of fisherfolk, some of whom live in stone-walled, thatched cottages many years old. Their cemetery is unusual in that most of the graves, though laid out in orderly rows, are ornamented with strange, untidy piles of rough stones.

From Melkhoutfontein continue 53,4 km eastward to Gouritsmond, passing the left turn to Albertina after 22 km. At first well inland, the road runs near the coast from the lighthouse at Ystervarkpunt, and there is a constant crash of breakers against strange rock formations covered with ochre-coloured lichens. Dairy herds along the way perpetuate the reputation this coastal strip acquired at the time the early Portuguese navigators were naming places such as Rio dos Vaqueiros ('river of the cowherds'), Rio das Vaccas ('river of the cows') and Angra das Vaccas ('bay of the cows'), a name which survives in Cape Vacca.

GOURITSMOND, occasionally known as Avondsrust, is a resort with holiday homes, a camping site and an hotel on a sandy seafront on the west bank of the Gourits River. The river, with its main tributaries of the Groot – formed by the Buffels and Touws – the Gamka, Olifants and Kammanassie, drains most of the Karoo and central Cape. Although Bartolomeu Dias first set foot ashore at Mossel Bay, the coast cut by the Gourits River was the first landfall he made after having been blown off course in 1488. When he sailed northward after the storm the sight of land to the west confirmed that he had rounded the tip of Africa.

Drive north-westward from Gouritsmond between some of the farms of the Gourits River valley. After 10 km turn right (SP Mossel Bay) and 1,6 km further on cross the river at Johnson's Post. Turn right (SP Mossel Bay, Vleesbaai) after 800 m, pass the right turn to Kanonpunt 2,3 km further on and after another 4,4 km turn right (SP Vleesbaai) to reach Vleesbaai after 4,8 km.

VLEESBAAI Originally Vleeschbaai, this inlet was named by the Dutch mariner Paulus van Caerden because when he came ashore here in search of slaughter stock in 1601 he could obtain as many cattle as he wanted to replenish his two-ship flotilla. He had actually been pre-empted in his naming by Portuguese navigators who, having also found the Hottentots of the region only too eager to barter cattle, called the inlet Angra das Vaccas. It was, however, the Dutch name that stuck, although the Portuguese designation is perpetuated in the alternative name for nearby Kanonpunt – Cape Vacca. There is a caravan park overlooking the bay, but the resort of shacks clinging to the slopes running down to the sea is on private property. The cannon after which Kanonpunt and Kanonstrand are named were from

62. A fisherman sits outside his cottage at Stilbaai

the French ship, *La Fortune*, wrecked in 1763 at Fransmanshoek which separates Vleesbaai from Visbaai. Both bays are renowned for the hauls anglers have made in their waters.

Return to the last intersection before Vleesbaai, turn right and drive 13,6 km north-eastward. Turn right (SP Mossel Bay) on to the N2 for the remaining 17,8 km back to the post office in Mossel Bay.

63. Holiday homes overlook Vleesbaai, an anglers' paradise

23
80 km

MOST BEAUTIFUL LAND

From George two routes run eastward through countryside described by
early travellers as the most beautiful they had seen. One hugs the coast,
while the other winds up and down the wooded foothills of the Outeniquas.

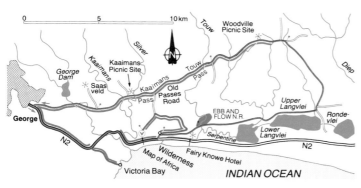

GEORGE The earliest report on the region in which George was to be founded was by the distinguished naturalist and traveller Francois le Vaillant who in 1780 wrote of the privilege of seeing here 'the most beautiful land in the universe'. He added: 'In the distance we espied the mountain range, covered with proud forest, that had cut off our horizon. . . below us lay the extensive valley, enhanced by shapely hills alternating with innumerable undulating formations down to the sea.' In 1813 John Campbell of the London Missionary Society said of the site on which George now stands: '. . . a more pleasant one I have not seen in Africa; it abounds with wood, water and majestic scenery'. And the novelist Anthony Trollope regarded the settlement that had developed a century after Le Vaillant passed this way as 'the prettiest village on the face of the earth'. Although George is now a thriving business and educational centre with most of the appurtenances of a twentieth-century town, it has retained in its spacious layout and pretty gardens much of its early charm, while the surrounding countryside is largely unspoilt and little different from the landscape so admired by those early travellers. Named in honour of George III and originally Georgetown, the place was laid out by Adriaan van Kervel, the first magistrate of what in 1811 was declared a separate district. It was he who planted along the wide streets he had planned avenues of oaks, and one of these stately trees – in front of the Public Library in York Street – is now a national monument. Embedded in its trunk is a length of chain which perhaps lends credence to the belief that slaves were once fastened to it before being sold in its shade. Before the British occupied the Cape there had been a Dutch East India Company outpost here, and one of the sandstone beacons asserting the company's dominion over its possessions was set up in 'Outeniqualand' in 1785. It, too, is a national monument and is preserved in the library.

Trees of the indigenous forest were for many years the basis of George's economy, but by 1936 indiscriminate exploitation had so depleted the wealth of standing timber that the government was obliged to impose a 200-year ban on further felling. Apart from conserving what indigenous trees had survived, the Department of Forestry established in the district extensive plantations of exotic species, the State Sawmills and the Saasveld College of Forestry. In recent years the district has gone over to dairy and vegetable farming, and is the only region in South Africa producing hops for the brewing industry. One of the country's most scenic railway journeys starts in George at 06h55 every morning except Sundays.

The steam engine, hauling carriages and freight cars, ascends through the forest and then loses height near Victoria Bay where, rounding sharp bends, it clings to the precipitous mountainside above the sea. The Outeniqua Express, as it is known, runs across the spectacular curved bridge high over the Kaaimans River where breakers crash against the foundations at high tide, puffs on through Wilderness, skirts the series of lakes further east, traverses Swartvlei on a long, low causeway to reach Sedgefield and arrives at its destination – theoretically 3 hours and 22 minutes after departure – by means of a bridge more than 2 km long over the middle of the Knysna Lagoon.

Leave George by driving south-eastward along Courtenay Street and on to the N2. Turn right (SP Victoria Bay) 7,8 km from the Dutch Reformed church in Courtenay Street and follow the steep, winding road 3 km down to Victoria Bay.

VICTORIA BAY This small but pretty, secluded cove with its cluster of holiday cottages is a popular surfing spot, and its little beach, which is usually sheltered from the wind, is safe for bathing.

Return to the N2, turn right (SP Knysna) and drive 4 km to cross the Kaaimans River by the first curved bridge of its kind built in South Africa. Continue for 2,3 km, at first along the eastern bank of the river and then along the coast, to the left turn to the Wilderness Hotel. But pause at the crest of the hill high above the mouth of the Kaaimans River for the splendid view of the coastline with its long beaches stretching away to Gericke's Point in the east.

WILDERNESS One of the most fashionable holiday resorts in the country, Wilderness is noted for its extensive golden Leentjiesklip and Wilderness beaches which are, however, safer for walkers and sun-worshippers than for bathers. Its drives into the hinterland, which afford some magnificent views, and its proximity to the Garden Route lakes, on which the opportunities for boating and angling are almost limitless, also contribute to its popularity as a holiday venue.

Take the road winding up past the Wilderness Hotel, turn left 100 m from the hotel, left again 2,1 km further on, and left yet again (SP Map of Africa) after another 300 m to reach this splendid viewpoint after 2,5 km.

'MAP OF AFRICA' The name of this viewpoint derives from the resemblance of the northern vista from here – between the Kaaimans River and the mountains in the north-east – to the outline of the continent. To the south the panorama embraces the Garden Route lakes and an extensive stretch of coastline. Hang-gliders launch themselves from this hill for graceful flights down to the Leentjiesklip beach.

Return to the Wilderness Hotel, turn left (SP Fairy Knowe) and then right

64. The Outeniqua Express puffs across the bridge over the mouth of the Kaaimans River

ENJOY A FUN DAY ON OUR VINTAGE STEAM TRAIN
MAGALIESBURG EXPRESS
JOHANNESBURG TO MAGALIESBURG
SUN 26 FEB 1989

FOR BOOKINGS (from 9 am to 5 pm)
(011) 888-1154/5
Fares: Adults R25. Children (3-12) R15

Braai fires ready lit. Meat packs on sale. Salads on sale. Individually reserved seats. Catering car with light take-away meals. Lounge car with full bar service. Live music by Dave Dale. Registered with Museums Association of SA.

PO BOX 1419, ROOSEVELT PARK 2129
NB: OUR NEXT STEAM TRAIN IS ON SUN 12 MARCH

PRESERVATION GROUP
RAILWAY SOCIETY OF S.A.
SPOORWEGVERENIGING VAN S.A.
BEWARINGSGROEP

303

East Rand Bureau

A major breakthrough has been made in an investigation into theft of company products by a security chief at a Wadeville, Germiston, company which produces non-ferrous alloys.

Mr Colin Brown said he became suspicious when a truck from their firm, which was due to make a delivery in Pretoria recently, was hijacked and the entire cargo stolen.

The abandoned vehicle was later recovered in Boksburg.

Mr Brown said he contacted at least 12 scrap metal dealers between Springs and Boksburg but was unable to trace the product, which arrived the following day at a scrap metal dealer in Johannesburg.

Members of the Pretoria Murder and Robbery Unit and Mr Brown went to the scrap metal dealer in Johannesburg where it was discovered the goods had been purchased from a Boksburg dealer.

Police swooped on the Boksburg scrap metal dealer and arrested a 62-year-old woman.

She was later convicted by a Boksburg regional magistrate on the charge of receiving stolen goods and for not keeping a register as is required by law.

The woman was sentenced to a fine of R10 000 or 400 days' imprisonment with a further 12 months' imprisonment conditionally suspended for five years.

The court heard she bought the goods for R8 000 and immediately sold the non-ferrous metals for R12 000.

In another breakthrough, a security guard and a shop steward were arrested at the Wadeville factory in connection with the alleged theft of baled copper wire valued at R56 000.

The two are expected to appear in court this week.

EET
'S)

33

Councillors

Own Correspondent

TZANEEN — The cou
were packed recently
town councillors met th
ter of Gazankulu, Prof
Ntsanwisi, Governor Nel
of Lebowa and represent
interested parties.

The occasion was ph
five-year plan to achie
aims for Tzaneen and its
Management committ
Councillor Vic Borcher
that they were all prese

65. Wilderness

(same SP) after 2,2 km. Continue 1 km eastward, cross the Touw River – taking care on the bridge which is shared by road and rail, with trains having the right of way – and after 100 m reach the left turn into the Ebb and Flow Nature Reserve.

EBB AND FLOW This nature reserve along the tidal reach of the Touw River is a delight for bird-watchers and canoe enthusiasts. There are picnic spots, camp sites and rondavels in the forested reserve.

From the Ebb and Flow Nature Reserve turn left and drive along the northern bank of the Serpentine.

SERPENTINE This natural channel, which snakes across mainly marshy land, allows the waters of the three linked lakes to the east of it – Lower Langvlei, Upper Langvlei and Rondevlei – to flow by way of the Touw River estuary to the sea at Wilderness. There can be few more peaceful pleasures than messing about in boats on the still water of the Serpentine, which gives access to the Ebb and Flow reserve, a source of delightful birdsong.

The road – which now veers away from the Serpentine – runs along the northern shores of both Lower and Upper Langvlei. After travelling 11 km from Wilderness turn left and drive 5 km to the T-junction at Woodville. Turn left, and 500 m further on turn left again on to the Old Passes Road. Continue 2 km before taking a short track to the

right and drive through the forest to the Woodville picnic site where there is one of the region's famous yellowwood giants. Return to the Old Passes Road and continue 13 km westward, through the Touw and Kaaimans passes, to reach the Kaaimans River picnic spot.

KAAIMANS RIVER Crossing the Kaaimans River, with its steep banks and at times torrential flow, was an arduous undertaking for early travellers and it presented the engineer Thomas Bain with his most serious problem when, in 1867, he started replacing the hazardous track between George and Knysna with a properly

constructed road. Until Bain completed his task a wagon coming from the east slid on its brakeshoes down the precipitous Trek-aan-Touw ('haul on the rope', as the approach to the Kaaimans River was known) and usually needed three spans of oxen to drag it up the Swartrivierhoogte on the western side. The channel gouged by braked wheels and the slithering feet of oxen was in parts nearly 3 m deep, and in places so narrow that the drivers could not walk alongside their wagons.

Continue 6,8 km westward from the Kaaimans River picnic site to the N2, passing the right turn to

Saasveld after 2 km, and turn right (SP George) on to the N2 to drive the remaining 2,9 km to the Dutch Reformed church in George.

SAASVELD The only college of forestry in South Africa, Saasveld, was established in 1906 in what is now the Tokai State Forest on the eastern slopes of the mountainous spine of the Cape Peninsula. The earliest students received their training in scientific subjects at the South African College in Cape Town. In 1932 the college was transferred to its present site, where a graduate receives a diploma after two years of theory and two years of practical training.

66. The Old Passes Road crosses the Kaaimans River by way of an old dressed-stone bridge

THE LAKES AND THE OLD PASSES ROAD

Sea, golden beaches, lakes and forest compose a landscape of beauty between George and Knysna. Many travellers speed along the coastal highway, unaware of the equally scenic route further inland.

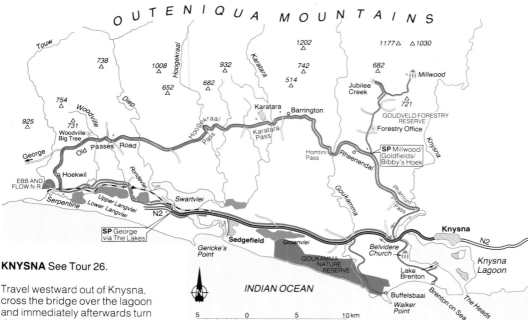

KNYSNA See Tour 26.

Travel westward out of Knysna, cross the bridge over the lagoon and immediately afterwards turn right and right again (SP Belvidere) to double back under an archway. Turn left (same SP) 1,8 km further on and reach Holy Trinity Church after another 700 m.

BELVIDERE

was once the estate of Thomas Duthie who came to South Africa as an ensign in the 72nd Highland Regiment. In 1830 he spent his leave as a guest of the Knysna landowner George Rex at Melkhoutkraal (see Tour 26), fell in love with his host's daughter Caroline, married her in 1833 and acquired this part of his father-in-law's domain. He retired from the army as a captain in 1834 to devote his energies to the development of Belvidere, where he died in 1857. Duthie's home, Belvidere House, is still a private dwelling, but visitors are welcome to look around the beautiful little Holy Trinity Church that he and his friends built in eleventh-century Norman style on the estate. Its timberwork is of local stinkwood and yellowwood, and the rose window installed in the west wall in 1955 is composed of stained glass salvaged from churches bombed in World War II, notably Coventry Cathedral. Duthie, his wife and a number of their descendants are buried in the graveyard of Holy Trinity.

From Belvidere continue southward and then eastward for a pleasant drive with splendid views along the ridge of the peninsula known as Brenton. After 5 km turn left to Lake Brenton and 1,6 km further on turn right to the water's edge.

BRENTON

was named after Sir Jahleel Brenton, the Admiralty Commissioner in Simon's Town who, at George Rex's persuasion, was sent in 1817 to investigate Knysna's suitability as a harbour and who gave a favourable report. At the edge of the lagoon, on the northern side of the peninsula, there is the Lake Brenton caravan park and holiday camp, while on the seaward side the holiday resort of Brenton-on-Sea has an expanse of fine beach for bathing, surfing and fishing.

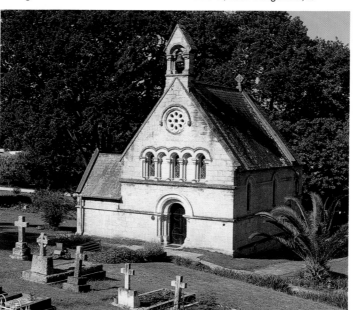

Backtrack 1,6 km from Lake Brenton and turn left to drive 2,6 km to Brenton-on-Sea. Return along the peninsula road, pass under the archway to the Belvidere turn-off from the N2, turn right and continue 5,8 km on the N2 before turning left towards Buffelsbaai. The entrance to the Goukamma Nature Reserve is 6,2 km along this road.

GOUKAMMA NATURE RESERVE

This 2 330-ha sanctuary, which stretches along the coast from Platbank, near Sedgefield, to Buffelsbaai, includes the estuary of the Goukamma River and part of the southern shore of Groenvlei, the only freshwater lake in the series which distinguishes this region. There are eland, bushbuck, bontebok and smaller antelope at Goukamma, but its main fascination is in its birdlife, of which there are some 170 recorded species. Visitors may spot jackal buzzard, various hawks, yellow-billed duck, Egyptian goose, pied, giant and brown-hooded kingfishers, marsh harrier, blacksmith plover, fish eagle, sunbirds and dikkops. No vehicles are allowed beyond the picnic site at the entrance but there are many walking trails through the reserve.

From the entrance to the reserve continue 4,3 km to the resort of Buffelsbaai. Return to the N2, turn left and drive 14,3 km before turning left again (SP Beach) into Sedgefield. The start of Sedgefield's short marine drive is 2,5 km along this road.

SEDGEFIELD

This prettily situated municipality beside the tidal Swartvlei estuary has been steadily developed as a haven for the retired and as a holiday resort where bathing, boating and angling may be enjoyed in peaceful surroundings. There are several caravan parks and numerous holiday cottages as well as the fine homes of the permanent residents.

Return to the N2 and drive westward across the estuary of Swartvlei and along its southern shore.

SWARTVLEI,

a large, scenically beautiful lake at the eastern end of which is a Veld and Vlei Adventure School, affords excellent opportunities for yachting, powerboating, waterskiing and angling for the fish, such as grunter, steenbras and mullet, with which it teems. Like the other expanses of water in the Garden Route's 'Lake District', Swartvlei has an abundance of birdlife.

Turn right (SP George via The Lakes) 6 km after rejoining the N2 at Sedgefield and immediately afterwards fork left along the southern shore of Rondevlei.

RONDEVLEI

This is the most easterly of the three lakes which are linked, its overflow running into Upper Langvlei. The Lakes Conservation Station, where estuarine and freshwater life is studied, is in a small reserve – open to the public only by special arrangement – at the eastern end of Rondevlei.

67. Holy Trinity Church at Belvidere

Continue along the eastern shore of Upper Langvlei and, 5,5 km after leaving the N2, cross the railway at the Rondevlei station. Turn left (SP George), travel along the northern shore of Upper Langvlei and recross the railway at Duiwerivier 1,4 km further on. Drive along the northern shore of Lower Langvlei, then turn right (SP George) over the railway again.

UPPER AND LOWER LANGVLEI

Upper Langvlei spills over into Lower Langvlei, where the George Lakes Yacht Club is based, and the combined overflow of these two lakes and Groenvlei, all of which are interlinked, runs into the Serpentine. As its name suggests, this channel snakes at first through marshy land and then luxuriant vegetation to join the Touw River estuary at Ebb and Flow.

The road now runs through Hoekwil Pass, at the top of which is a viewpoint off to the left. Pass the right turn into Hoekwil 3,1 km from the last railway crossing and 4,6 km further on join the Old Passes Road where the signpost to the left points to George.

OLD PASSES ROAD This scenic drive, sometimes called the Seven Passes Road, is gravelled but maintained in good condition. The original highway between George and Knysna, it had to be forced through terrain densely wooded with primeval forest and traversed by numerous rivers which have gouged deep ravines in the landscape. The road winds down these gorges, crosses the rivers and streams by way of narrow bridges, and ascends again to link a series of small settlements and forestry stations. The seven passes are the Swart River, Kaaimans, Touw River, Hoogekraal, Karatara, Homtini and Phantom.

After joining the Old Passes Road drive 3,4 km eastward and then turn left (SP Big Tree, Picnic Spot, Collins Hoek) to the Woodville Big Tree, which is 33 m tall, has a crown spread of 29 m and is estimated to be 800 years old. Continue eastward, passing at 2,1 km a left turn to Bergplaas, at 2,7 km a right turn to Rondevlei, and at 9,7 km a right turn to Ruigtevlei. Start the Hoogekraal Pass 13,7 km from the Woodville Big Tree, the Karatara Pass after another 9,4 km, and reach Barrington 3 km further on.

BARRINGTON The hamlet of Barrington is on what was once a farm owned by the Honourable Henry Barrington, son of the 5th Viscount Barrington. A lawyer by profession, he came to South Africa in 1842 and bought from Captain Duthie the Knysna estate of

68. Knysna Lagoon

Portland where he experimented, mainly unsuccessfully, with silkworm cultivation, honey production and growing apples for cider. He achieved more success as an administrator and public figure, holding several government appointments before he was elected Member of Parliament for George in 1869.

Continue 7,3 km eastward and then southward to the start of the Homtini Pass which meanders, climbs and descends through the forest, affording wonderful views, particularly of the spate of the Homtini River in the valley far below. Pass the right turn into Rheenendal 13,4 km from Barrington and 1,1 km further on turn left (SP Millwood, Goldfields, Bibby's Hoek). After 2,4 km take the middle of three ways (through white gateposts) and stop 500 m further on to sign the visitors' book at the Goudveld forestry office. Fork right (SP Jubilee Creek) 1,7 km from the office, 500 m further on take the left of three ways and after 2,5 km fork left to reach the beautiful picnic spots in clearings at Jubilee Creek, Natbos and Droerug. From Jubilee Creek return to the last junction, turn left (SP Millwood) and follow the signs to the mines.

GOUDVELD The Goudveld, or 'Goldfields', byway runs through dense forest carpeted in places with ferns and intersected by streams in which, as the area's name suggests, prospectors panned for and found gold in the nineteenth century. The scene of the Knysna gold rush of the 1880s, however, was nearby Millwood. Some thousand diggers materialised here in 1886 after the discovery of a reef in a hill overlooking terrain in which

only alluvial gold had previously been found. The mining camp that sprang up developed into the town of Millwood, with shops, banks, hotels, a police station, a post office and several newspapers. It even boasted the first Methodist church in the Knysna area, founded by the Reverend C S Franklin who had been sent to minister to the roughcast community. The gold soon petered out and the diggers were lured to the new goldfields of Barberton and the Witwatersrand, leaving the forest to swallow up most traces of their presence. Now it is necessary to ferret through the undergrowth to find rusty remnants of the machinery that once clankingly disturbed the tranquillity of the woodland, the adits sunk with

such optimism into the hillsides and the foundations of the buildings in which the lives of the fortune-hunters were centred.

Return to the Old Passes Road, turn left and drive 8,8 km south-eastward before turning left again (SP Knysna, Phantom Pass). Continue 4 km down the Phantom Pass, turn left over the Knysna River at the head of the lagoon, after about 4 km turn left again on to the N2 and travel 7 km along the northern shore of the lagoon to the centre of Knysna.

69. One of Rheenendal's forestry workers at the doorway of his home

IN AND OUT OF THE LANGKLOOF

All the engineering skill, imagination and endurance of South Africa's early road-builders are epitomised in Prince Alfred's Pass and the Montagu Pass, both of which link the Langkloof and the coastal plain across the Outeniquas.

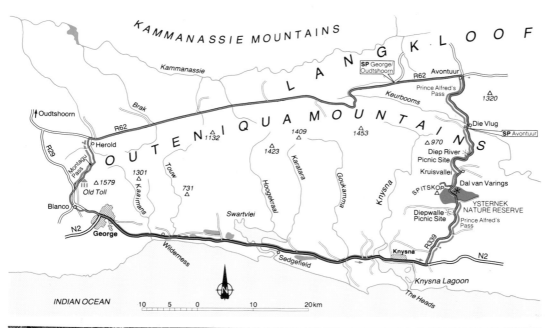

70. Ferns dwarf a visitor to the Dal van Varings

KNYSNA See Tour 26.

Leave Knysna driving eastward along Main Street on to the N2 and after 6,9 km turn left (SP Uniondale) on to the R339. The tar ends after 5,5 km and Prince Alfred's Pass starts about 10 km from the N2.

PRINCE ALFRED'S PASS There are those who regard Prince Alfred's Pass as the greatest achievement of road-builder Thomas Bain. After surveying the terrain in 1856 his father, Andrew Geddes Bain, was of the opinion that a 70-km road could be constructed through the dense forest to a height of more than

900 m over the Outeniqua Mountains to Avontuur in the Langkloof. However, it was only in 1863 that the scheme was approved and the younger Bain was able to start the project. It took four years of hacking through the seemingly impenetrable vegetation, of blasting through rock massifs, crossing innumerable streams, and building extensive dry-stone embankments before the tortuous but scenically spectacular route was completed. At Die Vlug, where his road crosses the Keurbooms River, Bain set up home for his young family while the pass was being constructed. Soon after the road was completed the first Duke

of Edinburgh, Prince Alfred, in whose honour the pass was subsequently named, visited Knysna and was accompanied by Bain on an elephant hunt led by members of George Rex's family. It is recorded that the engineer made an extremely favourable impression on the royal visitor, who sent him a gold pen-and-pencil set in appreciation of his services.

The path to the Diepwalle picnic spot and the tree known as King Edward's Tree is on the left, 16,4 km from the N2.

KING EDWARD'S TREE Named in honour of King Edward VII, this is one of the Knysna Forest's famed yellowwood giants. The tree is 39 m tall, has a crown spread of 24 m and is estimated to be 620 years old. It is in this part of the forest that the last of the elusive Knysna elephants roam. A comfortable 18,2-km trail leading from here through beautiful natural woodland is indeed known as the Elephant Walk, although the chance of the visitor encountering one of the great animals is minimal.

Continue northward from the Diepwalle picnic spot, pass the Kom se Pad turn-off to Gouna after 1,4 km and turn left to Spitskop 9 km further on.

SPITSKOP The winding road to the top of this 933-m peak is rough and daunting for the nervous, with sharp bends and steep drops away from it, but the 360° view from the summit is so breathtaking that anyone who accepts the challenge of the 1,4 km drive is amply rewarded. From here the splendour and vastness of the indigenous forest can be really appreciated. The north-south vista from Spitskop stretches some 30 km from the Outeniqua Mountains to Knysna, and from east to west it is possible to see more than 60 km of coastline reaching beyond Plettenberg Bay.

Return from Spitskop and cross the R339 into the Dal van Varings, a dale of giant ferns which dwarf those who care to follow one of the enchanting walks under the canopy of the cool, damp forest. Return to the R339 and continue 7,7 km northward through Prince Alfred's Pass to Kruisvallei. After another 6,4 km reach the Diep River picnic spot where the Outeniqua Naturalist and Historical Society erected a memorial on the 150th anniversary of the birth of Thomas Bain 'to whose dedication and skill as a road engineer the people of South Africa owe this fine mountain pass and several others in the Cape'. Fork right (SP Avontuur) 11,7 km beyond the picnic site, pass Die Vlug where the road crosses the Keurbooms River a short distance further on and reach the top of the pass 14,6 km from the last fork. At Avontuur, 72,2 km after turning off the N2 near Knysna, turn left (SP George, Oudtshoorn) on to the R62.

AVONTUUR is the terminus of the 'Apple Express' line, the narrow-gauge railway through the Langkloof from Port Elizabeth (see Tour 30). The village was laid out on part of the farm Avontuur, which had been granted as a loan farm to Matthys Zondagh in 1756. Part of the rest of the original farm, renowned for its apples, is still owned by members of the Zondagh family, who have given their name to nearby Zondaghberg and Sondagsnek.

Remain on the R62 by turning left (SP George, Oudtshoorn) 12,3 km after joining it at Avontuur and drive through the Langkloof on a mainly straight road which is relieved in springtime by the colour of apple blossom in the many orchards along the way and by the constantly changing views of the Kammanassie Mountains to the north and the Outeniquas to the south.

THE LANGKLOOF Once the preserve of Bushmen and the Gonaqua Hottentots, the 160-km Langkloof was put on the Europeans' map by Ensign Izaq Schrijver in 1689 and settled by white people from about 1770 onwards. Since then this long valley has become second only to the western Cape in the production of deciduous fruit, particularly apples. Its fertile floor, which is bounded to the north by the Kammanassie and Kouga mountains and in the south by the Outeniqua, Langkloof and Tsitsikamma ranges, varies in width between 8 km and 15 km.

Drive 65,1 km from the last junction, turn left (SP Herold, Montagu Pass) off the R62 and pass the hamlet of Herold 1,8 km further on before descending through the Outeniqua Mountains by way of the Montagu Pass.

MONTAGU PASS Until the Montagu Pass was completed in 1847 by Henry Fancourt White, an Australian engineer brought specially to South Africa for the undertaking, the only direct route through the Outeniqua Mountains from the farms of the Upper Langkloof to George was by way of Cradock's Pass. This earlier route, constructed in 1811 with more good intention and haste than competence, ascended in succession the steep slopes of George Peak, the 1 579-m Skurwekop and Cradock Berg. It was plotted by the first magistrate of George, Adriaan van Kervel, and was so ill-conceived that an ox wagon took three days – without halts for repairs – to negotiate its 9 km, while even a horseman could do it in no less than 3½ hours. The rough, tortuous pass acquired such a daunting reputation that some who were obliged to use it regarded it as fit only for baboons, and there were Langkloof farmers who chose the two-week trek to Algoa Bay with their produce rather than the shorter but more hazardous trip to George. On the recommendation of Colonel Charles Michell, Surveyor-General of the Cape, work on the Montagu Pass, which was named after Colonial Secretary John Montagu,

was started in 1844, several years after its dreaded predecessor had been braved by the Voortrekkers from the George area at the start of their northward migration. Part of this arduous route through the Outeniquas, which some now prefer to call the Voortrekker Road, was picked out with white beacons at the time of the Voortrekker Centenary in 1938 and can still be seen. Whereas Van Kervel had taken his road straight up the high slopes, White at first kept low in the valley and then, only when climbing was unavoidable, took his road this way and that to follow the contours as closely as possible. It was a prodigious engineering feat, entailing the gunpowder-blasting of rock and the construction of extensive dry-stone retaining walls. Though some maps indicate a maximum gradient of 1:8 and the narrow road is characterised by many sharp bends, the Montagu Pass enabled ox wagons to cover in three hours what had taken three days by the old route. The new way took its toll, however, both in wagon wear and in the fees demanded by the toll-keeper, W K Smith – 3d a wheel for a vehicle without brakes, three-farthings a wheel with brakes, a penny a draught animal, a ha'penny for small stock and tuppence for bigger animals. A reminder of the toll in wagon wear is the ruin of a blacksmith's shop halfway up the pass, and still to be seen at the start of the ascent on the George side is the old tollhouse. Although the mountain range can now be traversed at high speed by way of the modern Outeniqua Pass, the gravel road of the Montagu Pass, being a more direct route to the Langkloof, is still maintained. The railway line over the range runs close to the upper stretches of the road and affords passengers one of South Africa's most thrilling train rides.

Fork right (no SP) 12,7 km after leaving the R62, cross the R29 (Outeniqua Pass road) 800 m further on to join the R404 (SP Blanco) and drive 2,1 km into Blanco.

BLANCO The settlement of Blanco grew from the construction camp, stores and convict labour quarters established by Henry Fancourt White when he started building the Montagu Pass. The homes of the artisans, storemen and labour supervisors he employed became the nucleus of the picturesque village that developed, but the most impressive building to have survived is Fancourt, the stately mansion White built for himself. The property was bought and sold many times after his death in 1866 and after a succession of absentee-owners became dilapidated. However, it was bought and

restored to its original stateliness by the distinguished Transvaal neurosurgeon Mr R A Krynauw when he retired to the George district in 1958.

From Blanco drive south-eastward, forking left into George after 1,6 km and then passing the George Hospital on the right. Reach the intersection of Courtenay and York streets 1,3 km from the last fork.

71. Dry-stone walls and a simple bridge are features of Prince Alfred's Pass

GEORGE See Tour 23.

Drive south-eastward out of George along Courtenay Street on to the N2 for the remaining 59 km to Knysna.

72. The road of Montagu Pass winds past the toll house

26

170 km

GIFT OF GOD

Knysna's lovely surroundings – the rivers, lakes and islands, beaches and lagoons, mountains and indigenous forest – fully deserve the motto on the town's coat-of-arms: *Pulchra terra Dei donum* – Beautiful land, a gift of God.

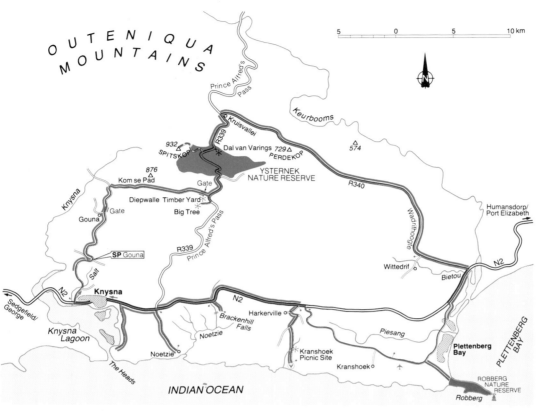

KNYSNA As intriguing a facet of Knysna's history as any is the legend that George Rex, on whose large estate the town developed, was the son of George III and the beautiful Quaker Hannah Lightfoot – either in or out of wedlock. But legend it certainly is. Diligent research has disclosed no evidence of his royal lineage. On the contrary, he has been shown to have been the eldest son of Mr and Mrs John Rex of London. He was a lawyer of Doctors of Commons and was appointed Marshal of the High Court of Vice-Admiralty at the Cape in 1797, retiring in 1804 to Melkhoutkraal, the farm he had bought east of the Knysna Lagoon. Whatever his origins, though, Rex was a remarkable man, a man of vision, determination and enterprise who became the biggest landowner in the area, a successful farmer, harbour pilot, and builder and owner of at least one ship, the *Knysna*. It was he who persuaded the Admiralty to investigate the suitability of Knysna as a harbour and helped to pioneer the port once it had been authorised, although the Norwegian Thesen family – boat-builders and shipping line founders

– did most to ensure the maritime prosperity it enjoyed until the railway reached the town in the 1920s. The economy of the district then became almost entirely dependent on its timber, which was now transported overland, the manufacture of furniture from local woods, and the developing tourist industry. Knysna, on the northern side of the broad, enchanting lagoon formed by the Knysna River and other streams, had indeed been a busy port of call for many a coaster which brought supplies to the area and sailed away with timber, but now only fishing boats and the Thesen family's boat-building concern maintain the town's maritime links. A more recent economic development has been the cultivation in the lagoon of oysters to feed gourmets all over South Africa. The number of pleasure boats and private fishing craft moored or, at low tide, lying on the mud in the lagoon testifies to its reputation as an angling and watersport paradise. And for those who prefer to remain ashore and drive along the road skirting most of this glorious expanse of water, the lagoon is a visual treat. It is hardly surprising that the number of people who avail themselves of Knysna's numerous holiday amenities every year is always on the increase.

Drive 2,2 km westward along Knysna's Main Street from its intersection with Grey Street, turn right (SP Gouna Forest Station) along the eastern bank of the Salt River and then left at the electricity substation 500 m further on. Pass the left turn to the Vrede Nursery after another 5,2 km and fork left (SP Gouna) 400 m still further. The road now runs through a gorge 200 m deep in parts, with countless tall trees of the Gouna Forest crowding each other to reach a sky that can rarely be seen through the canopy they form. Pass the Gouna forestry village 6,6 km from the last fork and turn right through a gate ('Closed from 6 pm to 6 am') on to Kom se Pad, which has a notice: 'Private road – Use at own risk', although its gravel surface is good. Reach the start of the Ystervark trail through the forest after 2 km, fork right 1,4 km further on and drive 9,2 km before turning right through another gate on to the R339. At the Diepwalle timber yard 1,3 km further on turn right again to reach the Diepwalle picnic spot and 'King Edward's Tree' next to the timber yard (see Tour 25). Return to the R339, turn left and continue north-wards, passing the turn-off to Gouna via Kom se Pad after 1,3 km and reaching the left turn to Spitskop or the right turn to the Dal van Varings (see Tour 25) after another 9,1 km. From the Spitskop turn-off continue 7,6 km to Kruisvallei and turn right (SP

73. One of the 'castle' homes at Noetzie

64 THE SOUTHERN CAPE

74. Looking towards Plettenberg Bay from near Perdekop

Plettenberg Bay) on to the R340 to drive along the inland limit of the forests on a ridge overlooking the deep valley between the Kranskop Forest highland and the Outeniqua Mountains. Reach Perdekop on the right 8,1 km from Kruisvallei.

PERDEKOP From the summit of Perdekop, 729 m above sea level, there are splendid views of the Langkloof Mountains over the deep Keurbooms River valley to the north, and to the south the whole sweep of Plettenberg Bay. The 20-minute climb is worthwhile not only for the distant views, but also for the wealth of flora close at hand, particularly in springtime when there is a magnificent variety of veld flowers.

Start the descent of the Wadrifhoogte 32,4 km from Kruisvallei, pass the right turn to Wittedrif 2,7 km further on and after another 5,1 km turn right (SP Knysna) across the Bietou River on to the N2. Travel 4,4 km on the N2 before turning left (SP Plettenberg Bay) on to the R346 to reach Plettenberg Bay after 1,4 km.

PLETTENBERG BAY See Tour 27.

To leave Plettenberg Bay, cross the Otto du Plessis Bridge over the Piesang River, which runs down to the sea at Beacon Island, turn right (SP Airport) into Piesangvallei Road 200 m further on, left into Robberg Avenue after another 300 m and left again (SP Robberg) 3,5 km still further to reach the entrance to the Robberg Nature Reserve after another 2,7 km.

ROBBERG, the 'mountain of seals', juts out into the sea to enclose the southern end of Plettenberg Bay. It was named by the Swedish scientist-explorer Carl

Thunberg who observed hundreds of seals on the rocks in the shadow of the mountain promontory when he was in the area in the 1770s. Innumerable anglers now haunt the same rocks, and have given imaginative names to a profusion of rewarding fishing spots. From the end of the road at the entrance to the Robberg Nature Reserve, which encompasses the peninsula, walks lead along both the northern and southern sides. The one on the latter slope is more rewarding for, apart from affording grand vistas, it leads to huge overhangs where strandlopers sheltered and left huge middens long ago.

Return 2,7 km to the last junction, turn left, pass Plettenberg Airport after 1,4 km and the left turn to Kranshoek 4,3 km further on.

KRANSHOEK is a settlement of about a thousand Griquas descended from a group who,

under Andries Stockenstrom le Fleur, left Kokstad (see Tour 51) for Plettenberg Bay and after a three-month trek in carts and wagons settled here in 1928. The grave near Robberg of 'The Reformer' – as Le Fleur, a deeply religious man and son-in-law of Adam Kok III, was known – is hallowed by the Griquas.

Continue 9 km north-westward from the Kranshoek turn-off, turn left on to the N2 and drive 1,5 km before turning left (SP Harkerville) again. Fork left 1,2 km from the N2, turn right 600 m further on, fork left after 1,2 km and reach the Kranshoek picnic spot 3,1 km still further.

KRANSHOEK RIVER MOUTH After crossing the Kranshoek River, where there is a delightful picnic spot, the road runs up to a parking area at the edge of a high cliff. From this point there is a spectacular view of the Indian Ocean pounding on to Romangat and Grootkop, the rocky promontories on either side of the river mouth 200 m below.

Return from the Harkerville Forest to the N2, turn left and left again to the Brackenhill Falls 8,1 km further on.

BRACKENHILL FALLS The Brackenhill Falls start as a series of minor cascades and end in a sheer drop of awesome height into the gorge of the Noetzie River. There are shady picnic spots at the falls.

Return to the N2, turn left, and left again (SP Noetzie) after 5,6 km. Drive 5,3 km – keeping an eye open to the west for a fine distant view of the Knysna Lagoon – to the parking area above Noetzie.

NOETZIE This delightfully situated seaside hamlet in a rock-girt bay has, in addition to a fine surfing beach and a shady lagoon, the distinguishing feature of holiday homes that have been built like miniature castles. To the Noetzie aficionados the spot is doubly attractive because the road ends at the cliff top and hordes of trippers are deterred from invading the pleasant beach by the prospect of the steep climb down to it.

Return to the N2, drive 4 km westward and turn left to follow the 4-km road down the eastern side of the Knysna Lagoon to The Heads.

THE HEADS Apart from the advent of the railway, the tricky narrow passage between the beautiful headlands at the entrance to the Knysna Lagoon was an important factor in the decison to abandon Knysna as a port. So hazardous did seamen regard the channel after several ships had been wrecked on their way in that the first official pilot was withdrawn in 1827. So determined, on the other hand, was George Rex that the port should survive that he and his sons served as pilots until an official was again appointed to the post in 1858. Had access to Knysna from the sea been less perilous there is no doubt that the port would have survived competition from the railway, that the Thesen Line would still have its headquarters on the lagoon, and that other ships would be regular callers. The headland on the eastern side of the narrows has been marred in recent years by insensitive residential development but, with admirable concern for the environment, the owner of the farm on the western side is determined that its beauty should be preserved and has taken steps to have it proclaimed a nature reserve.

Return to the N2 on the road along the eastern shore of the lagoon, turn left and continue into Knysna.

75. Millwood House, an original building from the gold town of Millwood, is preserved in Knysna

TSITSIKAMMA FOREST

Perhaps the most enchanting of South Africa's indigenous forests is the Tsitsikamma, the name of which is as beautiful as its towering trees, dense undergrowth, clear streams, vociferous birdlife and magnificent river gorges.

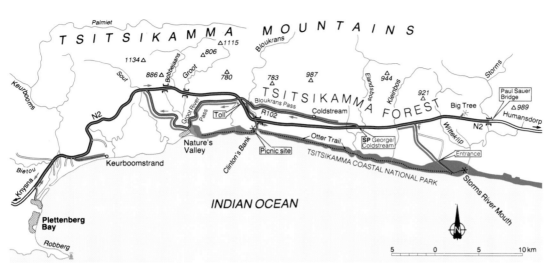

PLETTENBERG BAY The 'Bay of Lagoons', the 'Beautiful Bay' and the 'Bay of Content' – are all names aptly descriptive of this, one of South Africa's most attractive maritime playgrounds. Its recorded history started in the fifteenth century when early Portuguese explorers named it Angra das Alagoas ('Bay of Lagoons'). Their successors preferred to call it Bahia Formosa ('Beautiful Bay'), however, and the name is perpetuated in, among other things, the Anglican parish at Plettenberg Bay, a nearby mountain and a local variety of erica. The Dutch mariners in their turn knew this as the Bay of Content, as well as Keurbooms River Bay and Piesangs River Bay. The first Christian church in Plettenberg Bay dates from 1630 and was a wooden structure

erected by the 100-odd survivors of the wreck of the *São Gonçalo*. The castaways stayed for eight months before they could complete two boats, in one of which some set sail for India and in the other the rest headed for Portugal. As a memento of their sojourn at Formosa Bay the *São Gonçalo* men left an inscription on a cube of sandstone found near Beacon Island in the nineteenth century. What remains of the wording reads: 'Here was lost the São Gonçalo in the year 1630. They built two vessels. . .' A replica of the stone, which is now in the Cultural History Museum in Cape Town, stands on private property where the original was found. Another replica at Plettenberg Bay is that of the slate beacon erected by Governor Joachim van Plettenberg who, with scant regard for modesty,

gave his name to the place in 1778. The original (NM) is also preserved in the Cape Town museum. The first permanent resident in these parts, Cornelis Botha, was already an established farmer in the Piesang River valley by the time Van Plettenberg called, but a community came into existence only after the Dutch East India Company started exploiting the surrounding forest in 1787 and shipping timber to the Cape the following year. Above the beach near the Plettenberg beacon is the ruin (NM) of a timber storehouse built at this time. Next to it stands the 'Old Rectory', now called Van Plettenberg Park, which was in existence in 1777 and subsequently became, in succession, a barrack house and military store, the home of a whaleman and, until 1939, the home of Anglican clergymen. Another of the town's national monuments is the little yellowwood church of St Andrew which local landowner William Newdigate built on his farm in 1851. Although the early development of Plettenberg Bay was prompted by the demand for timber, industry has left it with few scars. Happily, a Norwegian whaling station established in 1912 on Beacon Island – so named because it was once the site of a navigation beacon – lasted less than a decade and what might have remained is buried under a luxury hotel, the flagship of tourism, the only industry the bay still has. Indeed, the resort, with its 10 km of unsurpassed beaches, exquisite setting, splendid rock, surf and deep-sea fishing, its hotels, holiday flats and cottages, balmy weather and modern shopping centre, has acquired a worldwide reputation as a holiday centre.

At the eastern exit from Plettenberg Bay turn right on to the N2 and cross the Bietou River after 4,1 km and then the Keurbooms River 1,1 km further on.

KEURBOOMS RIVER The first and possibly the most attractive public resort developed by the Cape Provincial Administration is on the western bank of the Keurbooms River. On lush lawns which run down to the water's edge there are charming, fully-equipped wooden chalets, a fine caravan park under a canopy of trees, and sites for campers.

From the Keurbooms River continue 2 km eastward on the N2, passing right turns to a caravan park and an hotel on the eastern bank of the lagoon-like estuary of the Keurbooms and Bietou rivers, and turn right to drive 4 km to Keurboomstrand.

KEURBOOMSTRAND From the end of the road to Keurboomstrand a walk of less than half an hour ends at the Matjies River Cave in front of which there is a huge midden. Since 1929 archaeologists have uncovered more than 30 000 objects that have contributed immeasurably to the study of South Africa's primeval peoples, some of whom occupied the cave more than 11 000 years ago. The sandy beaches of Keurboomstrand, popular with surfers, are interrupted by rocky outcrops from which many anglers cast their lines.

Return to the N2 from Keurboomstrand and turn right (SP Humansdorp) for the drive through the Tsitsikamma Forest.

TSITSIKAMMA FOREST Until the 1860s the Tsitsikamma Forest between the mountains of the same name and the Indian Ocean was regarded as impenetrable. In 1869, however, a fire which devastated most of the natural vegetation between Swellendam and Uitenhage made it possible for the famed road-builder Thomas Bain to report favourably on the possibility of constructing a 160-km route from Plettenberg Bay to Humansdorp. The road was completed in 1884 – but only after prodigious effort. While the fire had destroyed the forest on the plateau over which much of the road runs, the deep gorges of the Groot, Bloukrans and Storms rivers which had to be traversed were still covered with dense vegetation. It is, indeed, the indigenous forest which survived in these gorges that makes so delightful the old road winding deep down to each of the rivers and high up the other side again. Until recently there had been minimal deviation from the road Bain constructed, but the volume of

76. One of the Garden Route trio of arches, the Bloukrans River bridge

traffic has led to the construction of a freeway which avoids the Groot and Bloukrans passes, the Storms River Pass having been replaced by the 130-m Paul Sauer Bridge in 1950. Since 1982 the gorges of the Groot and Bloukrans rivers, as well as the Bobbejaans River, have been spanned by three of South Africa's most exciting bridges, and what takes nearly an hour by the Bain road can be covered on the freeway in a few minutes. But those who love the more leisurely drive among the venerable yellowwood giants and other indigenous trees, the flowering shrubs, and the ferns and creepers which together form a tunnel for the road, still take the old route.

To save the more interesting Bain road for last, remain on the N2 where it becomes a toll road (R1,50 a car) 13,3 km after turning on to it at Keurbooms River. Cross the Bobbejaans River Bridge 18,2 km after rejoining the N2 at Keurboomstrand, and the Groot River Bridge after 20,3 km. Reach the toll gate 7,4 km further on and cross the Bloukrans River Bridge after another 2,9 km.

GARDEN ROUTE TRIO OF ARCHES
The graceful concrete arch of each of these three new bridges was started with simultaneous construction from either side of the gorge it spans. Such is the precision of modern engineering that when, for instance, the two quadrants of the 272-m arch which was to support the 451 m of roadway 216 m above the Bloukrans River were ready to 'lock in', there was a discrepancy of a mere 10 mm.

From the Bloukrans River Bridge continue 26,6 km eastward to the the Paul Sauer Bridge over the Storms River.

PAUL SAUER BRIDGE A walk along one of the paths near this bridge enables the visitor to appreciate the grandeur of the Tsitsikamma Mountains, the forest, the mighty gorge through which Bain had to construct the Storms River Pass and the engineering skills of those who build modern bridges like this one. At the restaurant near the bridge there is a small forestry museum and a photographic display illustrating the construction of the bridge.

Backtrack 3,3 km from the bridge to the sign on the right to the 'Big Tree' of the Tsitsikamma Forest National Park.

TSITSIKAMMA FOREST NATIONAL PARK
Of the 30 or more species of beautiful indigenous trees in this park the most striking is the Outeniqua yellowwood which may attain a height of 50 m and live for hundreds of years. Such a giant is the 'Big Tree' 360 m from the N2. It is possible to drive to it, but a leisurely walk through tunnels in the rank vegetation – trees garlanded with moss, lichens and creepers and at their feet ferns and shrubs in profusion – is like an elementary lesson in forestry. This particular yellowwood giant is 36,6 m tall, has a crown spread of 32,9 m and is estimated to be 800 years old. Tabs on other trees in the reserve enable the uninitiated to identify, among others, the alders, stinkwood, ironwoods, redwood, wild olive, white pear, candlewood and the Cape ash.

From the turn-off to the 'Big Tree' continue westward on the N2 and after 9 km turn left (SP Storms River Mouth, Tsitsikamma Coastal National Park). Drive 6,1 km to the entrance to the park (R2 a car) and continue 3,9 km to the restaurant

77. Through the Tsitsikamma Forest

and car park at Storms River Mouth.

STORMS RIVER MOUTH The Storms River mouth is roughly in the middle of the Tsitsikamma Coastal National Park, a narrow strip of land and sea between the mouths of two rivers of the same name but 80 km apart – the Groot at Nature's Valley and the Groot at Oubosrand. The short, easy trail through coastal vegetation from the end of the road to the suspension bridge over the river climbs gently up and down, giving splendid views of the restless sea. Trees along the way are marked for easy identification, and there are information displays featuring the natural life of the park. For those who have more time there are other trails, such as the Lourie Trail, Blue Duiker Trail, Tsitsikamma Underwater Trail and, most famous of all, the 45-km Otter Trail.

78. The mouth of the Storms River, spanned by a suspension bridge

Return to the N2/R102, turn left (SP Knysna) and drive 7,4 km before turning right (SP George, Coldstream) to remain on the R102, or the old Bain road. The Bloukrans River Pass starts 9,5 km from the last turn.

BLOUKRANS PASS Several picnic spots beside the winding road through the pass enable the appreciative traveller to enjoy the sound of tumbling water and birdsong, and the sheer majesty of the scenery.

Turn left off the R102 at the top of the western side of the pass and drive through gateposts at the Bloukrans Forest Station. Turn left just short of more gateposts at the top of an avenue of oaks and right 600 m from the R102. After 1,8 km cross the bridge over the Toll Road (N2) and continue 2 km through indigenous forest to the parking area and picnic site at the top of the cliffs overlooking Koos se Bank, Clinton's Bank and Grootbank. The seascape is magnificent, and there is a circular drive along the cliffs which rejoins the road back to the R102. Turn left on to the R102 again, cross the Toll Road (N2) 400 m further on and start descending the Groot River Pass 5,6 km from the Toll Road, reaching the bottom after another 3,1 km. Continue 1 km before turning left into Nature's Valley.

NATURE'S VALLEY The combination of sea, river, lagoon, mountains and luxuriant vegetation gives Nature's Valley a charm of its own, and it seems appropriate that the whole resort, even the holiday homes, should lie within a small nature reserve. From the beach and in the lagoon the bathing is safe.

Return from Nature's Valley to the R102, turn left and emerge from the Groot River Pass 3,3 km further on. Continue 8,2 km westward, turn left (SP George) on to the N2 and after another 21 km turn left into Plettenberg Bay.

CHAPTER THREE

The Eastern Cape and Border Country

PORT ELIZABETH'S WEST COAST RESORTS

The site of the 1820 Settlers' landing in South Africa, Port Elizabeth has become one of the country's major industrial centres, yet has much to offer the seaside holiday-maker.

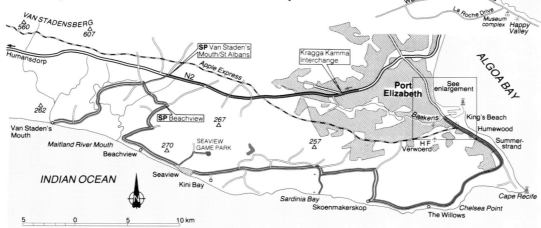

PORT ELIZABETH Citizens of Port Elizabeth aver that the city's soul is epitomised in two monuments. One, the stone pyramid on 'The Hill' overlooking the city, is to a woman who never saw the place. It was erected in 1820 by the Acting Governor of the Cape, Sir Rufane Donkin, and his tribute to the young wife of whom fever had robbed him in India two years previously reads: 'To the memory of one of the most perfect of human beings who has given her name to the town below.' The other monument is a bronze group (NM) depicting a British soldier kneeling with a water bucket before a horse. An inscription on the plinth of this memorial honouring the mounts who suffered and died in the Anglo-Boer War reads: 'The greatness of a nation consists not so much in the number of its people or the extent of its territory as in the extent and justice of its passion.' The people of Port Elizabeth believe that the sentiments expressed in these two tributes convey the humanity of their community and justify their claim that theirs is the 'Friendly City'.

In 1488 Portuguese navigator Bartolomeu Dias became the first European to visit Algoa Bay – or 'Bahia de Lagoa', as the bight on which Port Elizabeth is sited was named by the Portuguese.

For 311 years after Dias called little of significance happened in Algoa Bay. Then in 1799 Lieutenant-General Francis Dundas established Fort Frederick (NM) – named after the Duke of York – both

to guard the landing place in the bay and to keep an eye on the burghers who had settled in the Graaff-Reinet area. This fort, at the southern end of Belmont Terrace overlooking the Baakens River valley, is believed to be the oldest building of British construction in Africa south of the equator. By 1819 no more than 35 people were living on the shore of the bay, but the following year saw the arrival of the 1820 Settlers, most

of whom were destined to farm in the district of Albany. Their landing was supervised by Captain Francis Evatt, commandant of Fort Frederick where his gravestone records that he treated the newcomers with the 'greatest kindness and hospitality'. Also on hand to welcome them was Sir Rufane, whose responsibility it was to supervise their settlement, and the care and thoroughness with

which he carried out this duty made a deep impression on the new arrivals.

The 55-m, 23-bell Campanile, which was modelled on the Campanile of Venice and dominates the entrance to the docks, was erected to mark the centenary of the settlers' landing. Other historical buildings which recall the period include the home built in 1827 at 7 Castle Hill (NM) for the Reverend Francis McCleland, chaplain to some of the settlers. Said to be the oldest surviving dwelling in the city, it is now a social history museum that is well worth visiting. Three streets to the north of it is the Donkin Reserve (NM), where stands the pyramid memorial to Elizabeth Donkin. On the north side of the reserve Donkin Street is graced with a steep terrace of Victorian-style houses that contribute to the character of this historic part of the city. Like McCleland's rectory, the terrace is a national monument. And in Cora Terrace off Bird Street restored Regency-style houses, built in the early 1830s and often referred to as Military Row, are also typical of the dwellings of Port Elizabeth's earliest citizens.

After the arrival of the 1820 Settlers, Port Elizabeth grew rapidly to become an important market and harbour for the export of wool, mohair and ostrich feathers, while its residential areas began to sprawl in all directions over the plateau stretching away from the top of 'The Hill'. Port Elizabeth is now the second biggest city and port in the

79. Rondavels at The Willows provide accommodation for holiday-makers

Cape Province and a major industrial centre. Among the city's most famous attractions are its snake park and oceanarium, both of which are part of the seafront complex at Humewood which has as its nucleus the Port Elizabeth Museum. Few who visit the city miss a performance by the oceanarium's dolphins or a demonstration by one of the snake park attendants handling some of the world's most deadly reptiles.

Leave Port Elizabeth from the Kraggakamma Interchange, driving 18 km westward on the N2 before taking the exit SP Van Staden's Mouth, St Alban's. Turn left (SP Van Staden's Mouth) 900 m further on to drive 15 km through rolling hills – mainly along a high ridge which affords fine, varied views both inland and towards the sea – to the Van Staden's River mouth.

VAN STADEN'S RIVER MOUTH
The Van Staden's River ends in an expansive lagoon that provides sport for the angler, boating enthusiast and swimmer. On the north bank a delightful resort with holiday bungalows, caravan and camping sites and a restaurant has been laid out on greensward which slopes gently down to the river, while on the southern shore spectacular sand dunes plunge steeply to the water's edge. In contrast to the grandeur of Van Staden's gorge upstream (see Tour 29), long lines of breakers roll gently in to miles of silvery shore on either side of the blind river mouth.

Retrace the route towards the N2 for 12,9 km and turn right (SP Beach View). At the junction 3,6 km further on turn right (SP Beach View) and after another 3 km right again (SP Maitland River Mouth, Beach View, Sea View) to reach the Maitland River mouth after 3,5 km.

MAITLAND RIVER MOUTH Like the Van Staden's River mouth, the Maitland River mouth is popular with anglers intent on catching steenbras and musselcracker. The expanse of beautiful beach stretching away on either side of the mouth is dominated by high sand dunes down which, as at the Van Staden's River mouth, the young enjoy sliding. The 'disused mine' symbol on the official survey map of the area testifies to the late eighteenth-century discovery and the subsequent exploitation of lead deposits in the form of galena 3 km from the mouth of the river.

The road continues eastward as a pleasant marine drive, reaching the Beach View holiday resort 3,2 km from the Maitland River mouth and a T-junction at Sea View 3,6 km further on.

SEA VIEW was the pleasant setting during World War II for the training in South Africa of officers for the Royal Navy. After the war the training establishment, HMS *Good Hope,* reverted to being an hotel.

At the Sea View T-junction turn left (no SP) and 2,5 km further on turn right to drive a short distance to the Sea View Game Park.

SEA VIEW GAME PARK A wide variety of wildlife, both animals and birds, may be seen in the Sea View Game Park, which is particularly noted for its cheetahs.

Return to the T-junction in Sea View and continue 13,6 km eastward before turning right on to gravel (SP Sardinia Bay). After 800 m turn right again and drive 2,6 km to the parking area at Sardinia Bay's long stretch of beach. Return to the last intersection and keep straight on for 5,5 km, then turn right at the T-junction (SP Skoenmakerskop). At another T-junction 3,6 km further on turn right into Skoenmakerskop, a rock angling resort and residential area. From the last T-junction return to Port Elizabeth along the Marine Drive, passing or perhaps tarrying at The Willows, which with rondavels, caravan park, tidal swimming pool, restaurant, sweeping lawns and good fishing is one of the most popular of the holiday resorts close to the city; Summerstrand; Humewood; Happy Valley; King's Beach; and, at the boundary of the harbour area, the terminus of the narrow-gauge railway, the Apple Express (see Tour 30) which runs through the Langkloof to Avontuur.

HUMEWOOD Tucked away within the horn of Algoa Bay, Humewood is Port Elizabeth's principal playground for holiday-makers. The seafront highway with its attractive flower beds is flanked on one side by homes, flats and hotels, and on the other by splendid beaches running down to water which is rarely colder than 17 °C and is more likely to be around 24 °C. The amenities and attractions by day and by night are numerous and imaginative. They include the Princess Promenade; an amusement park with all the fun of the fair; lawns with swings and roundabouts; a miniature railway; tidal swimming pools; paddling pools; changing rooms; seafront cafés and restaurants; and the Port Elizabeth Museum complex, which includes the city's renowned snake park, tropical house and oceanarium with its performing dolphins and a fascinating variety of other marine life.

HAPPY VALLEY Barely a step away from the beach, Happy Valley is a combination of natural beauty

80. The Donkin Reserve, with its lighthouse and monument to Lady Elizabeth Donkin

and landscaping art. What was once a marsh has been converted into an enchanting garden of lawns and winding paths, water gardens with lily ponds and banks of massed flowers. Like the seafront, Happy Valley is bright with coloured lighting after dark and alive with the happy sounds of promenaders.

KING'S BEACH This magnificent stretch of golden sand – a continuation of the Humewood Beach towards the harbour – is where King George VI and his daughters bathed not far from the spot at which their White Train was parked during the royal visit to Port Elizabeth in 1948.

81. A cheetah feeding at the Sea View Game Park resents disturbance

29
250 km

SURFERS' NIRVANA

Today a mecca of surfers and shell-collectors, St Francis Bay takes its name from the Portuguese title 'Bahia de São Francisco' which was accorded it by Manuel de Mesquita Perestrelo in 1575.

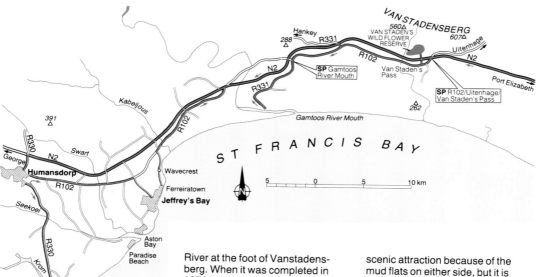

HUMANSDORP originated in 1849 and owes its name – at first Human se Dorp – to Matthyus Gerhardus Human who gave the land to the Dutch Reformed Church on which to establish a church village. Its development was accelerated by the construction of the narrow-gauge railway which links it with its fruitful hinterland in the Langkloof.

From the stop street at the northern entrance to Humansdorp continue southward (SP St Francis Bay) through the town on the R330. The Krom River mouth is 17 km from the stop street.

KROM RIVER MOUTH This is the mouth of one of the 20 'crooked' rivers in South Africa, only one of which is not in the Cape Province. This one, which probably owes its name to the number of times travellers had to cross it, flows eastward down the Langkloof for more than 100 km before entering St Francis Bay. During World War II the Churchill Dam was built on the Krom River to provide Port Elizabeth, 125 km to the east, with its main water supply. At the river mouth a colony of European mute swans was started by a pair which appeared 'from nowhere' in 1918 and settled on a small farm dam. The farmer cared for them and, with the introduction of an extra male after some time, the colony grew and spread to other nearby estuaries. Good angling in the tidal reaches of the Krom River led to the development of holiday homes on the bank of the estuary.

82. The Gamtoos River mouth

PORT ELIZABETH See Tour 28.

Leave Port Elizabeth from the Kraggakamma Interchange on the N2, travelling 28,8 km westward before taking the exit SP R102, Uitenhage, Van Staden's Pass. After 400 m turn left on to the R102, 900 m further on turn right (SP Van Staden's Wild Flower Reserve) and cross the N2 into the reserve.

VAN STADEN'S WILD FLOWER RESERVE AND BIRD SANCTUARY This 372-ha reserve lies on the east side of the beautifully forested gorge through which the Van Staden's River flows. It is noted for the indigenous *Protea neriifolia* which grows in abundance and for its ericas, crassulas, *Cyrtanthus* lilies and numerous ground orchids. Pleasant walks lead through the reserve, from which there is a splendid view of the Van Staden's River bridge. There is also a picnic area for visitors.

From the reserve return over the N2 to the R102, turn right and drive down the old Van Staden's Pass, from the bottom of which, 2,8 km from the reserve, there is another fine view of the bridge.

VAN STADEN'S BRIDGE One of South Africa's most remarkable bridges crosses the Van Staden's

River at the foot of Vanstadensberg. When it was completed in 1971 its arch was the second largest of its type in the world. With a height of 125 m and a length of 325 m, the bridge cost R1,5 million to build – just to save the motorist five minutes. However, as it is on the trunk road between Cape Town and Port Elizabeth and it obviated the need to use the steep Van Staden's Pass, the expense was deemed worthwhile. Until the 1880s the original road, nearer the sea than the present route, had been a traveller's nightmare, but then it was so improved in gradient and condition that it was regarded as excellent – with the bonus of running through attractive, heavily forested scenery at the bottom of the gorge. The traveller who speeds over the bridge is now oblivious of the beauty below, but anybody with the time and inclination may take the old road to experience the pleasure those who used to pass this way once enjoyed.

Continue 2,1 km up the western side of the pass and 13,3 km from Van Staden's Reserve pass the right turn to Hankey, Patensie and Humansdorp. After another 2,1 km turn left off the R102 (SP Gamtoos River Mouth) on to the R331 and drive 9,9 km to the Gamtoos River mouth, pausing at the brow of the last line of coastal hills to observe the fine view of St Francis Bay.

GAMTOOS RIVER MOUTH The Gamtoos River, which drains the Willowmore region of the Karoo, is said by some to have been named by Hottentots who regarded it as being 'wily as a lion' because it so often flooded its banks when least expected. Others maintain that the name meant 'water' in the Hottentot tongue. The river mouth is not a

scenic attraction because of the mud flats on either side, but it is good for fishing. It has camping facilities and there is an hotel not far upstream.

Backtrack 9,9 km from the Gamtoos River mouth and turn right (SP Port Elizabeth) on to the R102. After 5,1 km turn left (SP Port Elizabeth, Hankey, Humansdorp) on to the R331 and 100 m further on rejoin the N2 (SP Humansdorp). Drive 35 km before turning left (SP Humansdorp) on to the R330, and continue for 2,5 km to the stop street at the northern entrance to Humansdorp.

From the Krom River mouth continue southward for 2,8 km to St Francis Bay (formerly Sea Vista).

ST FRANCIS BAY As recently as 1950 access to St Francis Bay and the beaches on either side of it was by mule wagon. Until then only anglers and beachcombers frequented this stretch of coast and made use of the cluster of rondavels built by Leighton Hulett, the pioneer of the subsequent development which has resulted in St Francis Bay becoming one of South Africa's most splendid recreational areas. Visitors and the owners of the numerous luxury homes at the resort now cruise most of the way from Humansdorp on a fine tarred road, and it is no longer only beach fishermen who revel in what there is to offer. They have been joined by deep-sea anglers and by those who delight in the facilities that have been provided for golf, tennis, waterskiing, horse-riding and powerboating – to say nothing of the surfers who since 1961 have been 'hanging ten' in the wake of Bruce Brown. Whether or not Bruce Brown actually discovered what is regarded as *the* perfect wave, rolling in as it does off a powerful swell that surges towards Cape St Francis from thousands of miles away, it was he who showed the world of surfers in *Endless Summer*, some of which he filmed at Cape St Francis, just what the wave is like. The adepts who take its long, fast ride when the winter north-westerly wind combines with a ground swell at low tide call it 'Bruce's Beauty'.

Continue 7,6 km southward to the hamlet of Cape St Francis.

CAPE ST FRANCIS The cluster of holiday homes known as Cape St Francis – a popular spot with anglers – and the Cape St Francis lighthouse are at Seal Point, a rocky promontory marking the westerly limit of the whole bight designated St Francis Bay. To add to the confusion of spots named after St Francis, the Cape St Francis headland lies across a small bay to the north of Seal Point.

Retrace the route to the stop street at the northern entrance to Humansdorp and turn right (SP Paradise Beach, Jeffrey's Bay) into Voortrekker Street (R102). After 6,7 km pass the right turn to Paradise Beach, turn right (SP Jeffrey's Bay) 5,8 km further on and drive 3 km before turning right (SP Kabeljous) into Reyger Street at Jeffrey's Bay. At the stop street 300 m ahead continue straight on to the beach.

JEFFREY'S BAY Four hundred years after Dias had named this bay 'Golfo dos Pastores' it assumed the

83. Boardsailing in St Francis Bay, at the mouth of the Kabeljous River

84. Proteas in Van Staden's Wild Flower Reserve and Bird Sanctuary

name of a former whalerman, J A Jeffrey, who had come from St Helena and, with a partner, set up shop near the seashore, trading under the style 'Jeffrey and Glendenning'. By the middle of the nineteenth century the firm was supplying Port Elizabeth with fresh produce, much of which was transported by coasters which loaded and discharged goods directly from the beach. The coasters ceased their visits after the construction of the narrow-gauge railway between Port Elizabeth and the bountiful larder of the Langkloof, but Jeffrey's Bay has survived as a fishing village and holiday resort. The beach, with its seemingly endless stretch of glorious white sand and the great rollers that break

on to it, was popular long before it became an essential port of call on the world surfing circuit. The surfers, some of them professionals seeking 'the perfect wave' or training for yet another championship, lend colour to the Jeffrey's Bay scene. Others who are not up to the standard that would ensure them a living from surfing sustain their easy-going lifestyle by making leatherware and other handcrafted goods for sale. World champions and run-of-the-mill surfers alike, however, afford the shorebound spectator thrilling displays as they ride their boards just ahead of the white water or even in the tubes of the waves that have made St Francis Bay world famous. As popular as Jeffrey's Bay is with surfers, so is it with conchologists: its seashells are celebrated for their variety, beauty and number. It is

here that the famous Charlotte Kritzinger Seashell Collection, housed in the C J Langenhoven Library on the seafront road, was gathered. Jeffrey's Bay, which has several hotels as well as caravanning and camping facilities, is a town of rapidly increasing numbers of holiday homes.

Return from the seafront to the last stop street mentioned, turn right (SP Kabeljous) and, at the stop street 5,7 km further on, right again (SP Port Elizabeth) on to the R102, having driven through the seaside residential areas of Ferreiratown and Wavecrest. Cross the Kabeljous River 1,1 km after joining the R102 and continue for 9,7 km before turning left (SP N2, Port Elizabeth) and then right 400 m further on to return to Port Elizabeth on the N2.

NORTH-WESTERN HINTERLAND

Port Elizabeth's north-western hinterland includes the valleys of the Gamtoos, Kouga, Groot and Baviaanskloof rivers, its scenery ranging from the pleasant farmland of the Gamtoos valley to the rugged grandeur of Baviaanskloof.

The distance given allows for about 30 km on the gravel road into Baviaanskloof.

Leave Port Elizabeth from the Kraggakamma Interchange and drive 40 km westward on the N2 before taking the exit SP Hankey, Gamtoos. Turn right (SP Hankey) on to the R331 600 m further on and drive 11,4 km past rolling hills before passing under the cableways at Loerie.

LOERIE This village in the foothills of the Cockscomb Mountains takes its name from the Knysna lourie or

it is in places a spectacular run as the Langkloof extends westward between the Tsitsikamma and Langkloof Mountains in the south and the Kouga Mountains in the north.

From the Loerie cableways continue 15,3 km north-westward on the R331 — mostly along a ridge overlooking more rolling hills – to Hankey.

HANKEY Now a centre for citrus fruit, tobacco, lucerne, potatoes and other vegetables as well as the site of the factory producing the largest

precast cement pipes in Africa, Hankey originated as a mission station on the farm Wagensdrift which was bought by the London Missionary Society in 1822. The mission, named in honour of the treasurer of the society, William Alers Hankey, was founded to accommodate some of the numerous Hottentots who had given up their nomadic ways and overpopulated Bethelsdorp, a community the society had established near Port Elizabeth in 1802. It was at Hankey that South Africa's first major tunnelling project was undertaken by the versatile William Philip, a former marine officer who had turned surveyor and then missionary to follow in the footsteps of his father, the well-known John Philip.

Continue westward through Hankey on the R33 and 16,2 km from the Loerie cableways cross a tributary of the Gamtoos River. Turn left (SP Philip Tunnel, Milton) 800 m from the tributary, cross the railway line 900 m further on and recross the tributary after another 900 m, leaving the tarred road as it turns right 400 m from the second bridge across the tributary. Drive about 1 km along a farm road, following power lines at the foot of the high ridge through which Philip's team burrowed. The tunnel, somewhat obscured by undergrowth, is 100 m off the farm road.

WILLIAM PHILIP IRRIGATION TUNNEL (NM) When the practical, enterprising William Philip took over the Hankey mission station in 1841 he originated a variety of projects designed not only to keep his flock busy but also to feed them. In addition to opening a smithy and wagon works he put his mind to extending the community's agricultural activities. Although by the time he arrived some of the mission's land was already under irrigation by means of furrows from the Klein River which runs through Hankey, Philip envisaged a far more ambitious scheme. He planned to water a large fertile tract in an oxbow of the Gamtoos River north-west of the settlement by building a tunnel through a 90-m high ridge between the tract and the river. With his congregation providing the labour and himself acting as surveyor, engineer and clerk of works, he set to work in 1842 with such confidence in his measurements that tunnelling was undertaken simultaneously from either side of the ridge. Progress was slow with the primitive

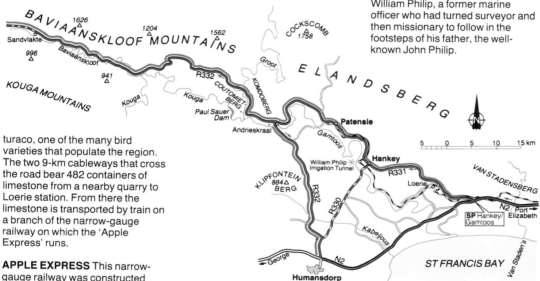

turaco, one of the many bird varieties that populate the region. The two 9-km cableways that cross the road bear 482 containers of limestone from a nearby quarry to Loerie station. From there the limestone is transported by train on a branch of the narrow-gauge railway on which the 'Apple Express' runs.

APPLE EXPRESS This narrow-gauge railway was constructed mainly to transport goods to the farming communities in the fertile Langkloof and bring back to Port Elizabeth the area's agricultural produce, which consists mainly of fruit, and apples in particular. Passenger transport on the 285-km line has always been a minor function and is now limited to a handful of labourers, but holiday excursions occasionally encourage the nostalgia of railway buffs and others who hanker after the romance of travel in trains hauled by steam-powered locomotives. From the harbour in Port Elizabeth the fussy little engines with their shrill whistles chug through the dormitory municipality of Walmer and then haul their wagons through the bush of the coastal plain towards the valley between the Suuranys Mountains and the Kareedouw range. On their way the trains cross a bridge over the Van Staden's Gorge so high that they look like models. Beyond the bridge

85. The Apple Express on its way back from the Langkloof

equipment available, especially as 88 m of the tunnelling was through solid rock, but after nearly a year the men burrowing from either side could hear each others' pick, chisel and hammer blows. Encouraged by these sounds, the tunnellers laboured day and night with even greater enthusiasm. At 2 am on 13 August 1844 the pick wielded by the best of Philip's 'moles', Jan Bosman, broke through the last remaining section of rock. When the news reached the mission by way of a gun shot pandemonium erupted in the form of laughing, weeping, cheering, bell-ringing, torch processions and 'music' struck from pots and pans. Although later in the day Philip opened the sluice only partially to allow water through the tunnel, the flow was strong enough, he reported, to have powered the biggest mill in the country. Within a year the man responsible for this historic project was dead – drowned in inexplicable circumstances in the Klein River. Floods caused extensive damage to the tunnel three and 23 years after it was completed, but it was repaired on both occasions and remained in use for more than a century.

Return from the tunnel to the R331, turn left and drive 12 km further up the Gamtoos River valley to come abreast of the Dutch Reformed church in Patensie.

PATENSIE The terminus of the narrow-gauge railway's branch line on which Hankey is the only other station, Patensie's *raison d'être* is the packing and export of oranges grown in the Gamtoos River valley. Its name is probably a corruption of a Hottentot word for 'resting place for cattle'. At certain times of the year pink and red poinsettia add spectacular splashes of colour to the orange groves round Patensie.

Continue through Patensie on the R331 and 18 km from the Patensie Dutch Reformed church start driving past a great mass – indeed a mountain which appears pockmarked – of conglomerate rock. Pass the left turn to Humansdorp at Andrieskraal 20,4 km from the Patensie Dutch Reformed church and continue westward, now on the R332, to pass the left turn to the Paul Sauer Dam after 4,1 km. The tar peters out 200 m further on, but the roughness of the following 100 km of road is eclipsed by the magnificence of the scenery as the route runs through the spectacular Grootrivierkloof between the Coutomietberg and the Komdo-berg, and then through the rugged beauty of Baviaanskloof (Baboon's Gorge).

GROOTRIVIERKLOOF AND BAVIAANSKLOOF Rising sheer on either side of the road, the mountainsides are cleft by deep gorges, some the courses of clear streams that at times become cascades. During various seasons red hot pokers, oleanders, agapanthus and pelargoniums splash the rock with colour, while many bird species make their vociferous contribution to the pleasure of those who are prudent enough to cut their car engines and listen.

The drive through Baviaanskloof may be terminated after any distance, although there is grandeur in the scenery all the way to the western end of the Baviaanskloof range. The entire distance would, however, be too great to be included in a one-day tour. Return to the turn-off to Humansdorp at Andrieskraal, turn right and drive southward on the rough gravel of the R332. After 33,6 km turn right (SP Humans-dorp) on to the R330 and after another 4,2 km left on to the N2 to

86. Farmlands under spray irrigation near Patensie

return to Port Elizabeth. If, however, the rough road of Baviaanskloof has been so demanding that relief is desired, continue through Andrieskraal to Hankey and turn right (SP Humansdorp). Drive 24,5 km in comfort on the tarred R330 before turning left on to the N2 for the return to Port Elizabeth.

87. Grootrivierkloof

31
225 km*

ELEPHANT COUNTRY
North of Port Elizabeth lie the fertile Sundays River valley and the Addo Elephant National Park, where Africa's most southerly surviving herd of elephant, once almost exterminated, is protected in its natural habitat.

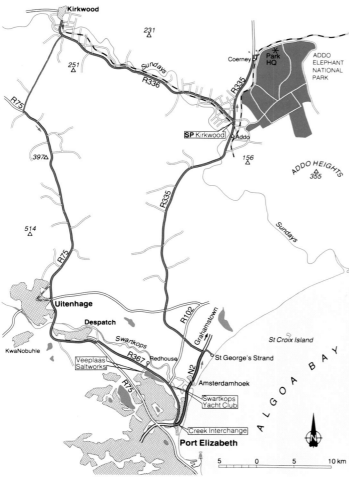

*This distance allows for about 30 km in the Addo Elephant National Park.

PORT ELIZABETH See Tour 28.

From the Creek Interchange on the Port Elizabeth seafront travel north on the N2 and after 7 km take the exit to Amsterdamhoek.

AMSTERDAMHOEK This pleasant seaside suburb of Port Elizabeth lies on the north bank of the Swartkops River estuary, where numerous private jetties and landing stages jut out into the placid water. Although it has been remarked that Amsterdamhoek's name may stem from the hamlet's resemblance to a typical Dutch village, it more probably originates from the Dutch vessel *Amsterdam* which was wrecked near the mouth of the river early in the nineteenth century. Nobody who stops at Amsterdamhoek should miss a stroll down the narrow road which skirts the waterfront to the 'meeting of the waters' where sea meets river in restless frolic. The best time to visit this charming settlement is in the late afternoon, when sunset tints the scene, the dinghies of anglers swing lazily to their moorings, the colourful wings of boardsailers glide across the placid water and gulls wheel overhead.

Rejoin the N2 and 3,9 km north of Amsterdamhoek take the exit to St George's Strand.

ST GEORGE'S STRAND A vast stretch of silvery sand and a popular camping area make St George's Strand another fine resort for surf-fishing, bathing, surfing and picnicking on the Algoa Bay coast.

Return to the St George's Strand Interchange, take the R335 (SP Addo) and after 51,9 km, at Coerney station, turn right off the tarred road (small SP Addo Elephant National Park).

ADDO ELEPHANT NATIONAL PARK It was in the Addo Elephant National Park that one of the most extraordinary operations in the history of animal conservation was conducted. In 1919, when the encroachment of civilisation had made the peaceful co-existence of man and elephant impossible, the celebrated big-game hunter Major Jan Pretorius was commissioned to exterminate the herd of pachyderms that frequently

emerged from the Addo bush to devastate the groves of the citrus farmers. Battling through almost impenetrable vegetation, the major shot 120 of the animals in less than a year, and the remaining 15 retreated into the densest part of the bush where they became man-shy, wily and dangerously aggressive. Public indignation both in South Africa and abroad resulted in the hunt being called off, and the survival of the herd was assured in 1931 when the government proclaimed 9 712 ha of the Addo bush a national park. It fell to the lot of Harold Trollope, a former Kruger National Park game ranger, to herd the elephants into the proclaimed area, a phenomenal task in which he succeeded by acting calmly but systematically. Keeping the ill-tempered herd there was another problem, and it was only after a 20-year period of experimenting with electrified fences, fires, torches, night patrols, trap guns and trenches that a solution was found. A team of workers headed by Graham Armstrong, Trollope's successor, spent two years constructing the world's strongest fence out of old lift cable and disused tramlines. The result, the Armstrong Fence, is elephant-proof. Within the enclosure boreholes were sunk, dams were dredged and conditions made as attractive as possible not only for elephants but for as many other forms of wildlife as could be returned to an area in which they were once indigenous. Black rhinos from Kenya and hippos from the Kruger National Park have since been introduced to the Addo Park and the many other varieties of game include Cape buffalo, bushpigs and several species of antelope. The wide variety of birds, ranging from ostriches to songbirds, adds to the attractions of the park. For a long time visitors were able to observe the elephant herd, which has re-established itself to viable strength, only from outside the Armstrong Fence, but now it is possible to drive on roads within the enclosure right up to waterholes and revel in the spectacle of adults, mischievous juveniles and infants emerging from the bush almost every day to gambol, splash, squirt, wallow and cover each other in red mud.

Return from the elephant park and turn left on to the R335. After 10,3 km turn right (SP Kirkwood) and follow the R336 for 30 km before turning right again and continuing 2,5 km to Kirkwood.

SUNDAYS RIVER VALLEY Stretching from Addo away to the north-west between the Sundays River (originally Zondags River, a name probably associated with the many members of the Zondagh

88. Amsterdamhoek

89. A young elephant bull disturbed at his browsing in the Addo Park

90. The rest camp in the Addo Elephant National Park

family in the region) and the foothills of the Suurberg and Klein Winterhoek ranges is a region boasting attractive homesteads set among orange groves and fields of green lucerne. Fertile soil and irrigation have made what was once semi-arid land into one of the country's most productive agricultural regions. Cultivation began towards the end of the nineteenth century when pioneers such as Port Elizabeth auctioneer James Kirkwood realised the potential of the valley and started using the flood waters of the Sundays River for irrigation. The irregularity of the floods made irrigation farming precarious but, just before World War I, the conservation of water which had run unused from the Sundays River into the sea was made possible through the energy and vision of Sir Percy FitzPatrick. The financier, politician and author of *Jock of the Bushveld* had been enchanted with the area, bought property, and he and his associates spent about £450 000 on irrigation development. Stimulated by Sir Percy's dynamic personality and drive, irrigators banded together and obtained government assistance for the building of Lake Mentz, a dam which transformed the valley into one of the country's principal citrus fruit regions. Lucerne is another important product of the Sundays River valley, also noted for its dairy products and cattle stud herds.

KIRKWOOD, the terminus of a branch of the railway between Port Elizabeth and Alice and principal town of the Sundays River valley, was founded in 1913 on the farm Gouvernmentsbeloning and named after James Kirkwood who pioneered irrigation farming in the valley.

Return 2,5 km along the Kirkwood road and continue southward (SP Uitenhage). After 12,3 km turn left on to the R75 (SP Uitenhage) and wind through rolling hills thick with prickly pear, aloes and scrub. Remain on the R75 when it becomes a freeway north-east of Uitenhage, and either take one of the Uitenhage exits to visit the town or continue on the freeway to skirt it.

UITENHAGE Although the district of Uitenhage was proclaimed in 1804 and named after Commissioner-General Jacob Abraham Uitenhage de Mist who had been sent to the Cape by the Batavian Government in 1802, the founder of the town was Captain Jacob Glen Cuyler of the British expeditionary force which occupied the Cape in 1806. Captain Cuyler was appointed *landdrost* of Uitenhage and commandant of the eastern frontier forces later that year, and the town developed around his headquarters. The history of the town from 1804 to the second half of the twentieth century is pictorially recorded in a collection of photographs in the Uitenhage Africana Museum, which came into existence in 1960 through the efforts of Tom Fowlds, a former mayor. Among its prized exhibits are articles once owned by Cuyler, as well as the De Mist Bible sent from Holland in 1817 to the citizens of Uitenhage in gratitude for their kindness to the survivors of the *Amsterdam,* a Dutch vessel which had run aground at the mouth of the Swartkops River. Today Uitenhage is an important railway and industrial centre, with factories for the assembly of motor vehicles, wool-scouring and the production of tyres and textiles.

Returning to the R75 from Uitenhage, continue south-eastward and either stay on the freeway or take the appropriate exit to visit the town of Despatch.

DESPATCH It is uncertain how Despatch, principally a residential town for people who work in Port Elizabeth and Uitenhage, acquired its rather strange name. There is a theory that it is related to the fact that when brickfields were established in the vicinity early in the community's history, it was from here that the bricks were despatched. It has also been suggested that it might have something to do with the despatch of trains at a time when the town was developing as a railway centre.

At the interchange east of Despatch take the R367 (SP Redhouse, Swartkops), after 8,7 km turn left to Redhouse, and 400 m further on turn right to the river.

REDHOUSE is a peaceful riverine suburb of Port Elizabeth on a stretch of the Swartkops River where yachting and fishing are popular.

From Redhouse return to the R367 and continue south-eastward to Swartkops, passing the Veeplaas salt pans and mountains of salt on the right of the road. At the junction 4,3 km from Redhouse turn right to Swartkops and 400 m further on left to the river and the Swartkops Yacht Club.

SWARTKOPS Situated on a wide stretch of water 3 km from the river mouth, Swartkops is one of South Africa's premier yachting venues. Indeed, the river attracts watersport enthusiasts of all kinds and is not only the scene of many a rowing regatta, but has elbow room for powerboating and waterskiing as well. Anglers, too, either on the banks of the river or in boats, enjoy the sport the river offers and may catch a variety of fish – and, boast the locals, some of the biggest of their kind. Swartkops was also noted at one time for the hot mineral water which, at 55 °C, has been gushing up at the rate of a quarter of a million gallons a day ever since an oil prospecting drill plunged into a subterranean river 1 200 m down in 1919. The spa hotel, built with a swimming pool and slipper baths to cater for those who came to seek relief in the waters, has not been replaced after being destroyed by fire.

Leave Swartkops on the R102 for the remaining 10 km back to Port Elizabeth.

A LEGACY OF FORTS

The territory north of Grahamstown still bears the character stamped on it by the 1820 Settlers. Surviving forts, bridges and military barracks are reminders of the endurance of those who lived here during the frontier wars.

Take the R63 from Bedford and drive 22,4 km eastward to Adelaide.

ADELAIDE Like many other towns in the eastern Cape, Adelaide originated as a military post during the frontier wars. A certain Captain A B Armstrong chose the site for this fort on the Koonap River in 1834 and he named it in honour of the consort of King William IV. Farmers gradually settled the area and now, as well as having a proprietary medicine industry, Adelaide is the centre of an agricultural district. Its museum has a fine collection of glassware and old furniture that reflects the lifestyle of the mid-nineteenth century settlers.

Another old stone church still in use may be seen at Glen Thorn 26 km north of Adelaide on the road to Tarkastad. Thomas Pringle's brother John was granted the farm Glen Thorn and in 1840 he built on it a small church that has been in uninterrupted use as a Presbyterian place of worship ever since.

GRAHAMSTOWN See Tour 33.

Leave Grahamstown on the R350 and travel 101 km north-westward from the Cathedral of St Michael and St George to Bedford. This is a pleasant drive which includes the Helspoort Pass and then a longish stretch through typical Karoo countryside.

BEDFORD Centre of a well-established cattle and sheep stud area, Bedford was founded in 1854 on the farm Maasstroom below the well-wooded Kaga Mountain at the southern end of the Baviaans River range. Many of the Scottish families among the 1820 Settlers had gravitated to the district and local place names testify to the Caledonian origins of those who were farming there when Andries Stockenström, Lieutenant-Governor of the Eastern Cape, named the new settlement after his friend the Duke of Bedford.

In the Baviaans River valley about 29 km north of the town is Glen Lynden, where stands the sturdy little stone church built in 1828 by Scottish settlers and their Dutch neighbours. Director of the project was the writer Thomas Pringle, leader of a party of Scottish settlers from Roxburghshire. From the outset the church, which is now a mission church, was Dutch Reformed, although it retained its connections with the Scottish settlers.

Continue south-eastward from Adelaide on the R63. After 37,6 km turn right over the Kat River and drive into Fort Beaufort.

FORT BEAUFORT In 1822 Lieutenant-Colonel Maurice Scott established a military post on the Kat River to keep in check the marauding Xhosa chief Makoma. He named the fort after Lord Charles Somerset's father, the Duke of Beaufort. Fort Beaufort played as important a part in the defence of the eastern frontier as any of the series of forts that were built along South Africa's first military highway – the Queen's Road – to maintain the land between the Great Fish and Keiskamma rivers as a buffer zone between the white settlers and the Xhosa tribes. It was, indeed, the storm centre of the confrontations of the Sixth Frontier War. When that conflict was over Sir Benjamin D'Urban ordered the erection at Fort Beaufort of even more sturdy fortifications than there had previously been, and remnants of the newer redoubt are still to be seen in Bell Street, near the Tower Mental Hospital. The most important and picturesque part of the surviving fortifications is the martello tower, a stout round structure of dressed stone with particularly fine brick upperwork. Apart from its function as a fortress, it served at times as a refuge for town and country folk. Next to the martello tower, the former officers' quarters now house a museum. In view of the military history of Fort Beaufort, it is hardly surprising that emphasis in the museum is on weapons used by both sides during the frontier wars. A large, splendid relief map in this museum enables a visitor interested in the military history of the eastern Cape to visualise the defence system organised by successive leaders of the government forces ranged in the area. Fort Beaufort's other museum – where there are, among other exhibits, fine collections of African beadwork, pottery and basketwork – is housed in what used to be the Officers' Mess in Durban Street and is now, like both the martello tower and the museum next to it, a national monument. Another building of indirect historical interest in Durban Street is the block of apartments called Emgwenyeni Flats. It was built on the site of Charles Holliday's shop, from which the axe that triggered the Seventh Frontier War was stolen in 1846. The conflict, also known as the War of the Axe, broke out when a patrol sent to arrest the tribesman suspected of stealing the axe was ambushed, and a colonial force under Colonel John Hare

91. The martello tower at Fort Beaufort

92. Relics of the eastern Cape's frontier days are displayed at the Adelaide museum

subsequently invaded Xhosa territory. Yet another structure which has received recognition from the National Monuments Council is the Victoria Bridge, access to which is from the south-western end of Campbell Street. Designed by Major Charles Selwyn of the Royal Engineers, this bridge over the Kat River was an important link in the Queen's Road. The foundation stone was laid in 1840 by Lady Napier, wife of the Governor of the Cape, and the bridge was completed in 1844.

From Fort Beaufort take the R67, the Queen's Road, and travel southward for 52 km, passing the Andries Vosloo Kudu Nature Reserve on the left, before reaching the turn-off left to Fort Brown.

FORT BROWN The largest stronghold on the Queen's Road, Fort Brown was built in 1835 to replace a smaller one at Hermanuskraal, so named after the Hottentot freebooter Hermanus Xogomesh. The later construction bears the name of Lieutenant Robert Brown of the 72nd Highland Regiment who was in command here during the Sixth Frontier War. It consisted of a group of buildings which provided spacious accommodation for men and horses and were enclosed by high walls. In one corner the Royal Engineers built a loopholed tower 3,5 m high, atop which was mounted a swivel gun, while between the foundations was located a magazine. The square tower and part of the redoubt walls may still be seen at

Fort Brown, which has been a police post almost since it ceased to be garrisoned in 1861.

Rejoin the R67 and travel the remaining 27 km to Grahamstown, driving en route over the Ecca Pass. A memorial to Andrew Geddes Bain lies at the Grahamstown end of the pass.

ECCA PASS No more appropriate site for a memorial to Andrew Geddes Bain could have been chosen than at Ecca Pass, for this was the first mountain gateway he constructed after becoming a professional road-builder. He had come to South Africa from the Scottish town of Thurso in 1816 as a 19-year-old saddler who read Shakespeare for relaxation. Having spent six years in Cape Town, in 1822 he moved to Graaff-Reinet

and there opened a saddlery. A born, though untrained, engineer and an amateur geologist of note, he took a lively interest in the affairs of the local community. So it was that he cooperated with other citizens who, at their own expense, were building the Oudeberg Pass north of Graaff-Reinet. It was, however, in supervising without charge the construction of the Van Ryneveld Pass on the road from Graaff-Reinet to Murraysburg that Bain established his reputation as a road-builder. The immediate consequence was his appointment as superintendent of military roads by the Royal Engineers in 1837. His most important work in this capacity was the Queen's Road, connecting a string of forts from Grahamstown to the foot of the Katberg. It was hewn out of mountainsides, traversed embankments thrown up in deep ravines and was supported on bridges – one of them, over the Great Fish River, the biggest bridge in the country at the time. The most difficult section had to be constructed over the heights just north of Grahamstown and was named the Ecca Pass after an insignificant river north of the heights that is now called the Brak River. Bain's services were dispensed with when the Royal Corps of Engineers was reorganised in 1845, but they were snapped up by the Colonial Administrator, John Montagu, who appointed him Inspector of Roads. Among Andrew Geddes Bain's subsequent achievements were the construction of Michell's Pass, near Ceres; Bain's Kloof, near Wellington; and the Katberg Pass, near Fort Beaufort – to say nothing of the training he gave his son and learner-assistant Thomas Bain who also became a renowned road engineer.

93. Helspoort Pass between Grahamstown and Bedford

33

150 km

SETTLER COUNTRY

Grahamstown, the 'Settler City', is an admirable starting point for a tour of the once-inhospitable countryside to which the 1820 Settlers were translated from the crowded industrial towns of Britain.

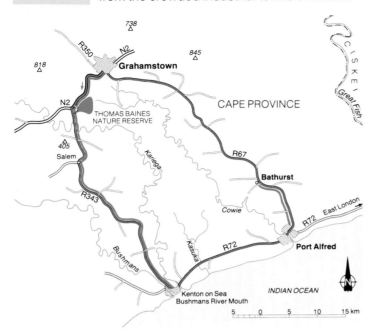

94. Near Grahamstown's 1820 Settler memorial, a statue depicts a pioneer couple surveying the land they were to farm

GRAHAMSTOWN It was in 1812, just after the fourth of the frontier wars between the white trekkers who were on the move from the west and the Xhosas who were expanding from the north-east, that the Governor of the Cape, Sir John Cradock, sent the intrepid Colonel John Graham to clear the Xhosa from a buffer zone that had been proclaimed east of the Fish River. To maintain his advantage after completing his mission, Graham established a military post on the abandoned farm De Rietfontein above the Qoyi (Xhosa for 'rushing', but corrupted to Kowie) River. A memorial in the High Street, opposite Fisher's Building, marks the place at which he chose the site for his base. In 1819 the post, commanded by Lieutenant-Colonel Thomas Willshire, played a vital role in the Battle of Grahamstown, one of the most significant incidents in the history of the eastern Cape. Thousands of Xhosa warriors who attacked the settlement under the leadership of the prophet Makana were repulsed by Willshire's garrison of 301 men. Makana was eventually captured and he drowned while trying to escape from imprisonment on Robben Island. However, his name is perpetuated by the hill known as Makana's Kop, on the northern outskirts of the city, where a plaque commemorates the battle.

The arrival of the British settlers the following year at first made little difference to the size or status of Grahamstown, for the settlers were sent to farm in the districts of Albany, Bathurst and Alexandria. When, however, they were allowed to leave their farms and move to Grahamstown, many to pursue their original occupations as artisans, their enterprise and diversity of skills helped what had been a nondescript cluster of camp-followers' shops, canteens and dwellings to develop into a thriving centre. Some of the homes of these early craftsmen have been beautifully restored in the part of the city known as Artificers' Hill. Progress, especially with the start of wool production, was so rapid that by 1831 Grahamstown had become the principal town of the eastern Cape and, in the colony as a whole, second in importance only to Cape Town.

Three more frontier wars afforded the town the opportunity of enhancing its reputation as a military base, but when peace eventually came to the region the garrison was withdrawn. The Old Provost, Fort Selwyn, Fort England (the name of which is perpetuated in the local mental hospital) and the Military Hospital (now part of Rhodes University) remain as monuments to Grahamstown's erstwhile military importance. The city is characterised not only by its atmosphere of 'old England' and the number of churches and ecclesiastic-style educational buildings that has led to another nickname, the 'City of Saints', but also by the wide streets which in the original layout were intended to allow ox wagons to turn in them. Among the historic monuments in the city are the Drostdy Gateway, now the entrance to Rhodes University and all that remains of the Drostdy completed in 1842; Fort Selwyn on Gunfire Hill where the 1820 Settler Memorial with its two conference halls, theatre and restaurant was opened in 1974; the Old Provost near the Albany Museum; the organ installed in Wesley Church in Market Street in the 1830s, the first pipe organ in the eastern Cape; and the Huntley Street School, which in 1849 became the first Anglican school in South Africa.

Leave Grahamstown on the N2, travelling south-westward for 13 km from the Cathedral of St Michael and St George before turning left (SP Alexandria, Kenton on Sea) on to the R343. The turn-off left to the Thomas Baines Nature Reserve is 2 km along the R343.

THOMAS BAINES NATURE RESERVE This 975-ha reserve is the home of such animals as the white rhino, eland, buffalo, bontebok, mountain reedbuck, wildebeest and impala, while the birds to be observed include a variety of kingfishers and the red-billed hoopoe.

Return to the R343, turn left and travel 12,2 km to Salem.

SALEM After an abortive attempt to settle elsewhere, the party of 344 Londoners led by Hezekiah Sephton was relocated at what is now Salem, so named by their chaplain, the Reverend William Shaw, who took the word for 'peace' from Psalm 76. Although the Salem settlers' first church was demolished only 10 years after it had been built, it was immediately replaced in 1832 by the more substantial thatched building which is still a place of worship and a monument to the pioneers of Methodism in South Africa. On a hill opposite the church is a memorial to the Quaker Richard Gush. By virtue of his dignity and courtesy Gush succeeded in mollifying a band of Xhosa warriors intent on burning down the village in the Sixth Frontier War.

From Salem continue 34,6 km southward on the R343 – from which there are splendid views of the kind of terrain the 1820 Settlers pioneered – to the mouth of the Bushman's River.

BUSHMAN'S RIVER AND KENTON ON SEA On either side of the Bushman's River mouth are the seaside resorts of 'Bushmans', as it is known, to the west and Kenton on Sea to the east. Both afford excellent opportunities for boating, waterskiing and fishing as well as for swimming from fine beaches.

From Kenton on Sea take the R72 and drive north-eastward for 24 km to Port Alfred. The road runs between rolling hills, some of which have been cleared of indigenous vegetation for pasture, creating a landscape which might have been familiar to settlers who hailed from the Downs of England – had it all happened in their time.

PORT ALFRED Now exclusively a pleasure and holiday resort nicknamed 'The Kowie', Port Alfred did indeed have its day as a port, though never an important one. It started off in 1825 as Port Frances, named in honour of Lord Charles Somerset's daughter-in-law, but was renamed in 1860 to mark the visit of Queen Victoria's second son. The 1820 Settlers were the first to use the mouth of the Kowie River to land cargoes, and repeated attempts were subsequently made by the government to establish a viable harbour. Private enterprise also took a hand, and in 1876 as many as 101 vessels landed a total of almost 13 000 tons of cargo. However, while deep water upstream is navigable for a meandering 24 km, the bar at the river's mouth proved to be a ships' graveyard, with the result that Port Alfred ceased to be a port just before the turn of the century. And all for the best, say those who love its restful setting amid enchanting scenery, its temperate climate, the placid water of its river and the superb swimming, fishing, yachting and surfing in which they can indulge.

From the Nico Malan Bridge over the Kowie River, drive 2 km north-eastward along Albany Road and turn left into Bathurst Street to visit the Settlers' Church.

96. Kowie River craft at Port Alfred, with the Nico Malan bridge in the distance

95. The 1820 Settlers' Methodist church at Salem

SETTLERS' CHURCH The thatched 1820 Settlers' Church with its clay pulpit was built in 1823 at the instigation of the Reverend William Shaw, was twice burnt down in the frontier wars and twice rebuilt. After falling into a state of dilapidation it was beautifully restored in 1938.

Continue up Bathurst Street for 1,3 km, turn right on to the R67 and drive 14,4 km to Bathurst.

BATHURST, founded in the year the 1820 Settlers landed and named by Sir Rufane Donkin in honour of the Secretary of State for the Colonies, was initially the administrative centre for the Albany district but soon lost this status to Grahamstown. It was, however, the religious and community centre for the majority of settler parties who, allocated farms in a belt leading

north-westward from Port Alfred to Grahamstown and immediately to the west of the Great Fish River, bore the brunt of the Xhosa incursions. The two places of worship built by the settlers – St John's Anglican church, which was dedicated in 1838 and the Methodist church – are both buildings of historical note, the first being a national monument and the other bearing the bronze plaque of the National Monuments Council. Both served as refuges for women and children during times of war, St John's while still unfinished during the Sixth Frontier War in 1834. As congenial an inn at which to slake one's thirst as could be found anywhere is another national monument, the Pig and Whistle in Bathurst. One of the oldest licensed hotels in the country, it was built in 1821 and originally called the Bathurst Arms.

Deep in a beautiful gully 1,4 km south of Bathurst is the wool mill (NM) that weaver Samuel Bradshaw, the head of a party of 64 settlers from Gloucestershire,

set up soon after his arrival. The mill provided the settlers, who were deprived of some of the most elementary necessities of life, with blankets and with kersey material with which to make clothing. It was bought by the Simon van der Stel Foundation in 1962 and restored.

The Bathurst district saw the beginnings of the eastern Cape's 70 million-plant pineapple industry, a venture that was pioneered in 1865 by Charles Purdon, member of an 1820 Settler family, on his farm, Thorndon. While having his hair cut in Grahamstown Purdon was fascinated by a row of pineapple tops set on the rims of jars of water in the barber's shop. The barber, a man named Green, gave him the tops and they grew so well at Thorndon without irrigation that other farmers were encouraged to follow Purdon's lead on a grand scale.

Return to Grahamstown, continuing north-westward for 45 km on the R67.

34 INTO CISKEI FROM EAST LONDON

260 km

The south-western coastal route from East London takes the traveller past seaside resorts and hut-dotted hills of Ciskei. Swinging inland from Hamburg, this tour includes a visit to the former fortified outpost of Peddie.

EAST LONDON See Tour 36.

Cross East London's Buffalo Bridge southward into Dr Zahn Road, turn left into Bank Street 900 m from the bridge and right (SP West Coast Resorts) into Strand Street 1 km further on. After running briefly between a depressed residential area and railway property which blocks out any view of the coast, the route follows the seafront as Molteno Drive. From Shelly Beach the drive swings inland for half a lap of East London's Grand Prix Circuit and back to the coast at Fuller's Bay. It then continues as the Prince

97 On the beach near Hamburg

George Circuit before swinging inland again at Leach Bay to join the R72. Turn left on to the R72 and 14 km from the Buffalo Bridge turn left on to the 2,7-km gravel road to Cove Rock.

COVE ROCK is a residential and holiday seaside resort dominated by a mighty headland of rock known to the early Dutch mariners as 'Doodkist' because of its resemblance to a coffin when seen from the sea. It is referred to by this name in the log of the *Centaurus*, the vessel built by some of the survivors of the *Stavenisse* which was wrecked about 112 km south of where Durban now stands in 1686. When the *Centaurus* sailors

reached Cape Town Governor Simon van der Stel bought their vessel and sent it back up the coast, ostensibly to search for the remaining 47 *Stavenisse* castaways who had elected to try to walk to the Cape. According to one record, the rescue party aboard the *Centaurus* sighted a group of animated 'savages' at Doodkist, but the crew of a boat which was lowered to investigate found that the 'savages' were some of the *Stavenisse* overlanders for whom they were supposed to be searching. The same record tells that the survivors at Doodkist and their companions, who were living at a nearby kraal, were all rescued – a total of 22. Other accounts have it that only 21 of the 47 were still alive after the long trek, that three of them paddled out to the *Centaurus* lying at anchor off Doodkist and that all but three of those ashore were taken aboard the ship before rough weather prevented further rescue work. The English who settled in the area many years later translated the name 'Doodkist' directly as 'Coffin Rock', which in turn was corrupted to Cove Rock, although to this day there are still people who refer to it as Coffin Rock. The area to which Cove Rock eventually gave its name was granted to Colonel John Maclean when he retired from the lieutenant-governorship of Natal in 1865 and he called it Cove Farm. It was on part of the farm that the pleasant resort of today, with its fine

beach and shallow lagoon, was established.

From Cove Rock return to the R72, turn left and drive about 17 km to the left turn to Kidd's Beach.

KIDD'S BEACH No matter how diligently they may hunt, beachcombers will find no pirate treasure buried at Kidd's Beach. Although Captain William Kidd voyaged around the Cape of Good Hope, this was not one of the stretches of coast visited by the notorious buccaneer. This Kidd's Beach is less evocatively named after Charles Kidd, a mayor of East London in the 1860s. Though an example of the undisciplined building of holiday cottages that in the past has marred many an attractive spot on the South African coast, Kidd's Beach has many aficionados, particularly among the people of King William's Town. An expansive beach and excellent waves ensure its popularity among surfers and boardsailors while the rocky part of its coastline, from which quite a variety of fish are reeled in, attracts many anglers. Boating on the lagoon is popular and there is also a tidal pool.

Return to the R72 from Kidd's Beach, turn left and continue westward through undulating parkland interspersed with orderly fields of pineapples and occasional Xhosa kraals. The road makes a steep descent through the Cayenne Hills, presenting many a splendid view as it enters Ciskei. At the fork 50,4 km from the Kidd's Beach turn-off keep left (SP Port Elizabeth, Hamburg) to remain on the R72, and 4,7 km further on turn

98. Barracks once used for the cavalry at Peddie

left (SP Hamburg) on to the R345. This good gravel road runs down through pleasant, undulating countryside to the broad Keiskamma River valley and reaches Hamburg after 14 km.

HAMBURG is a charming little village on the south bank of the wide stretch of placid water which the Keiskamma River becomes just before it reaches the coast. The settlement, 3 km from the mouth of the river, was founded in 1857 by members of the party of Germans who settled in the eastern Cape after fighting for Britain in the Crimean War. It has a small permanent population and is popular as a holiday resort. Facilities for river boating are excellent and so are the opportunities for fishermen. Keiskammapunt, 1,7 km beyond Hamburg, has a glorious curve of golden beach backed by dense indigenous coastal vegetation.

Return from Keiskammapunt and Hamburg to the R72 and turn right (SP East London, Peddie). After 4,7 km turn left (SP Peddie) on to the R345 and travel 25,8 km before crossing the N2 into Peddie.

PEDDIE In 1835, after the Sixth Frontier War, Sir Benjamin D'Urban as Governor of the Cape Colony annexed the territory between the Keiskamma and Kei rivers and called it Queen Adelaide Province.

At the same time he moved 17 000 loyal Fingo people with their 22 000 head of cattle from Gcalekaland to what was to become the Peddie district, with the intention that the Fingos would serve as a buffer against further incursions by the Xhosa. Sir Benjamin also ordered the building of a series of forts from Fort Willshire in the north to Fort Peddie in the south, the latter being named after Lieutenant-Colonel John Peddie of the 72nd Highland Regiment, who was in command of the British troops in the area at the time. These forts were moated earth stockades which had sturdy stone buildings within them to accommodate both cavalry and infantry. When the British Government repudiated the annexation of Queen Adelaide Province the following year most of the troops were withdrawn. Fort Peddie, however, was retained to maintain order in the region and protect the loyal Fingos, and in 1837 it played an extremely important part in the defence of the eastern frontier. The eight-pointed, star-shaped fort, which had now been strengthened by having its earth walls replaced with loopholed walls of stone, had its baptism of fire when the Xhosa, who hated and despised the Fingos, attacked the redoubt. The assault was repulsed, but Fort Peddie's most severe test came in 1846 when the British troops and their Fingo wards were attacked with even greater force by

the Xhosa chiefs Pato, Umhala, Seyolo and Stokwe. The enemy was again beaten off with the loss of only one defender, and Fort Peddie was henceforth regarded by the Xhosa as unassailable. The remains of the double-storey tower which was added to the fort in 1841 are to be seen on the ridge overlooking Peddie. The tower, a national monument, had a cannon emplacement on top, a single door which was 3 m from the ground and a retractable ladder. Another historical feature in Peddie is a stone tablet noting that Dick King passed this way in 1842 on his famous ride from besieged Durban to summon a relief force from Grahamstown.

Leave Peddie on the N2, travelling 54,2 km north-eastward to King William's Town.

KING WILLIAM'S TOWN See Tour 37.

From King William's Town drive the remaining 53 km back to East London on the N2.

99. A Xhosa student who has just undergone the circumcision rite is attended by a young companion

35
THE ROMANTIC COAST
130 km

Smooth white sand on expanses of unspoilt beach, blind rivers that penetrate perennially green coastal hills to form placid lagoons, and rocky promontories from which anglers reel in a variety of fish characterise East London's 'Romantic Coast'.

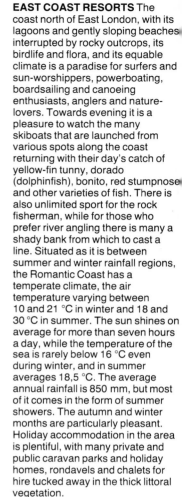

EAST LONDON See Tour 36.

From the Nahoon Interchange leave East London on the N2 (SP Umtata, Gonubie) and drive through pleasant undulating farmland and coastal bush. After 4 km take the exit SP Gonubie, East Coast Resorts, and 500 m further on turn right (SP Gonubie) to reach Gonubie 6,4 km away.

100. Holiday cottages at Haga Haga

GONUBIE lies on the south bank of the Gqnube River which takes its name from the local bramble berries known to the Xhosa as 'gqunube'. It is a rapidly-developing, self-sufficient seaside town with a population of almost 5 500, a thriving business community, caravan parks, holiday cottages and the homes of many permanent residents. Originally a resort favoured by retired people, it has also become popular as a residential area for many younger couples who work in East London but prefer to raise their families away from the frenetic environment of the city. Gonubie's splendid beach, which is safe for swimmers, presents a barrier to the river and forms an enchanting lagoon. This tranquil stretch of water is flanked to the north by a high, thickly-vegetated bluff and to the south by a comparably high bank on which there are numerous homes – with beautiful views – that property agents would describe as 'desirable'.

Return from Gonubie to the N2, cross it and 500 m further on turn right (SP East Coast Resorts) on to the R102 to drive for almost 10 km through a charming agricultural 'valley' between the high bush-covered dunes along the coast and the uplands to the west. From here the R102 runs through beautiful countryside, and one may branch off to any of about 20 delightful and mostly unspoilt spots at which resorts have developed.

EAST COAST RESORTS The coast north of East London, with its lagoons and gently sloping beaches interrupted by rocky outcrops, its birdlife and flora, and its equable climate is a paradise for surfers and sun-worshippers, powerboating, boardsailing and canoeing enthusiasts, anglers and nature-lovers. Towards evening it is a pleasure to watch the many skiboats that are launched from various spots along the coast returning with their day's catch of yellow-fin tunny, dorado (dolphinfish), bonito, red stumpnose and other varieties of fish. There is also unlimited sport for the rock fisherman, while for those who prefer river angling there is many a shady bank from which to cast a line. Situated as it is between summer and winter rainfall regions, the Romantic Coast has a temperate climate, the air temperature varying between 10 and 21 °C in winter and 18 and 30 °C in summer. The sun shines on average for more than seven hours a day, while the temperature of the sea is rarely below 16 °C even during winter, and in summer averages 18,5 °C. The average annual rainfall is 850 mm, but most of it comes in the form of summer showers. The autumn and winter months are particularly pleasant. Holiday accommodation in the area is plentiful, with many private and public caravan parks and holiday homes, rondavels and chalets for hire tucked away in the thick littoral vegetation.

Typical of the East Coast resorts is Kwelera, the turn-off to which (SP Sunrise on Sea, Kwelera) comes 9 km after joining the R102.

KWELERA, a cluster of holiday homes and a caravan park near the mouth of the Kwelera River, has a short but pleasant marine drive along a rocky seafront favoured by anglers. The drive leads to a fine beach where the river percolates into the sand and surfers are in their element.

From the road down to Kwelera there are branches to the right to Rainbow Valley and Sunrise on Sea, a private caravan park.

RAINBOW VALLEY One of the most picturesque of the Romantic Coast resorts, Rainbow Valley is sheltered from the wind on all sides by tall trees and sand dunes, and lies in beautiful surroundings with pleasant nature walks. Attractive cottages and a caravan park nestle in the woodland.

From Kwelera return to the R102 and continue for 6,5 km before turning right. Follow the road and at the fork bear left to Glengariff, a cluster of homes on a high bluff

overlooking the sea. The right fork leads to Yellow Sands, where there is a private caravan park and a beach from which the surfing is excellent. Return to the junction and turn right on to a loop road (Schafli Road) which eventually leads back to the N2. From the loop road take the turn-off right to the Eastern Beach resorts.

EASTERN BEACH is a series of spots whose names reflect a strong Caledonian influence. They include Glen Muir, a group of holiday homes; Glen Navar and Glen Eden, both of which have caravan parks as well as private homes; and Marina Glen, a caravan park. Other Eastern Beach resorts are Krause's Beach; Four Seasons, which has a caravan park and fully-equipped cottages for hire; and Queensberry Bay.

Return from the Eastern Beach resorts to the loop road and 2,6 km further on turn right to Cintsa West.

CINTSA WEST There are fully-equipped cottages and rondavels, a caravan park, horses to ride and safe bathing from a beautiful beach at Cintsa West on the south bank of the Cintsa River.

Return from Cintsa West to the loop road and 3 km from the junction turn right to Cintsa Mouth (at the end of the fork to the right further on) and Cefane Mouth (at the end of the fork to the left).

CINTSA MOUTH AND CEFANE MOUTH At the mouths of both the Cintsa and Cefane rivers there are excellent beaches where the swimming and fishing are good. Both resorts have caravan and camping sites, and at Cintsa Mouth there is also a cluster of time-sharing holiday chalets.

Return to the loop road, continue north-westward for 7,2 km to rejoin the N2, drive 9,7 km northward to Mooiplaas and turn right on to the R349. After 11,6 km fork right to Haga Haga.

HAGA HAGA Haga Haga's 2 km of gently sloping beaches, from which there is safe access to the sea for swimming and fishing, are said to be a shell-collector's dream. And, with a little luck, a beachcomber taking one of the several pleasant walks along the coast on either side of the village may pick up something even more exciting – 'treasure' from one of the Indiamen wrecked hereabouts, such as a cornelian bead from India, a shard of Chinese porcelain or even a gem. Many a vessel has been wrecked along this, the Wild Coast, and mariners tell of enormous walls of water and huge 'holes' in the sea which may account for some of the

101. The river mouth at Gonubie

disasters. Constant wind action on the Agulhas Current causes waves of different origins to be super-imposed on others and thus form a 'freak' wave. The current creates a deep trough at the foot of the wave, and when a vessel falls into it she is unable to rise again to meet the oncoming wall of water. This could have happened to the 10 000-ton *Waratah*, flagship and pride of the Blue Anchor Line, which left Durban on 26 July 1909, was positively sighted for the last time on 27 July by another ship off the mouth of the Bashee River 130 km north-east of East London, and then vanished

with 221 people on board. Each of the many efforts to trace the wreck – the most recent in 1983 – and to ascertain why she went down has failed. But the ship *does* lie somewhere out there on the ocean bed off this coast, whose pounding surf is supposed to be simulated by Haga Haga's onomatopoeic name. The *Waratah's* fate remains the greatest unsolved mystery of South Africa's seaboard and one of the most tantalising enigmas in the annals of the sea.

Return towards the N2 from Haga Haga, but at the fork mentioned in the last route direction turn right and drive 11 km to a T-junction.

Turn right again and travel 16 km to the fork from which Morgan's Bay is 7,1 km to the right and Kei Mouth 8,7 km to the left.

MORGAN'S BAY, which is named after the master of the survey ship HMS *Baracouta*, lies on the bank of a lagoon formed by the Nchara River. The lagoon is admirably suitable for swimming, waterskiing and boardsailing, and there are cottages and boats for hire, a safe bathing beach and excellent fishing, both in the sea and in the river. Deposits of black sand known as ilmenite, from which titanium is extracted, were discovered near Morgan's Bay in 1953 and have been exploited by a company which also mines rutile and zircon.

KEI MOUTH At Kei Mouth, where the visitor looks across the Great Kei River to Transkei, there is another of the Romantic Coast's expansive beaches which is safe for swimming and a paradise for shell-collectors. Deep-sea fishing expeditions are organised from Kei Mouth, but the resort is equally popular with anglers who prefer to keep their feet on terra firma.

From Kei Mouth return on the R349 to the N2 for an easy drive of less than 50 km back to East London.

102. Morgan's Bay

A CITY FOR ALL SEASONS

Although founded by people of British stock, South Africa's only major river port and its hinterland have benefited considerably from the skills, labour and resolve of settlers from Germany.

EAST LONDON The first people, apart from indigenous nomads, who spent any significant time at the mouth of the Buffalo River, where East London was established nearly two centuries later, did so reluctantly. When the Dutch East Indiaman *Stavenisse* was wrecked 112 km south of what is now Durban in 1686 60 of her crew of 71 reached the shore. Of these, 13 stayed in the area for some time and, in partnership with survivors of the British ships *Bona Ventura* and *Good Hope* which had also been wrecked in the vicinity, built another vessel, the *Centaurus*. More than two years after the *Stavenisse* disaster the *Centaurus* completed an 11-day voyage without compass

to Table Bay harbour, where the Dutch authorities bought her to search for the 47 *Stavenisse* castaways who had set out towards Cape Town on foot. The *Centaurus* found and rescued some 20 of the overlanders 10 km south of the Buffalo River, where they had settled and were living among the Xhosa (see Cove Rock, Tour 34). The information brought back by

these survivors about the region between the estuaries of the Tugela and the Buffalo rivers and about its black population was invaluable to the Dutch authorities at the Cape.

However, it was only some 150 years later, when the British were experiencing trouble on the eastern frontier of the Cape and needed a port closer to the area of conflict

than Algoa Bay, that a survey of the Buffalo River mouth was made. In 1836 the brig *Knysna*, owned by the family of George Rex, was chartered to transport supplies and ammunition to what now came to be known as Port Rex. In 1847 a further survey was conducted by HMS *Beagle*, the port was renamed East London and Fort Glamorgan was established on a height on the west bank as a base for the 73rd Highland Regiment, which eventually became the Second Battalion of the Black Watch. Trade followed the British flag, but the settlement received its greatest early impetus in 1857 when 2 362 veterans of the German Legion who had been recruited by Britain for the Crimean War arrived with 361 women and 195 children to be settled in British Kaffraria. Although more than a thousand of the veterans were called up again later the same year to serve in the Indian Mutiny and only 386 returned, the German settlement was strengthened in 1858 by the arrival of 2 315 more settlers from the same country. For this reason many border towns have names such as Berlin, Potsdam, Breidbach, Frankfort, Hamburg, Hanover and Stutterheim, which was named after the leader of the settlers, Baron Richard von Stutterheim. Although the reports of the surveys of the river mouth, which by 1848 had a stone jetty, had been favourable and the port had been in regular use, it was only in 1856 that work on a proper harbour was started and 1886 that a sorely-needed suction dredger was employed. The main construction was started in 1872, after which development was rapid and the depth of the water in both river and harbour was soon sufficient for the largest ships on the South African coast. East London is now the country's only river port of importance. The 305 m-long double-deck bridge built over the Buffalo in 1935, which has the railway above and a now-disused road below, is also unique in South Africa. The first public ceremony at which England's young Princess Elizabeth officiated was the opening of East London's Princess Elizabeth Graving Dock in 1948.

Although East London and its fine harbour are of great importance to the industry of the eastern Cape, and the city itself has seen considerable commercial and industrial development since the 1960s, its temperate climate, warm sea, beautiful safe beaches along an evergreen coastline and numerous holiday resorts make it one of the country's premier

103. South Africa's only river port, East London, straddles the Buffalo River

maritime playgrounds. Among the wide variety of amenities available to the holiday-maker is the East London Museum which has, as well as the reputation of being among the country's best, the distinction of having on display the only known dodo egg in the world and the first recognised coelacanth caught in modern times. The latter, a prehistoric fish thought to have been extinct for millions of years, was caught off the mouth of the Chalumna River south of East London in December 1938 and identified amid great excitement by the well-known ichthyologist, Professor J L B Smith of Grahamstown.

Leave East London from the Nahoon Interchange on the N2 (SP Umtata, Gonubie). After 55 km turn left (SP Komga, King William's Town) on to the R63 and drive 5,4 km to Komga.

KOMGA During the Seventh Frontier War in 1847 the site of the present town of Komga – the name being a corruption of the Xhosa designation 'iQumra' which in turn was a corruption of the Hottentot term for the area's brown clay – was used as an army camp. In the Ninth Frontier War in 1877 it became a permanent police camp and a town was laid out to serve as a centre for the increasing number of farmers settling in the region. Today it is the hub of a peaceful cattle and sheep farming district.

Continue on the R63 from Komga, driving 12,5 km westward to the monument on the left commemorating the first award of the Victoria Cross for gallantry in South Africa.

FIRST VC WON IN SOUTH AFRICA At Bleakmoor, a railway siding 20 km from Komga, is a memorial which records the courage of Colonel Hans Garrett Moore of the Connaught Rangers who, at the time of the Ninth Frontier War, was in command of British troops at Komga. On 29 December 1877 Moore, then still a major, received word that an Ngqika (Gaika) force of 300 warriors, many of them mounted, was on the warpath. He and 32 men of the Frontier Armed Mounted Police set out to stem the Gaika advance and sighted the enemy at Draaibosch, near Bleakmoor. The Gaika launched a mighty attack with great courage, compelling Moore to retire. In the retreat a member of his patrol, Trooper Giese, had trouble with his horse and was overhauled by the enemy. The major, accompanied by Sergeant Dan Harber, Corporal J Court and a Private Martindale, heroically rode back to try to rescue him. Moore, whose mount had been wounded,

104. Xhosa kite-flyers

had his forearm pierced by an assegai, but he and his men managed to drive the Gaika back. With the assegai blade still in his arm he rode back to Komga where it was removed by an army doctor, but he returned to the fray the following day when 600 mounted warriors and another thousand on foot attacked. Displaying calm conduct, exceptional courage and brilliant strategy, he put the enemy to flight and averted disaster, although he lost two men and his remount was wounded three times. His valour won him the Victoria Cross, the first to be awarded for action in South Africa. Major Moore, who had fought with the Connaught Rangers in the Indian Mutiny, in the Ashanti War and the Egyptian Campaign, was subsequently promoted to colonel and commanded the Frontier Armed Mounted Police. While the role played by Sergeant Harber and Corporal Court in the Battle of Draaibosch is recognised in the wording on the memorial at Bleakmoor, Private Martindale's name is, strangely enough, omitted.

Continue westward for 30,7 km before turning left off the R63 into Kei Road.

KEI ROAD, which is little more than a railway station with a community of few more than a thousand souls, has seen little development since its days as a staging post on the way from King William's Town to British Kaffraria (which was annexed by Britain in 1847, proclaimed a Crown colony in 1860 and made a separate province of the Cape in 1866), Transkei and Natal. It was given its name because it was on the military route between King William's Town and the Kei River.

Returning to the R63 from Kei Road, continue south-westward for 25 km to reach King William's Town.

KING WILLIAM'S TOWN See Tour 37.

Leave King William's Town on the N2, travelling 18,7 km eastward to reach Berlin.

BERLIN, which was incorporated into East London in 1970, was founded in 1857 by those of the German settlers who were led by Count Carl von Lilienstein and Lieutenant-Colonel von Hacke. The homes of these two leaders are still intact, and other reminders of Berlin's German origins are the interesting Hoffman Square, the Round Tower and two national monuments, the home of Rudolph von Ronnow and Moser's cottage. For many years Berlin was no more than a small rural settlement but, with the development of Ciskei, it has recently seen considerable industrial development.

Continue eastward on the N2 to return about 40 km to East London, passing the huge Ciskei resettlement town of Mdantsane on the right.

105. Hans Garrett Moore, the first man to be awarded the Victoria Cross in South Africa, is commemorated by a plaque at Bleakmoor

SCENIC DRIVE FROM KING WILLIAM'S TOWN

To the north-west of King William's Town, once an important military centre, are the forest-clad ravines of the Amatole range, into which the Xhosa armies withdrew after successive setbacks in the frontier wars of the last century.

KING WILLIAM'S TOWN It is fitting that one of the few places in South Africa, if not the only one, where toy soldiers have been made should be King William's Town, for the early history of this one-time royal borough was almost exclusively military. The town began as the Buffalo Mission Station and was established on the east bank of the Buffalo River in 1825 by the Reverend John Brownlee of the London Missionary Society. In 1835, when Brownlee was driven out by the Xhosa in the Sixth Frontier War, the Governor of the Cape, Sir Benjamin D'Urban, sent a military force to oust the tribesmen and replace them with a garrison.

He named the outpost in honour of the reigning monarch, William IV, and made it the capital of Queen Adelaide Province, the newly-annexed territory between the Keiskamma and the Kei rivers. However, the British Government refused to ratify the annexation, the troops were withdrawn and in 1846 the missionaries who had returned met further disaster when the town was sacked by the Xhosa in the Seventh Frontier War. In consequence, the new Governor, Sir Harry Smith, re-annexed the area between the two rivers, proclaimed it the colony of British Kaffraria with King William's Town the capital and the old mission house, which stands in Reserve Street, as Government House. The fortifications of 'King', which were now strengthened, were at one time in the early 1830s the headquarters

of eight regiments, and the town remained a vibrant military base – with all the hectic martial and social activity characteristic of a garrison town – until long after the last of the nine frontier wars. It was still a military base at the time of Prince Alfred's visit in 1860, in consequence of which it was accorded royal borough status, and was still garrisoned by British troops until the outbreak of World War I. Many of the troops whose military service ended at 'King' settled in the area, as did a considerable number of Baron Richard von Stutterheim's German veterans of the Crimean War.

Among the buildings which recall the early days is the imposing town hall of dressed stone. Another old building, erected in 1898, is the Kaffrarian Museum, most fascinating of whose exceptional mammal exhibits is Huberta. The odyssey of Huberta, the female hippo which ambled more than 1 500 km from Zululand to the Keiskamma River is one of South Africa's best-loved animal stories. The great beast was first reported to be on the move late in 1928. She wandered southward, munching her way through canefields, and whenever she tarried for a while near a public road attracted crowds of fans, some of whom had availed themselves of special bus excursions. She delighted holiday-makers when she stopped over at a lagoon north of Durban and occasionally took a stroll along the beach, but the most extraordinary aspect of her peregrination was her appearance in areas of human habitation, such as the Durban Country Club, where she gatecrashed a party on the veranda one night. She even ventured into West Street in the busy centre of Durban early one morning. The public adored her, the drivers of engines and lorries would slow down to nudge her out of their way rather than harm her if they found her obstructing a railway or road, and the Zulu, Indian and Xhosa folk through whose territories she trekked regarded her with such reverence that she was able to trundle on unharmed – until she reached the Keiskamma River where she was shot by hunters in 1931. Her body might have rotted and disappeared had not the staff of the Kaffrarian Museum hauled it out of the river and mounted it among the 200 other exhibits of their world

famous mammal collection of 19 000 specimens. The museum also has valuable collections of Bushman and other African cultural history material as well as, not surprisingly, extensive displays which recall the town's military associations, not only with the frontier wars but also with the Anglo-Boer War and both world wars. Part of the museum is a building which has been reconstructed as a trading station typical of the stores that were established by some of the British and German settlers and maintained by generations of their descendants. Like its models, this store stocks everything from the blankets so coveted by the Xhosa and rolls of chewing tobacco to boots and three-legged pots. Now King William's Town, with factories producing footwear, sweets, candles and soap – although the one-man toy soldier workshop is no longer in existence – is a major element in the South African Government's border industry policy for Ciskei.

From its intersection with Alexandra Road drive south-westward along Cathcart Street to leave King William's Town on the N2. Having travelled 1,4 km from the starting point, turn right (SP Alice, Fort Beaufort) on to the R63 and after 2,7 km right again (SP Keiskamma-hoek) on to the R352 just beyond Dimbaza, another of Ciskei's border industry growth points. This gravel road runs for 21,5 km through the beautiful cultivated Rabula River valley, with its innumerable Xhosa huts, to Keiskammahoek.

KEISKAMMAHOEK, in the heart of the Amatole Mountains, is yet another town that originated as a military frontier post. It was here that the Xhosa chiefs Sandile and Anta surrendered to the Redcoats in 1847 and, in doing so, brought the War of the Axe, the Seventh Frontier War, to a close.

At Keiskammahoek the R352 turns right and is tarred for the remaining 41,3 km to Stutterheim. It climbs out of the Rabula River valley by way of the Dontsa Pass, passing among thickly-wooded mountains on to a plateau of rolling pastureland interspersed with indigenous vegetation and occasional small conifer plantations.

STUTTERHEIM On the ridge overlooking Stutterheim, just north of the railway station, is the little church of the Bethel Mission, founded in 1837 by the Reverend Jacob Ludwig Dohne of the Berlin Missionary Society. The mission station was sacked in the Seventh Frontier War, rebuilt by the Reverend Albert Kropf and again

106. Colonial-style architecture survives in King William's Town

burnt down in 1850. Kropf, who compiled the first Xhosa-English dictionary and was chief translator for the Xhosa Bible, was a doughty man, though, and started all over yet again. Some of the German veterans of the Crimean War who settled in the eastern Cape in 1857 made their homes around Fort Dohne, which had been established near the mission station. They named the settlement in honour of their leader Baron von Stutterheim and it is now the centre of a district producing cattle, timber, citrus fruit and fine wool.

From Stutterheim's main traffic intersection drive north up Maclean Street on to the R30 (SP Cathcart) and reach Cathcart after 50,9 km, having passed an 1820 Settlers' Milestone on the left about 7 km before entering Cathcart.

CATHCART See Tour 38.

From the southern entrance to Cathcart take the R345 south-westward (SP Hogsback, Fort Beaufort) and after 2,1 km turn left (SP Hogsback, Happy Valley) to remain on the R345 which now becomes gravelled. At the three-ways near Dunskye 35,6 km further on turn right (SP Hogsback) and after another 8,4 km turn left (SP Hogsback, Alice). From here it is 6,1 km to the village at the Hogsback where directions to the starts of the marked forest walks and to the various waterfalls are available.

HOGSBACK The Xhosa, whose term for 'carrying on the back' is 'uku-beleka', are reminded by one of the three Hogsback peaks of a woman carrying a child. So they call it Belekezana, although their name for the wider area is Qabimola, which means 'face painted with clay'. The name used by white people is popularly believed to have been coined by someone to whom the three peaks looked like the back of a pig – even to the bristles which the crags of one of them resemble. It is more probable, however, that the name of the Hogsback is linked with the Captain Hogg who founded the village when he was in command of nearby Fort Mitchell. Whatever the name, the scent of the dense indigenous forest which makes this part of the Amatole range so attractive, could be no sweeter. Those who have discovered the Hogsback return again and again to delight in that scent and every other soothing sensation offered by the forest, with its entrancing walks and rides down long, winding glades lined with giant yellowwoods; its sensational mountain scenery; its azaleas, rhododendrons and daffodils growing wild in a sylvan setting; its abundance of hazelnuts,

107. The road leading up to the Dontsa Pass

raspberries and other berry fruits; and its clear water tumbling down numerous falls with such imaginative names as the Swallowtail and Boiling Pot, the Madonna and Child, the Thirty Nine Steps and the Bridal Veil. One waterfall, the Kettle Spout, does not in fact always tumble *down*; at times

108. Madonna and Child Falls in the Hogsback

when the wind blows strongly enough up the valley the water actually 'falls' about 10 m *up* and lands behind the lip of the fall. The enchantment of the Hogsback is that it is unspoilt, and those who live there and those who welcome guests to their hostelries are determined that it should remain

this way; even the amenities for holiday-makers are of such rustic character that they detract only minimally from the natural environment.

From the Hogsback resort there is a glorious tarred 30,8-km drive through indigenous forest and the scenic Hogsback Pass to the R63. Turn left and follow the R63 eastward for 60 km back to King William's Town.

38

240 km

THE NORTH-EASTERN CAPE

A tour of the countryside south of Queenstown takes in a region of beautiful mountain scenery and towns and villages that played significant roles in the conflict between black and white people in the nineteenth century.

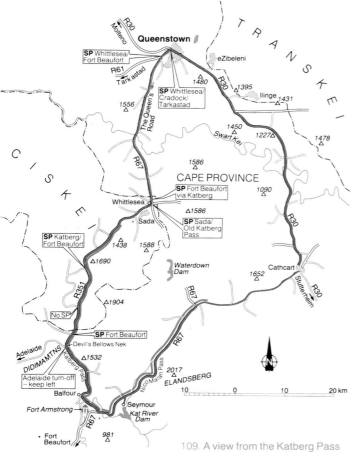

109: A view from the Katberg Pass

QUEENSTOWN What distinguishes Queenstown from other South African towns is the hexagonal open space at its centre, a feature which recalls its military origin. In 1835, when Governor Sir George Cathcart ordered the establishment of a stronghold on the Komani River below the Hangklip Mountain in a newly-annexed region, Assistant Surveyor-General M R Robinson, who was responsible for the layout, planned the Hexagon with six streets radiating away from it as a defence measure. The plan allowed speedy access from the centre of the stronghold to any point on the periphery and provided uninterrupted firing lines from the central command post. The Hexagon has survived as an attractive open space around a fountain in the business centre of the town. Ensuring visitors a pleasant welcome to Queenstown, which is now the commercial and educational centre of the north-eastern Cape, is the Walter Everitt Sunken Garden through which the approach road from East London passes. The garden has a series of pools for water birds, including swans, and is named after the former superintendent of parks and gardens who was principally responsible for pioneering the horticultural beautification of Queenstown. Places worth visiting include the Frontier Museum in Shepstone Street which has exhibits recalling the early struggles of those who pioneered the Border region; the Public Library in Lamont Street where, apart from the well-stocked bookshelves, the Lock Shell Collection is exhibited; and the Queenstown Art Gallery.

From the Hexagon in Queenstown drive north-west along Cathcart Street and after 1 km turn left (SP Whittlesea, Cradock, Tarkastad). Drive for another 1,8 km, then fork left (SP Whittlesea, Fort Beaufort) on to the R67, the Queen's Road, and continue through the flat grassland which contributes to Queenstown being the centre of a major cattle-ranching area. After crossing the Swart Kei River the R67 continues southward and on into Ciskei to Whittlesea. Take the left fork (SP Fort Beaufort via Katberg) to the village 37,5 km from Queenstown.

WHITTLESEA, an important defence outpost in the Eighth Frontier War, was established in 1849 and named after the birthplace of Governor Sir Harry Smith. In 1851 it was the objective of a mighty onslaught by a combined force of Hottentots and Xhosa of the Tembu tribe. Main credit for the repulse of the attackers, who attempted to storm the outpost by driving 3 000 head of cattle before them, has been accorded to Thomas Bowker, whose heroic defence of Whittlesea is said to have stemmed the Xhosa incursions for some time. But there were other heroes of the battle, among them Thomas Webster. When, after what appeared to be a withdrawal by the attackers, a young English officer, Lieutenant Robert Jefferson, was dismounted as he rode out in pursuit and then ambushed, Webster galloped after him, told him to grab a stirrup and carried him back to safety as bullets hissed all around them. A romantic sequel to the rescue was the marriage between Jefferson and Webster's sister, of whom the young officer had seen a great deal during the siege of Whittlesea. Some of the old fortifications of the settlement are still to be seen.

At the turn-off 1 km south of Whittlesea turn right on to the R351 (SP Sada, Old Katberg Pass) and pass Shiloh and Sada on the left.

SHILOH In 1828 the Governor of the Cape, Lord Charles Somerset, requested that a mission be established on the eastern frontier and his call was heeded by three Moravian missionaries, J Lemmerz, F Hoffman and J Fritsch. They started their ministry on the Klipplaat River, naming the community they founded Shiloh

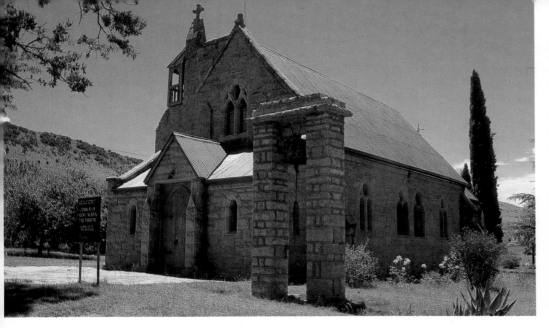

110. St Alban's Church in Cathcart, with its strange balcony

after the ancient village on the eastern slope of Mount Ephraim in Palestine. From here the work of the Moravian Church was extended to Tembuland and East Griqualand. The settlement now has a population of about a thousand and is the seat of the headquarters of Ciskei's important Shiloh Irrigation Works.

SADA is one of Ciskei's proclaimed industrial growth points.

The tar ends about 5 km from Sada and the R351 becomes rough. Fork left (SP Katberg, Fort Beaufort) 21,7 km from Sada and 8,6 km further on left again (no SP). At the T-junction 8,6 km from the last fork keep straight on (SP Fort Beaufort), passing the right turn to Tarkastad. From here the road climbs Devil's Bellows Nek, part of the Old Katberg Pass, into the Great Winterberg range. Pass the right turn to Adelaide 2,8 km from the last T-junction and start the descent of the southern slopes of the Winterberg by way of the rest of the Katberg Pass.

KATBERG PASS The Katberg Pass, another of the mountain gateways on which Andrew Geddes

Bain worked, is a splendid scenic drive that leads at first through grassy uplands and then through the forested escarpment between the Didima Mountains of the Great Winterberg range and the 2 017-m Elandsberg in the Amatole Mountains, the scene of many a battle during the frontier wars. From the 1 700-m summit of the pass, the construction of which was started by Bain in 1860, the road meanders down to the valley of the Kat River through what at times seems like a green tunnel of the vegetation which festoons the cliffs. Byways off the road lead to beautiful picnic spots, drives and walks, a caravan park and the Katberg Hotel.

Travel 17,3 km from the Adelaide turn-off (62 km from Whittlesea) and then fork right to Balfour (SP, almost illegible, Balfour).

BALFOUR The village of Balfour, centre of a citrus fruit and tobacco area, has hardly grown since the missionaries Ross and McDiarmid of the Glasgow Missionary Society established their base here in 1828 and named it after Robert Balfour, first secretary of the society. A short

distance south of the village on the road to Hertzog is the hill on which Camp Adelaide was established to afford the Hottentots settled by the Colonial Government in the upper Kat River valley in 1829 protection against the Xhosa. As part of Sir Benjamin D'Urban's frontier defence scheme the outpost was converted into a fort in 1835 and named after Captain A B Armstrong whose task it was to ensure that the Hottentots remained loyal to Britain during the Sixth Frontier War. In the Eighth Frontier War, however, the Hottentots turned against the government and in January 1851 captured the fort, although they allowed its white occupants to depart in safety. Fort Armstrong now became the headquarters of Uithaalder, leader of the rebels, but a month after he had taken it an 840-strong British, Boer and Fingo citizen force, joined by 1 800 artillery-supported regulars under Major-General Henry Somerset, retaliated. The fort was destroyed by artillery fire, but the rebels fought valiantly until only nine were left. The attacking force was obliged to resort to hand-to-hand fighting before the nine diehards were

eventually killed. Fort Armstrong was never rebuilt and all that remains is the main tower, which survived the 1851 artillery barrage and is now a national monument.

From the crossroads at the southern entrance to Balfour drive 4,6 km, then turn left on to the R67. Turn right into Seymour 8 km further on.

SEYMOUR Like so many other villages and towns in the region Seymour has a military origin, starting off as a stronghold known as Elands Post. A sundial fashioned from sandstone in 1839 by a soldier named Cross was erected within the fort, which in 1853 was laid out as a town and named in honour of Lieutenant-Colonel Charles Seymour, military secretary to the Governor of the Cape, Sir George Cathcart. The sundial is now in the Kaffrarian Museum in King William's Town, but part of the walls of the fort, its powder magazine and other outbuildings still stand in the grounds of the magistrate's home, which was built on the site of the original drostdy.

Return to the R67 and drive north-eastward over the Nico Malan Pass which, with its excellent cambered road surface, gentle gradient, easy curves and open vistas, is an example of the contrast between modern engineering developments and the skills and techniques on which Bain had to rely for projects such as the Katberg Pass. At the junction 30,7 km from Seymour turn right (SP Cathcart, Hogsback) off the R67 and drive 26,9 km to Cathcart.

CATHCART Yet another former military outpost, Cathcart, which was named in honour of Sir George Cathcart, was established in the 1850s at the foot of the Windvogelberg, the mountain named after the leader of a tribe of local Bushmen. The surrounding hills and the thermals that develop in them have made Cathcart popular with glider pilots. The handsome stone Anglican church of St Alban's, which was patterned on a church in England of the same name, has a strange roofed balcony breaking the symmetry of its upper façade. It is believed that the structure, to which there is no access, was intended as a belfry, although it has never had a bell.

From Cathcart drive 61,5 km northward on the R30 to return to Queenstown.

111. Part of the wall and the powder magazine of the old fort, Elands Post, at Seymour

WILD COAST

A tour to Coffee Bay and nearby Hole in the Wall has all the charm characteristic of a coastline that is 'wild' both in its rugged, unspoilt beauty and in the fury of the sea that sometimes lashes it.

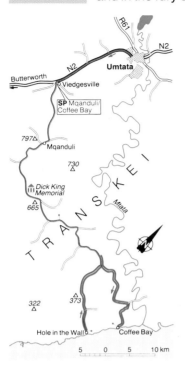

UMTATA See Tour 40.

From the Bunga in Umtata drive south-westward along Alexandra Road on to the N2 towards East London. At Viedgesville, 19,9 km from the city, turn left (SP Mqanduli, Coffee Bay) and travel 14 km to Mqanduli.

UNCHANGING LANDSCAPE The road to Coffee Bay runs through a beautiful landscape composed of what seem to be a thousand rolling hills liberally dotted with many more thousands of kraals. It is a landscape that has remained unchanged for hundreds of years, notwithstanding the vast numbers of people who populate the region. Their uniformly patterned rondavels, built with the same earth on which they stand and thatched with the grass that grows all around, are a natural part of the prospect and certainly create no impression of intrusion on the environment as do the structures of mankind in so many other areas of the world. In this part of the country the kraals are far less spoilt than elsewhere in Transkei by the junk of the western world, such as derelict car bodies and – where there should traditionally be thatch – sheets of rusted corrugated iron. Although, with a few exceptions, the places on the way to the coast have no designation boards, their evocative names are singularly euphonious when enunciated by those whose tongues and teeth are agile enough to cope with the clicking consonants – names like Mqanduli, Ngqungu, Ngqwara, Lutubeni and Ngcwanguba. While the tar of the road to Coffee Bay is more conducive to speed than the corrugated, potholed and sometimes muddy surfaces of most

other Transkei routes off the highway, it is a wise motorist who heeds what even the Department of Commerce, Industry and Tourism calls the 'Transkei robots' encountered along the way. These are the seemingly untended cattle, sheep, goats and little black pigs that wander unpredictably and with absolutely no sense of impending danger into the path of any approaching vehicle. With the grazing unfenced and common to all, it is amazing that anybody knows to whom what cow, sheep or goat belongs, although the ubiquitous little black pig – the Transkei's scavenger, for in such an unsophisticated society there is no sewerage reticulation – will regularly return to the kraal at which it was born.

MQANDULI The only village of any size on the way to Coffee Bay is Mqanduli, the name of which means 'the place of the grindstone-maker'. It was at Mqanduli that the first magistrate in the area established his office in a tent in 1876.

At the fork 57 km from the N2 keep left (SP Coffee Bay), noting for later reference that the right fork leads to Hole in the Wall, and drive for another 22 km through scenery that is soft and beautiful. The first glimpse of the sea is through a spectacular valley with yet more undulating hills, the steepest

slopes of which are densely bushed. Innumerable Tembu huts either stand like sentinels atop high summits or cling to the falling ground far below.

COFFEE BAY is believed to have been given its name because of the small coffee trees that at one time grew along this part of the coast. Some people say the trees were planted by men who plundered a wrecked ship laden with coffee beans while others believe they grew without human intervention from the beans in a barrel that was washed ashore and battered to pieces by the surf. Nestling in natural coastal forest and flanked by mighty bush-covered cliffs, Coffee Bay, with its rural tranquillity, is a village of considerable charm and one of the most popular resorts on the Wild Coast. The beach, about 1 km long, is fairly safe for swimming but, while the resort is a paradise for those who love sunbathing, rambling through an unspoilt environment or simply lazing about, it is most renowned for the sport it affords anglers. One of the walks from Coffee Bay is along the coastal hills to Hole in the Wall, but to include a visit to this spectacular phenomenon of nature in a one-day tour it is necessary to drive.

From Coffee Bay return to the fork 22 km up the road, then turn sharply left (SP Hole in the Wall) and drive 19 km back towards the sea. The road is extremely rough but the destination is ample reward for enduring the slow, uncomfortable ride.

HOLE IN THE WALL The Hole in the Wall is one of southern Africa's most fascinating and most photographed spectacles, a huge rock massif standing a short distance out to sea. Its sheer sides tower above the surf to the east and the sandy shallows to the west, while its mostly flat top, which could probably accommodate several rugby fields, is thickly covered with perennially green vegetation. Halfway along its extensive length the sea has scoured a tunnel through which light streams and the surf thunders so dramatically that to Xhosa-speaking people the Hole in the Wall is known as 'esiKhaleni' – 'the place of the sound'. The hole, through which a double-decker bus could pass if it were on dry land, has long been known to mariners, among them the Captain Vidal whose ship, HMS *Baracouta*, was part of the flotilla under Captain William Owen sent by the British Admiralty in the early 1820s to survey the east coast of southern

112. The dusty road to Hole in the Wall

113. Hole in the Wall

Africa. It was Vidal, in fact, who gave Hole in the Wall its English name. He was careful in his approach to it and *Baracouta* was able to sail away without mishap, but many another vessel has come to grief in these parts. Indeed, for the imaginative the Wild Coast is steeped in the romance of ships – some of them Dutch and English Indiamen heavily laden with wares and treasure from the East – that have been battered on to its rocks in stormy weather. Beachcombers have come upon lozenge-shaped agate beads that have been drilled longitudinally to take a string, and the finds have led some antiquarians to theorise that Phoenicians, whose craftsmen were among the few capable of drilling such hard material, were the earliest mariners to round the Cape and sometimes be wrecked on this inhospitable shore.

Belief in magic has tremendous power over the Xhosa, and some say that Hole in the Wall featured in the most disastrous episode recorded in their history – 'Nong-qause' as they term it – which was the result of the credence they accorded a soothsayer. Nongqause was the name of a child who reported having 'seen' strange men on the banks of the Gxara River in 1856 when the Xhosa were spoiling for more conflict with the white people. Her uncle, Mhlakaza, who had ambitions as a prophet, seized on her revelation and spread the word that the strangers were Russians, whom his people assumed were black because they were fighting against the British in the Crimea. With the shades of long-dead Xhosa warriors, the Russians were going to lead the nation in a war which would end in

all white men being thrown back into the sea whence they had come – but only, Mhlakaza insisted, after his compatriots had killed all their cattle and ceased planting crops. Vast herds of cattle would materialise to replace those slaughtered and the grain pits would be replenished many times over, but all who disregarded the prophecy would be blown into the sea by a great wind after the sky had fallen on them. It has been suggested that this interpretation of Nongqause's vision was a ploy devised by Mhlakaza and Kreli, paramount chief of the Xhosa, to

eliminate the main obstacle to mustering a really mighty army against the British – the tribesman's obsessive desire to tend his stock.

It has been estimated that more than 30 000 head of cattle were killed in the ensuing months, 30 000 Xhosa are believed to have starved to death and many more flocked to the territory of the white people whom they had planned to annihilate, begging for food and work. This 'national suicide', as it has come to be known, resulted not only in a great decrease in the tribal numbers but the extensive geographical redistribution of the

Xhosa. Had the day of reward promised by Mhlakaza ever dawned, however, the liberating warrior spirits and their Russian allies would, according to some versions of the Nongqause incident, have made their entrance through the Hole in the Wall.

From Hole in the Wall return to the N2 and Umtata.

114. South of Mqanduli a horseman greets travellers on the way to Coffee Bay

TRANSKEI, LAND OF THE XHOSA

Transkei – the land of Xhosa-speaking peoples such as the Xhosa themselves, the Tembu, Pondo, Fingos and Bhaca – is a well-watered country of undulating landscape intersected by numerous rivers.

115. Old and new buildings in Umtata, capital of Transkei

UMTATA, the capital of Transkei, was founded towards the end of the 1860s when Ngangelize, paramount chief of the Tembu, granted land on the south bank of the Mtata River to a group of white settlers who, he hoped, would be a buffer between his subjects and the warring Pondo. The Pondo at the same time gave similar land rights to white colonists on the north bank as a cushion against the Tembu. A village developed on the banks of the river and, after a military post had been established in 1882 to control the continuing conflict, a village management board was called into being. The city, as Umtata was proclaimed by President Kaiser Matanzima in 1981, took its name from the river on which it was founded. It is generally accepted that the river's name was derived from the Xhosa word 'thata' which means 'to take'. Some ascribe the derivation to the fact that a Tembu clan who buried their dead in the river used to entreat the gods to 'mThate Bawo' – 'Take him, Father' – but others believe the name was given because the Mtata took so many people to their death when it came down in flood.

By the turn of the century the village had become a thriving town, with schools, shops, churches, hotels, a hospital, sporting facilities, a library, a newspaper and several minor industries. It was here that the stately building of the Transkeian Territories General Council, the Bunga, was erected in 1903, giving Umtata the status of

capital, a status that was retained when Transkei was granted self-government in 1963 and independence in 1976. Rapid development, which started after the attainment of self-government and led to a self-generating economy, has resulted in the population of the city increasing from about 7 000 to some 42 000, and the rateable valuation of properties from R4,3 million to R118,8 million. Umtata is the principal educational centre of the country and apart from having numerous schools, is the seat of the

University of Transkei, which was established in 1976 as a branch of Fort Hare and gained its own identity in 1977.

Leave Umtata on the R61 and travel 2 km westward to the Izandla Pottery and the Transkei Hilmond Weavers.

IZANDLA POTTERY The meaning of the name 'Izandla' is 'many hands', and among the hands that have moulded the local clay are those of some of the country's best-known potters, such as Florida

116. Adding a finishing touch to wares at the Izandla Pottery

Xintolo and Miriam Ndabeni. The clay that is used is specially prepared to withstand the white-hot temperatures to which it is subjected. At around 1 350 °C it matures into intensely hard stoneware of a warm brown colour. The high temperature at which the ware is baked eliminates the need to use lead in Izandla's glazes, which are prepared mainly from finely ground rocks and clay. The atmosphere in the kiln and the intense heat combine to give the glazes depth and quality, some being glossy and others satiny or matt. Complete dinner services are included among Izandla's products.

TRANSKEI HILMOND WEAVERS Pure mohair tablecloths, cushion covers, wall hangings and curtaining material are among the handwoven products of the Transkei Hilmond Weavers, one of the oldest factories in Transkei. The raw mohair, which is spun at Umtata's Efata School for the Blind, is dyed at the Hilmond factory.

Continue westward on the R61, passing the palatial South African Embassy on the left 3 km out of Umtata and then driving across a densely-populated plain that is distressingly scarred by erosion. From time to time there is evidence of efforts to arrest the process by dumping derelict cars – which are a common sight in Transkei – into some of the worst dongas. Engcobo is 85 km from Umtata.

ENGCOBO, situated on a spur of the Kumba Mountains, is one of the prettiest towns in Transkei and the centre of one of its cattle-raising and crop-farming districts.

At the T-junction in Engcobo turn right and travel north-westward for about 13 km before starting the run along Satansnek.

SATANSNEK is a pass from which some of the most magnificent vistas in southern Africa are to be seen. In particular, there are splendid views of the vast canyon slashed through northern Transkei by the Xuka River, but further along the pass, as the road runs out of Transkei, the scenery unbelievably becomes even more breathtaking. And, far from detracting from the panorama, the thousands of traditional Xhosa rondavels which dot the hilltops and slopes as far as the eye can see appear as attractive and natural a feature of the landscape as if they had been there as long as the hills themselves.

At Qiba, 43 km from Engcobo, turn right on to the R393, drive 5 km north-eastward to join the R56 and 8,6 km further on reach Elliot.

ELLIOT See Tour 41.

Leave Elliot on the R56, driving eastward along Maclear Road, the main thoroughfare, from its intersection with Voortrekker Street. The 50 km to Ugie affords a splendid scenic drive between well-husbanded farms in the foothills of the Drakensberg where numerous herds of prize dairy cattle graze.

UGIE At the foot of the Prentjiesberg – 'picture mountain' – Ugie lies in surroundings that have been described as an artist's paradise. It was founded in 1863 by the missionary William Murray who, because the pretty Inxu River flowing through the grassland of the area reminded him of the Ugie River in his native Aberdeenshire, chose the name that has been retained to this day. In the 1870s other white people began to settle near the mission station and it became the nucleus of a community that was granted village management board status in 1916. Ugie is widely known for the Smit Children's Haven, a large undenominational institution established by the Reverend M T R Smit to care for children orphaned in the great influenza epidemic of 1918. It is still a home for destitute youngsters from all over South Africa.

Continue north-eastward on the R56 with still more splendid views of the southern end of the Drakensberg range in the north. Van Riebeeck Street in Maclear is 20 km from Ugie.

MACLEAR was named after Sir Thomas Maclear, the distinguished Astronomer Royal based in Cape Town from 1834 to 1870. The town began as a military outpost established by Captain J R Thompson in 1876 when he and a body of troops on their way to Matatiele were held up on the northern bank of the Mooi River for some time. The area around Maclear was first known to white men as Gatberg on account of the large hole through the top of a mountain near the south-western border of what is now the magisterial district of Maclear. The Xhosa name for the mountain is Untunjinkala, meaning 'the opening of the crab'. The name of the district and the town was changed when the magistracy was proclaimed in 1881. Teeming with trout as the streams and rivers – such as the Mooi, Pot, Tsitsa and Wildebeest – in the vicinity do, Maclear has become one of South Africa's most popular fly-fishing resorts.

From the intersection of the R56 and Van Riebeeck Street in Maclear drive 17,7 km south-eastward on the R396 to cross back into Transkei. Continue 40 km to the police station in Tsolo.

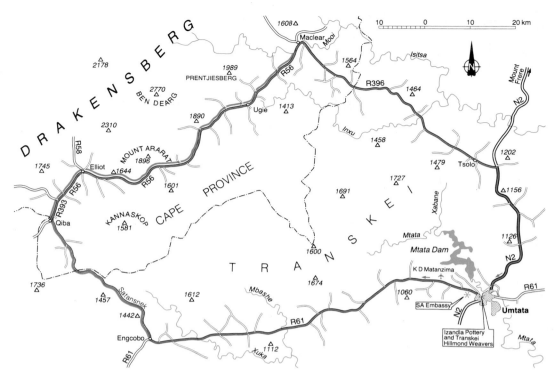

TSOLO, an administrative and trading centre in the area sometimes called East Griqualand, takes its name from the adjective 'pointed' which the Xhosa apply to the sharply pointed hills in the vicinity. The seat of the first magistracy was at one of these 'tsolo' near the Inxu River until the magistrate, some 30 other white people and five Fingos were besieged during the Pondomisi uprising in 1880. By the time the beleaguered had been rescued from the small stone building which had previously been the jail, some of them were delirious as a result of privation. The magistracy was subsequently moved to its present, safer site on the Xokona River but retained its original name. Near Tsolo is the Jongelizwe College where the sons of chiefs are trained in the art of government.

From the Tsolo police station continue 4,9 km south-eastward and turn right on to the N2 for the remaining 37 km back to Umtata.

117. The Xuka River valley, seen from Satansnek

41

400 km

HOT WATER AND COLD TOWNS

From Aliwal North where hot mineral water gushes from the earth the road runs eastward to the southern limits of the Drakensberg and some of the highest – and coldest – places in South Africa.

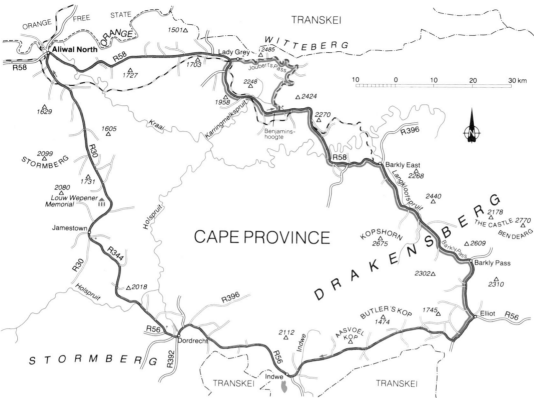

118. Taking the waters in the 'Wonder Pool' at Aliwal North

ALIWAL NORTH In 1849, the year after Governor Sir Harry Smith had proclaimed that the northern boundary of the Cape Colony was to be the Orange River, he founded Aliwal North on its left bank, commemorating in the name his decisive victory over the Sikhs at Aliwal in India in 1846. 'North' distinguished this town from Aliwal, which was subsequently renamed Mossel Bay. The site, at the confluence of the Orange and Kraai rivers, was chosen by Sir Harry's secretary, John Centlivres Chase, who was appointed civil commissioner and magistrate of the new district. His choice was influenced by the ford, known as Vlotfontein, which had been used by Bushmen and Voortrekkers to cross the Orange at this spot. Soon after the town came into being a ferry service was established, but the pont used to transport vehicles and passengers over the Orange was replaced in 1881 by a bridge which in turn was superseded by the Hertzog Bridge in 1938. The anchors used for the pont, instituted in 1862 by two men named Butler and Smith, were obtained from a wrecked ship and are now preserved at the Aliwal North Town Hall.

The town was the venue for the signing of the treaties of Aliwal North, the first of which, after conflict between the Republic of the Orange Free State and the Basotho in 1858, increased the territory of the black kingdom, while the second, in 1869, ratified the British annexation of what is now Lesotho and extended the territory of the Free State. Juana Square, in the centre of this pleasant town with its colonial-style architecture, tree-shaded streets and attractive gardens, was named after Sir Harry Smith's Spanish wife. He had married Juana Maria de los Dolores de Leon when, at the age of 14, she had thrown herself at his mercy after fleeing from the atrocities being perpetrated at the fall of the city of Badojoz to the British in the Peninsular War.

Aliwal North's main claim to fame – and, by virtue of the 160 000 visitors it attracts annually, its principal economic asset – is the hot mineralised water which gushes up through two springs to the earth's surface at the rate of about 4,36 million litres a day from an estimated depth of 1 280 m. The springs were first exploited for their therapeutic value in 1877. Since then development has been extensive and now, in an attractive setting of lawns and trees, there are swimming pools as well as private baths, saunas, Turkish baths, pools for children, picnic areas, holiday cottages, playgrounds, a caravan park and a treatment block. In one of the swimming pools, which is of Olympic standard, the temperature of the water is almost 28 °C, and in another pool right over the eye of one of the springs it is just over 31 °C. The 'Wonder Pool', which is enclosed, contains effervescent water at 34,4 °C. Many of those who 'take the waters' for therapeutic reasons testify to their efficacy, especially in the treatment of rheumatic conditions.

Leave Aliwal North travelling eastward on the R58 and after 53 km turn left into Lady Grey.

LADY GREY The first plots on the farm Waaihoek, which the Dutch Reformed Church had bought for the establishment of a new congregation, were sold in 1858. The settlement thus established in a beautiful setting at the foot of the Witteberg range was named after the wife of the Governor at the time, Sir George Grey. It is now the centre of a farming area in which sheep predominate, although wheat and maize are also grown in the district. The gorge from which Lady Grey's water is drawn is of great scenic beauty and the reservoir is surrounded by a nature reserve. Beyond the reservoir the road becomes rough as it climbs out of the gorge by way of Joubert's Pass and winds its way through 47 km of mountain grandeur before joining the road between Aliwal North and Barkly East.

To avoid the rough but spectacular drive through Joubert's Pass, return to the R58, turn left and continue southward. Pause after about 10 km to look back from the elevation of Wolfhuis – part of the Karringmelkspruit – at the splendid views of the terrain from which you have just come. Keep an eye open too for some of the varieties of raptorial birds and vultures which may be seen nesting on the towering rock faces of the kloof. After another 12 km the road starts climbing Benjaminshoogte, and 28 km further on traverses the 8,3-km Kraai River Pass, high above the valley through which the tree-lined Kraai River flows. An extraordinary reversing railway, a branch line between Lady Grey and Barkly East, is rarely far from the road. The line zigzags up exceptionally steep gradients, and trains have to make use of eight reversing stations, shunting backwards and forwards up the mountainsides. Barkly East is 70 km from Lady Grey.

BARKLY EAST, on the western slopes of the Drakensberg, is one of the highest and, at times, coldest places in South Africa. The highest mountain in the Cape Province, the 3 300-m Ben Macdhui, towers above the north-eastern part of the Barkly East district – at the corner where the borders of the Cape, Lesotho and the northern pocket of Transkei run together – only 48 km from the town. Barkly East, the centre of a rich wool-producing region, was laid out on the farm Rocky Park in 1874 and named after the Governor, Sir Henry Barkly. Anyone with the right rod, the flies and the time might well find rewarding a cast in the trout-rich waters of the Langkloofspruit and other streams near Barkly East.

From Barkly East continue south-eastward on the R58 for 67 km to Elliot. For a considerable distance the road follows the sometimes rugged but always beautiful valley of the Langkloofspruit with its fine sheep farms and huge, grotesque rock formations that resemble the heads of prehistoric monsters. From the top of the valley the road descends the southern end of the Drakensberg by way of the Barkly Pass.

BARKLY PASS This is one of the highest mountain passes in the country. About 6 km long, it crosses the southern end of the Drakens-berg and affords a magnificent view of the Castle of Giants and, at 2 770 m, another of the Cape's highest peaks, Ben Dearg.

ELLIOT Another town with a backdrop of Drakensberg grandeur is Elliot, founded in 1885 and named after the Chief Magistrate of Tembuland at the time, Sir Henry Elliot, a former Royal Marine officer who was highly decorated in the Crimean War.

Turn left (SP Cala, Engcobo, Indwe, Queenstown, Umtata) off the R58 on to the R56 in Elliot and drive 8 km south-westward to pass a left turn to Cala. Cross the Tsomo River 13 km further on, pass another left turn to Cala 34,7 km from the river and a left turn to Lady Frere (Cacadu) 1,7 km further on. Reach the Indwe post office after another 1,4 km.

INDWE 'Indwe' is the Xhosa name for the blue crane which at one time abounded along the stream known as Ndwe east of the town. The locality was known as Indwe long before the mining of low-grade coal was started in 1867, and the name was taken for the town in 1896, when it was laid out 15 km south-west of the towering Xalanga crags at the southern end of the Drakensberg. The boardroom of the old Indwe Coal Company has been preserved in the town and still contains its original furniture.

From the Indwe post office continue westward on the R56, pass the right turns to Lady Grey (R392), and Rossouw and Barkly East (R396) after 33 km and reach the Dutch Reformed church in Dordrecht's main thoroughfare, Grey Street, 3,2 km further on.

DORDRECHT Boschrand, a farm on the northern slopes of the Stormberg range, was bought by the Dutch Reformed Church of Aliwal North in 1856 to establish a

119. The Dutch Reformed church in Lady Grey

new congregation. The settlement which developed around the church was named to commemorate the historic Synod of Reformed Churches held in the Dutch city of Dordrecht in 1618 and 1619.

Drive 1,3 km south of the Dordrecht Dutch Reformed church and turn right (SP Jamestown, Molteno, Sterkstroom) out of Grey Street on to the R56. Continue 4,1 km before turning right (SP Jamestown) on to the gravel-surfaced R344 to reach Jamestown after 39 km.

JAMESTOWN James was the nickname of Jacobus Johannes Wagenaar, the original owner of the farm on which he and some of his friends laid out the town of Jamestown on the northern slopes of the Stormberg in 1874. Once a staging post for transport riders travelling northward, it is now the rural centre of a fertile region in which cattle, sheep and wheat are farmed.

From Jamestown drive 61 km northward on the R30 to return to Aliwal North, keeping an eye open to the left after 13.3 km for the memorial to Commandant Louw Wepener.

LOUW WEPENER MEMORIAL Lourens Jacobus Wepener was a Cape burgher officer whose military ability and fearlessness won him distinction in the frontier wars of 1835, 1846 and 1851. In 1858 he fought with the Orange Free State Commando in the First Basotho War, and in the second conflict he achieved further distinction as Commandant-in-Chief of the Free State's southern commando. After his heroic death at the storming of Thaba Bosiu his Basotho enemies were so impressed by his valour that they roasted and ate his heart in the belief that they would thus acquire some of his courage.

120. Rock formations in Barkly Pass

CHAPTER FOUR
The Cape Interior, Orange Free State and Lesotho

42
390 km

THE CAPE MIDLANDS

Historic frontier towns of the early Cape, tucked away in the eastern highlands of the province, are connected by routes that penetrate the ranges by way of scenic mountain passes.

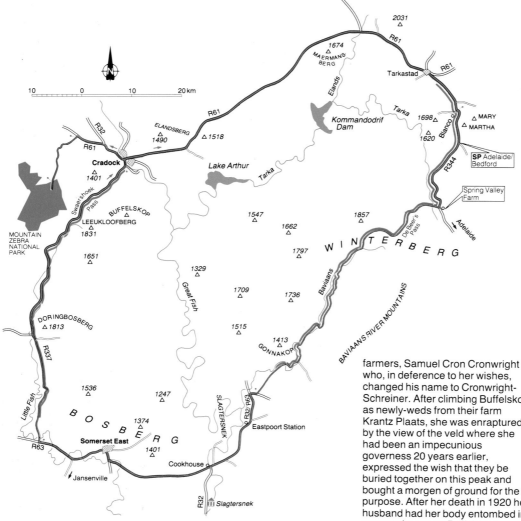

CRADOCK The vaguely defined part of the Karoo between the Suurberg range and the Great Fish River is known as the Cape Midlands and has as its 'capital' Cradock, a pleasant, tidy town with broad, tree-lined streets. Strategically situated on the eastern bank of the Great Fish River, the settlement originated on the farm Buffelskloof in 1813 as a frontier outpost under the command of Ensign Andries Stockenström (later Sir Andries and Lieutenant-Governor of the Eastern Cape) who acted as deputy to the *landdrost* at Graaff-Reinet. After a visit by the Governor of the Cape, Sir John Cradock, the following year it was proclaimed a town and named, at Stockenström's suggestion, in Sir John's honour. The agricultural community of the district, started by frontier pioneers even before the outpost was established, prospered and Cradock is now a major centre

of wool and mohair production as well as cattle farming. One of the town's three national monuments is the handsome 1867 stone Dutch Reformed church, modelled on the design by James Gibbs for St Martin's-in-the-Fields in London. The other two are the Old Parsonage in High Street and the Congregational church. Other places of interest are the ovoid mass of dolerite known as the Egg Rock on the commonage north-east of the town, a visit to which entails a call at the municipal offices for a permit; the Karoo Sulphur Springs to the north; the huge holm oak (*Quercus ilex*), reputed to be the world's oldest, in Dundas Street; and the Van Riebeeck Karoo Garden. The authoress Olive Schreiner spent six years in the 1870s as a governess on farms around Cradock, and it was when she was revisiting the area in 1894 that she met and married one of its

farmers, Samuel Cron Cronwright who, in deference to her wishes, changed his name to Cronwright-Schreiner. After climbing Buffelskop as newly-weds from their farm Krantz Plaats, she was enraptured by the view of the veld where she had been an impecunious governess 20 years earlier, expressed the wish that they be buried together on this peak and bought a morgen of ground for the purpose. After her death in 1920 her husband had her body entombed in a sarcophagus on Buffelskop together with the remains of their baby girl, who had died 16 hours after birth.

Drive 500 m northward along Stockenström Street from its intersection with Church Street in front of the Dutch Reformed church, turn left (SP Colesberg, Graaff-Reinet, Middelburg, Mountain Zebra Park) into Park Street, cross the Great Fish River on to the R32 after 400 m and pass the right turn to the Karoo Sulphur Springs 100 m from the river. Turn left (SP Graaff-Reinet, Mountain Zebra Park) on to the R61 3,9 km further on, left again (SP Mountain Zebra Park) after another 5,6 km and drive 12,9 km to the entrance to the park, with another 1,8 km to go to the rest camp and reception.

MOUNTAIN ZEBRA NATIONAL PARK One of the rarest of the world's large animal species, the

mountain zebra, is protected in this delightful 6 536-ha national park. Some 200 specimens roam the reserve, together with black wildebeest, several antelope species, caracal, black-footed wild cat, African wild cat, bat-eared fox, black-backed jackal, Cape fox and aardwolf. The rare booted eagle has also been spotted in the park. Accommodation is in superb, fully-equipped chalets – with fireplaces for which wood is provided – or in the restored homestead of the farm Babylonstoren, on which the park was established in 1937 to save the mountain zebra from extinction. The secluded homestead, with three double bedrooms, has been entirely refurnished with antiques of the region.

Return to the Dutch Reformed church in Cradock, drive 200 m southward along Stockenström Street and turn left (SP Cookhouse, P E, Bedford, Tarkastad, Queenstown) into Voortrekker Street. Turn right (same SP) into Hospital Street (R32) 400 m further on, left (SP Tarkastad, Queenstown) on to the R61 after another 1,3 km and cross a grassy plain to the hills of the Elandsberg. Pass the 1 674-m Maermansberg on the right about 50 km after joining the R61, cross the Elands River 10 km further on and reach the Dutch Reformed church in Tarkastad 16,9 km from the river.

TARKASTAD Established by the Dutch Reformed Church on the farm Boschfontein in 1862, Tarkastad derives its name from the Tarka River which flows into the Kommandodrif Dam south-west of the town and then Lake Arthur before joining the Great Fish River. And the Tarka River is thought to take its name from the Hottentot word 'taraxa!as', meaning 'a place rich in women'. The double-storeyed Dutch Reformed pastorie in Grey Street, built soon after the Reverend J G S de Villiers was appointed first minister to the congregation, has unusual cast-iron lattice-work and, though sadly dilapidated, is a national monument.

Turn right (SP Adelaide, Bedford, Blanco) out of Grey Street into Cathcart Street 500 m beyond the Dutch Reformed church, left (same SP) on to the R344 at the stop street 200 m further on and continue towards two high rock-crested, flat-topped hills known as Martha and Mary. Pass the right turn to Blanco where the tar ends 10,4 km from the last stop street, fork right (SP Adelaide, Bedford) 6,8 km from the start of the gravel and run into the valley of the poplar-lined Tarka River 10 km further on. Turn right (SP Quaggaskirk, Bedford via Baviaans River) at the farm Spring

Valley 17,9 km from the last fork, cross the Tarka River 1,7 km further on and climb the winding road of De Beer's Pass into the Winterberg range. From the top of the pass, 11,9 km from the Tarka River, descend by way of many sharp curves into the Baviaans River valley and follow its meandering course for another 11 km, with the Baviaans River Mountains – a blaze of aloe flame from about June – on the left.

BAVIAANS RIVER The Baviaans River, with the Tarka and Great Fish rivers, formed the eastern frontier of European civilisation in South Africa when the new district of Graaff-Reinet was proclaimed in 1785.

Turn right (SP Cookhouse) 47,6 km from the top of De Beer's Pass, right again (no SP) on to tar 14,1 km further on, left (SP Kookhuis, Somerset-Oos) on to the R32/R63 after another 800 m and pass Eastpoort station on the right 6,8 km still further. The defile known as Slachtersnek can be seen about 5 km to the west of Eastpoort.

SLACHTERSNEK Following repeated complaints by his Hottentot shepherd, Booi, to the magistrates at Cradock and Graaff-Reinet in 1815, Frederik Bezuidenhout, a Baviaans River farmer, received several summonses to appear in court on charges of ill-treatment. A request to settle the matter on his farm, which he pleaded he could not leave unattended, was ignored and a posse of coloured troops of the Pandour Corps under white officers was sent to arrest him. When he resisted and was shot dead by a Pandour, his brother Hans and other farmers, among them Hendrik Prinsloo, swore vengeance and vowed to expel the British from the country. Prinsloo was arrested at his home and other rebels surrendered, but some of the leaders who held out were ambushed by a force of Boers under Commandant W Nel and Major G S Fraser. Hans Bezuidenhout was mortally wounded and Prinsloo and four others who were captured were clumsily hanged in public, four of the ropes suspended from the single gallows breaking at the first attempt. The inhumanity of the execution has been given as one of the reasons for the Great Trek.

Cross the Great Fish River 19,6 km after joining the R32/R63, turn right (SP Cookhouse, Somerset East) on to the R63 300 m from the river and continue into Cookhouse.

COOKHOUSE Strangers – and particularly railway passengers who in high summer have had to endure long waits in the station of this important junction – could be forgiven for thinking Cookhouse was named because it feels at times like the inside of an oven. The name, in fact, dates back to the time when there was a small, solitary building of stone here on the western bank of the Great Fish River where troops crossing the border took shelter and prepared meals. The building was known as 'the cook-house', and when Christiaan van Aarde was allocated a loan farm here it was called Kookhuis, although it had the name Roodewal by the time the town was established on the property. About 11 km south of Cookhouse, on the left of the R32, is a monument marking the spot where the gallows were erected for the execution of the leaders of the Slachtersnek Rebellion.

From Cookhouse continue 24,1 km westward on the R63 to the intersection of Worcester and Charles streets in Somerset East.

SOMERSET EAST At the foot of the densely-bushed Bosberg range in the heart of the Cape Midlands, Somerset East is a pleasant, tranquil place in a lovely setting. In the rainy season 16 waterfalls can be seen from the town, and the 33-km Auret Drive up into the mountains affords splendid views of the countryside. Part of the farm on which the town was founded in 1825 was occupied by Louis Trichardt before he embarked on the Great Trek. He grew tobacco so successfully here that the Governor of the Cape, Lord Charles Somerset, established Somerset Farm both for experimental purposes and as a produce source for his frontier forces. The farm was abandoned, however, the year before Somerset East was established. Now the local agriculture is based on merino sheep, angora goats, citrus fruit and dairy farming. Of note among the town's historic buildings is the Old Parsonage (NM) in Beaufort Street, a fine example of a Georgian manor house which for three years from 1829 was the place of worship for the community's Wesleyans, and for the next hundred years the Dutch Reformed pastorie. It is now a provincial museum.

Drive westward along Charles Street from its intersection with Worcester Street (SP Pearston, Graaff-Reinet, Swaershoek Pass) on to the R63, cross the Little Fish River for the first time after 5,1 km, for the second time 3,9 km further on, and for the third time after another 3,6 km. Turn right (SP Cradock) off the R63 on to the

gravel of the R337 3 km further on and travel between the Groot Bruintjieshoogte Mountains in the west and the Bosberg in the east. Cross the Little Fish River once more 1,4 km from the R63, pass the 1 813-m Doringbosberg on the right after another 27,1 km and run alongside the headwaters of the Little Fish River to the start of the Swaershoek Pass, with the 1 831-m Leeukloofberg on the right, 27,8 km further on. The road meanders for another 2,5 km to the top of the pass, from where there are magnificent views over Cradock to the north-east of thousands of hills rolling away as far as the eye can see. Towards the end of the pass,

121. The original homestead of the farm Babylonstoren on which the Mountain Zebra National Park was established

11 km from the top, look out for cliffs of weird, pillar-like rocks which appear to be precariously balanced on top of each other. Cross the railway line 18,9 km from the top of the Swaershoek Pass and turn left (no SP) on to the R390 after another 100 m. Turn right at the stop street 2,2 km further on, cross the Great Fish River into Church Street in Cradock and drive 400 m to the Dutch Reformed church.

122. Cradock's Dutch Reformed church was patterned on St Martin's-in-the-Fields in London

43
380 km

GEM OF THE KAROO
From Graaff-Reinet a variety of landscapes can be traversed, from the barren and flat Karoo of popular concept to mountain areas covered with vegetation.

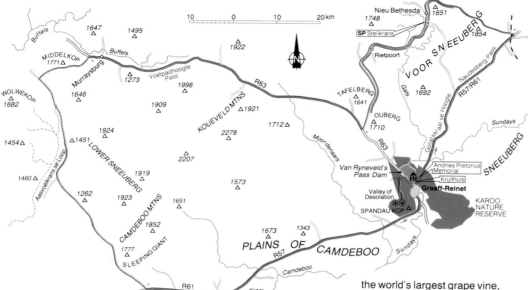

GRAAFF-REINET Numerous elegant buildings of historic note which have been meticulously restored, gardens, orchards and vineyards whose greenery is a welcome contrast to the harshness of the surrounding countryside, and the retained charm of a nineteenth-century rural town have earned Graaff-Reinet the sobriquet 'Gem of the Karoo'. When it was founded within an oxbow of the Sundays River among the foothills of the Sneeuberg range in 1786 – a lone outpost in a barren, untamed region during the troubled frontier days – it was named in honour of Governor Cornelis Jacob van der Graaff and his wife Cornelia Reynet. Less than a decade later, when the British occupied the Cape, an armed band of burghers demonstrated their mettle by expelling the *landdrost* and proclaiming Graaff-Reinet a republic. Independence was short-lived, however, for necessity compelled the republicans to accept

British authority within a year – although their maverick spirit brought them into conflict with the government again in 1799 and 1801. Finally the British yoke became intolerable and many left the area under the guidance of the Great Trek leaders Andries Pretorius and Gerrit Maritz. Because of its strategic position, the immigration of British and German settlers and the introduction of merino sheep and angora goats, the town became the second most important agricultural and commercial centre in the Cape in the latter half of the nineteenth century. Since then prize cattle and horse studs have added to the prosperity of the district and therefore the town. Among the many national monuments dating from Graaff-Reinet's pioneer days the most notable is Reinet House, for many years the Dutch Reformed parsonage and now a museum. In the garden of this stately building is

the world's largest grape vine, planted in 1870 by the Reverend Charles Murray, who – as his father, the Reverend Andrew Murray, had done – lived in Reinet House. Other outstanding buildings which are national monuments include the Drostdy, designed by Louis Thibault in 1806 and carefully restored in 1976 to its original elegance; the 1821 Dutch Reformed Mission church which is now the Hester Rupert Art Museum; the majestic Dutch Reformed church, the design of which is a copy in miniature of Salisbury Cathedral; and the Graaff-Reinet Pharmacy, a fine example of a Victorian chemist's shop. Most enchanting, perhaps, is what was at first appropriately called Vrijstraat, then Stretch Court and now Drostdyhof, a mall of 13 cottages given by Captain Charles Stretch, a one-time owner of the Drostdy, to his slaves when they were emancipated. Exquisitely restored, the cottages now form, with the Drostdy, a charming hotel complex. Other precincts, such as Cradock Street, Pastorie Street, Donkin Street, Stockenstroom Street and Somerset Street are endowed with many private dwellings that have been proclaimed national monuments. On a hill north-west of the town is a powder magazine ('kruithuis') which was built in 1853 and is now a mini-museum.

A particular feature of Graaff-Reinet is its relationship to the Karoo Nature Reserve. Nowhere else in the world is there a town of historical importance completely surrounded by a nature reserve – a living museum at the heart of a

conservation area. The South African Nature Foundation, which established the reserve in 1975, has pioneered wilderness trails, built birdwatching hides on the western shore of the Van Ryneveld's Pass Dam and is gradually restocking the veld with at least some of the wildlife that inhabited the Karoo in the days when a single herd of a million or more migrating springbok might take three days to pass one farm.

From the Dutch Reformed church in Graaff-Reinet drive 600 m westward along Caledon Street, turn right (SP Valley) into Stockenstroom Street and leave town on the R63. Cross the Sundays River 1,2 km from the church and pass the Van Ryneveld's Pass Dam and the memorial to Gideon Scheepers, the leader of a commando which harried British communication lines during the Anglo-Boer War. Scheepers was captured by his enemies, court-martialled, shot and buried in the bed of the Sundays River. Turn left (SP Valley of Desolation) 3,8 km from the river, fork left (SP Valley) 1,5 km further on and drive steeply up to the viewing site at the Valley of Desolation.

VALLEY OF DESOLATION
Focal point of the Karoo Nature Reserve is the Valley of Desolation (NM), a deep, awe-inspiring cleft in the Sneeuberg facing Spandau Kop. The canyon, which is flanked by a confusion of precariously-balanced columns of basalt rising to heights of 120 m and by other extraordinary, even grotesque rock formations, is among the most remarkable sights in southern Africa. From it the view of the Plains of Camdeboo and the surrounding mountains seems boundless.

Return to the Dutch Reformed church in Graaff-Reinet, drive to the eastern end of Caledon Street and turn left (SP Middelburg, Johannesburg, Cradock) on to the R57/R61. After 1,6 km pass the left turn to the Kruithuis and, 800 m further on, the memorial to Andries Pretorius and other Voortrekkers from the region. Pass the first left turn to Nieu Bethesda 25,6 km from the memorial, traverse the Naudesberg Pass 10 km further on and, 20 km from the first turn-off to Nieu Bethesda, turn left (SP Nieu Bethesda). Cross the railway 700 m from the R57/R61 and climb the Voor Sneeuberg by way of a good gravel road with steep gradients and hairpin bends. The 2 502-m Kompasberg can be seen to the north-west across a hilly plateau. Turn right into Hudson Street to reach the Dutch Reformed church in Nieu Bethesda 27,3 km after crossing the railway.

123. Graaff-Reinet's powder magazine overlooks the town

NIEU BETHESDA, at the foot of the Kompasberg, the highest peak in the Karoo, is a quaint little town which did not originate as a mission station, as is widely believed. It simply developed on a farm on which so many 'bywoners' (sharecroppers) congregated that it was eventually deemed necessary to establish a new parish of the Dutch Reformed Church. So out of the way is the town and so infrequent was the traffic at one time that the authorities allowed certain streets to be used for growing potatoes and lucerne. Nieu Bethesda is becoming known for its Owl House, the home of Helen Martins. This eccentric artist was obsessed with ground-glass ornamentation and, by the time she died in the 1970s, had spent 25 years creating a gardenful of extraordinary cement figures, many life-size, depicting religious and literary subjects. Mrs Claassens, former Town Clerk of Nieu Bethesda and now curatrix of the Owl House, conducts visitors around this Karoo oddity.

At the stop street in Hudson Street turn left (SP Graaff-Reinet) into Martins Street, after 2,3 km turn right (SP Steilkrans) and 800 m further on bear left for a drive high above the Gats River and then through fine merino and angora stud farms. After 20,2 km fork right on the farm Rietpoort and after another 2,7 km turn left (SP Graaff-Reinet) at a T-junction to curve around the 1 641-m Tafelberg on the right about 10 km further on and the 1 710-m Ouberg on the left after another 7 km. Turn right (no SP) on to the R63 19,2 km from the T-junction and continue 46 km to the top of the Voetpadhoogte Pass. Travel along the south bank of the Buffels River and drive into Leeb Street in Murraysburg 69,5 km after joining the R63.

MURRAYSBURG Two men are commemorated in the name of this town: Andrew Murray, the distinguished clergyman who was the minister at Graaff-Reinet when Murraysburg was founded by the Dutch Reformed Church in 1855; and Barend Burger who was known as the 'father of Murraysburg'. The Dutch Reformed community bought the farm Eenzaamheid, sold much of it off as plots and built the church and parsonage with the proceeds. Since then the town has prospered on the wool and mohair produced in the surrounding district, but what distinguishes Murraysburg from all other towns is its claim to have the longest stretch of quince hedge in the world. This usually quiet Karoo town leapt into prominence, became frenetically active and

assumed a carnival atmosphere for a brief period in 1966 when a farm in the district was chosen as the first South African site on which to erect a giant oil-exploration rig.

Turn right into Pastorie Street 300 m after running into Leeb Street, after another 200 m turn left into Voortrekker Street and continue westward on the R63. After 2,9 km turn left (SP Aberdeen, Nelspoort) off the R63, 13,3 km further on bear left (SP Aberdeen) and, after passing the 1 682-m Wolwekop on the right, descend Jonkersnek into the valley of the Aasvoëlkrans se Loop. Continue towards the Camdeboo Mountains, at the southern end of which is the imposing 1 777-m Sleeping Giant whose summit, composed of solid rock cliffs, indeed looks from the west like a supine colossus. Turn left (SP Aberdeen) on to the R61 76,7 km after leaving the R63 and at the intersection 17 km further on carry straight on into Aberdeen.

ABERDEEN The name of this town is another link with the Reverend Andrew Murray, a native of Aberdeen in Scotland, who ministered here for a brief period after the new church community was established on the farm Brakkefontein in 1855. As in most South African country towns, Aberdeen's landmark is the Dutch Reformed church, but this one has a steeple with the double distinction of being claimed by the townsfolk to be the highest in the country and of being 45 cm out of plumb.

Return to the intersection at the northern entrance to Aberdeen and turn right on to the R57 to drive 57 km across the Plains of Camdeboo back to Graaff-Reinet.

124. Some of Helen Martins' strange sculptures in Nieu Bethesda

PLAINS OF CAMDEBOO The Plains of Camdeboo, the subject of a book of the same title by Eve Palmer and a prolific source of archaeological material, stretch

from the catchment area of the Camdeboo River which rises in the Camdeboo Mountains north-west of Aberdeen, to the Groot Bruintjieshoogte Mountains in the east. The name of the region, through which the old wagon route from the Cape to Graaff-Reinet ran, is said to be a Hottentot word meaning 'green hollow'.

125. A corner of Aberdeen typifies the character of a Karoo town

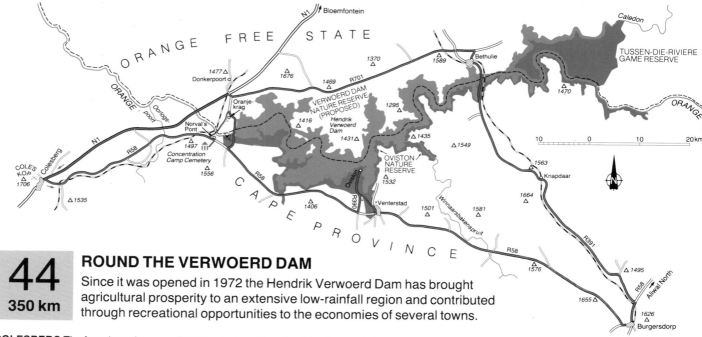

Bloemfontein
N1
1370
1477△
Donkerpoort
1676
1469 R701
1589 Bethulie
Caledon
TUSSEN-DIE-RIVIERE
GAME RESERVE
Oranje-
krag
VERWOERD DAM
NATURE RESERVE
(PROPOSED)
1416
Hendrik
Verwoerd
Dam
1295
1470
ORANGE
Norval's
Pont
1431△
1435
1549
10   0   10   20km
1497
Concentration
Camp Cemetery
1556
OVISTON
NATURE
RESERVE
1532
1563
Knapdaar
N
COLE'S
KOP
1706
Colesberg
N1
R58
1535
1406
Venterstad
1501
1581
Winnaarsbakensgruit
1664
R391
Aliwal North
R58
1576
1495
R58
1655△
1626
Burgersdorp

44
350 km

ROUND THE VERWOERD DAM

Since it was opened in 1972 the Hendrik Verwoerd Dam has brought agricultural prosperity to an extensive low-rainfall region and contributed through recreational opportunities to the economies of several towns.

COLESBERG The founders of the first settlement on the site of present-day Colesberg would have been less than pleased to know that in the twentieth century one of its claims to fame would be as a racehorse-breeding centre, for they were members of the London Missionary Society. They were forced by the government to close their station because the many Bushmen attracted to the mission were regarded by the frontier farmers as a threat to their security. However, a town was established at the site of the abandoned mission station in 1830 and named in honour of the Governor of the Cape, Sir Lowry Cole. Like Graaff-Reinet, Colesberg has retained much of the charm of an early Karoo town, and for such a small place has a remarkable number of national monuments. Several of them are in

Bell Street where there is a blend of Cape Dutch and Georgian architectural styles. Other national monuments include the Dutch Reformed church and the Old Horse Mill, which the chairman of the Colesberg Historical Society, Taetse Vorster, moved from Sewefontein, 10 km away, restored and installed in what was once a coach-house. As fascinating an antiquity as any, though, is a pane of glass in the Colesberg Museum on which in 1866 the magistrate, Lorenzo Boyes, scratched the letters 'DP' with a stone brought to him by John O'Reilly (see Northern Cape Diamond Fields, Tour 46). He told O'Reilly that the scratching seemed to confirm that the stone was indeed a diamond, the first recognised one found in South Africa. The Colesberg area was the scene of considerable fighting

during the Anglo-Boer War, including the Battle of Colesberg in 1900, and the town was actually held by Boer forces for some time.

From the Dutch Reformed church drive northward (SP Bloemfontein, Verwoerd Dam) up Church Street on to the R58, keeping straight on (SP Venterstad) at the fork on the outskirts of town to remain on the R58. Pass Gary Player's stud farm 26,4 km from the church, the left turn to Norval's Pont 12,7 km further on and after another 900 m turn right (SP Konsentrasiekamp Kerkhof) to drive 1,1 km to the Norval's Pont Concentration Camp cemetery.

NORVAL'S PONT, little more than a railway station on the southern bank of the Orange River, is where the main line to the north crosses from the Cape into the Orange Free State by way of an 11-arch bridge. The spot acquired its name when a Scot called Norval built a ferry here in 1848 for Governor Sir Harry Smith to cross the river on his march on the Orange Free State. The cemetery of the Norval's Pont Concentration Camp, established by the British in the Anglo-Boer War, has been paved over with slate to form an unusual monument commemorating the 278 adults and 88 children buried here.

ORANGE RIVER South Africa's major river, which was named in honour of the Prince of Orange in 1779 by Colonel Robert Gordon, commander of the garrison at the Cape, flows 2 300 km from its headwaters in the Drakensberg to the Atlantic. After a rapid drop from

3 350 m above sea level to 1 300 m in its first 640 km, it takes another 1 600 km to make the rest of its descent to the sea. In spite of its magnitude little use could be made of its water until the Orange River Project came into operation in the 1970s. This scheme entailed the construction of the Hendrik Verwoerd and P K le Roux dams and the Orange-Fish Tunnel – at 82,5 km the longest of its kind in the world – which transfers water from the Verwoerd Dam to the Teebus River, a tributary of the Great Fish River. A system of canals, inverted siphons and another tunnel conduct some of the supply further from the Great Fish to the Sundays River in the eastern Cape. The Orange River Project has brought unprecedented agricultural activity and prosperity to a region where the rivers are seldom more than dry, dusty beds.

Return to the R58, turn left and 900 m further on turn right (SP Norval's Pont, Oranjekrag). After 500 m pass the Glasgow Pont Hotel, another reminder of the hamlet's Caledonian connection, and cross the Orange River into the Orange Free State by a single-lane bridge 1,3 km further on. Continue 3,7 km, turn left (SP Springfontein, Bethulie) and at Oranjekrag 1,3 km still further turn right (SP Venterstad via Verwoerd Dam) to reach the dam wall after 4,7 km. Turn left to drive across the wall back into the Cape Province.

HENDRIK VERWOERD DAM
The Hendrik Verwoerd Dam, the country's most extensive stretch of inland water, has a dam wall that at 914 m is the second longest in Africa. Places like Oranjekrag and

126. The small town of Colesberg nestles among hills

Oviston which started as housing camps for workers on the project have become towns, and within a decade of the completion of the dam existing towns such as Venterstad and Bethulie had been injected with extra life through tourism. The dam is virtually surrounded by nature reserves – the Verwoerd Dam Nature Reserve on the Orange Free State shore, the Oviston Nature Reserve on the Cape shore and the Tussen-die-Riviere Game Reserve in the triangle formed by the confluent Orange and Caledon rivers. At the western end of the northern shore there is a resort with an hotel, rondavels, holiday cottages, a restaurant and a recreational area.

At the control boom 2,3 km from the start of the drive over the dam wall turn right to climb 1,6 km to the main viewing site above the dam. Return to the viewing site turn-off, turn right and after 2,7 km turn left (SP Venterstad) back on to the R58. Drive 32,9 km before turning left (SP Oviston) on to the R390, turn left again (SP Caravan Park) 3,7 km further on and drive 6,6 km to the intake of the Fish River Tunnel on the southern shore of the Hendrik Verwoerd Dam.

OVISTON, whose name is an abbreviation of *Oranje-Vis-Ton*nel, was established in 1964 to house workers on the tunnel which conducts water from the Verwoerd Dam via two other rivers to the Sundays River in the eastern Cape. The name is also applied to the nature reserve on the dam's southern shore, where animals are bred to stock other conservation areas. It is open at weekends and on public holidays, and has large herds of most antelope species, Burchell's zebra and black wildebeest.

Backtrack 6,6 km from the tunnel intake and, instead of turning right back on to the R390, continue straight on through the Oviston Conservation Station gate to drive to the intersection in the centre of Venterstad 5,1 km from the gate.

VENTERSTAD Although Venterstad was laid out on the farm of Johannes Venter in 1875, it really came into its own only a century later when the Verwoerd Dam pushed the water of the Orange River, previously 11 km away, to the 'doorstep' of the town. As a result Venterstad, for long no more than the small centre of a sheep-farming area, now has the status of a holiday resort with the added income that brings.

Turn right (SP Steynsburg, Bloemfontein, Verwoerd Dam) at the last-mentioned intersection and after 300 m turn left (SP East London, Burgersdorp) on to the R58. Travel 59,3 km to reach the intersection of Coligny and Van der Walt streets in Burgersdorp.

BURGERSDORP, which was founded when about 300 families between the Stormbergspruit and the Kraai River were given permission to form their own Dutch Reformed congregation, is steeped in national history. In 1847 the burghers – after whom some historians believe the new settlement was named – laid out a village where, less than a decade later, the powerful campaign for the recognition of Dutch as an official language originated. After the second British occupation of the Cape in 1806 English had been proclaimed the only official language, but in 1857 and 1858 the voters of Burgersdorp petitioned the Legislative Assembly on four occasions for an amendment to the constitution that would permit the use of Dutch in its deliberations. After yet another appeal from Burgersdorp, now the focus of a countrywide crusade, the requested amendment was passed in 1882. With funds collected all over the country the Taalmonument ('Language Monument') was erected in Burgersdorp, but it was badly vandalised during the Anglo-Boer War and Lord Milner added insult to injury after the war by having it removed altogether. In 1907 the British Government provided a replica of the marble figure pointing with one hand to the inscription on the tablet she holds in the other. The remnant of the original statue, found in 1939 during excavations in Kimberley where Milner had ordered it to be buried, has been erected next to the replica on Burger Square. Another reminder of those troublous times – in which the Boers defeated a large British force in the Battle of Stormberg, not far from Burgersdorp – is the 'Brandwag' (NM), a British blockhouse in the chain of forts from Queenstown to Bethulie. Burgersdorp was also the original seat of the theological seminary of the Gereformeerde Kerk (Reformed Church) which seceded from the Nederduitse Gereformeerde Kerk (Dutch Reformed Church) in 1859. The seminary has since been transferred to Potchefstroom and has developed into the Potchefstroom University for Christian Higher Education. The parsonage outhouse in which the seminary started is a national monument.

Turn left (SP Aliwal North, Bethulie, Bloemfontein) at the intersection of Coligny and Van der Walt streets in Burgersdorp, right (same SP) into Taylor Street after 100 m and left after another 100 m into Piet Retief Street to leave town on the R58.

127. The H F Verwoerd Dam

128. The 'Taalmonument' in Burgersdorp, with the vandalised statue on the central plinth and its replacement on the left

Turn left (SP Bethulie, Dreunberg) on to the R391 5 km further on, follow the signs to Bethulie and after 35 km turn left (SP Bethulie) over the railway line at Knapdaar. Descend Knapdaarhoogte to the Orange River valley and, having crossed the river back into the Orange Free State, turn left into Bethulie 34 km from the railway reaching a stop street in Voortrekker Street after another 2,3 km.

BETHULIE is a town whose name has been changed probably more than any other in South Africa. When the London Missionary Society established a post in 1829 the area was called Moordenaarspoort because of the many Bushmen and Griquas killed there by the Basotho. The name was changed to Caledon by the Reverend Jean Pierre Pellissier when he took over the station on behalf of the Paris Evangelical Society in 1833. Because there was another Caledon in the country Pellissier renamed the settlement Verhuellpolis in honour of the president of his society in 1835, but the society preferred something

biblical and Bethulia ('chosen of God') was selected. Yet another change, to Heidelberg, was effected when a new Dutch Reformed congregation was established near the mission, but as there were already two other Heidelbergs the developing town reverted to Bethulia, and since then only the spelling has altered. The home Pellissier built and added to during his ministry from 1833 to 1865 has been preserved as Pellissier House (NM) and is used as a local history museum. Since the completion of the Verwoerd Dam Bethulie has also benefited from the increased numbers of holiday-makers visiting the area.

Continue northward from the last-mentioned stop street and after 3,3 km turn left (SP Verwoerd Dam, Donkerpoort) on to the R701. Travel 48,2 km, turn right (SP N1, Donkerpoort) and after another 500 m turn left (SP Colesberg) on to the N1. Cross the Orange River back into the Cape Province 8,1 km further on, turn left (SP Colesberg, Petrusville, Venterstad) 34,7 km from the river and turn right into Colesberg after another 400 m.

45
270 km

OASIS IN A MOONSCAPE

For most of its length the Orange River is deeply channelled, but from the Boegoeberg Dam to the spectacular Augrabies Falls the valley opens out, giving the river a luxuriant green border.

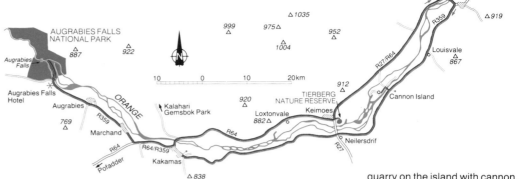

UPINGTON There was a time in the nineteenth century when the depredations of the nomadic Korana Hottentots, who raided farms in the northern Cape and retreated with rustled cattle and sheep to the densely-wooded islands of the Orange River, became intolerable. Klaas Lukas, the most powerful Korana chief, was at this time less troublesome, however, and at his request a missionary, the Reverend Christian Schröder of the Inland Mission, was sent from the Cape in 1871 to establish a station at Olyfenhoutsdrift. Eight years later the Cape Government established a Baster settlement here as a buffer between the Korana and white farmers, with Schröder as spiritual and secular mentor. And it was to his design that Japie Lutz constructed the first irrigation canal in the lower Orange River valley, a scheme which developed to the economic benefit of not only Olyfenhoutsdrift but the entire region. The settlement, renamed in honour of the Prime Minister of the Cape Colony, Sir Thomas Upington, when he visited it in 1884, has become the centre of a prosperous agricultural area concentrating on the production of high-grade cotton, vast quantities of lucerne, the finest sultana grapes in southern Africa, wine, deciduous fruit, grain, cattle, wool and mutton. The Kalahari region north of the town also produces South Africa's richest output of karakul pelts. Even palms, which produce large, delicious dates, thrive along the river, but they have not been extensively cultivated because of cheap imports from the Middle East.

National monuments in Upington include the Dutch Reformed and Roman Catholic churches, the Old Water Mill in the grounds of the museum (Schröder's home) at the western end of Schröder Street, and Palm Tree Avenue, at 1 041 m the longest avenue of palms in the southern hemisphere. But the most evocative memorial is the stone in the cemetery on the grave of the legendary brigand 'Scotty' Smith, who spent the last years of his roguish life here. Member of a noble Scottish family, Scotty fought in India with a Highland regiment, in the Franco-Prussian War and in Spain with the Carlists before coming to this country as a member of the Frontier Armed and Mounted Police. He deserted from the force and became a highwayman, stock thief, ivory-hunter, confidence trickster and gun-runner, earning for himself the somewhat dubious title

of South Africa's Robin Hood. He was also an ally of the Hottentots in their wars against the Germans in South West Africa, and a filibuster on the side of one or other of the warring chiefs in what was then Bechuanaland. He served time for a few of his misdeeds, but most went unatoned when he was pardoned in reward for the service he rendered as a Kalahari guide and spy in the Anglo-Boer War and World War I.

Upington is a starting point for visitors to the Augrabies Falls National Park, the Kalahari Gemsbok National Park and the Fish River Canyon. Near the town is the Spitskop Nature Reserve, which has a population of various antelope species, wildebeest, giraffe, zebra and the progeny of camels once used in the Kalahari by the police.

Leave Upington by turning left at the western end of Schröder Street, crossing first the bridge over the northern channel of the Orange

River to The Island, where there is a pleasure resort and the celebrated Palm Tree Avenue, then the bridge from The Island over the southern channel of the river. Turn right (SP Louisvale) on to the R359 1,1 km from the entrance to The Island Resort and after 13,6 km reach the Dutch Reformed church in Louisvale, one of the Orange River agricultural villages. Turn right (SP Keimoes, Kanoneiland) 12,3 km further on and left (SP Kanoneiland Dorp) after another 1,1 km to drive through the lush vineyards and orchards of Cannon Island.

CANNON ISLAND At 14 km long and more than 3 km wide, Cannon Island (Kanoneiland) is the largest island in the Orange River. Its name originated in one of the punitive expeditions against the Korana freebooters when, in 1878, the Cape Field Artillery under Colonel Zachary Bayly and a contingent of police and burghers attacked their

quarry on the island with cannon. When the Korana tried to retaliate with a home-made wooden fieldpiece it exploded, killing six of them. The intensive cultivation now characteristic of Cannon Island started in the Depression when 52 land-hungry men seized the island in defiance of authority, resisted attempts to dislodge them and, after illegally clearing the dense vegetation, constructing irrigation canals and furrows, planting crops and reaping bumper harvests, so impressed the government with their industry that they were eventually allowed to buy their holdings. To replace the boat (now preserved on pillars in the grounds of the Cannon Island Primary School) and rafts they first used to reach the island, the settlers constructed the Orange River's largest pont, which was used until the Eendrag Bridge was built across the southern stream in 1940. The double-carriageway bridge over the northern stream was constructed in 1954.

129. A paddle wheel at Kakamas is part of the system that irrigates the Orange River farmlands

Return from Cannon Island to the R359, turn right (SP Neilersdrif) and continue 19,6 km westward to cross the R27 at Neilersdrif, another of the Orange River agricultural villages. Travel 41 km before turning right (SP Kakamas), and at a stop street 1,7 km further on turn left on to tar to reach Kakamas after another 2,3 km.

KAKAMAS Mention South African canned peaches and you are probably talking about the famous Kakamas clingstone variety which originated here in the lower valley of the Orange River. The Kakamas community was established in 1898 by the Labour Colony Commission of the Dutch Reformed Church on a reservation provided by the Cape Government for the resettlement of those impoverished by the disastrous drought and rinderpest plague that lasted from 1895 to 1897. The same Christian Schröder and Japie Lutz who provided Upington with its first irrigation canals initiated the construction of furrows on the banks of the Orange River at Kakamas. Some of the areas now under irrigation are able to support so many sultana, lucerne, cotton, legume, grain, deciduous fruit and stock farmers that they look like extended villages. The Kakamas peach was propagated from material from a tree of the 'Transvaal' variety growing here and descended from the St Helena peach, which was probably imported from the island of that name by Jan van Riebeeck. The propagation was undertaken by the University of Stellenbosch with material sent to Professor Reinecke in 1933 by one of his former students, A D Collins.

At the stop street at the north-western end of the main street through Kakamas turn left (SP Pofadder, Augrabies Falls National Park) on to the R64/R359 and after 8,2 km turn right on to the R359. Reach the right turn into Marchand 4,7 km further on.

MARCHAND The agricultural village of Marchand was named after the Reverend B P J Marchand of Knysna who, through pleading with the synod of the Dutch Reformed Church for assistance for its poor white members, played a major role in the establishment of the Kakamas irrigation settlement in 1898.

Continue north-westward from the Marchand turn-off, passing the right turn into the town of Augrabies after 10,3 km and the Augrabies Falls Hotel 8,4 km further on. After another 1,3 km turn right (SP Augrabies Falls National Park) to drive 4,7 km to the park gate. Before setting off through the moonscape around the falls, collect

a map and study the enormous relief model of the park at the information centre.

AUGRABIES FALLS NATIONAL PARK After losing altitude at a mean rate of only 66 cm in the previous 1 660 km of its crawl across southern Africa, the Orange River suddenly plunges about 147 m over a massive barrier of granite. First there is a series of cascades and rapids over which the flow gathers momentum, then a rushing flood through a narrow channel and finally a sheer fall of 56 m which is awe-inspiring, especially after rain. The roar of this final fall accounts for the name Augrabies, a corruption of a Hottentot word which means something like 'the place of great noise'. Apart from the main drop there are several secondary falls from branches of the stream, one of which disappears underground before gushing out of the cliff face as the Bridal Veil. Even after that roaring final plunge the Orange continues its rampage, careering on down a series of rapids. A suspension bridge above the main cataract affords access between viewing points on both banks of the river. The 9 000-ha Augrabies Falls National Park provides a habitat for most locally indigenous flora, a wide variety of birdlife, and an increasing population of antelope, reptiles and wild cats. A major attraction for the energetic is the park's Klipspringer Hiking Trail.

Return eastward on the R359 and 23,4 km beyond the Augrabies Falls Hotel turn left (SP Kakamas) on to the R64/R359. Pass the right turn to Kakamas 8,2 km further on

and 1,4 km still further cross the Kakamas Bridge over the Orange River on to the R64, passing the left turn to the Kalahari Gemsbok Park after 800 m and reaching the Keimoes Hotel after another 39 km.

KEIMOES Now a major agricultural centre in the lower valley of the Orange River, Keimoes was originally one of the villages established by Klaas Lukas, the Korana chief who had asked for a mission station to be founded at Upington. Keimoes also has its special peach, the Keimoes variety, although it is not as famous as the Kakamas. Unimpeded views of the valley under irrigation reward those who visit the sheltered lookout at the summit of the Tierberg,

130. The gorge of the Orange River below the Augrabies Falls

overlooking the town. The nature reserve in which the Tierberg is located is noted for its abundance of aloes.

At the traffic lights in Keimoes keep straight on, turn right (SP Tierberg Nature Reserve) 2,4 km further on and follow the 1,4-km road to the top of Tierberg. Return to the traffic lights, turn right (SP Upington) on to the R27/R64 and drive 49 km back to the centre of Upington.

131. Hanging sultana grapes to dry on a farm between Cannon Island and Neilersdrif

46

180 km

DIAMOND FIELDS

Hundreds of mounds which dot parts of the northern Cape symbolise the hopes and despair of thousands of men who flocked to South Africa late in the nineteenth century to search for diamonds.

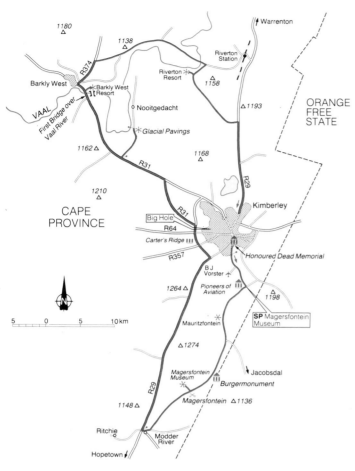

132. The Big Hole at Kimberley

NORTHERN CAPE DIAMOND FIELDS South Africa's first recognised diamond was found in the 1860s by a child on the farm De Kalk near Hopetown. In 1866 a neighbour, Schalk van Niekerk, showed the stone to a trader and transport rider named John O'Reilly who offered to have it identified and took it to the magistrate at Colesberg, Lorenzo Boyes. After succeeding in scratching the letters 'DP' on a pane of glass, Boyes said he believed it was indeed a diamond and sent it to Dr William Atherstone, a Grahamstown physician with a knowledge of mineralogy, who confirmed his opinion. The 21,25-carat gem was valued at £500, and bought for that sum by the Governor of the Cape, Sir Philip Wodehouse. The excited prospecting activity evoked by this and subsequent finds had no spectacular result until three years later when the same Schalk van Niekerk paid a Griqua named Booi 10 oxen, a horse and 500 sheep for a stone which he resold to Hopetown dealers for £11 200. The 82,5-carat 'Star of Africa', as the diamond was named, was eventually bought by the Earl of Dudley for £25 000. This started the first major rush to the northern Cape, and by 1870 there were 10 000 people encamped along the banks of the Vaal River, whither Koranas had guided the first organised party of prospectors. The mushroom community included traders, artisans, hoteliers, bankers, brewers and even journalists who started newspapers. While the Orange Free State, the Transvaal Republic and the local Griqua chief, Nicolaas Waterboer, all laid territorial claim to the diamond fields, the diggers themselves established their own republic which ceased to exist only when the British annexed Griqualand West to the Cape Colony after arbitrating the rival claims to the region in favour of Waterboer. The alluvial diggings along the Vaal were soon producing £3 million worth of diamonds a year, but spectacular finds on farms south of what was to become Kimberley were yet to be made. It was these finds that led to the 'dry' diggings, to a stampede that dwarfed the rush to the Vaal, and to the establishment of the Diamond City.

KIMBERLEY Though not one of South Africa's major cities, Kimberley for many holds the most allure, for it has an atmosphere of

adventure and romance – the romance of diamonds, of intrigue, and of fortunes made and lost by those who came to search for the gems. It was a series of successively more exciting finds on the farms Bultfontein, Dorstfontein, Alexandersfontein and particularly Vooruitzicht some distance from the early alluvial diggings along the Vaal River that determined the siting of Kimberley. Vooruitzicht had been bought for £50 by the brothers Johannes and Diederick de Beer, whose name has become synonymous with diamonds through the mighty De Beers company, although they gave up their share of the £90 million worth of treasure which was to be unearthed on their property after they sold Vooruitzicht for £6 000 within a few months of the rush to it. Among those involved in the rush was a group led by Fleetwood Rawstorne, who found diamonds in such quantities on Colesberg Kopje that within a short period thousands of diggers were swarming over the hillock to dig by hand a pit 400 m deep and 500 m wide, the biggest man-made hole in the world. Many of the fortune-hunters became fabulously wealthy overnight; for others there was only despair from the first shovelful of soil they turned over. Theirs were claims staked beyond the perimeter of the kimberlite pipe in which the diamonds were to be found, and a man might watch his immediate neighbour picking up a fortune in gems but never see one in his own sorting tray. In the wake of the diggers came the camp followers, the entrepreneurs and the madams who set up bars, dance halls, boxing booths, fairgrounds, sweepstake 'offices' and most of the other amenities for which such a *nouveau riche* society was only too happy to pay. Without any sort of organisation or control conditions at both the Big Hole and the town – named Kimberley in honour of the British Colonial Secretary, the Earl of Kimberley – were chaotic until the more successful diggers formed themselves into syndicates. These, in turn, were eventually amalgamated by the moguls Cecil Rhodes and Barney Barnato and later consolidated by Sir Ernest Oppenheimer into the renowned De Beers Consolidated Mines. When the price of diamonds plummeted during World War I mining in the Big Hole came to an end, and Kimberley, though still the diamond 'capital' of South Africa, has never been the same since. Happily, some of the atmosphere of the early days has been retained in reconstructed or restored buildings and in a quaint town-like museum near the Big Hole which has a wealth of memorabilia evocative of the excitement, the hurly-burly and the glamour of the infant city.

In the Anglo-Boer War Kimberley was an early target of the Boers, who besieged the town and kept it under sporadic fire for four months with a 6-inch gun known as 'Long Tom'. The defenders, under Lieutenant-Colonel Robert Kekewich, retaliated with 'Long Cecil', a 4-inch gun made in the De Beers workshops. The 30 000 people under siege endured the privations of starvation and disease, the infant mortality rate among whites soaring to 50 percent at one stage and among the black people to a horrifying 93,5 percent. The edifice on Memorial Hill, at the foot of which stands 'Long Cecil', pays tribute to 'the Honoured Dead' of the siege, and another memorial, in Belgravia Park, commemorates the police who fell during it. A statue in the grounds of St Cyprian's Cathedral depicts Sister Henrietta Stockdale, a pioneer of nursing in South Africa and the first in the world to institute a nurses' register, and is a tribute not only to her, but to her profession as a whole. Most notable of the city's functional memorials is the McGregor Memorial Museum in Egerton Street.

From the Honoured Dead Memorial in Memorial Road drive south-south-eastward (SP Magersfontein, B J Vorster Airport) along Oliver Road and then southward out of Kimberley. Pass the entrance to the B J Vorster airport after 4,2 km and reach the Memorial to the Pioneers of Aviation 3,4 km further on.

PIONEERS OF AVIATION This national monument on the site of South Africa's first flying school comprises a symbolic memorial, a reconstruction of the hangar and a replica of the Compton Paterson biplane used in early flight training in 1913.

Continue southward from the memorial, after 700 m turn right (SP Magersfontein Museum) and pass the entrance to Mauritzfontein, the Oppenheimer stud farm, 7,2 km further on. Pass the left turn to Jacobsdal after another 2,7 km and drive 7,3 km to the left turn to the Burgermonument.

BURGERMONUMENT In the shadow of the pyramidal Burgermonument lie the remains of many members of the Boer forces who died at Magersfontein, at Modder River and around Kimberley. Originally buried in scattered graves, the bodies were exhumed and reburied here in the 1920s. One of the numerous headstones preserved at the monument is not, however, that of a Boer. It is 'in memory of a young unknown Scottish bugler who died of wounds and was buried by the burghers'.

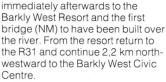

133. The mine museum preserves some of Kimberley's original atmosphere

Return to the Burgermonument entrance, turn left and after 3,5 km turn right to the Magersfontein Battlefield Museum.

BATTLE OF MAGERSFONTEIN
When the Boer forces under General Piet Cronjé and General Koos de la Rey, who were resisting Lieutenant-General Lord Methuen's advance towards besieged Kimberley, made a tactical withdrawal from Modder River on 28 November 1899, they took up positions at Magersfontein. Instead of following the more usual Boer procedure of digging their trenches on high ground, they chose the foot of a ridge of low hills and there awaited the British who delayed 11 days before setting off in pursuit from Modder River. When Methuen's 12 000 soldiers eventually advanced on Magersfontein at dawn on 11 December, poor reconnaissance resulted in their being caught unawares by withering fire from the unexpected trench sites of the Boers, of whom there were no more than 8 500. Thousands of Britons were pinned down without cover on the open veld for hours under the blazing sun. At the end of a day of confusion Methuen broke off the engagement and moved his battered regiments back to Modder River. Among the dead was Major-General Andy Wauchope, commanding the Highland Brigade, to whom there is a memorial near Matjiesfontein (see Matjiesfontein Cemetery, Tour 18). The Magersfontein Field Museum was established to protect the battlefield (NM) and its memorials, and to

provide information for visitors by means of descriptive displays, a large relief model at a forward viewing post and exhibitions of photographs, equipment and uniforms.

Turn right out of the field museum and travel 9,7 km before turning right again (SP Modder River). Turn right again (SP Ritchie, Kimberley, Hopetown) at the stop street 700 m further on, and right once more (SP Kimberley) on to the R29 after another 400 m. Continue 29,9 km and turn left (SP Barkly West, Griquastad) on to the R31. Cross the R357 2,9 km further on and after another 2,2 km the R64 at Carter's Ridge, where among other war graves in Gladstone Cemetery are those of George Labram, who designed 'Long Cecil', and the intrepid Lieutenant-Colonel Henry Scott-Turner, who was killed storming a Boer position here in the Kimberley siege. Turn right (SP Nooitgedacht Glacial Pavings) 18,6 km from the R64 to drive another 5,8 km to the glaciation site.

NOOITGEDACHT GLACIAL PAVINGS About 300 million years ago stony rubble carried by the vast ice sheet moving from South Africa's highlands to the coast scored many underlying rock surfaces, creating what are known as glacial pavements. These at Nooitgedacht (NM) are also marked by the engravings of stone-age man.

Return to the R31, turn right (SP Barkly West) and cross the Vaal River after 12,7 km. Turn right

immediately afterwards to the Barkly West Resort and the first bridge (NM) to have been built over the river. From the resort return to the R31 and continue 2,2 km north-westward to the Barkly West Civic Centre.

BARKLY WEST One of the first alluvial diamond camps sprang up at this spot, then known as Klipdrift, when numerous gems were found at Canteen Kopje (NM) on the north bank of the Vaal River in 1869. The following year, while governments were wrangling over territorial rights to the diamond fields, the diggers at Canteen Kopje established the Republic of Klipdrift with the colourful Stafford Parker as their first and only president. Of mighty physique and a questionable past, President Parker maintained order in an unruly community with a system of rough justice. A Transvaal commando led by President Marthinus Pretorius arrived to lay claim to the diamond fields in 1870, but was ignored by the diggers and, finding itself powerless, withdrew. The republic's history ended with the annexation of the territory to the Cape in 1871, and the camp from which the diggers were now flocking to Colesberg Kopje assumed the name of the Governor, Sir Henry Barkly. Apart from its place in diamond history, Canteen Kopje is also a celebrated archaeological site, yielding numerous fossil remains of extinct animal species and sacksful of stone-age implements that have been distributed to museums all over the world.

Drive north-eastward (SP Windsorton) from the centre of Barkly West on to the R374 and after 4,2 km turn right (SP Riverton). Continue 18,5 km, cross the Vaal and turn right (SP Riverton) at the stop street 4 km further on to drive another 300 m to the entrance of the Riverton Resort.

RIVERTON, a resort with 30 km of navigable river behind a weir, is owned by the Kimberley Municipality, but was once the property of a syndicate of diamond magnates which included Cecil Rhodes.

From the Riverton Resort continue 11,4 km south-eastward to the R29, turn right (SP Kimberley) and drive 15 km back to the centre of the city.

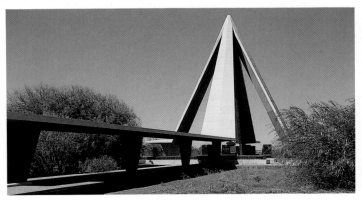

134. The Burgermonument at Magersfontein

47

HEART OF THE ORANGE FREE STATE

440 km

A road from Bloemfontein to the north-west leads through the characteristically flat maize and cattle country of most of the Orange Free State to shady resorts on the banks of the Vaal River.

BLOEMFONTEIN Contrary to popular belief, Bloemfontein's origins are more British than Afrikaans, although trekkers had used the perennial spring, Bloem Fonteyn, and Rudolph Brits had farmed on the surrounding land for a brief period. It was Major Henry Warden who founded in 1846 what is now the capital of the Orange Free State and the judicial capital of South Africa. Having been sent as British Resident to the Transgariep, the land north of the Gariep, as the Orange River was once known, he bought as his headquarters the farm Bloem Fonteyn from Johan Nicolaas Brits, nephew of the original owner. Irate republicans of the Transgariep resented his presence, however, and expelled him in 1848, but within months the ebullient Governor of the Cape, Sir Harry Smith, having proclaimed the territory British and named it the Orange River Sovereignty, sallied forth, defeated the republicans at the Battle of Boomplaats and re-instated Warden as British Resident. The sovereignty lasted only until 1854, when the British decided that it was a worthless expense and ceded it to the republicans, but by then Warden had established the sound administration on which the model republic of the Orange Free State was founded. The Old Raadsaal (NM) he built to serve as schoolroom as well as council chamber still stands in St George's Street and Queen's Fort (NM), with which he replaced his original stronghold, Fort Drury, also survives.

Bloemfontein became an open city during the Anglo-Boer War and Lord Roberts, who commanded the British forces, made it a supply and communications base. The incongruous name of the flat-topped hill in the centre of the city, Naval Hill, dates from this period, when the Royal Navy party accompanying Roberts on his march on Bloemfontein emplaced their guns on it. The white horse depicted on the side of the hill was laid out by men of the Wiltshire Regiment to remind them of the Cherhill Horse on the downs near Calne back home. When the Orange Free State became the Orange River Colony after the war Bloemfontein remained the capital, and it became the provincial capital of the region and judicial capital of the country when South Africa became a Union in 1910. The National Women's Monument in Monument Road commemorates the 26 370 women and children who died during the Anglo-Boer War, and the War Museum below it relates to this and other South African conflicts. Other buildings which have national monument status include Die Presidensie, the Fourth Raadsaal, the Fountain, the Gnome aircraft engine in the National Museum and the Tweetoringkerk. Atop Naval Hill is the Franklin Nature Reserve, from which there is a fine view of the city.

From J B M Hertzog Square in Bloemfontein drive north-eastward along President Brand Street and follow the R700 signs through Kloof Street, Aliwal Street and Milner Road to the traffic circle 3,4 km from the square. Continue on the R700 (now Eeufees Road), cross the N1 5,9 km from the circle and travel through flat savanna stretching from horizon to horizon. Pass the right turn into Bultfontein 87 km from the N1 and 3,2 km further on the giant Bultfontein maize elevator on the right.

BULTFONTEIN is the centre of one of the country's foremost maize-producing regions, although the production of wool, wheat, groundnuts and sunflower seed, as well as cattle farming, is also important. The maize elevator is the largest in the country. The committee appointed by the men who bought the farm Bultfontein in 1873 intended to call the village they planned 'Fairplay', but the Orange Free State Volksraad rejected the proposal and the name of the farm was adopted for the new community. The village was occupied by the British in the Anglo-Boer War and the vicinity saw heavy fighting.

135. The Old Raadsaal of the Orange Free State in Bloemfontein

Fork left (SP Hoopstad) 800 m north-east of the Bultfontein elevator to remain on the R700. Cross the Vet River after 54,8 km and reach the right turn into Hoopstad 900 m further on.

HOOPSTAD The village founded in 1876 on the farm Kameeldoorns alongside the Vet River was indirectly named after A P Haupt who surveyed the town. Instead of naming it Hauptstad ('chief town'), however, and thereby causing possible confusion with the capital, the new settlement was named Hoopstad. Several Anglo-Boer War skirmishes were fought in the surrounding veld. Maize, Afrikander cattle, wool and wheat are important products of the area.

From the intersection at the entrance to Hoopstad drive north-westward (SP Bloemhof) on the R34 through country that becomes more bush-covered. Enter the Sandveld Nature Reserve and cross the Vaal River arm of the Bloemhof Dam into the Transvaal 31,5 km from the entrance to Hoopstad.

SANDVELD NATURE RESERVE Waterfowl abound on the sandflats on either side of the bridge linking the Orange Free State with the Transvaal across the Vaal River arm of the Bloemhof Dam. This is part of the Sandveld Nature Reserve, and birdlife is indeed one of its features. Species include, near the water, the red-billed teal, spur-winged goose and yellow-billed duck, as well as the yellow-billed hornbill, kori bustard, white-backed vulture and long-tailed shrike. The thornbush vegetation is also the habitat of several antelope species and giraffe. There are camping and picnic sites in the reserve.

BLOEMHOF DAM Originally called the Oppermansdrif Dam, the Bloemhof Dam at the confluence of the Vaal and Vet rivers is the fifth largest in the country and, with a capacity of 1 270 million litres, is about a fifth of the size of the H F Verwoerd Dam. Swimming, boating and angling have become popular at the dam.

Turn left (SP Bloemhof) on to the R29/R34 7,4 km from the Bloemhof Dam bridge and enter Bloemhof after another 1,1 km.

BLOEMHOF, the second oldest town in the Transvaal, started as a village in 1864 on the farm Bloemhof, bought from John Barclay, a survivor of the wreck of HMS *Birkenhead* which foundered at Danger Point in 1852 (see Gansbaai, Tour 15). The town enjoyed a brief period of prominence in 1871 when the court

of arbitration sat here to consider the rival claims to the diamond fields and decided in favour of the Griqua chief, Nicolaas Waterboer. There was little more than a shop, a small hotel and a few houses here until the search for diamonds was extended to unoccupied plots in the hamlet. Now diamond digging in the immediate vicinity has almost ceased and the town's economy relies on malt factories, a creamery, the surrounding district's maize production and tourism, which is based on the Sandveld Nature Reserve on the Orange Free State shore of the Bloemhof Dam, and camping and watersport facilities in the Bloemhof Dam Nature Reserve along the Transvaal shore.

BLOEMHOF DAM NATURE RESERVE The 14 000-ha Bloemhof Dam Nature Reserve stretches 136 km eastward from Bloemhof along the northern shore of the Vaal River arm of the dam. More anglers than game-spotters frequent the reserve, although several animal species are protected within its boundary. These include eland, red hartebeest, springbok, black wildebeest, zebra and ostrich. Among the fish to be caught in the dam are carp, barbel, yellowfish and mudfish.

From the crossroads at Bloemhof's eastern exit drive south-westward (SP Christiana) on the R29 and after 49,2 km reach the entrance to the Rob Ferreira Mineral Baths Holiday Resort.

ROB FERREIRA RESORT The imposing Rob Ferreira spa, with a restaurant, cocktail bar and shop, is the focal point of a fine modern resort with many chalets, a large caravan park and picnic sites on lawns along the tree-shaded banks of the Vaal River. In addition to an indoor pool of hot mineralised water that offers relief to rheumatics, an outdoor swimming pool and a paddling pool, the resort offers various sporting facilities, horses to ride and an adjacent game reserve stocked with eland, gemsbok, red hartebeest, blesbok, springbok, impala, black wildebeest, zebra and a few white rhino. The spa was named after Rob Ferreira who, as a member of the Executive Committee of the Provincial Council, promoted the development of public spas in the Transvaal.

Continue 2,3 km westward on the R29 from the Rob Ferreira Resort, turn left (SP Jan Kempdorp, Christiana) into Christiana and reach the first stop street in the town 1,5 km further on.

CHRISTIANA Generally accepted to be named after Christina, daughter of the Transvaal President

136. The grain silo at Hoopstad

Marthinus Pretorius, Christiana was laid out in 1870 on part of the farm Zoutpansdrift. Some people believe that the town owes its name to Christiaan Hattingh, the original owner of the farm. Diamonds have been found in the vicinity since 1872, and there were rushes in 1891 and 1903. There are still important diggings in the district, although its economy is now more agricultural. The first British general to invade the Transvaal in the Anglo-Boer War, Sir Arthur Hunter, crossed the Vaal River at Christiana. There are Bushman paintings (NM) at Stowlands (Stow's Kopje) about 3 km from the town.

At the stop street 400 m from the first reached in Christiana turn left (SP Hertzogville) into Voortrekker Street (R708) and 800 m further on cross the Vaal River back into the Orange Free State. Continue on the R708 and pass the right turn into Hertzogville 40,4 km from the river.

HERTZOGVILLE is one of the country's youngest towns, having been established in 1915 and named after the Boer general and statesman J B M Hertzog, who was the Prime Minister of South Africa from 1924 to 1939.

From the first right turn into Hertzogville continue 1,8 km south-eastward on the R708 to its junction with the R59 (SP Hertzogville to the right and Hoopstad to the left). Carry straight on and continue on the R59, passing left turns to Bultfontein after 1,6 km and 32,2 km. Turn left (SP Dealesville) on to the R64 58,3 km from the R708/R59 junction and drive another 18,1 km to the Dutch Reformed church in Dealesville.

DEALESVILLE John Henry Deale, on whose farm, Klipfontein, the town was laid out and proclaimed in 1899, gave his name to Dealesville, now the centre of a flourishing sheep-farming and maize-producing area. The municipality recovers salt from the large pan on its commonage and exploits as a spa a sulphur spring about 1,6 km from the town.

Drive 300 m south-eastward from the Dealesville Dutch Reformed church and turn right (no SP) to remain on the R64. Pass a left turn to Florisbad after 23,5 km and reach J B M Hertzog Square in Bloemfontein 44,6 km further on, having followed the Charles Street signs from the outskirts of the city.

137. Camping on the shore of the Bloemhof Dam

48

220 km

MOUNTAINS OF THE ORANGE FREE STATE

East of Bethlehem the rolling Orange Free State prairie gives way to a remarkably beautiful mountain landscape, in the midst of which is the Golden Gate, a colossal slash through the Rooiberg's red and yellow sandstone.

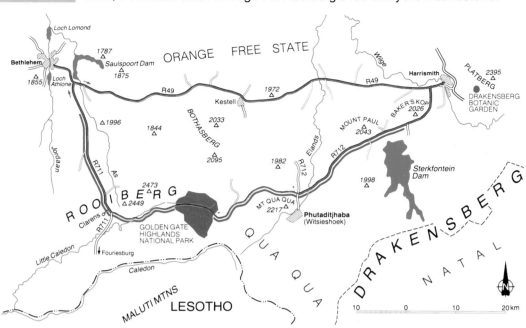

BETHLEHEM, in the scenic eastern Orange Free State, was founded in 1860 on the farm Pretoriuskloof and handed over to the Dutch Reformed Church in 1874. Because the earliest settlers had found that wheat flourished in the area the new village was named after Christ's birthplace, which means 'house of bread'. And to be consistent, the river which flows through the town was named the Jordaan. While Bloemfontein was occupied by the British during the Anglo-Boer War Bethlehem became the temporary capital of the Orange Free State. It is now the centre of a district renowned for its dairy herds and has one of the largest creameries in the country. Other factors in the economy are the maize and other grains produced in the region, flour mills, a furniture factory and a major railway workshop complex, the town being one of the most important railway junctions in the province. It is also a pumping station on the Durban-Johannesburg oil pipeline.

As well as being a centre for visitors to Lesotho, the Golden Gate Highlands National Park and other parts of the Drakensberg, Bethlehem is a popular tourist venue in its own right and has been a winner of the Administrator's Cup for the Free State's best inland resort. There are pleasure resorts at Loch Lomond north of the town, Loch Athlone to the south and at Kloof Park in Pretoriuskloof, where there is also a bird and game sanctuary. At the edge of Loch Athlone a restaurant, built in the form of a Union-Castle liner in traditional red-funnel, lavender-hull livery, is 'equipped' with a number of navigational aids and other maritime relics saved from the *Athlone Castle* when she was scrapped. The Nazareth Mission church, a graceful building of dressed blue ironstone which is now the home of the Bethlehem Museum, was the second Dutch Reformed Mission church to be built in the province. Its exhibits include old farm implements and furniture, harmoniums, barrel-organs and an Edison 'talking machine', Voortrekker clothing and weapons, and a Sharp-Stewart railway locomotive that went into service on the line between Cape Town and Mafeking in 1896. Another fine building is the Town Hall (NM), which is floodlit at night.

From the traffic circle at the eastern end of Church Street in Bethlehem take the R49 exit (SP Durban, Golden Gate). Pass a right turn to

Golden Gate after 6,9 km, take the exit left to Kestell 38 km further on and drive under the R49 into the town.

KESTELL Established on the farms Driekuil and Mooifontein in 1905, Kestell was named after the Reverend John Kestell, an 1820 Settler's son who became a diamond digger, then studied at Stellenbosch and Utrecht and was ordained a Dutch Reformed minister. He served as chaplain to General Christiaan de Wet's forces in the Anglo-Boer War, was appointed Chancellor of the University of Stellenbosch in 1939 and was so venerated a national hero that he is among the few men buried at the foot of the National Women's Monument in Bloemfontein. During one of the bloodiest confrontations of the Anglo-Boer War, the battle of Wagon Hill (see Ladysmith, Tour 59), he tended the wounded and dying of both sides, and his compassion is commemorated by a granite monument at the battlefield. John Kestell was the Dutch Reformed incumbent at Harrismith when the town named after him – now a commercial, educational, church and administrative centre for a prosperous farming community – was established within his parish.

Return to the R49 and continue through rolling grassland and expanses of maize and wheat, passing the 2 043-m rock-topped Mount Paul away to the south about 25 km from Kestell. Ahead is the long, flat-topped 2 395-m Platberg which dominates Harrismith. Pass a right turn to Qua Qua and Bergville 41 km from the Kestell turn-off, turn left (SP Harrismith) after another 2,6 km, cross the Wilge River by a single-lane bridge 500 m further on and drive 900 m to the centre of Harrismith.

HARRISMITH Once an important staging post on the wagon road from Durban to the Kimberley diamond fields and later to the Transvaal goldfields, Harrismith is a town that got off to a false start. In 1848 the popular Governor of the Cape, Sir Harry Smith, gave instructions for a village to be established in the British sovereignty he had proclaimed between the Orange and Vaal rivers. The magistrate he appointed chose a site about 16 km west of present-day Harrismith and called it Vrededorp, but after only a few buildings had been erected it was decided to move the village to the banks of the Wilge River where the water supply was more reliable. Although Sir Harry favoured the retention of the name Vrededorp, others decided to name it in his honour. A blockhouse (NM) on the slopes of the Platberg recalls the

138. Baling hay near Kestell

139. Golden Gate

importance of Harrismith as a British base during the Anglo-Boer War. Of far greater antiquity, a 30-m petrified tree, *Dadoxylon solerosum* of the Triassic Age and estimated to be 150 million years old, is situated in the centre of the town. The resident Brand Park on the Wilge River is an attractive spot, while on the Platberg is the Drakensberg and eastern Free State Botanic Garden, a regional garden under the control of the National Botanic Gardens at Kirstenbosch. A curiosity of Harrismith history is South Africa's

longest recorded Christian name. It was borne by 'Vrees niet, gij wormpje Jakobs, gij volkje Israels! Ik help u, spreekt de Here, en uw Verlosser is de Heilige Israels' Schoeman, who was born here in 1879 and died in 1947. At the behest of his parents, Mr and Mrs H N Schoeman, 'Oom Jacob', as the boy was known later in life, was baptised by the Reverend A van der Lingen in 1879 with the entire text in Nederlands of Isaiah 41:14 – 'Fear not, thou worm Jacob, and ye men of Israel; I will help thee, saith the Lord, and thy redeemer, the Holy One of Israel'.

Drive south-westward out of Harrismith, returning to the R49, and turn right (SP Kestell). Turn left (SP Qua Qua, Bergville) on to the R712 2,6 km further on to curve around the south of 2 026-m Baker's Kop. Pass a left turn to Bergville and Sterkfontein Dam 8,7 km from the R49, and 29,5 km further on pass the left turn to Witsieshoek (SP Qua Qua). After another 600 m pass under a highway which, to the north, is a continuation of the R712. The tar lasts for another kilometre and the road ahead, which at first runs along the northern slopes of 2 217-m Mount Qua Qua, is not recommended for caravans.

MOUNT QUA QUA, a flat-topped sandstone massif which encloses the northern side of a rugged 47 385-ha mountain enclave bordered on the south by the Maluti Mountains, is the habitat of a colony of Cape vultures. Their droppings make the cliffs on the mountain as white in summer as the snow does in winter, hence the name Qua Qua, meaning 'white white'. For many years the enclave was known as Witsieshoek, a corruption of Oetsi (Wetsi), the name of the chief of the Makholoko tribe which dwelt here in the first half of the nineteenth century. Now a homeland, it has taken its name from Mount Qua Qua. The people of Qua Qua are the Bakwena and Balokwa, whose seat of government is at Phutaditjhaba.

Turn left (SP Golden Gate, Clarens) 15,7 km from the R712 and 9,6 km further on reach the eastern entrance to the Golden Gate Highlands National Park.

140. Chickens come to town – a market scene in Bethlehem

GOLDEN GATE HIGHLANDS NATIONAL PARK This nature reserve, which is more remarkable for its scenery than its wildlife, gives access to the highest plateau in South Africa. The twin massifs of multicoloured sandstone that form Golden Gate itself stand on either side of the road along the deep valley gouged through the Rooiberg range over many millions of years by the vigorous Little Caledon River. The valley with its surrounding bluffs, ramparts and weird rock formations in shades of russet, ochre and purple is a paradise of walks, hiking trails and bridle paths. One trail leads from the Glen Reenen rest camp to the crest of the Brandwag, a towering sandstone butte that resembles the prow of a ship of such tonnage that it would dwarf the biggest supertanker afloat. Wherever there is soil – and there is ample on the rolling slopes below the crags – a high annual rainfall ensures a wealth of vegetation to nourish the game with which the park has been restocked. The species include eland, blesbok, springbok, red hartebeest, grey rhebok, oribi, black wildebeest, Burchell's zebra and warthog. The black eagle and the lammergeyer are among the many bird species to be seen. Between them, Glen Reenen (3,7 km from the eastern entrance to the park) and the park's luxury rest camp, Brandwag Lodge (1 km further west), have facilities for campers and caravanners, for a variety of sports and for horse-riding.

Leave the park by the western gate, 7,2 km from the eastern entrance. Continue westward, pass a left turn to Fouriesburg after 17,6 km where the road from the Golden Gate joins the R711, and turn left to Clarens 400 m further on.

CLARENS Snuggling in a glen surrounded by towering sandstone mountains of the southern aspect of the Rooiberg range, Clarens was founded in 1912 and named after the Swiss resort on the shore of Lake Geneva where Paul Kruger, President of the Transvaal Republic, died in exile in 1904. The village is one of the most picturesque in the Orange Free State and, because of the Bushman art in the vicinity, its scenic surroundings and its bracing climate, it has become popular enough to support several holiday farms.

Return to the R711, turn left and drive 28,8 km northwards before forking left (SP Bethlehem) on to the R49. After ascending around the south-western shore of Saulspoort Dam reach the first traffic lights in Bethlehem 6,1 km from the last fork and turn left to the centre of town 800 m further on.

49
280 km

MOUNTAIN ENCLAVE

Because most of Lesotho is mountainous, it does not yet have an extensive network of modern roads, but the roads there are pass through splendid mountain scenery.

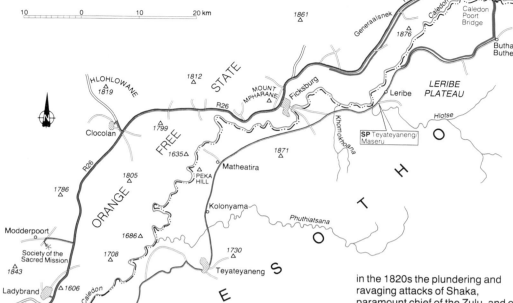

LESOTHO At the end of the sixteenth century this mountainous region was the domain of the Bushmen, but early in the following century migrant tribes and clans started arriving from other parts of southern Africa, some at first intermarrying with the Bushmen and all living in relative peace. Then in the 1820s the plundering and ravaging attacks of Shaka, paramount chief of the Zulu, and of Mantatisi, the warlike chieftainess of the Batlokwa, disrupted the tribal life so recently established. The courageous young chief Moshoeshoe, who had only just been able to withstand assaults on his people at Butha Buthe, moved his entire following at dead of night to Thaba Bosiu, 'the mountain at night', about 20 km south-west of present-day Maseru. This flat-topped mountain with precipitous sides proved to be an almost impregnable stronghold from which he was able to repel not only warring tribes, but later the attacks of the Boers and British. Remnants of other tribes fleeing from the warmongers sought refuge at Thaba Bosiu and together with his original followers were welded by Moshoeshoe into the nucleus of the Basotho nation. Conflict of a different kind ensued, however, as white settlers to the west cast covetous eyes at the narrow fertile plain east of the Caledon River, while the Basotho in turn envied the whites their cattle. The constant border skirmishing and the series of wars which resulted persisted until Britain annexed Basutoland in 1884.

MASERU Although Basutoland was formally annexed only in 1884 it had, at Moshoeshoe's request, been placed under the authority of the High Commissioner at the Cape in 1868. The agent representing the High Commissioner established his 'camp' at Maseru, the 'place of red

sandstone' on the east bank of the Caledon River, the following year, and when the territory was sent its own Resident Commissioner in 1884, Maseru was retained as Basutoland's administrative base. For its first 37 years the capital was little more than an informal village with a few trading stores and churches. From 1905, however, as a result of the pont previously used to cross the Caledon River being replaced by a bridge, Maseru experienced considerable growth. Of the variety of haphazard building styles, old and new, structures that stand out are of modern design but based on traditional forms, such as the church of the Paris Missionary Society, which is modelled on the early beehive-shaped huts of the Basotho, and the thatched craft centres, one of which is in the form of the traditional woven Basotho hat, while the other has the shape of a shield.

From the Caledon River border post at the western limit of Maseru drive 12 km generally northward on the R64 before turning right (SP Ladybrand) on to the R26. Turn left 1,5 km further on and run into Piet Retief Street in Ladybrand.

LADYBRAND See Tour 50.

Return to the R26 by the same route taken into Ladybrand and turn left (SP Clocolan). Pass another turn-off to Ladybrand after 2,4 km and take the left turn to Modderpoort 8,7 km further on. Drive 4,9 km, turn left 1 km beyond the grain elevator and left again after another 300 m.

MODDERPOORT Noted for the sandstone cave rock art and the wealth of stone-age implements in the neighbourhood, Modderpoort is also the site of a cave distinguished not as an art gallery but as a place of worship. Anglican missionaries of the Society of St Augustine used it for about a year in the 1860s until they were able to erect a conventional church. Services are still occasionally held and candles constantly burn in the cave church, although there are now imposing dressed-stone churches at the Modderpoort mission, which falls under the authority of the Society of the Sacred Mission. The cave church is a short walk from the mission, from which permission to visit it should be sought.

Return to the R26, turn left (SP Clocolan) and drive past hills and clusters of trees that break up a rolling plain used for cattle ranching. After 24 km turn left on to the R708 and drive into Clocolan.

CLOCOLAN The name of this town is thought to derive from the white man's pronunciation of 'Hlohlowane', as the 1 819-m

141. A door closes the entrance to the cave near Modderpoort used as a church in the 1860s

mountain 8 km to the north-west was known to local tribes. Clocolan is the centre of the Orange Free State's principal wheat region, which is also noted for its heavy potato and maize yield as well as its fine cattle. The town was established in 1906.

Return to the R26 and continue 29,9 km north-eastward before bearing right (SP Ficksburg, Lesotho) into Ficksburg.

FICKSBURG Lying between the Caledon River and Mount Mpharane, Ficksburg is one of the three towns that were established to defend the 'Conquered Territory', from which the Basotho were driven eastward over the Caledon River in the last of the Basotho Wars. It was named in honour of Johan Fick, Commandant-General of the Orange Free State and a hero of those wars. During the town's early existence each of its citizens was obliged by the authorities to have available at all times a rifle, 200 rounds of ammunition, 5 lb of powder and rations for 10 days. Most of the willow trees that grace the town have grown from cuttings taken from a tree on Napoleon's grave by Methodist missionaries who ministered here. The Old Prison (NM) in the cabbage patch of Ficksburg's modern jail was where one of the town's teachers, Charles Swart, was incarcerated for a week after being arrested on a charge of espionage at the time of the 1914 Rebellion following South Africa's declaration of war against Germany. Swart later became the first State President of the Republic of South Africa. Ficksburg is now an important trade link between South Africa and Lesotho and, with adequate water and labour from the neighbouring sovereignty, an industrial centre of some note. It is also the centre of a district which produces wheat, potatoes and deciduous fruit, including the famous Ficksburg cherries.

Drive north-westward in Fontein Street from its intersection with Kestell Street, turn second right into McCabe Street and after swinging north-westward over the railway line turn right (SP Fouriesburg) on to the R26. Travel 23 km between rock-crested hills and mountains to Generaalsnek, the rendezvous of the generals of two Boer commandos when they joined forces against the Basotho in 1865. At the crossroads 44,8 km after rejoining the R26 turn right (SP Fouriesburg, Lesotho, Clarens) into Fouriesburg.

FOURIESBURG Established on Christoffel Fourie's farm, Groenfontein, and named after him in 1892, Fouriesburg became a stronghold of the Boer forces in the

Anglo-Boer War. It was the last seat of the Orange Free State's republican government and as such was almost completely destroyed by the British army. One of the proud elements of the Boers' 'flying press' – a print shop producing newspapers in a railway carriage as it moved from Kroonstad to Heilbron, Frankfort, Vrede, Reitz and Bethlehem – found its way to Fouriesburg and fell into disuse for a while. Mels Meijer, a Netherlander fighting with the Boers, resurrected it, however, and, without any printing experience, contrived to publish three editions of *De Brandwacht* in Fouriesburg before the press had to be moved several more times, each move being one jump ahead of the British. Meijer printed the tenth and last edition of the newspaper in an open cave and then in a bamboo hut high in Schoemanskloof, north-east of Fouriesburg.

Turn right (SP Butha Buthe) 600 m east of the last-mentioned crossroads, fork left (SP Thabuti) after 800 m and drive 7,6 km, part of the distance through a spectacular mountain gateway, to the most northerly Lesotho border post at Caledon Poort Bridge. Enter Butha Buthe 8,7 km from the border.

BUTHA BUTHE was the stronghold where Moshoeshoe started welding the Basotho into a nation in the 1820s. The name means 'place of lying down', possibly a reference to the lying down and resting that took place after Moshoeshoe persuaded various warring tribes to become reconciled. It could also refer to three nearby hills that resemble reclining lions. Butha Buthe is an undistinguished administrative and commercial village, although its setting among sandstone hills and mountains is splendid.

Turn right (SP Leribe, Maseru) 1 km after entering Butha Buthe and after about 10 km start a 12-km curve around the north-western end of the Leribe Plateau into the fertile valley of the Caledon River. Here intensive farming is practised and there is evidence of diligent efforts to curb the erosion that plagues much of Lesotho. Turn right into Leribe 26,5 km from the right turn in Butha Buthe.

LERIBE Major Charles Bell, one of the four Basutoland magistrates appointed by the British in 1871, was a much-loved and respected figure among the Basotho, who called him Majorobello. In 1877 he moved his seat of office to Leribe, or Hlotse as it was once known, and when the War of the Gun, caused by an attempt to disarm the people of the territory, broke out three years later, the fort he had built

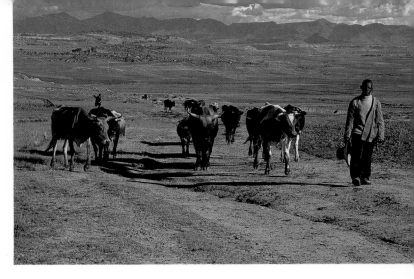

142. Herding cattle along a road between Teyateyaneng and Maseru

there played an important part in the conflict. With complete disregard for its historic significance, the authorities allowed most of the fort to be demolished in 1956, leaving only the tower in the main street. One building that has survived, the oldest in Leribe, is the mud-walled Anglican church built in 1877 by the Reverend John Widdicombe.

Continue southward on the Butha Buthe-Maseru road and keep straight on (SP Teyateyaneng, Maseru) at the three-ways 2,5 km from Leribe. Cross the Hlotse River 3 km further on, the Khomokhoana River after another 8,6 km, and pass the right turn to Ficksburg 2,8 km from the Khomokhoana. In Matheatira, 18,8 km still further, pass the right turn to Gum Tree and reach Kolonyama, where there is a pottery crafts centre, 10,4 km from Matheatira. Cross the Phuthiatsana River 3,3 km from Kolonyama and drive 8,2 km to the right turn in Teyateyaneng to the Handwoven Rugs and Tapestries Factory.

TEYATEYANENG 'TY', as the town used to be called during Lesotho's colonial era by those who could not pronounce its name, has

acquired a reputation among tourists for its weaving industry. This started as an effort by the wife of a Teyateyaneng inn-keeper to provide destitute women and emaciated children with an occupation by teaching them to spin, colour with local vegetable dyes and knot Lesotho mohair into articles of quality for their own profit. Unhappily, she did not live to see the small undertaking in the back yard of the hotel develop into a lucrative industry, with proper factory premises, efficient administration and an eager market. Another magnet that draws tourists to this bustling commercial and administrative centre, which was founded as a magisterial seat in 1886, are several caves and rock shelters with Bushman paintings.

Continue generally south-westward on the Butha Buthe-Maseru road through splendid scenery, scarred by dreadful soil erosion, between maize fields in which the tribal allocations of land are clearly demarcated, and reach the dressed-stone, twin-towered Roman Catholic Cathedral of Our Lady of Victories in Maseru 40 km from Teyateyaneng.

143. The Roman Catholic Cathedral of Our Lady of Victories in Maseru

50
250 km*

THE LESOTHO PLAIN AND 'CONQUERED TERRITORY'

The Lesotho highway runs across a plain between the Caledon River and the Lesotho mountains. West of the river is the 'Conquered Territory' from which the Basotho were driven into their mountain enclave.

*The distance given allows for about 10 km on the Mountain Road.

MASERU See Tour 49.

Take the south-eastern exit from the traffic circle in front of the Cathedral of Our Lady of Victories in Maseru and after 2,1 km pass the left turn to Teyateyaneng, Leribe and Butha Buthe, keeping straight on (SP Roma, Mafeteng, Quthing). Turn left (SP Roma) off the Lesotho highway 11,7 km further on and at St Michael's, after another 12,1 km, turn left (SP Mantsonyane) on to Lesotho's celebrated Mountain Road.

MOUNTAIN ROAD The winding, untarred Mountain Road, which climbs high into the Central Range of Lesotho, demands careful driving in wet weather or in winter when there may be snow, but the scenic splendour through which it passes makes the 96-km drive – or at least part of it – to Mantsonyane amply rewarding. It is intended that

beyond Mantsonyane the road, in places now little more than a track, will eventually be improved to continue what will become the Trans-Maluti Highway eastward across the Central Range to the valley of the Senqu, as the Orange River is known in Sesutho, and then southwards through the Qachasnek border post into East Griqualand in the eastern Cape.

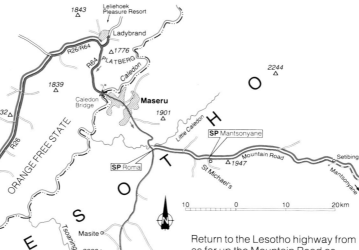

Return to the Lesotho highway from as far up the Mountain Road as time and inclination permit, turn left, pass a left turn to Matsieng after 18 km, pass the right turn to Masite 5,5 km further on and cross the Lerato River after another 3,1 km. Pass another left turn to Matsieng 700 m from the river, cross the Tsoaning River into Motsekuoa 10,2 km further on and travel past the western foothills of the Thaba Putsoa range, with the 'spired' Thaba Ts'oeu in the foreground to the left about 10 km from the Tsoaning River. Pass the right turn to Ha Sephula 19,1 km from this river, reach the first stop street in Mafeteng 6,5 km further on and turn right.

MAFETENG was originally the name of a village on the Caledon River where a Cape Mounted Police base was established in 1871 after the British had assumed control of Basutoland. Refugees from regions plundered and ravaged by the *impis* of Shaka and Mantatisi (see Lesotho, Tour 49) had settled at the place now called Mafeteng, but in 1874 they exchanged their site for that of the police camp on the river. When the mounted police transferred their post and the newly-established magistracy, the name

Mafeteng was transferred to the new location too. The village came under constant attack and was besieged for a time in the War of the Gun in 1880. In the cemetery graves of members of the garrison who were killed during this conflict may still be seen. Mafeteng today is an untidy village of dusty streets, undistinguished shops and a market where there is much designed for the unwary tourist.

At the traffic circle 600 m from the last-mentioned stop street follow the exit SP Van Rooyen's Gate. Pass through the village of Ha Ralintsi after 14,1 km and reach the Van Rooyen's Gate border post 2,7 km further on. At the stop street 7,7 km from the border post turn left (no SP) into Spies Street in Wepener.

WEPENER, with Ladybrand and Ficksburg, was one of the three towns established to protect the 'Conquered Territory' from which the Basotho were driven eastward over the Caledon River in the last of the Basotho Wars. The first plots were granted in 1869 on condition that occupation was immediate. A monument in the town commemorates the man after whom it was named, Commandant Louw Wepener (see Louw Wepener Memorial, Tour 41). Wepener is the centre of an agricultural district producing maize, wheat, sheep and cattle.

Cross the Sandspruit by a single-lane bridge 900 m west of the last-mentioned stop street, turn left 400 m further on, cross the railway after 200 m and turn right (SP Dewetsdorp, Hobhouse, Smithfield) on to the R26/R702 600 m from the railway. Pass the left turn to Smithfield immediately after crossing the Caledon River 6,8 km further on, drive 1,5 km from the river and turn right (SP Jammerdrif, Hobhouse) to remain on the R26. Pass the right turn into Jammerdrif after another 900 m.

JAMMERDRIF The site of large wheat and maize mills today, Jammerdrif, or Jammerberg Drift, on the Caledon River was the scene of the Siege of Wepener in the Anglo-Boer War. In April 1900 General Christiaan de Wet attacked a force of 1 900 troops of the Cape Mounted Rifles and Brabant's Horse under the command of Colonel E H Dalgetty, which was encamped at the drift. The Boer attackers were spurred on by the galling knowledge that Dalgetty's men were mainly Afrikaners from the Cape Colony who were accepting five 'tainted' British shillings a day. However, the colonial force had dug itself in with skill and was able to hold out for 16 days, until Field Marshal Lord

144. Ladybrand's dressed-stone Dutch Reformed church

Roberts' infantry divisions lifted the siege. An attempt was made by the relieving force to trap De Wet, but the wily Boer general with his remarkable sense of timing, direction and confidence evaded capture and returned to the eyrie from which his bold sorties were made.

Continue 28,1 km north-eastward from the Jammerdrif turn-off and turn right (SP Hobhouse). Cross the Leeu River 600 m further on and reach the Dutch Reformed church in Hobhouse 1,1 km from the river.

HOBHOUSE If the unimposing little town of Hobhouse, another wheat, maize and dairy-farming centre, has a claim to fame it is its name, which it was given in honour of Emily Hobhouse. As a result of her philanthropic work among the women and children in British concentration camps in the Anglo-Boer War this courageous woman was regarded by some as infamous but by thousands of others as illustrious. Prominent in pro-Boer circles in Britain, she became secretary of the women's branch of the Conciliation Committee dedicated to averting conflict and, when war was declared, established a relief fund and reported on conditions she found in the concentration camps during a five-month visit to South Africa in 1901. She was reviled by many Britons for her compassion for the enemy but, in spite of being denied further access to the camps and of being deported from South Africa when she arrived for a second visit, she continued her campaign with considerable success. After the war she organised rehabilitative training for Boer women, initiated more relief funds and became so revered among those she sought to succour that after her death in her native Cornwall in 1926 her ashes were brought to South Africa for burial at the National Women's Monument in Bloemfontein. Regardless of whatever gratification she may have derived from her indefatigable humanitarian work, she was never able to subdue her sorrow over the failure of her own people to recognise that one of her principal motives had been to uphold the honour of Britain in its treatment of the wives and children of its enemies.

Return to the R26, turn right (SP Ladybrand) and after 39,6 km turn right again (SP Ladybrand, Maseru) on to the R26/R64. Pass the right turn to Maseru after 12,2 km and turn left into Ladybrand 1,5 km further on.

145. The Caledon River forms the border between Lesotho and the Orange Free State

LADYBRAND was laid out at the foot of the 1 778-m Platberg in 1867 and named in honour of the wife of Sir Christoffel Brand, first Speaker of the Cape Legislative Assembly, and mother of Sir Johannes Brand, President of the Orange Free State. Like Wepener and Ficksburg, it was established specifically to defend the 'Conquered Territory' against marauding Basotho. The town and its district lie in an amphitheatre formed by an imposing crescent of mountains capped by sandstone cliffs in which there are numerous caves with 'galleries' of rock art. People of succeeding cultures lived for many millennia in these caves and the art and vast number of stone implements they left behind make this one of the continent's most rewarding regions for archaeological research. Leliehoek, an area of trees, shrubs and flowers at the northern edge of the town, has been developed as pleasant recreational parkland with a swimming pool. On the way from the centre of town to Leliehoek there is a statue of Antjie Scheepers, a remarkable Voortrekker woman who, after the death of her second husband, spent her last years with her son in the Ladybrand district. First widowed on the Great Trek, this courageous, independent spirit who was noted for her common sense continued the northward journey, brought up the nine children of her first marriage with uncompromising discipline, tended her own cattle all the way to Port Natal with the Trichardt party, and with two other women pioneered a route over one of the mountain chains the party had to cross.

From Ladybrand return to the R64, turn left and drive 12 km to the Caledon Bridge border post at the eastern outskirts of Maseru.

146. Looking down from Lesotho's Mountain Road

CHAPTER FIVE
Natal

LOWER SOUTH COAST AND HINTERLAND

From Port Shepstone a tour of the Lower South Coast of Natal and its hinterland is mostly scenic, particularly through the Oribi Gorge and between Stafford's Post and Magusheni.

PORT SHEPSTONE See Tour 52.

Leave Port Shepstone from the mosque in Escombe Street, travel south for 3,3 km, then turn right (SP Izingolweni, Harding) on to the N2. Turn right again (SP Oribi Gorge) 9,5 km after joining the N2 and 12,6 km further on turn left to the viewing sites (SP Fair Acres Viewing Sites). There is a small charge to go to Fair Acres.

Return to the viewing sites turn-off, turn left to the Oribi Gorge Nature Reserve, and 7,4 km further on turn left again to drive through the Oribi Gorge Pass.

ORIBI GORGE PASS At times the road through the pass becomes all but a tunnel through the luxuriant growth of lofty trees reaching up towards the sunlight, of ferns tumbling down the cliffs in green cascades, and of monkey ropes, palms and creepers. And there can be few sights more exciting than that of a crowned eagle swooping down out of one of the patches of sky visible through the verdant canopy to settle on a high branch and brood over the forest below.

Drive 9,6 km from the turn-off to the nature reserve before turning right (SP Izingolweni, Harding) on to the N2. Bypass Harding and at Stafford's Post, 63 km after

rejoining the national road, keep left (SP Kokstad) to remain on the N2. At the intersection 40,3 km further on turn right to drive 3 km into Kokstad.

KOKSTAD William Dower of the London Missionary Society chose the site for Kokstad in scenic surroundings on the slopes of Mount Currie. He founded the settlement in 1872 and named it in honour of Adam Kok III, the Paramount Chief of the Griquas. Kok was the great-grandson of a slave, Adam Kok I, a good cook – which probably accounts for his surname – who was freed early in the eighteenth century and became a man of considerable influence. Several groups of detribalised Hottentots chose the first Adam Kok to be their leader, a position that was handed on to his descendants. When Adam Kok III became chief in 1837 the tribe was settled at Philippolis but Kok quarrelled with the Cape Government and he and his people moved on. After years of wandering they settled in an area that had been designated no man's land but henceforth became known as East Griqualand.

Kokstad, with its broad streets lined with oaks and water furrows, its bracing climate, the trout-stocked Mzimhlava River which embraces part of the town, and its numerous sporting facilities, has become a popular health and holiday resort. A building of interest is the Griqua National Independence Church which, with its castellated tower, was built by Dower and his congregation and dedicated in 1877.

ORIBI GORGE The Oribi Gorge, carved through a rugged landscape by the Mzimkulwana River, is one of South Africa's most exciting beauty spots. Even the best of photographs cannot induce the vertiginous thrill experienced by anyone standing at the brink of one of the dizzily high walls of this majestic cleft in the earth's surface. The gorge – 25 km long, 5 km wide and in places 400 m deep – and its surroundings comprise a nature reserve alive with a wide variety of birdlife. It is also the home of leopard, blue and grey duiker, bushbuck, monkeys and the oribi antelope from which it takes its name. The road to the viewing sites from the top of the gorge is through private property, but to see to the best advantage such majestic wonders of nature as Baboon's Castle, the Pulpit and Leaning Tower, Ola's Nose, the Sphinx, Lehr Falls, Echo Valley and the Oribi Heads or to venture out on to one of the overhanging rocks is well worth the fee charged.

Return from Kokstad to the N2 and travel southward (SP Mount Ayliff, Umtata), crossing the border into Transkei at Brook's Nek 6,9 km from the Kokstad Interchange. After 6,8 km turn left (SP Bizana, Port Edward) and at Magusheni, after another 35,5 km, turn left again (SP Bizana, Port Edward) on to the R61. Drive 30,7 km further before turning right (SP Port Edward, South Coast). Transkei's casino resort, the Wild Coast Sun, lies on the south bank of the Mtamvuna River, 54 km further on. Remain on the R61, returning to Natal by the C D Mitchell Bridge over the Mtamvuna (Zulu for 'reaper of mouthfuls' because of the crop damage caused when it floods) and drive 4 km northward before turning right to Port Edward.

PORT EDWARD The southern-most of the South Coast resorts, this village is set in luxuriant subtropical forest and fronted by an expansive protected beach. It was named by its developer, T K Pringle, in honour of the Prince of Wales who was to become King Edward VII.

147. 'This is the resting place of Adam Kok III, Paramount Chief of the Griqua people. . .' reads the inscription on this monument in Kokstad

From Port Edward drive the remaining 50 km to Port Shepstone on the R61, branching off on the way to such resorts as Glenmore Beach and Munster, Trafalgar, Marina Beach, Southbroom, Ramsgate, Margate, Uvongo, Shelly Beach and Oslo Beach.

GLENMORE BEACH AND MUNSTER The three scalloped beaches here afford enjoyable bathing, surfing and angling, and there is a walk through pleasant scenery to the mouth of the Tongazi. It was at the mouth of this river that the barque *Ivy*, carrying a cargo of liquor, was wrecked in 1878, and beachcombers from afar were able to indulge in a party of bacchanalian proportions.

TRAFALGAR is an unspoilt village with a splendid beach from which the bathing is excellent.

MARINA BEACH This resort was named after Princess Marina of Kent who came to South Africa in the 1930s. It is situated between two lagoons – at the mouths of the Mkobi and Mhlangulu rivers – and its magnificent stretch of beach, 5 km long and up to 180 m wide, is protected for bathers by shark nets. Marina Beach also has a tidal pool.

SOUTHBROOM With its wide golden beaches and wooded park-like surroundings between two river mouths, elite Southbroom – named after the Wiltshire home of the family of Alfred Eyles on whose farm the resort was laid out – is ideal for those who appreciate rustic serenity, although it has all the attractions and amenities for a happy holiday. Sea bathers are protected from sharks, and there are two tidal pools as well as facilities for boating and waterskiing on the lagoon.

RAMSGATE A resort named with a depressing lack of originality in spite of its charm, Ramsgate affords the visitor a relaxed holiday in surroundings of lush subtropical vegetation which sweeps down to a broad expanse of beach, rocks and sandy coves. There is a tidal pool, bathing in the surf is protected, the angling is good and on the tranquil Blue Lagoon boats can be hired.

MARGATE Also named with no sense of originality, Margate is the mecca for throngs who, preferring their leisure time gingered up with organisation and entertainment in the holiday camp mould, stream from the Witwatersrand to its hotels, caravan parks and camping sites. The fine beach is protected from sharks. It is regrettable that Margate had to forego the distinctive name

of 'Nkongweni' given to it by Hugh Ballance who laid out the resort beside the Kongweni River on land for which he paid only £466 in 1919.

UVONGO, a municipality which includes St Michael's on Sea and Manaba Beach, is set among high, thickly wooded cliffs and lays claim to being one of the most attractive Lower South Coast resorts. The name of the river on which it is situated, Vungu, is derived from the Zulu verb 'vungazela', which means 'make a low rumbling sound'. This the stream does as it plunges over a 23 m waterfall into the beautiful Vungu Lagoon. At Uvongo shark nets provide protection for surf bathers, there is a tidal pool and, at the Thure Lilliecrona Park, boats can be hired for fun on the river. Manaba (Zulu for 'the place to relax') has a rocky front favoured by anglers, a big tidal pool and a skating rink, while at St Michael's on Sea, which also has a tidal pool, there is a splendid beach with protection for bathers.

SHELLY BEACH One of the less developed South Coast resorts, Shelly Beach has a glorious stretch of sand, backed by grass and trees.

OSLO BEACH The names of this hamlet and King Haakon Road, which runs through it, are reminders that the area owes much to its Norwegian settlers. The resort has a sandy beach running down to the sea from dense coastal vegetation.

149. Oribi Gorge

INTO KWAZULU THROUGH THE MZIMKULU VALLEY

Having followed the high eastern 'wall' of the beautiful Mzimkulu River valley, this tour returns to the sea at Park Rynie for a drive along the central stretch of the South Coast.

150. The lighthouse at Port Shepstone, a popular South Coast resort

PORT SHEPSTONE, at the mouth of the Mzimkulu ('big') River, is the administrative, commercial, educational and transport 'capital' of the Lower South Coast of Natal. Its earliest recorded history relates to the reluctant stay of about 300 Portuguese, survivors of the wreck of the *Nossa Senhora de Belem*, which ran aground near the estuary in 1635. The castaways built boats from the wreckage of their ship and managed to sail to Angola the following year. Settlement began only in the latter half of the nineteenth century and the town, named South Shepstone in honour of the highly respected Secretary for Native Affairs, Sir Theophilus Shepstone, was founded in 1867. Improvement of the river mouth for navigation was started in 1880 by engineer William Bazley with the backing of the Aiken family, but the creation of a harbour was left to the marine-minded 246 Norwegian settlers who arrived in 1886. Recognition as a fiscal port was accorded in 1893 when the name Port Shepstone was adopted, but its use as a harbour was of short duration. In 1901 a more reliable form of transport for the sugar, marble and limestone of the district became available with the completion of the railway line from Durban to the town. And in any event, the cost of dredging had become all but prohibitive. Silting has now reduced traffic on this, one of the most impressive stretches of water in Natal, to the sailing and rowing of shallow-draft pleasure boats. The shipping may have disappeared but, with its facilities for holiday-makers, safe bathing in a tidal pool and good fishing spots in beautiful surroundings, Port Shepstone is an attractive resort.

Leave Port Shepstone northwestward on the N2 from the sea end of Aiken Street and after 4,1 km turn left (SP Ixopo, St Faith's). The road runs at first along a corridor of subtropical vegetation and banana groves and then through undulating fields of sugar cane. Where the road forks into three 3,8 km from the N2 take the middle road (SP St Faith's) to pass St Faith's after 42 km and Highflats 42,8 km further on. The gravel road ascends rapidly into hilly country and overlooks deep valleys with vast numbers of Zulu settlements

clinging to the slopes. After running along the high eastern 'wall' of the Mzimkulu River valley, with one splendid vista unfolding after another, the route winds deep down to the river and then high up the other side of the valley. And while the road may be rough, the splendour of the scenery makes the drive well worthwhile.

HIGHFLATS has a station on the narrow-gauge railway which meanders a tortuous course from Donnybrook in the foothills of the Drakensberg through Ixopo to Esperanza south of Umzinto, with a branch line to Mandonela near the Umzimkulu border post between Natal and Transkei. The line is never far from the road between Highflats and Umzinto and one often sees a train being hauled by a huffing, puffing, straining and occasionally tooting steam engine.

At Highflats turn right (SP Umzinto) on to the R612 and after 57,8 km reach the left turn to the Vernon Crookes Nature Reserve.

VERNON CROOKES NATURE RESERVE The fauna in this reserve, which comprises three wooded valleys and a tract of higher grassland, includes eland, nyala, impala, bushbuck, zebra, wildebeest, porcupine, mongoose and black-backed jackal, while the wild flowers among the flora present a magnificent display in spring.

From the reserve drive 4,3 km further eastward on the R612 to Umzinto.

UMZINTO, whose name is derived from the Zulu 'um enzi we zinto' which means 'the kraal of things (achieved)' or 'kraal of achievement', is a major South Coast industrial town and the centre of one of the principal sugar-producing regions. It was around Umzinto that a group of Javanese, the first Asians brought to work as labourers in Natal's sugar industry, were employed.

From Umzinto continue 6,7 km eastward on the R612 before crossing the N2. After another 1,3 km cross the old South Coast Road (R102) into Park Rynie.

PARK RYNIE An attractive village surrounded by beautifully wooded countryside and canefields, Park Rynie was named after Rynie Hoffman, the wife of a partner in the firm which bought and developed the land on which the resort is situated. A whaling station operated here between the two world wars but all that remains is a breakwater and a landing ramp which is now found useful for the launching and hauling up of fishing boats. The spot is also popular with surfers.

51. Village scene at St Faith's, on the road between Port Shepstone and Highflats

IFAFA BEACH is a charming village and popular angling resort on the southern bank of the lagoon at the mouth of the Fafa ('sparkling water') River. Bathers in the sea are protected from sharks and the lower reaches of the river are suitable for boating.

MTWALUME This resort south of the Mtwalume River boasts excellent angling opportunities and an attractive beach which has anti-shark protection.

HIBBERDENE In an alluring setting, Hibberdene is the gateway to the Lower South Coast. The popular, tree-fringed beach at the mouth of the Mzimayi River affords protected bathing, and there are pleasant walks in the area. A tidal pool and various sporting facilities are among the amenities that have been provided.

UMZUMBE is almost hidden among palms and other subtropical coastal vegetation between the Mzumbe and Injambili rivers. The beautiful Pumula Beach, where there are anti-shark nets, is one of the attractions of this resort, and the adjacent coastline is popular with anglers, many of whom are kite-fishing experts. Umzumbe is also the starting point of pleasant walks through the subtropical vegetation along this unspoilt stretch of coast.

BANANA BEACH has a fine sweep of sandy beach and is popular with surfers who, together with bathers, are protected from sharks.

BENDIGO is four resorts in one, its components being Sunwich Port, Anerley, Southport and Sea Park. Sea bathers at both Sunwich Port and Southport are protected from sharks, and Sunwich, separated from Anerley by the Domba River and lagoon, has a rock-enclosed bay which ensures superb surfing. The scenery around Anerley is captivating, with a wide variety of plantlife growing alongside numerous streams. Southport and Sea Park are separated from each other by the picturesque Mhlangamkulu River.

UMTENTWENI A wide stretch of sandy beach and the mouth of the lovely Mtentweni River with its lagoon contribute to the charming surroundings of Umtentweni, where it is possible to swim either in a tidal pool or, protected from sharks, in the sea. Fine angling spots, such as Shaka's Rock, Shad Alley and Splash Rock, and pleasant walks through the countryside are among the resort's other attractions.

Leave Park Rynie southward on the R102 and after 9 km reach the left turn to Kelso, Pennington and Umdoni Park.

KELSO, PENNINGTON AND UMDONI PARK On a stretch of coast boasting several tidal pools and productive angling spots, these adjacent resorts cater specially for caravan enthusiasts for whom there are a number of parks. On the sylvan estate of Umdoni Park, which he had bought from the Pennington family, the sugar baron Sir Frank Reynolds built a gracious, white-gabled mansion and bequeathed it to the nation as the official holiday home of South Africa's prime ministers. Sir Frank's bequest included £50 000 a year for the maintenance of Botha House, as the mansion is known, and its surrounding parkland. In 1951 the South African Government offered the use of the mansion to King George VI for recuperation after his lung cancer operation, and extensive preparations were actually under way when the monarch died.

Return to the R102 from Pennington and drive 2 km westward and then 2,9 km southward to join the N2 for the remaining 45,5 km back to Port Shepstone, turning off left where the signposts indicate to visit resorts such as Ifafa Beach, Mtwalume, Hibberdene, Umzumbe, Banana Beach, Bendigo and Umtentweni.

152. Eland in the Vernon Crookes Nature Reserve

53 270 km START OF AN EPIC RIDE

It was along the route that subsequently came to be called the South Coast Road that Dick King set off on the first leg of his historic ride from Durban to Grahamstown in 1842.

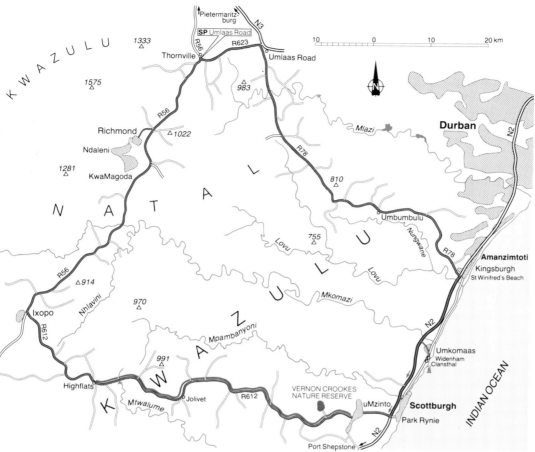

SCOTTBURGH Even unpopular public figures are sometimes honoured by having places named after them. Sir John Scott, who as Lieutenant-Governor of Natal was unsympathetic to the colony's representatives and clashed with them over matters of policy, had the first Natal town south of Durban named in his honour when it was surveyed in 1860. For some time after the establishment of Scottburgh coasters called to discharge and load cargo, but there was little protection in the bay and when the South Coast railway line was constructed marine activity ceased – except, until the early 1960s, for the launching and landing of fishing craft. Now Scottburgh, with its grass-covered 2,5-km beachfront backed by coastal forest, is almost exclusively a holiday resort, although a sugar mill and a rayon factory nearby, to which visits can be arranged, represent industrial activity. Surfers and swimmers are protected from sharks and, in addition to a filtered sea-water swimming bath, there are numerous sheltered rock pools, a miniature railway system which runs along the seafront, a paddling pool and several good angling spots.

Leave Scottburgh southward on the N2 and after 4 km take the exit SP Umzinto, Highflats on to the R612. Continue westward, passing Umzinto after 6,7 km and the right turn to the Vernon Crookes Nature Reserve (see Tour 52) after another 4,3 km before reaching Jolivet 51 km from the N2.

JOLIVET This hamlet, which consists of little more than a post office and a station on the narrow-gauge railway between Esperanza and Donnybrook (see Highflats, Tour 52), was named in honour of Charles Constant Jolivet. The Roman Catholic Bishop of Natal from 1874 to 1903, he founded several schools and missions, including Marianhill, the biggest Roman Catholic mission in South Africa.

Continue on the R612 and pass Highflats 29 km further on. Reach the R56 at Ixopo 92 km from the N2.

IXOPO The name 'Ixopo' is either of onomatopoeic origin, simulating the squelchy sound of a foot being withdrawn from the mud of a marsh, or derived from the Zulu word for a marsh 'ixhaphosi'. The town was laid out in its pleasing surroundings on the Ixopo River in 1870 and named Stuartstown after Marinus Stuart, the magistrate at the time, but was later given its Zulu name again. It is one of the more

153. Scottburgh

54. A Bhaca woman visits Richmond in the colourful garb of her people

important stations on the narrow-gauge railway line to Donnybrook.

From Ixopo take the R56 (SP Richmond) and drive 41 km north-eastward to the left turn into Richmond.

RICHMOND was founded in 1850 by British settlers from Beaulieu, the Duke of Buccleugh's estate at Richmond, Surrey, who were brought to Natal under the scheme organised by the Irish emigration promoter Joseph Charles Byrne. The settlers originally called their new home Beaulieu but subsequently changed the name to Richmond. The district has plantations of wattles and other timber, produces dairy products and has the double distinction of having two honey-flow seasons a year and of growing citrus fruit out of season. Visitors occasionally have the fortune to see women of the Bhaca tribe who have come to town to register their marriages. The brides deck themselves out for the occasion in colourful costumes of elaborate beadwork, for which the Bhaca are famous.

Return from Richmond to the R56, turn left (SP Pietermaritzburg) and drive 21,3 km before turning right (SP Umlaas Road) on to the R623. After 11,2 km turn right again on to the R78 to drive 43 km to Mbumbulu.

MBUMBULU The name of this rural village which serves as the administrative centre of the area means 'the place of the round knoll'. The knoll in question, the 619-m Mbumbula, is on the left 5 km further along the road.

Continue eastward on the R78 for 23 km, turn left into Almond Road and cross the N2 into Kingsburgh at St Winifred's Beach.

KINGSBURGH comprises the delightful holiday resorts of Doonside and Warner Beach on either bank of the Little Manzimtoti River; St Winifred's Beach; Winklespruit; and Illovo Beach and Karridene which are separated from each other by the Mzimbazi River. Doonside was originally a railway siding named Middleton after the engineer who constructed the South Coast line, but it was renamed to avoid confusion with Middleton in the Cape. Its present designation is a derivation of 'Lorna Doone', the name given by a man from Devon to his home overlooking the station. Karridene was named after Lieutenant-Colonel Walter Karri-Davis, the mining magnate who at about the time of World War I built a sanatorium for Rand miners suffering from silicosis; Warner Beach after T A Warner who surveyed it for a settlement – which failed – for pensioners and impoverished people; and Winklespruit – a corruption by English-speaking people of

Winkelspruit – after a temporary shop ('winkel') which was set up on the beach in 1875 to sell groceries salvaged from the wrecked schooner *Tonga*. Kingsburgh as a whole was named in honour of Dick King, the first leg of whose epic ride to Grahamstown was along this stretch of coast. An allusion to his heroic feat is the crest of the town's coat-of-arms, a representation of the Dick King equestrian statue on Durban's Esplanade. King, who landed in Algoa Bay as a boy with the 1820 Settlers and subsequently moved to Durban, was a lieutenant in the Port Natal Volunteers when the British garrison at Congella was besieged in 1842 by Voortrekkers intent on establishing a republic in Natal. He undertook to carry to Grahamstown despatches appealing for relief and, accompanied for half the distance by a young Zulu, Ndongeni, covered the 960 km of dangerous terrain on his horse Somerset in the amazing time of 10 days. Reinforcements were shipped from Port Elizabeth immediately, the Durban garrison was relieved and King, who was hailed as the saviour of Natal, was rewarded with a grant of land at Isipingo.

The area around Doonside and Warner Beach is ideal for outdoor recreation such as bathing and skiboating, walking through picturesque surroundings and boating on the Little Manzimtoti. Winklespruit is noted for its tiled sea-water pool and its charmingly laid-out picnic and camping sites, rock-angling opportunities and delightful walks. Illovo Beach and Karridene share the attraction of the wide Mzimbazi Lagoon where the fishing is good and powerboating is permitted. There is also a choice of swimming in the lagoon, a tidal pool or in the sea. Sea bathers at Warner Beach, Winklespruit and Illovo Beach are protected from sharks.

Leave Kingsburgh southward on the N2 to drive the remaining 26 km to Scottburgh, turning off where the signposts indicate to visit the resorts of Umkomaas, Widenham and Clansthal.

UMKOMAAS In the days before roads, bridges and the railway made overland transport along the South Coast possible, sugar-transporting coasters had to negotiate the tricky entrance at the mouth of the Mkomazi River, where the settlement of Umkomaas, originally known as South Barrow, developed. Now a popular resort, Umkomaas has as its special claim to fame one of the most scenic golf courses in the country. Other attractions are the waves surfers love to ride, a tidal pool which is illuminated at night, productive angling spots and the Mkomazi Lagoon.

WIDENHAM Primarily a residential town, Widenham also offers caravan enthusiasts pleasant camping sites against grass-covered slopes.

CLANSTHAL Although there is a lighthouse on the hill overlooking Clansthal for the specific purpose of warning ships of the Aliwal Shoal – Natal's most prolific deep-sea fishing ground 4 km out to sea – the new United States express cargo vessel *Aimee Lykes* ran aground here in calm weather in 1970. Had there been foul weather one might have been able to say it's an ill wind that blows nobody any good, for the damage caused by the shoal enabled South Africa's ship repair industry to show its mettle. The *Aimee Lykes* was back at sea after repairs in Durban, which included dismantling and resetting her engines, in far less time than American marine engineers had estimated would be necessary.

155. Zulu basketware at a market between Kingsburgh and Umkomaas

54

160 km

TO THE VALLEY OF A THOUSAND HILLS

Following part of the arduous course run by participants in the annual Comrades' Marathon, this tour includes stops at vantage points for views across the majestic Valley of a Thousand Hills.

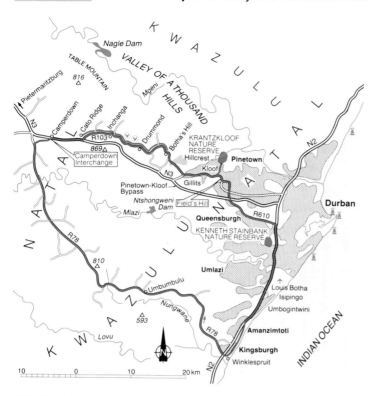

KINGSBURGH See Tour 53.

From the Winklespruit Interchange in Kingsburgh take the R78 (SP Pietermaritzburg) and drive 64,3 km westward and then north-westward before turning right (SP Camperdown), passing Umbumbulu (see Tour 53) 22,1 km along the way. Drive another 3,5 km to join the N3 at the Camperdown Interchange.

156. Drummond lies on the brink of the Valley of a Thousand Hills

CAMPERDOWN Until 1865 Camperdown was one of the estates of John Vanderplank, father of South Africa's wattle industry. It was probably because Vanderplank was steeped in maritime history, having been a master mariner before he settled in Natal, that he chose for his estate a name recalling the 1797 battle in which Admiral Adam Duncan of the Royal Navy defeated the Dutch fleet under Admiral Jan Willem de Winter off the tract of low sandy hills known as Camperdown on the coast of

Holland. Although Vanderplank had himself come from 'down under' – having sailed his schooner, the *Louisa*, from Tasmania in 1837 – it was his brother Charles who in the 1860s brought from Australia the first seeds of the black wattle (*Acacia mearnsii*) to be planted in South Africa. Since John Vanderplank's first plantings at Camperdown many millions of rands' worth of wattle bark and bark extract produced in this country have been used by the tanning industry both at home and abroad.

Continue 4,4 km eastward from Camperdown on the N3 (SP Durban) and at the Cato Ridge Interchange veer left on to the R103.

CATO RIDGE is a railway centre and junction named after George Cato, a descendant of a French Huguenot silk-spinning family, the Catons, who had settled in London. Cato came to South Africa with his parents in 1826 and as a young man moved to Natal where he became one of the pioneers of Durban and in 1854 the city's first mayor. He proved to be a man of great business acumen, achieving distinction as a merchant, ship-owner, legislator and churchman. It was he who, with his brother Christopher, rowed Dick King across Durban Bay when the intrepid horseman set off on his ride to Grahamstown in 1842 (see Tour 53). Due north of Cato Ridge is Natal's Table Mountain, known to the Zulu as 'emKhabathini', 'the place of the giraffe thorn tree'. This flat-topped mass of sandstone, which stands sentinel at the head of

the Valley of a Thousand Hills, was the refuge of the Debe people when they were being harassed by the Zulu. Their presence brought only disrepute to the mountain, for in their bitter struggle to survive they became cannibals, using hunting dogs to track down their victims.

From Cato Ridge continue eastward on the R103 from which, as it runs along the edge of the escarpment where Inchanga, Drummond and Botha's Hill are situated, there are signposted turn offs to the left to vantage points affording splendid views of the Valley of a Thousand Hills. While motoring along this section of the R103 – the old main road from Durban to Pietermaritzburg – have a care for the runners in the 86-km Comrades' Marathon who, with blistered feet and aching muscles and joints, pound up and down its exacting gradients every year.

INCHANGA The name 'Inchanga', a corruption of 'ntshangwe', the Zulu word for a long-bladed knife or sharp ridge, is appropriate for a place which, like Cato Ridge, Drummond, Hillcrest and Botha's Hill, is situated on the ridge forming the southern 'wall' of the Valley of a Thousand Hills. The ornamental shrubs which adorn many of the country's railway stations are supplied from the extensive South African Transport Services nursery at Inchanga.

DRUMMOND owes its name to F C Drummond, a London director of the Natal Land and Colonisation Company which bought up large tracts of the colony in the 1870s for the purpose of speculation, settling immigrants and exploitation. The town's present claim to fame is that it is one of the spots which afford magnificent views of the majestic Valley of a Thousand Hills, one of the most beautiful regions of Natal. The valley has been sculpted over millions of years by the Mgeni River which, strengthened by its many tributaries, feeds the Midmar Dam, roars spectacularly over the Howick Falls, runs into the Albert Falls Dam, tumbles immediately afterwards over the Albert Falls and then flows into the Nagle Dam before it reaches the sea just north of the city of Durban.

BOTHA'S HILL This village, from which there are also splendid views of the Valley of a Thousand Hills, takes its name from the Voortrekker Philip Rudolph Botha who once lived there. He was a grandfather of South Africa's first Prime Minister, General Louis Botha.

Drive 30,4 km from the Cato Ridge Interchange to the Gillitts Interchange and join the N3 (SP

Durban). After 3,7 km take the left turn to Kloof on to the Old Main Road and pass the Kloof Civic Centre on the right. Continue to the railway station and immediately east of it turn left across the bridge over the line and left again into Church Street. Turn first left into Abelia Road, first right into Kloof Falls Road and continue for 3 km to the Krantzkloof Falls and Nature Reserve.

KLOOF The name of this elite residential area is an abbreviation of the original Krantzkloof which was chosen because of the town's situation on the edge of a deep gorge between high cliffs carved by the Molweni River. The old name is retained, however, in the Krantz-kloof Nature Reserve, 448 ha of natural forest in the gorge which is inhabited by bushpig, reedbuck, duiker, bushbuck and a wealth of birdlife. The Molweni ('the place of high cliffs') tumbles into the ravine over the pretty Kloof Falls.

Leave Kloof eastward on the N3, follow the route down Field's Hill and then take the first exit to Pinetown on to the Old Main Road. Drive 1,5 km to the intersection with St John's Avenue in the centre of the town.

PINETOWN A bustling residential, commercial and industrial centre, Pinetown was laid out in 1849 on a farm owned by A K Murray who had acquired it from its first owner, Andries Marthinus Laas. The new town was named in honour of the Lieutenant-Governor of Natal at the time, Sir Benjamin Pine.

Leave Pinetown at the southern end of St John's Avenue, cross the N3 to join the R610 and drive 13,2 km to the N2, bypassing Queensburgh on the way.

QUEENSBURGH Although a separate municipality comprising several residential areas, Queensburgh constitutes part of Durban's urban sprawl. The most remarkable feature of this built-up zone is an 80-ha wilderness area with nature trails and picnic sites from which one may spot wildlife such as impala, zebra, bushbuck, duiker, nyala, smaller mammals and a variety of birdlife. The Kenneth Stainbank Nature Reserve is named in honour of the benefactor who gave the public this 'green lung' in 1963.

Turn right on to the N2 and drive 14 km to Isipingo.

ISIPINGO Isipingo Beach, a marine estate with a 5-km seafront and facilities for bathing and boating, has been reserved for Indian people since 1963. The resort was originally developed on part of the

157. A kraal occupied by traditionally dressed Zulus is a tourist attraction near Valley of a Thousand Hills

158. Valley of a Thousand Hills

estate granted to Dick King as a reward for his epic ride to Grahamstown (see Tour 53). King lived in the simple house, in front of which still stands the tamarind tree he planted, from 1850 until his death in 1871, and from it he ran his sugar farm and managed the small sugar mill he eventually owned. The house, on the South Coast Road, bears the bronze plaque of the National Monuments Council. Isipingo Rail, the village 2 km inland from the seafront, was founded by pioneer sugar planters.

Continue southward on the N2 and turn left into Amanzimtoti at the interchange 4,9 km from Isipingo.

AMANZIMTOTI 'Kanti amanz'a mtoti', the Zulu warrior chief Shaka is reputed to have said when encamped alongside the Manzimtoti River and his remark, meaning 'the water is sweet', gave rise to the name of the river and the resort now situated at its mouth. The beach, known as Inyoni Rocks, is protected by anti-shark nets and full-time professional life-savers are on duty throughout the year. A filtered sea-water swimming pool offers alternative bathing facilities,

and there is also a paddling pool. Skiboats are launched from the beach, and boats hired near the mouth of the Manzimtoti can be rowed upstream to tea gardens where refreshments are available. The river banks are attractively lined with subtropical flowers and dense bush teeming with birdlife. Many varieties of birds can also be seen in the Inyoni Sanctuary in Umdoni Road which leads off the freeway at the northern entrance to the resort.

From the lagoon at Amanzimtoti drive 5 km southward on Kingsway to return to Kingsburgh.

55
250 km
DURBAN'S HINTERLAND

From the urban sprawl between Durban and the historic city of Pietermaritzburg a drive across the Mgeni River valley to the Natal Midlands and back along the North Coast offers an ever-changing scene.

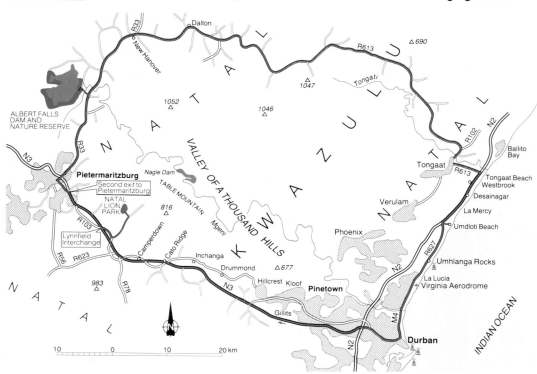

DURBAN See Tour 63.

Drive on to Durban's Western Highway – which becomes the N3 – from the beachfront end of West Street, cross the N2 after 7,7 km and continue on the N3, bypassing Westville, Pinetown, Kloof, Gillitts, Cato Ridge and Camperdown. Take the Lynnfield Park exit 55,4 km from the N2 and immediately afterwards turn right on to the R103. Turn left 1 km from the interchange and 5,3 km further on turn left again to reach the Natal Lion Park.

NATAL LION PARK The Natal Lion Park, established by the Chipperfield circus family and now run by the Boswells, is one place where there is a certainty of being able to see members of this great cat family. The park, with its 10 km of road up and down hilly scrubland and savanna, has a variety of other indigenous game, while there is also a zoo which houses many exotic animals.

Return to the N3 and turn right, driving another 10,3 km to the second exit to Pietermaritzburg. Veer left into Durban Road and after 3 km turn right into Commercial Street in the centre of the city.

159. The Old Pavilion in Pietermaritzburg's Alexandra Park

PIETERMARITZBURG As the first major party of Voortrekkers to reach Natal made its way down the slopes of what is now known as World's View, west of Pietermaritzburg, the travellers beheld a pleasant, green tract of land between the Msunduze River and one of its tributaries, the stream they subsequently named the Dorpspruit. They chose this fertile triangle for an encampment, and the village established by those who decided to stay was named after the Great Trek leaders Piet Retief and Gerrit Maritz. Following the Battle of Blood River in December 1838 the village became the seat of the Volksraad of the Voortrekker Republic of Natalia and was proclaimed a town in February 1839. Careful planning has been evident from the town's earliest days, and the orderliness of its core, around Market Square, is thanks to Commandant Piet Greyling who laid out a grid of eight broad streets intersected by six others. Furrows along the streets conducted water from the Dorpspruit for irrigation of the plots, on most of which thatched and whitewashed homes were built to create what was, by all accounts, a delightful settlement. Pietermaritzburg's status as capital lasted only until 1842 when Britain annexed Natal. In 1857, however, it was reinstated as capital of the colony and is to this day provincial capital of Natal.

From the outset Pietermaritzburg has been a leader in commerce and, as a major educational centre, it is the home of several faculties of the University of Natal as well as numerous schools and colleges. In spite of recent industrialisation, it is an appealing city of great natural beauty and charm, enhanced by luxuriant public and private gardens, an abundance of trees and many gracious old buildings whose survival is the subject of obvious civic concern. The Church of the Vow (NM), built in 1841 in terms of the covenant made by the victors of Blood River before they joined battle, stands at the north-eastern end of Market Square. After being replaced by a bigger church in 1861 it served successively as a school, smithy, mineral water factory, pharmacy and tearoom, but since 1912, having been bought for the nation and restored, it has been a Voortrekker Museum. At the other end of Market Square, on the site of the building where the Volksraad deliberated, is the imposing City Hall (NM), reconstructed in 1898 after being destroyed by fire when it was only five years old. It is said to be the largest all-brick building in the world. Another national monument recalling the city's Voortrekker origins is the road (now disused but still discernible) which the pioneers followed down World's View to the Msunduze valley.

Relics of the British regime include what was Government House (NM) in Longmarket Street, the home of several governors of the colony, and now part of the Natal Teachers' Training College; Fort Napier, south-west of the city, a garrison base after the British annexation of Natal and now part of a mental hospital; the Garrison Church near the fort; the Natal Parliament building (NM) in Longmarket Street, which has become the Natal Provincial Administration's headquarters; St Peter's Church in Church Street, completed in 1857; and Macrorie House, displaying period furniture, which was opened to the public in 1971 after purchase and restoration by the Simon van der Stel Foundation. It was once the home of Bishop John Colenso – whose views brought about the schism between the Anglican Church of the Province and the Church of England in South Africa – and of Bishop William Macrorie.

From the Pietermaritzburg City Hall drive northward along Church Street on to the R33. After 20,8 km turn left to the Albert Falls Dam and 1 km further on left again to the public resort.

ALBERT FALLS RESORT AND NATURE RESERVE The horse-shoe-shaped cliff over which the Mgeni River tumbles at the Albert Falls is in a pleasant sylvan setting, although part of the small hydro-electric installation below the

160. Albert Falls

with red, salmon pink and yellow poinsettia, bougainvillea of every shade, red-hot pokers, cannas and oleanders.

TONGAAT See Tour 63.

Turn right on to the R102 and drive 3,7 km southward before turning left on to the R613 again to travel 6,3 km to Tongaat Beach.

TONGAAT BEACH affords excellent sea bathing and angling and has a tidal pool. Sea bathers are protected by an offshore reef.

From Tongaat Beach continue southward on the N2 for 10 km and turn left to Umdloti Beach.

UMDLOTI BEACH is a pleasant, largely unspoilt resort with a rock-enclosed bathing pool, attractive beaches and rocky outcrops from which the fishing is good.

Leave Umdloti Beach on the R627 and drive 7,3 km to Umhlanga Rocks.

cascade is somewhat detracting. A picturesque suspension bridge at the end of a forest path leading to the falls, where optimists once panned for gold, collapsed under the weight of an overlarge party of visitors in 1983 and has been replaced by a more robust structure. The land surrounding the 3 012-ha Albert Falls Dam immediately above the cascade is a pleasure resort and nature reserve in which game such as oribi, blesbok, springbok, reedbuck, impala, duiker and zebra may be seen. Boating and fishing are allowed on the dam but swimming is discouraged because of possible bilharzia infection.

Return to the R33 from the resort and turn left (SP New Hanover) to drive 14 km to New Hanover.

NEW HANOVER In 1848 Jonas Bergtheil brought a party of North German settlers to Natal to cultivate cotton. The area north of Pinetown which they pioneered they called Neu Deutschland, although the name was subsequently Anglicised to New Germany. Their cotton project failed, but the industrious immigrants took to general farming and some moved to this region, where the German language is still commonly spoken. Today more wattle is produced in the New Hanover area than anywhere else in Natal, although an increasing amount of sugar cane is also being planted.

Leave New Hanover travelling eastward on the R613 and drive 91,9 km to reach the R102 north of Tongaat. As the R613 approaches the R102 it runs through canefields lined at certain times of the year

UMHLANGA ROCKS Not long ago Umhlanga Rocks comprised little more than an enchanting camp site and hotel tucked away in subtropical forest above the beach. In recent years, however, it has mushroomed into what some Natalians call the Bermuda of South Africa, a resort of high-rise buildings and almost every amenity demanded of a fashionable maritime playground. The name of the resort is taken from the reeds, 'hlanga', with which the foreshore used to be strewn after flooding of the Ohlanga River. Long sandy beaches afford every opportunity for bathing and surfing while the many rocky outcrops make excellent spots for anglers after salmon, shad and garrick. An attractive tea garden is the home of an extensive collection of 'talking' birds from all over the world.

From Umhlanga Rocks continue southward on the R627, which becomes the M4, and return to the Snell Parade in Durban, passing Virginia Aerodrome after 5,9 km.

VIRGINIA AERODROME, Durban's base for light aircraft, is named after Virginia Cheron, a prominent Natal singer of the early 1900s whose Mauritian father, Melidor Cheron, once owned the land. It was Virginia's third husband, Ancrum McCausland, who built the first hotel, the Virginia, at Umhlanga Rocks.

161. Umhlanga Rocks

56
380 km*

GATEWAY TO LESOTHO

From Howick, with its spectacular waterfall, a road runs south-westward to Underberg, one of the gateways to the Drakensberg, and to the ancient Sani Pass, the highest mountain pass on the African continent.

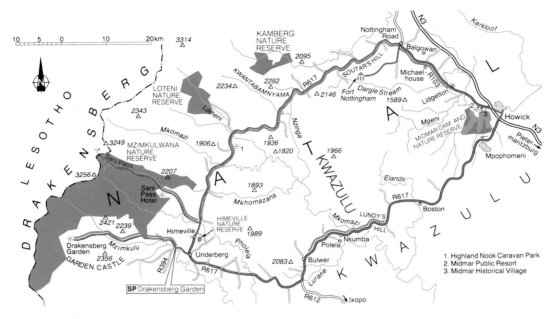

* The distance given allows for about 10 km beyond the Sani Pass Hotel.

162. The Mgeni River plunges 95 m over Howick Falls

HOWICK Until the middle of the nineteenth century Voortrekkers and early English settlers used a ford at Allemansdrif, about a kilometre upstream of the waterfall known to the Zulu as 'Kwa Nogqasa', 'the place of the tall one', and now known as Howick Falls. Because it was not an easy way to cross the Mgeni River, a more convenient ford was chosen immediately above the 95-m high waterfall, and in 1850 the government bought part of the property near the falls from its owner James Archbell, a retired Wesleyan missionary. A village was established and named in honour of the Secretary of State for the Colonies, Viscount Howick, later Earl Grey. As traffic along this inland route from Durban increased, Howick assumed importance as a staging post and now has a population of about 15 000. At the end of World War I the South African Rubber Company's first factory, which uses power from a small hydro-electric plant at the falls, was set up and since then industrialisation has been steady. But it is the Mgeni's spectacular plunge in a lush, green setting – one of the country's most beautiful natural phenomena – for which Howick is famous. To prevent despoliation the falls and the surrounding 32 ha were proclaimed

a national monument in 1951. An expansive picnic spot, a tearoom and a parking area right at the viewing point are located just above the waterfall, but for a different view a steep path to the riverbed below the falls rewards anyone energetic enough to undertake the climb, which is arduous both down and up. Numerous people have died at the falls, the first recorded being in 1851, when the 12-year-old son of Howick's first ferryman lost his hold on the horse he was leading through the river and was washed over the cascade.

From the library in Howick's main street drive southward, following the signs to Pietermaritzburg. Cross the Mgeni River 500 m from the library and, after another 1,4 km, pass the right turn to Midmar Dam before turning right (no SP) 2,1 km further on. After 300 m turn right again (SP Orient Park, Bulwer) on to the R617 to drive south-westward in and out of the fragments of KwaZulu. After 34,1 km pass the hamlet of Boston, cross the Elands River 300 m further on and pause at the top of Lundy's Hill 12 km from the river to view the magnificent panorama of the Mkomazi Valley to which the road now descends. Cross the Mkomazi (Umkomaas) River 22 km from the Elands River and reach the Bulwer Hotel 17,7 km further on. Continue through Bulwer – named after Sir Henry Bulwer, Governor of Natal from 1882 to 1885 – on the R617, cross the Lurane River 4,3 km from the hotel and 7,5 km further on breast one of the foothills of the Drakensberg for a breath-taking view of the main range ahead in the west, with the peak of Garden Castle prominent. Cross the Pholela River 20 km from the Bulwer Hotel and 18,2 km further on reach the right turn in Underberg to Himeville.

UNDERBERG Situated in well-watered grassland at the foot of the Drakensberg, Underberg is an appropriately named village. It is not only a junction from which roads branch out to several mountain resorts, but also a popular place in its own right, especially with trout anglers.

From the intersection of the R617 (Underberg's main street) and the R394 drive north-westward (SP Drakensberg Garden, Boesmansnek, Swartberg) on the R394 and after 4,1 km turn right (SP Drakensberg Garden) to drive up the Mzimkulu River valley. About 10 km from Underberg the rock formation at the summit of the 2 239-m Bamboo Mountain, south of which the road will pass, looks like a colossal lizard. On the other side the road passes the 2 356-m Wintershoek Peak before crossing the Mzimkulu River 26,3 km from

Underberg and reaching Drakensberg Garden 7,2 km further on.

DRAKENSBERG GARDEN
Deep in the foothills of the mighty range in a combination of splendid scenery and exhilarating atmosphere, Drakensberg Garden is a delightful resort at which simply to relax in a lush, green, tranquil setting, swim, fish for trout or embark on walks, hikes, climbs or horse-rides into the mountains.

Return to the intersection of the R617 and R394 in Underberg and turn left (SP Himeville, Sani Pass) on to the R617 to drive 5,3 km northward to the museum in Himeville's main street.

HIMEVILLE
Named in honour of Sir Albert Hime, the road engineer who became Prime Minister of Natal in 1889, Himeville is another centre of superb trout-fishing country and a pleasant resort at which to be based for trips into the Drakensberg. The Himeville Museum is housed in a fort built in 1899 in which the wives and children of farmers in the area could take refuge from the recalcitrant Griquas, although defence of the structure was never necessary. The well-preserved building complex became a prison in 1902, was used as such until 1972 and now houses numerous exhibits reflecting local history. The 105-ha Himeville Nature Reserve is reached by turning eastward from the museum.

Continue north-eastward through Himeville and 3,5 km from the museum turn left (SP Sani Pass) to ascend 11,6 km through a rolling landscape to the Sani Pass Hotel.

SANI PASS
The hotel, from which lead walking trails to some fine rock art, also offers facilities for bowls, tennis, golf, swimming and horse-riding. At a point 2,6 km further on the road enters the 22 751-ha Mzimkulwana Nature Reserve which abounds in flora and provides a habitat for several antelope and bird species, the latter including in particular raptors such as the martial eagle, black eagle, lammergeyer, Cape vulture and jackal buzzard. The road continues to climb the foothills of the Drakensberg and by the time it reaches the bottom of the Sani Pass 23 km from Himeville the traveller has ascended 600 m. The following 14 km up the pass, the most spectacular into Lesotho and the only route from the east, entails a further 600 m rise over steep gradients, loose stones, solid rock and potholes, with dizzy drops alongside, sharp turns and numerous streams to ford. Indeed, so forbidding is the route that a notice 1,8 km from the entrance to

the Mzimkulwana Reserve warns that from that point drivers use the road at their own risk, while the last part of the climb into Lesotho is actually prohibited other than in a four-wheel-drive vehicle. Safaris in such transport are arranged from the Sani Pass Hotel and Himeville for parties who wish to indulge in the thrilling experience of travelling through magnificent scenery to the top of the pass. Indigenous people used this high-altitude route for centuries, and in 1912 the Basutoland Administration pioneered a bridle path for pack animals conveying supplies into Lesotho and wool, mohair, peas and other products the other way. It was first negotiated by a motor vehicle in 1949.

Return to the R617 from as far up the Sani Pass as one's nerves and the prohibition on ordinary vehicles permit, turn left and after 6,5 km pause for another panoramic view on the left, with The Holm (2 207 m) in the foreground. Cross the Mkomazana River 8,7 km from the Sani Pass turn-off, then descend into the deep wide valley of the

Mkomazi and cross the river 8,5 km further on. Drive 6,1 km before passing the Highland Nook Caravan Park, from which there is a magnificent view of the Lotheni River valley far below. Descend to the valley, cross the river 4,9 km further on and pass the left turn to the Loteni Nature Reserve after another 1 km. After a season of rain the gentle contours of the Drakensberg foothills appear to be upholstered with light green plush which has been brocaded with the darker green of thickets. Climb the eastern side of the valley on to an eastward-stretching spur of the Drakensberg, with the 1 936-m hump of Carter's Hill to the south, and cross the Nkoleni River 19,8 km from the Lotheni and the Nzinga River 2,5 km further on. Continue on the R617, crossing the Rooi Draai River 6,1 km from the Nzinga, the Amanzinyama River 1,7 km further on, and finally descending from the Drakensberg foothills by way of Soutar's Hill. In the village of Nottingham Road 87,1 km from the Sani Pass turn-off turn right and take the right turn to Fort Nottingham 500 m further on.

164. Drakensberg scenery on the way to the Sani Pass

FORT NOTTINGHAM
About 14 km from Nottingham Road are the ruins of Fort Nottingham, to which is attached the bronze plaque of the National Monuments Council. It was built in 1856 and manned by a unit of the 45th Regiment to protect the farmers in the area from the marauding Bushmen who descended from their caves in the Drakensberg to steal cattle. The fort was also a base for military operations against the Hlubi leader, Chief Langalibalele, when he defied colonial authority in 1873.

Return to the junction in Nottingham Road, turn right and after 400 m turn right again on to the R103. After another 10,2 km pass the right turn to Michaelhouse, 200 m further on the left turn to the village of Balgowan and 8,4 km still further pass through the hamlet of Lidgetton. All are situated in undulating farmland grazed by prize cattle and horses and patched with occasional clumps of eucalyptus trees and indigenous forest, the valleys between the low hills providing courses for clear streams interrupted by babbling cascades. From Lidgetton continue 12,8 km south-eastward and turn right to the Midmar Resort.

MIDMAR PUBLIC RESORT NATURE RESERVE
This 2 831-ha resort on the northern shore of the Midmar Dam has facilities for both land and water sports, a camping site, accommodation in chalets, a restaurant and riding trails as well as a park in which there are rhino, various antelope, zebra and wildebeest.

Return to the R103 and 400 m east of the turn-off to the resort turn right to the Midmar Historical Village.

MIDMAR HISTORICAL VILLAGE
This 'living museum' consists of some old Natal buildings which have been moved to the site as well as replicas of others. There are, for instance, replicas of a Victorian-style railway station with rolling stock at the platform, of the Eshowe branch of the Natal Bank Ltd, the tollhouse at which riders and vehicles entering Durban by way of Berea Road were levied, a Victorian dwelling, a corrugated iron Hindu temple once used by the Indians of Groutville and – original but high above the Midmar Dam and dry – the Durban tug *J E Eaglesham*.

Return from the village to the R103, turn right and after 2,7 km turn left to cross the N3 200 m further on. Turn left again 2 km from the N3, cross the Mgeni River after 1,4 km and drive another 500 m to the Howick Library.

57

185 km

BARRIER OF UPLIFTED SPEARS

Estcourt is a convenient starting point for excursions to the mountain range the Zulu call Qathlamba, the 'barrier of uplifted spears'.

ESTCOURT Originally called Bushman's Drift because this was the name of a ford across the Bushmans River at this point, Estcourt was laid out in 1848 and renamed in 1863 in honour of T H S S Estcourt, the member of the House of Commons who had sponsored the immigration of the area's early settlers. A year before the town was laid out a unit of the 45th Regiment had been sent to Bushman's Drift to protect the farmers along the river from the depradations of cattle-thieving Bushmen. Rough breastworks of stone were constructed on a hillock just south of the river, opposite Saailaer where Gerrit Maritz had repulsed the rampaging Zulu *impi* intent on slaying every Voortrekker in Natal after the murder of Piet Retief in 1838. After the alarm caused by Langalibalele's defiance of colonial authority in 1873 the Estcourt breastworks were replaced by a more substantial sandstone fort with twin towers which was named after Lieutenant-Colonel A W Durnford, officer commanding the force that had been sent to deal with the recalcitrant Hlubi chief. Fort Durnford, having served various purposes since the region became peaceful, is now a museum. Because of its situation on the main route from Durban to the Transvaal, Estcourt grew rapidly and now has several major industries, some of which – and particularly the meat-processing factory famous for its bacon and sausages – are based on the farming activities of the surrounding countryside.

Drive north-westward along Albert Street from its intersection with Harding Street in Estcourt (SP N3, Central Berg), passing the left turns to Pietermaritzburg and Ladysmith on the N3 after 9,7 km and 9,9 km respectively. Continue for 11,6 km before turning left (SP Draycott, White Mountain) on to gravel. Cross the railway at Draycott siding after 900 m, drive up a rugged pass between two fragments of KwaZulu on to a great grassy plain where there is a wonderful 180° view of the central part of the Natal Drakensberg, and reach the White Mountain Resort 24,8 km from the railway.

WHITE MOUNTAIN RESORT The White Mountain Resort nestles in seclusion between two mountains – in the west the 2 153-m Manzimahle and in the east the 1 983-m Ntabamhlope, which in Zulu means 'white mountain'. There is a delightful guest farm with

sporting facilities, a small dam for boating and angling, and horses to ride to the numerous beauty spots in the area, while the Bushmans River, which rises near the resort, is a joy to trout fishermen. Hikes organised at the resort include a climb up Ntabamhlope, from the summit of which there are splendid views of the surrounding landscape. Other attractions in the vicinity include a waterfall accessible by car, one of several South African cascades known as the Bridal Veil; The Camel, a group of rocks on the slopes of Ntabamhlope which resembles a 'ship of the desert'; Pigeons' Pool, a pretty tarn of clear mountain water; and, south of Ntabamhlope, the 305 m-deep Skeleton Canyon, which is said to derive its gruesome name from the bones of a Zulu *impi* that was annihilated in it.

165. Fort Durnford at Estcourt

Turn right (SP Giant's Castle) 200 m south of the White Mountain Resort and 3,7 km further on right again to drive 5 km to Hillside, a Natal Parks Board camping site and base from which to set out on horse-riding or trout-angling expeditions. Return to the turn-off to Hillside, turn right and after 8 km cross the Bushmans River. Turn right at the T-junction 200 m further on in the KwaZulu village known as Mahlutshini and travel alongside the pretty Bushmans River. After rain the river can be spectacular, although the road at such a time demands concentration and a reliable vehicle. Reach the entrance to the Giant's Castle Game Reserve 11,5 km after crossing the river.

GIANT'S CASTLE GAME RESERVE It is said that 40 percent of the rock art discovered in South Africa is in the Giant's Castle Game Reserve – which includes the

3 314-m peak from which it takes its name – and in the Ndedema Gorge below Cathedral Peak. At the Bushman's Cave Museum in a rock face below Giant's Castle there are, indeed, some 700 rock paintings as well as a collection of replicas of Bushman artefacts that have recently been discovered, life-like models of the people who inhabited these mountain fastnesses until a century ago and a tape-recorded lecture on their history and culture. The reserve abounds in wildlife such as eland, bushbuck, blesbok, oribi, red hartebeest, reedbuck, mountain reedbuck, grey rhebok and klipspringer, black wildebeest, black-backed jackal and baboon, as well as some leopard and smaller predators such as the serval and caracal. In addition to a wealth of indigenous flora – of about 800 flowering species, 63 are ground orchids – the birdlife is prolific and includes the black eagle, martial eagle, lanner falcon, giant kingfisher, orange-breasted rockjumper, Natal sugarbird and lammergeyer. The world's only hide from which the lammergeyer can be observed is in the reserve. Easy and more arduous walks, hiking trails and horse trails lead through the magnificent scenery, and there is also ample scope for mountaineering and trout angling.

Return the 11,3 km from the entrance to the reserve to the T-junction in Mahlutshini, turn right and drive past 2 000-m Hlatikulu to the south about 16 km further on. Turn left (SP Mooi River) 19,4 km from Mahlutshini to head away from the mountains across a wide plateau of rolling grassland used

166. The Bushmans River, which rises on the slopes of Giant's Castle, flows towards Estcourt

for cattle ranching. After 12,5 km pass a left turn to the Moor Park Nature Reserve and Estcourt, another left turn to Estcourt 4,6 km further on and after 18,9 km reach the Argyle Hotel in Mooi River.

MOOI RIVER The town of Mooi River is of relatively recent origin, having been laid out on the farm Mooirivier – once owned by Jacobus Nicolaas Boshoff who was to become the esteemed second President of the Orange Free State – and proclaimed a township in 1921. Boshoff lost his post as principal clerk at the Graaff-Reinet Magistrate's Court through overstaying his leave at the end of a visit to the Natal Voortrekkers. He threw in his lot with his holiday hosts and, as a result of his flair for administration, became both chairman of their Volksraad and Pietermaritzburg's first *landdrost*. After the annexation of Natal he joined the British service and was Master of the Supreme Court when he accepted the presidency of the Orange Free State in 1855. Once more his administrative ability came to the fore, he created order in the hitherto chaotic civil service and, as

President, commanded both affection and respect. The settlement on the farm Boshoff once owned – on the 'beautiful' river which rises in the foothills of the Drakensberg and flows through a green fertile valley with extensive irrigation before joining the Tugela River – has grown into a town

serving the stockbreeding community of the district. Its industries produce cheese, bacon, textiles and treated skins and hides. With its bracing climate, sporting facilities and good trout water, Mooi River is another of the popular Natal Midlands pleasure and health resorts.

At the intersection 400 m from the Argyle Hotel in Mooi River turn left (SP Pietermaritzburg, Estcourt) into Claughton Terrace and pass the left turn to Estcourt on the N3 after 1,8 km and the right turn to Pietermaritzburg 200 m further on. Turn left at the T-junction after another 1,2 km and drive the remaining 27,7 km on the R103 back to Lorne Street in Estcourt.

167. The Bushman's Cave Museum in a rock face below Giant's Castle

58

325 km

AMPHITHEATRE SPLENDOUR

The colossal Amphitheatre, an arc in a wall of basalt cliffs flanked by two majestic peaks, is the focal point of the Royal Natal National Park, one of the most splendid of the numerous Drakensberg nature reserves.

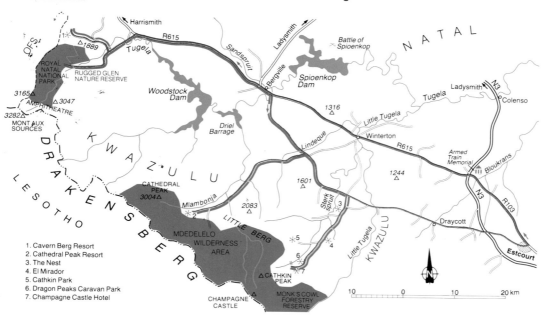

1. Cavern Berg Resort
2. Cathedral Peak Resort
3. The Nest
4. El Mirador
5. Cathkin Park
6. Dragon Peaks Caravan Park
7. Champagne Castle Hotel

ESTCOURT See Tour 57.

From Estcourt's Civic Buildings in Harding Street head north-eastward and out of town on to the R103 to drive 19,7 km to the spot where Winston Churchill was taken prisoner in the Anglo-Boer War.

ARMOURED TRAIN MEMORIAL The wording on this memorial to the right of the road reads: 'This marks the spot where the armoured train

was wrecked and the Rt Hon Winston Churchill captured by Boer forces, Nov 15th 1899.' Colonel Charles Long, commanding the Estcourt garrison, had ordered regular patrols by an armoured train of the railway between his base and Colenso. Being unaccompanied by mounted troops – 'inconceivable stupidity', as General Sir Redvers Buller described the patrol – the train steaming between Chievely and Frere was a sitting duck for the

field guns of General Louis Botha's commando. By putting rocks on the line just north of the rail bridge across the Bloukrans River, the Boers halted the locomotive and derailed all three of the train's wagons. Churchill, on board the train as war correspondent of the *Morning Post*, was among the 58 Britons taken prisoner.

168. The Amphitheatre in the Royal Natal National Park

Turn left (SP Winterton) off the R103 300 m north of the memorial and right (SP Winterton, Bergville, Berg Resorts) 2,4 km further on to cross the N3 on to the R615. Drive across a grassy plain of dairy farms and maize fields and reach the post office in Winterton's main street after 22,4 km.

WINTERTON Originally known as Springfield, the village of Winterton on the Little Tugela River was renamed in 1910 in honour of H D Winter, the Secretary for Agriculture in Natal at the time. It is the centre of an agricultural area important for the large-scale production of dairy products, while the streams which are a feature of the mountainous landscape afford trout anglers infinite pleasure.

Drive straight through Winterton on the R615, passing a left turn to Cathedral Peak and Champagne Castle 100 m from the post office and crossing the Little Tugela River 300 m further on. The right turn 800 m from the river leads to Ladysmith and Spioenkop Dam, north of which is the hill of the same name from which General Sir Charles Warren's force was driven in January 1900 by General Louis Botha after 243 Britons had been killed and 1 257 wounded or captured in one of the most furious battles of the Anglo-Boer War. Continue past the Spioenkop Dam turn-off and 18,9 km further on pass another left turn to Cathedral Peak before reaching the southern entrance to Bergville on the right, 22,2 km from the Winterton post office.

BERGVILLE Another gateway to beautiful mountain resorts, Bergville, at the confluence of the Tugela River and the Sandspruit, is as close to the towering Drakensberg escarpment as Estcourt. The town, which was laid out in 1897 on the farm Klein Waterval owned by retired mariner Captain Wales, is the centre of another maize and dairy-farming region and has a factory producing evaporated and condensed milk. In the grounds of the Bergville Magistrate's Court stands the Upper Tugela Blockhouse (NM), which was built by the British in the Anglo-Boer War and is now a Moth Shellhole.

Return from Bergville to the R615 by the same access road, turn right (SP National Park, Oliviershoek Pass, Harrismith), after 200 m pass the second right turn into Bergville and, at the crossroads 100 m further on, the right turn to Ladysmith on the R616. Turn left (SP National Park, Mont aux Sources) 28,9 km further on, and after another 7,4 km reach the right turn to the Cavern Berg Resort. The

name is taken from nearby Cannibals' Cavern, which is said to have been inhabited by man-eating people in Shaka's time. From here paths lead to fern forests and other attractive spots and there are facilities for swimming, bowls, tennis and horse-riding. Cross the Tugela River 9,5 km from the turn-off to the Cavern Berg Resort and reach the entrance to the Royal Natal National Park after 200 m.

ROYAL NATAL NATIONAL PARK

The Royal Natal National Park and the contiguous Rugged Glen Nature Reserve, which have a combined area of more than 8 000 ha, incorporate what is generally acknowledged to be the most magnificent mountain scenery of the northern part of the Drakensberg, the most famous feature being the vast Amphitheatre between the 3 165-m Sentinel in the west and the 3 047-m Eastern Buttress. South of the Sentinel the 3 282-m Mont aux Sources, one of the highest mountains in southern Africa, marks the beginning of the Tugela River's journey across Natal to the Indian Ocean. A short distance from its source the river cascades 853 m in three stages over the edge of the Amphitheatre, forming the spectacular Tugela Falls. Expeditions in the area – for which guides may be engaged – have to be undertaken on foot or on hired horses. Of the many routes from which to choose one of the most thrilling is to the summit of Mont aux Sources, which affords a breathtaking spectacle of panoramic splendour over both Natal – with the 8-km long Amphitheatre in the foreground – and Lesotho's seemingly endless mountains. The last part of this excursion entails a chain-ladder ascent up the steep rock face. The Royal Natal National Park has the province's biggest trout hatchery, and there are facilities for angling in the crystal-clear streams, which also afford hot, weary hikers and climbers many an opportunity for a cooling dip or refreshing drink of unpolluted water. The fauna of the Royal Natal Park and the Rugged Glen Reserve, which is dominated by the 1 889-m Camel's Hump, include klipspringer, bushbuck, mountain reedbuck, grey rhebok, grey duiker, hares, porcupine, baboon and black-backed jackal, while among the 184 bird species recorded are the black eagle, Cape vulture and lammergeyer. Because there is so much for the energetic to see and do in the Royal Natal National Park, those undertaking this tour from Estcourt may choose to take two days over it, spending a night at one of the park's hotels, its caravan park or the Tendele hutted camp, or in any of the various types of accommodation at resorts still to be reached, such as Cathedral Peak, The Nest, El Mirador, Cathkin Park and Champagne Castle.

Return from the Royal Natal National Park to Bergville on the R615, bypass the town and turn right (SP Cathedral Peak) 300 m after crossing the Tugela River just east of it. After 14,7 km turn right again (same SP) for the 31-km drive through beautiful scenery, the last part of it up the Mhlambonja River valley, to the end of the road below Cathedral Peak.

CATHEDRAL PEAK

The 3 004-m Cathedral Peak dominates a skyline of mountains popular with climbers which includes, from north to south, The Bell (2 918 m), Outer Horn (3 005 m), Inner Horn (3 017 m), The Column (2 926 m), The Pyramid (2 914 m), Cleft Peak (3 281 m) and Ndumeni Dome (3 285 m) with the Organ Pipes below it. Part of the attraction of these peaks is the challenge they offer, and several experienced climbers have fallen to their death in this part of the Drakensberg. A resort at the eastern foot of Cathedral Peak has an hotel, camping site and facilities for swimming, sport and riding. Well-maintained paths lead to such attractions as Rainbow Gorge, Doreen Falls, Mushroom Rock and the Oqalweni Fern Forest.

Return the 31 km along the Cathedral Peak road, turn right and, after driving 13,7 km south-eastward, turn right again (SP Cathkin Park, Dragon Peaks, Champagne Castle). Continue 21,5 km to the Monk's Cowl Forestry Reserve at the foot of the 3 181-m Cathkin Peak, from which there is a pleasant walk to the beautiful Sterkspruit Waterfall and to the south-west of which towers the 3 377-m Champagne Castle.

On the way to the forestry reserve pass at 7,3 km The Nest, an hotel in exquisite surroundings with pleasant accommodation in rondavels and a stable of saddle horses; at 11,2 km El Mirador, another hotel with facilities for sport and horses for riding; at 11,3 km the Moth National Shrine at Mount Money; at 12,2 km the right turn to Cathkin Park where there is an hotel with sporting facilities and a swimming pool as well as a 15-ha lake for boating and angling, streams in which to bathe or catch trout, and paths leading to another fern forest and other beauty spots; at 15,7 km the right turn to the Dragon Peaks Caravan Park and the Drakensberg Boys Choir School, where the choristers sing to visitors late in the afternoon on Wednesdays; and, just before the end of the road, the Champagne Castle Hotel.

CHAMPAGNE CASTLE

As in the other parts of the Natal Drakensberg there are in the Champagne Castle region numerous bridle paths for walking and riding, clear streams to fish and facilities for a variety of sports. The region is another favoured by mountaineers, and there is a base camp for climbers at the head of the gorge leading up to one of the most difficult Drakensberg peaks to scale, the 3 261-m Monk's Cowl, between Cathkin Peak and Champagne Castle. To the north of Champagne Castle the ridge known as the Dragon's Back ends in the extraordinary 2 408-m Gatberg, so named because of the enormous hole through it. To the Zulu it is 'Ntunga', 'the eye'.

Return the 21,5 km from the Monk's Cowl Forestry Reserve, turn right (SP Estcourt) and after 6,4 km pass the right turn to the Injasuti Resort 32 km away on the western slopes of Champagne Castle. Pass the right turn to Draycott 12,2 km further on, cross the N3 after another 11,7 km and run into Albert Street in Estcourt to reach its intersection with Harding Street 9,8 km from the N3.

170. A memorial to those killed in the Boer attack on an armoured train near Frere in 1899

59

450 km

SOME NATAL BATTLEFIELDS

Tranquil and beautiful as the Ladysmith countryside may be, there were times when it was the scene of bitter warfare – between Zulu and Afrikaner, between Briton and Zulu, and between Afrikaner and Briton.

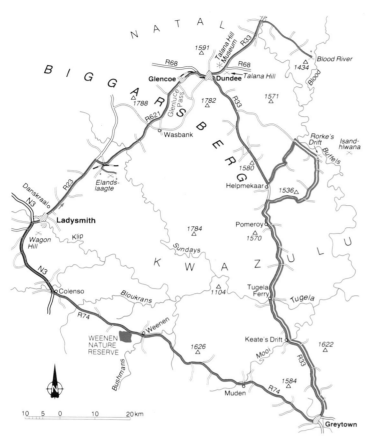

observance of the Day of the Covenant. But it was the Siege of Ladysmith in the Anglo-Boer War that gave the town world prominence. From 2 November 1899 to 28 February 1900 Ladysmith's 12 000-strong colonial garrison and many civilians, including some 250 children, were beleaguered by the Boers and subjected to severe privations, typhoid fever and constant shelling. The garrison made no effort to break out and, with one exception, the Boers made no major attempt to storm the defences. The exception was an attack on Wagon Hill (NM) and Wagon Point at the western end of the British forward fortifications on Platrand, a long, 200-m high ridge west of the town. In fierce fighting the Boers were repulsed with heavy loss, among those killed being their leader, Commandant Cornelis de Villiers.

From the Ladysmith Town Hall drive 900 m north-eastward in Murchison Street, turn right (SP Newcastle, Dundee) into Alfred Street and left (SP Dundee, Glencoe) into Newcastle Street (R23) 200 m further on. After 22,9 km turn right (SP Elandslaagte, Glencoe) on to the R621 and 2,5 km further on right again (SP Elandslaagte Battlefield). Cross the railway line after 1,3 km and 200 m beyond it turn left (SP Elandslaagte Battlefield) to drive 4 km on a rough road to the battle site.

BATTLE OF ELANDSLAAGTE
On 21 October 1899, 10 days after the outbreak of the Anglo-Boer War, a Boer force consisting of the Johannesburg Commando and the German and Hollander Corps was attacked by three British battalions led by General John French. The thousand or so Boers, who with only three field guns were no match for the 1 630 infantrymen, 1 314 cavalrymen, 552 gunners and 18 guns of the British force, were routed when 400 shouting, stabbing and slashing dragoons and lancers galloped among them inflicting such heavy losses that they scattered or surrendered. Their leader, General J H M Kock, was wounded and died in captivity nine days later.

Return from the battlefield to the R621, turn right and at the crossroads 18,1 km further on carry straight on. Drive about 15 km

through fine ranching country before climbing the Biggarsberg range by way of the Glenluce Pass. Turn left (SP Glencoe) to remain on the R621 16,7 km from the crossroads and reach the Glencoe Town Hall in Karel Landman Street 1 km further on.

GLENCOE, a coal-mining centre and railway junction with important railway workshops, was laid out at the Biggarsberg Junction in 1921 and renamed after the Argyllshire town whence some of the early colliers had come. There are numerous stock farmers in the country surrounding the attractive little town, where considerable attention is paid to landscaping and gardens.

Continue north-eastward in Karel Landman Street, following the road out of town, and after 7,2 km turn right (SP Dundee) on to the R68. Drive 1,8 km further to the traffic circle in the centre of Dundee.

DUNDEE Thomas Paterson Smith, the farmer who laid out Dundee in 1882 and named it after his birthplace in Scotland, was the first to exploit on any scale the high-grade coal deposits close to the surface in Natal. The town is now the centre of one of the two principal coalfields in the province.

From the Dundee traffic circle drive north-eastward in Victoria Street on to the R33/R68 and after 3 km turn left to the Talana Hill Museum, where the origins and development of coal-mining, brick-making, glass manufacture and confectionery in Dundee's first hundred years are illustrated. Near the museum is the neat little cemetery with a memorial on which are recorded the names of the British killed in the Battle of Talana Hill.

BATTLE OF TALANA HILL
On 20 October 1899 Talana (Zulu for 'little shelf') Hill was the scene of the first battle of the Anglo-Boer War. In a fierce engagement between a British force from Dundee, commanded by Major-General Sir W Penn Symons, and the Wakkerstroom and Utrecht commandos, under the command of General Lukas Meyer, the British drove the Boers from their position on Talana Hill, the latter losing 105 dead and wounded. It was a Pyrrhic victory, for although the British took the hill, they won nothing. After being shelled by artillery fire from another Boer force they withdrew to Ladysmith, leaving 51 dead, including their general and several other senior officers.

Return to the R33/R68, turn left and after 3,3 km pass the right turn to Nqutu on the R68. Turn right (SP Dejagersdrif) on to gravel after

LADYSMITH dates from 1847 when the village of Windsor was established on the Klip River and named after the trader George Windsor. The town, which was proclaimed three years later, was renamed in honour of the wife of Governor Sir Harry Smith. Lying on the main route from Durban to the Transvaal, it became a major railway centre and junction, and now has one of the largest and best-equipped marshalling yards in the country. Moreover, rich coal

deposits in the vicinity have led to the town becoming highly industrialised, and it has manufacturing or processing plants producing textiles, clothing, canvas, nuts and bolts, and bricks. Ladysmith has played a significant role in South Africa's history. It was at Danskraal, 4,6 km north-east of the town, that the Voortrekkers are said to have camped the week before the Battle of Blood River in 1838 and made their celebrated vow which resulted in the

171. Inscriptions left by cooks Hatch and Galley who took part in the Battle of Wagon Hill

Continue through Greytown on the R74 and pass through the village of Muden, Natal's major citrus centre, 27,7 km further on. Cross the Bushmans River after another 39,9 km and turn right into Weenen 400 m beyond the river.

WEENEN, whose name means 'weeping', was established in 1838 after the murder of Piet Retief's party and the subsequent Zulu attacks on Natal laagers, and is the second oldest settlement in the province. The local museum, where relics of the Voortrekkers are exhibited, is housed in a building dating from the town's first year. The district is one of Natal's major vegetable-producing regions.

Return to the R74, turn right and drive 29,4 km to the entrance to Colenso.

another 18,2 km, cross the Buffels River 1,2 km further on and reach the scene of the Battle of Blood River 18,5 km from the Buffels.

BATTLE OF BLOOD RIVER After the murder of Piet Retief's party at Ungungundlovu on 6 February 1838 and the subsequent *impi* attacks on Voortrekker laagers in Natal, Andries Pretorius arrived from the Cape to organise the 'Winkommando' ('Victory Commando'). When scouts reported the advance of a huge Zulu force on 15 December the commando of 470 men formed a laager on the bank of the Ngome River, tied the wagons together and set cannon in the only two openings. The Zulus, whose numbers were estimated at 12 500, attacked at dawn the following day and the Voortrekkers – who had made a covenant that if the Almighty granted them victory they would observe the day as a Sabbath and build a church as a memorial for future generations – opened fire with their muzzle-loaders and flintlocks. Wave after wave of assegai-wielding warriors stormed the laager, and each was repulsed. When the force of the hour-long final attack began to weaken Pretorius sent out a few hundred horsemen to put the survivors of the *impi* to flight. More than 3 000 Zulu bodies were left behind, but only three Voortrekkers had been wounded. The commando had proved that Dingaan's mighty forces could be defeated. From that day the river has been known as Blood River, and a granite monument by Coert Steynberg in the form of a wagon stands on the battlefield (NM), as does an enclosure of replica wagons drawn up in the same formation as Pretorius' laager.

Return from the battlefield to Dundee, turn left from Victoria Street into Wilson Street (no SP), drive 500 m south-eastward on the R33 and fork left. Pass a left turn to Rorke's Drift after 13,2 km and turn left (SP Rorke's Drift) 24,6 km further on. After another 18 km turn right (SP Rorke's Drift) and then left (SP Rorke's Drift) 5,1 km still further. The Rorke's Drift battlefield is 300 m along this road.

BATTLE OF RORKE'S DRIFT
What has been described as one of the most glorious exploits in British colonial history was enacted at Rorke's Drift on 22 January 1879. The British camp at Isandhlwana, 11 km away, had been overwhelmed by Zulu warriors earlier in the day and when two survivors brought news of the disaster the 110 men of the garrison at Rorke's Drift, under Lieutenant John Chard, barricaded and loopholed the Swedish mission buildings they had taken over. The 4 000-strong Undi *impi* swooped on Rorke's Drift at 4.30 pm, set fire to the building being used as a hospital and sustained their attack in the face of the garrison's rifles and bayonets throughout the night. At 4 am they withdrew, leaving some 300 comrades dead, while 17 men of the garrison were killed. Chard and 10 other members of the garrison which had held out until dawn were awarded the Victoria Cross for gallantry. A relief map at the scene of the battle, where the outlines of the mission buildings are picked out with low walls of rock, depicts the event.

Return the 300 m from the battlefield to the Rorke's Drift road, turn left and after 3,1 km pass the left turn to Fugitives' Drift where, in an effort to carry the colours of the force at Isandhlwana to safety, two courageous standard-bearers named Coghill and Melville lost their lives in the Buffels River. Turn right (SP Helpmekaar, Greytown)

172. Round the base of the memorial at Elandslaagte are gravestones of Boers killed here in 1899

14,1 km further on, and left back on to the R33 after another 14,5 km. Continue 82,9 km before turning right (SP Pietermaritzburg, Colenso) on to the R74 and into Durban Street in Greytown. Pass on the way at 10,8 km the untidy hamlet of Pomeroy, enter soon afterwards one of the most attractive fragments of KwaZulu, cross at 37,3 km the Tugela River at Tugela Ferry, pass at 53 km another untidy village at Keate's Drift and at 53,5 km leave KwaZulu, crossing the Mooi River.

GREYTOWN, which was laid out in pleasant surroundings on the Mvoti River in 1850 and named in honour of Governor Sir George Grey, was a rallying point with a stone-walled laager during the Zulu War of 1879 and the Zulu Rebellion of 1906.

COLENSO was laid out in 1855 on the site of one of the Voortrekker laagers attacked by Dingaan's *impis* in 1838, and was named in honour of John William Colenso, controversial Anglican Bishop of Natal from 1853 to 1883. In a battle fought along the banks of the Tugela River to the west and east of the town, General Louis Botha repulsed General Sir Redvers Buller's first attempt to relieve Ladysmith in December 1899. Lieutenant Frederick Roberts, the only son of Field-Marshal Lord Roberts, was killed in the fighting, a month before his father arrived from Britain to take over as Commander-in-Chief of the British Army in South Africa.

At the entrance to Colenso turn right on to the N3 and drive 28 km back to Ladysmith.

173. A Zulu village in one of the most attractive parts of KwaZulu, between Dundee and Greytown

FROM LAKE ST LUCIA TO HLUHLUWE

The greatest fresh-water lagoon in southern Africa and one of the oldest and most beautiful game reserves on the subcontinent are included in this tour from the St Lucia Estuary on the Zululand coast.

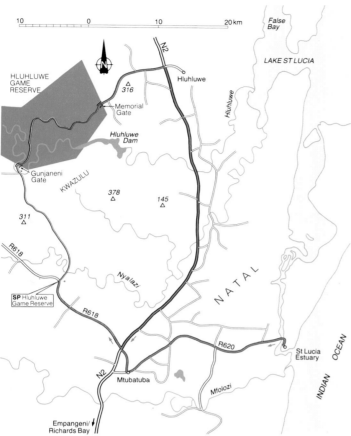

ST LUCIA The great lake of St Lucia, originally named Santa Lucia by Portuguese navigators who passed this way in 1507, is the largest fresh-water lagoon in southern Africa. It forms roughly the shape of the letter H, the western arm of which, False Bay, is connected to the eastern limb by a channel known as Hell's Gate. Of the four rivers that feed the lake the most important, the Mkuze, flows in from the north. At the southern end the Mfolozi also used to drain into this vast expanse of water, but it carried so much silt with it that in 1951 the mouth of the estuary became blocked – with disastrous effect on the estuarine ecology and once-splendid fishing. In the lake, too, fishing deteriorated since the seasonal migration of mullet and game fish no longer occurred between lagoon and sea. To remedy the situation, in the 1950s work was started on reopening the estuary and creating a new mouth for the Mfolozi so that it could empty directly into the sea. After the completion of the work in 1961 marine life started returning to Lake St Lucia, followed in due course by the water birds that had disappeared when their source of food had been destroyed. About 40 species of fish have since been recorded in the estuary, while

bream and catfish are caught in the fresh-water streams that flow into the lake.

The mangrove swamps at the estuary and the reedbeds and dense indigenous forest surrounding the lake provide a habitat for a great many species of wildlife which are protected in four reserves. Hippo and crocodiles abound in the St Lucia Game Reserve which comprises the lake and its islands, while St Lucia Park, a 1-km strip of land around the lake, is inhabited by vervet monkeys, black-backed jackal, duiker, reedbuck, bushpig and spotted hyena. The False Bay Park, on the western shore of the lake, is home to the only breeding colony of pink-backed pelican in southern Africa, as well as flocks of up to 20 000 flamingo and, in the surrounding parkland, nyala, duiker, bushbuck, reedbuck, steenbok, suni and bushpig. Denizens of the fourth sanctuary, the Eastern Shores Nature Reserve, include red duiker, bushbuck, vervet and samango monkeys, bushpig and cheetah, which have been introduced to control the prolific reedbuck population.

Camping sites, caravan parks and hutted camps are numerous in the St Lucia complex, and there are opportunities to take part in guided and self-organised wilderness trails. The angling is superb at times and boating, either in hired or

174. Members of an African Zionist church hold a service on the shore of Lake St Lucia

in privately-owned craft, is encouraged in the estuary and the lake, although swimming is prohibited even for those courageous or foolhardy enough to reckon with crocodiles. The Natal Parks Board crocodile research station, pool and museum near the resort of St Lucia welcomes visitors who, apart from learning about the great reptiles, may see displays interpreting the entire St Lucia area and its fauna and flora. Anti-malaria medication, which is available without prescription, should be taken before going to St Lucia and for four weeks after leaving.

From the bridge over the St Lucia Estuary drive 25,8 km westward on the R620 to Mtubatuba.

MTUBATUBA, surrounded by green rolling hills, is an attractive trading centre popular with the many cane and timber labourers in the area. On the outskirts of the village there are impressive views of the Mfolozi River and the scenic beauty of the countryside around.

From Mtubatuba drive 3,3 km north-westward on the R618 to the N2, cross it and continue on the R618 in the same direction. After 15,6 km turn right (SP Hluhluwe Game Reserve) and travel 14,8 km to Gunjaneni Gate, the southern entrance to the reserve.

HLUHLUWE GAME RESERVE
Even if none of the more exciting of Africa's big game is spotted in the

Hluhluwe Game Reserve, which was proclaimed a sanctuary as long ago as 1897, the splendour of its scenery and the wide diversity of its abundant birdlife make a visit an exceptional and worthwhile experience. The 23 000-ha reserve is hilly, with a range in altitude spanning almost 500 m from valley floor to hill summit, and more than 100 km of road meanders up and down the fascinating topography, presenting something new around nearly every bend. Dense forest covers the northern and higher parts of the reserve as well as the banks of the numerous streams, while the vegetation of the remaining areas varies between park-like savanna and thick scrub. Among the trees there are such

interesting species as the Cape chestnut, red ivory, tamboti, marula, tree fuchsia, cabbage tree and several species of acacia and coral tree, in addition to the plant from which the reserve derives its name, the thorny climber 'mhluhluwe' (*Dalbergia armata*) which grows along the banks of the Hluhluwe River. Zulu herdboys cut down the long, slender, liana-like branches and use them to muzzle calves to prevent them suckling while they are being weaned.

The wide variety of animal life at Hluhluwe includes lion, cheetah, leopard, elephant, both black and white rhino, giraffe, zebra, a number of antelope species, warthog, monkeys and hyena, and hippo and crocodiles in the rivers. Some of the animals may be observed from the hide at the Munywaneni waterhole. Among the birds in the reserve are the marabou stork, white-backed vulture, bateleur, crested guineafowl, emerald cuckoo, narina trogon, ground hornbill, lourie, blue quail and Delegorgue's pigeon.

From the Memorial Gate at the eastern boundary of the reserve drive 14 km eastward to the N2 and turn right (SP Durban, Mtubatuba). Travel 49,2 km southward before turning left (SP Mtubatuba) on to the R618 and reach Mtubatuba after another 3,3 km. Turn left on to the R620 and drive 25,8 km to return to the St Lucia Estuary bridge.

176. A rest camp at Hluhluwe Game Reserve

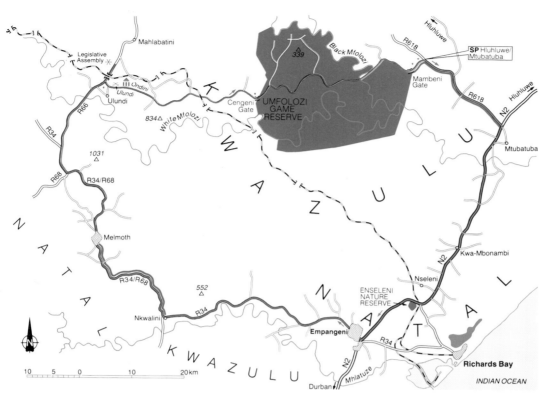

61

270 km*

WHITE RHINO SANCTUARY

As well as the Umfolozi Game Reserve, famous habitat of the white rhino, this tour includes the capital of KwaZulu and the battlefield on which the military might of the Zulu nation was finally broken.

MELMOTH The name of this village commemorates Sir Melmoth Osborn, resident commissioner of the area after Zululand was annexed to the British Empire in 1887.

From Melmoth continue on the R34/R68 into grassland interspersed with wattle and gum tree plantations. After 30 km turn right (SP Nongoma, Ulundi) on to the R66 and 12 km further on cross the White Mfolozi River by the replacement for the bridge which was washed away in the flood caused by Cyclone Demoina early in 1984. From the bridge drive 3,8 km and pass the right turn to Ulundi's dormitory village, then continue 2,6 km further to pass the right turn to the Umfolozi Game Reserve. Continue straight on under the railway bridge to the KwaZulu Legislative Assembly and Ulundi Holiday Inn.

ULUNDI The capital of fragmented KwaZulu, Ulundi is dominated by the imposing building of the KwaZulu Legislative Assembly, completed in 1984 at the cost of many millions of rands. The town was first established as capital of the Zulu nation when Cetshwayo became king in 1873, and it witnessed the great defeat that brought to an end the Anglo-Zulu War. In December 1878 Governor Sir Bartle Frere had given Cetshwayo an ultimatum to disband his troops and hand over the murderers of certain black subjects of Queen Victoria. The Zulu king ignored the command and the following month British forces under Lord Chelmsford invaded Zululand. They were routed at Isandhlwana and a number of confrontations followed, until in July 1879 Chelmsford – with his cavalry and African units surrounded by a rectangle of infantry led by Gatling gunners – advanced towards Cetshwayo's 20 000 warriors on the Plain of Ulundi. After watching his army being repulsed in successive attacks on the British and eventually defeated, Cetshwayo became a fugitive. The awesome military power of the Zulu was thus broken, and to commemorate the achievement a memorial (NM) now stands on the site of the battlefield.

Return to the railway bridge from the Legislative Assembly and immediately after passing under it turn left (SP Ulundi Battlefield, Ondini). Drive 2,5 km to reach Ondini.

ONDINI, which means 'the heights', is the site of Cetshwayo's second royal kraal of that name, the first having been destroyed by the

* The distance given allows about 35 km of travelling inside the Umfolozi Game Reserve.

EMPANGENI is the hub of Zululand's sugar industry, although there is also cattle farming in the district and cotton and timber are produced. The first of Natal's thousands of hectares of gum tree plantations, which now feed South Africa's paper and synthetic fibre

industries with cellulose pulp, were planted in this region. The town is an important railway centre and has seen modest industrial development. The beautiful, hilly countryside surrounding Empangeni is the land of the Mthetwa people, and it was here that the Zulu warrior chief Shaka grew up.

Leave Empangeni on the R34, travelling 45,3 km westward to

Nkwalini, at first through undulating sugar cane country and the valley of the Mhlatuze River. The route becomes increasingly scenic as more mountainous terrain is approached, the landscape enhanced at times by the splashes of colour that blaze from aloes and wild bougainvillea and poinsettia. At Nkwalini turn right (SP Melmoth) on to what for the 27 km to Melmoth and 30 km beyond is designated both as the R34 and R68.

177. Laundry day outside Ulundi, capital of KwaZulu

British after the Battle of Ulundi. The Zulu chief built the second kraal a short distance to the north of the original one after the British reinstated him in 1882, but this was sacked by the Swazi *impis* of Usibepu in 1883. The ruins of part of the kraal, including the floor of the royal hut which was 8,5 m in diameter, can still be seen. Ondini, which bears the bronze plaque of the National Monuments Council, is now the seat of the Zululand Cultural Museum, housed in a kraal much like Cetshwayo's 'great place' of traditional dome-shaped dwellings made of woven grass.

Continue eastward on the same road and reach Cengeni, the western gate of the Umfolozi Game Reserve, after 31,6 km. The helpful, immaculately uniformed Zulu on duty will supply a map showing the 85 km of road, the viewing sites, waterholes, hide and picnic sites in the sanctuary and, with the courtesy characteristic of Natal Parks Board staff, he will also answer the questions that are inevitably asked.

UMFOLOZI GAME RESERVE
The 48 000-ha Umfolozi Game Reserve, proclaimed in 1897, is the habitat of the densest population of white (square-lipped) rhino in the world. Although there was a time when the species had almost been wiped off the African continent, the 900-strong population is now healthy enough to permit the relocation of surplus animals to other reserves. It is in the acacia thornbush terrain which comprises most of the sanctuary that the white rhino thrives, its survival the achievement of the dedicated conservationists who protected the species here.

There is also an exciting variety of other wildlife in the reserve, both in the thornveld and in the riverine vegetation and other dense woodland. Some 50 animal species occur, including lion, cheetah, leopard, black rhino, buffalo, blue wildebeest, zebra, giraffe, several antelope species, bushpig, warthog, baboons, spotted hyena, black-backed jackal and crocodile. The lions of Umfolozi appeared long after trigger-happy hunters had exterminated the last of the breed in Natal. A single male made his way to the reserve from Mozambique in 1958 and several years later was followed by several lionesses who had also been able to survive the hunters' guns. The descendants of the progeny of these proud, errant beasts are now permanent denizens of Umfolozi. Among the 300 or more bird species with which the reserve teems are Shelley's francolin, black-bellied korhaan, yellow-billed stork, heron, Wahlberg's eagle, Temminck's courser, the little bee-eater,

178. A kraal like Cetshwayo's 'great place' on the site of the original at Ondini now accommodates the Zululand Cultural Museum

vultures, bustard, marabou stork and the crested barbet.

For those with the time and wisdom to do justice to Umfolozi there are rest camps at Mpila and Masinda as well as bush camps at Mhlogazana and Nselweni. At optimum times a hide at the waterhole on the Gqoyeni River, which is reached through a long, reed-walled passage, affords opportunities for close observation of some of the wildlife. Three-day wilderness trails which rangers conduct through acacia country

enable visitors to encounter at even closer range, among other creatures, the white rhino for which the reserve is famed.

From Mambeni, the eastern gate of the Umfolozi Game Reserve, drive 4,7 km eastward to the R618 and turn right (SP Hluhluwe, Mtubatuba). Travel 17,9 km to the N2, turn right again (SP Durban, Mtubatuba) and after 41 km (1 km beyond the left turn to Richards Bay) turn left to the Enseleni Nature Reserve.

ENSELENI NATURE RESERVE
This reserve, the haunt of many species of waterfowl and monitor lizards, also has a wealth of

plantlife. Wild fig trees along the river form a forest so dense that in places hardly any sunlight reaches the ground, while along the smaller streams there is concentrated coastal bush. Indigenous trees in the reserve include crotons, Cape ash, monkey thorn, coral trees, flat-crowns, and, along the reserve's swampland trail, mangroves and ilala palms. A game park, open only at weekends and on public holidays, is populated with bush-buck, nyala, impala, reedbuck and wildebeest.

Return to the N2 and drive 14 km southward before turning right on to the R34 for the remaining 2 km back to Empangeni.

179. White (square-lipped) rhino in the Umfolozi Game Reserve

62

320 km

HISTORY WAS MADE HERE

Once a region of violent conflict, the beautiful and now peaceful countryside around Eshowe is steeped in the history of the Zulu nation and the early white settlers.

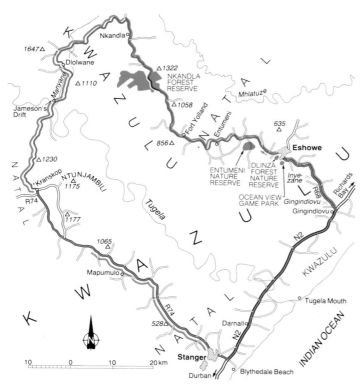

ESHOWE Situated on a hill with a splendid view of surrounding Zululand, Eshowe is one of the most beautiful towns in South Africa. It also has a beautiful name, for those who accept the most poetic of the three theories about its derivation – that it is 'the sound of the wind in the trees'. More prosaically, it has also been suggested that the name, which has been used since the Nguni tribes started settling the area in the

seventeenth century, simply means 'windy place'. And the third proposition is that it is a form of the Zulu name for a species of *Xysmalobium* bush – 'ishowe' or 'ishongwe' – which abounds in the region and, because of its repulsive smell, is used to keep dogs away from hides during the curing process. Preserved within Eshowe is the Dlinza, or 'place of tomb-like meditation', part of the indigenous forest that once covered the hill on

which the town is situated. From nature trails through the cool Dlinza Forest Nature Reserve it is sometimes possible to catch glimpses of its denizens, such as bushbuck, blue and red duiker, vervet monkeys and bushpigs. A second nature reserve in Eshowe is at the southern entrance to the town. Visitors, accompanied by guides, may explore the Ocean View Game Park on foot and perhaps encounter such wildlife as wildebeest, impala, duiker, reedbuck, kudu, zebra, bushpig, warthog and a wide variety of birds.

Much of the history of the Zulu people was enacted around Eshowe. Shaka had one of his kraals, Bulawayo, in this district, while the kraals of two other paramount chiefs, Mpande and his son Cetshwayo, were also not far from the town. Among the relics at Eshowe of Zululand's troublous times is Fort Nongqai, which was built by the British in 1883 to accommodate the Natal Native Police, mustered originally as a bodyguard to Sir Melmoth Osborn, British Resident for Zululand. Officially designated the Reserve Territorial Carbineers, the force also came to be known as the 'Nongqai', a name derived from a Zulu word meaning 'to seek' or 'to detect'. It served in the Zululand disturbances between 1883 and 1888, in the Anglo-Boer War from 1899 to 1902, and in the Bambatha Rebellion of 1906. The quadrangular fort, of brick construction and provided with loopholes, stands on a ridge on the commonage south-east of Eshowe and has crenellated, three-storey corner towers. It is a well-preserved national monument and houses the interesting Zululand Historical Museum.

East of the town and encircled by a deep moat – the remains of a fort – is a cemetery once used by the Norwegian Missionary Society of Kwa-Mondi, the name of which stems from the Zulu corruption of the name of the first pastor at the station, Ommund Oftebro. Kwa-Mondi was converted into a fort by Colonel Charles Pearson when he heard of the defeat at Isandhlwana of his general, Lord Chelmsford, in the Zulu war of 1879. Pearson's force, one of the three Chelmsford columns advancing into Zululand, was besieged in Fort Kwa-Mondi (also known as Fort Eshowe) for two months, and its provisions were

almost exhausted by the time Chelmsford's remustered force was able to relieve it. Iron crosses mark the graves of those who died of privation or were killed during the siege.

From the traffic circle where the John Ross Highway runs into Osborn Road in Eshowe drive 1,4 km north-eastward along Osborn Road – which continues as a fork to the left after 1 km – turning left into Kangela Street. Drive another 13,6 km generally westward to the left turn to the Entumeni Nature Reserve.

ENTUMENI NATURE RESERVE
In the surrounding countryside, from which most other wildlife has retreated as the ocean of sugar cane has advanced, the Entumeni Nature Reserve is a 436-ha forest sanctuary for birds and butterflies.

Continue westward from the reserve, passing after 9,6 km the left turn to Entumeni, where the Norwegian Missionary Society established another station in 1860. Fork right (SP Nkandla) 4,5 km further on, continuing on a gravelled surface after 2,2 km. Pass the right turn to Fort Yolland 7,7 km from the fork, the left turn to Cetshwayo's grave after another 6 km and enter the Nkandla Forest 12,9 km further on, although the KwaZulu Government notice defining the boundary of the forest reserve is another 3,6 km ahead.

NKANDLA FOREST RESERVE
Straddling a pass through the mountains 35 km north-west of Eshowe, this 1 620 ha of unspoilt indigenous forest is an enchanting part of Zululand where perennial mists promote the prolific growth of tree ferns, orchids, creepers, cycads and other moisture-loving plants. The forest shelters leopard, bushbuck, duiker, baboon and vervet monkey, as well as birds such as rameron pigeons, tambourine doves, chorister robins and the rare bronze-naped pigeon. It was in the almost impenetrable Nkandla Forest that the Zulu king Cetshwayo took refuge after his defeat in 1883 by Usibepu, and here that he died a year later. His grave, marked by a black marble stone, is in the Mhone Gorge at the end of a 25-km sidetrack from the Nkandla road to the forest's western edge. The forest was also the scene of furious fighting in the Zulu Rebellion of 1906 when the rebels, led by Bambatha, retreated to the Mhone Gorge to make their last stand.

After driving 10,2 km through the forest continue northward and, 44,1 km from the right turn to Fort Yolland, reach the Nkandla Hotel in Nkandla's only street, a stretch of

180. Ernest Ntombela, the guide at Fort Nongqai in Eshowe, wears the uniform of the Natal Native Police

tar on either side of which are a mission hospital, two banks, a post office, a police station and a few stores. Back on gravel 800 m beyond the hotel, turn left (SP Qudeni, Kranskop) 1,9 km from the end of the tar and cross the Nkanisa River 12,9 km further on. After another 3,8 km the road starts descending the enchanting scenic Manyane Pass to the Manyane River and runs alongside and above it for 3,1 km before crossing it by way of a low-level bridge. Keep left (passing a right turn to Nqutu, Dundee and Vryheid) 8,9 km after crossing the Manyane and drive another 6,7 km between sheer cliffs and more splendid mountain scenery to the Dlolwana trading post. Bear left (SP Kranskop) 1,1 km from Dlolwana, recross the Manyane River 5,1 km further on and cross it for the third time after another 6,3 km. Reach the bridge over the Tugela River at Jameson's Drift 1,4 km still further. From the bridge the road climbs the western slopes of the Tugela River valley and then, winding through cuttings and over embankments along the mountain slopes, enters tracts of eucalyptus plantation before reaching Kranskop 34 km from Jameson's Drift.

KRANSKOP takes its name from the dramatically precipitous red sandstone peak, Ntunjambili, which towers 1 175 m above the Tugela River valley to the east of the town. According to Zulu folklore, girls bearing water from the river to their kraals used to be enticed into a cave near the summit by the sound of revelry within and were never seen again. Kranskop was the site of the last in a series of seven forts stretching north-westward from Umhlali which the British manned during the Zululand conflict of the 1850s.

Turn right (SP Greytown, Stanger) 600 m from the start of the tar at the northern entrance to Kranskop and 2,1 km further on fork left (SP Mapumulo, Stanger) on to the R74. Drive through plantations of wattle, fields of sugar cane and beautiful mountain scenery as the road descends along the southern slopes of the vast Tugela River valley. Turn left into Reynolds Street in Stanger 70,8 km after joining the R74.

STANGER See Tour 63.

Leave Stanger travelling south-eastward on the R74 from the interchange at the northern end of Reynolds Street (SP Blythedale Beach). After 3,3 km turn left (SP Gingindlovu) on to the N2, cross

181. A Zulu settlement beside the road between Nkandla and Kranskop

the Tugela River by way of the John Ross Bridge 23,3 km further on and pass the left turn to Gingindlovu 23,5 km from the river.

GINGINDLOVU, which means 'the swallower of the elephant', was the site of one of Cetshwayo's military kraals and is said to have been named to commemorate his victory over his brother Mbulazi in their contest for the Zulu throne. The kraal was destroyed after

Cetshwayo's power was finally broken by the British in the Battle of Ulundi (see Tour 61) in 1879. The same year saw two other battles between the British and Zulus, which were fought near Gingindlovu. In the Battle of Inyezane Colonel Pearson's force of 4 400 defeated an *impi* of 5 000, and in the Battle of Gingindlovu Lord Chelmsford, with 6 000 men on their way to relieve Eshowe, vanquished an *impi* of 11 000. The

modern village is surrounded by extensive canefields in attractive countryside.

Fork left (SP Eshowe, Melmoth) 800 m north-east of the left turn to Gingindlovu and reach the Battle of Gingindlovu Memorial after 1,8 km. The left turn to the Inyezane Battlefield is 8 km further on and the Ocean View Game Park at the southern entrance to Eshowe is 11,3 km still further.

182. The cemetery at the Gingindlovu battlefield

63

145 km

WHERE THE OCEANS OF SWEETNESS STARTED

In the countryside once stamped by Shaka's *impis* South Africa's first sugar cane was planted more than a century ago. Since then sugar has become one of Natal's main economic assets.

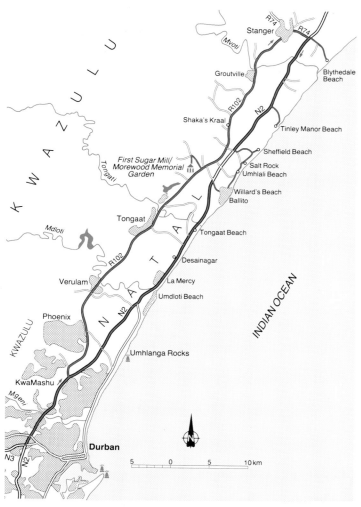

DURBAN The first entry in recorded history about the coast of Natal where Durban now stands was made in 1497 when the Portuguese navigator Vasco da Gama anchored off what the indigenous inhabitants called 'Thekweni', 'the lagoon'. By all accounts Da Gama did not go ashore but, having reached this part of the coast on Christmas Day, he named it 'Terra do Natal' while the entrance to the lagoon was given the name 'Rio de Natal'. Other exploring navigators came after, but the first group to stay for any length of time were some of the survivors of the *Good Hope* which in 1685 was wrecked on the sandbar off what is now called Durban Bay. These Britons elected to remain where they were when their shipmates sailed away in a reconstructed vessel, but they later joined the survivors of the Dutch East Indiaman *Stavenisse* which had foundered south of Rio de Natal. Together the Dutch and British built the *Centaurus* out of the wreckage and sailed to Cape Town (see Tours 34 and 36).

The first ship known to have passed the sandbar at the mouth of the Rio de Natal was the *Salisbury*, which in 1823 anchored off an island which has been known ever since as Salisbury Island. The vessel was on a trading mission under the command of two former Royal Naval officers, Francis George Farewell and John Saunders King, who returned the following year with 18 other adventurous Britons – including Henry Francis Fynn and Dick King who was to win fame on account of his epic ride to Grahamstown. They established a settlement on a large tract of land around the bay granted to them by Shaka, the Zulu king, and were joined a year later by Farewell's wife, the first white woman to make her home in Natal. The tiny settlement made little headway until 1835 when another former naval officer, Allan Francis Gardiner, presided over a meeting at which it was resolved to found a town and to name it in honour of the Governor of the Cape, Sir Benjamin D'Urban. Three years later, after the murder of Piet Retief's party of negotiating Voortrekkers by Shaka's successor, Dingaan, the settlement's situation became precarious. Zulu warriors sacked Durban and its inhabitants fled to Salisbury Island. However, with a stiffening of Voortrekkers who had proclaimed Natal a republic, the refugees returned and in 1839 laid out Durban's first streets. The British Government, which had previously refused to approve the establishment of a colony in Natal, now decided otherwise and despatched a garrison to occupy Durban. The now-antagonistic Voortrekkers besieged the town and it was only after they had been ousted by the relieving force summoned from Grahamstown by Dick King that Natal officially became British. From then on Durban grew, the entrance to the bay was improved and the port steadily developed to such an extent that it now handles more cargo than all other South African ports together. As the harbour developed so did the cultivation of sugar in the surrounding countryside. Labour was introduced from the Far East, mainly India, with the result that the present Asian population of Durban exceeds that of any other city in the Republic.

Now, as well as being South Africa's busiest port, third largest city and a major industrial centre, Durban is considered to be the country's principal pleasure resort. Factors contributing to the city's popularity as a holiday venue include its subtropical climate which ensures a year-round season, its proximity to the Transvaal and Orange Free State, and its glorious shoreline stretching away to the north and south with splendid beaches backed by indigenous vegetation. These attributes have been vigorously exploited not only in the city but also at the numerous resorts that have sprung up on the North Coast and, in particular, on the South Coast of Natal.

From Durban's N2/N3 Interchange follow the N2 11,3 km northward before taking the exit on to the R102. After 1,3 km turn right to remain on the R102, skirting KwaMashu and Phoenix, and reach Verulam 13,9 km after leaving the N2.

VERULAM was founded in 1850 by a group of British Methodists who were brought to South Africa in the barque *King William* under the patronage of the Earl of Verulam and settled along the Mdloti River. The newcomers were well equipped and established numerous small but well-run farms which have since been swallowed up by the great sugar estates. In 1967 Verulam was designated a town exclusively for Indians.

Continue northward on the R102 to reach the market in Tongaat 10 km after crossing the Mdloti River.

TONGAAT An important centre of the sugar industry, Tongaat takes its name from the Tongati River which in turn is named after the 'thongati' tree ('kafferklapper'), the

183. The Marine Parade, Durban

184. The garden at the headquarters of the Tongaat group of companies

185. Cutting sugar cane

dried fruit, or 'thonga', of which are used by the Zulu as snuff boxes or as rattles. The Tongaat group of companies has manifested its awareness of South Africa's cultural history in a complex of buildings in the Cape Dutch architectural style which houses a valuable collection of Gwelo Goodman paintings, furniture, silver, Dutch East India Company glassware and other Cape Dutch antiques.

From Tongaat continue northward on the R102 and 8,2 km after crossing the Tongati River turn left to the site of South Africa's first sugar mill. After 1,4 km turn left again and drive 1 km through a canefield to the Morewood Memorial Garden.

MOREWOOD MEMORIAL GARDEN It was here on the farm Compensation that Edmund Morewood planted the first sugar cane imported to South Africa and devised this country's first sugar mill. During extensive travel Morewood had visited the island of Bourbon, now Reunion, before he established himself as a merchant in Cape Town. Later he moved to Natal where the Volksraad of the Voortrekker republic of Natalia appointed him harbour master of Port Natal. After retiring from this office he was granted a farm which, because he regarded it as an inadequate substitute for property he would rather have had, he named Compensation. A 'sweet reed known to the Zulu as 'umoba' or 'imphi' which grew prolifically in the region caught his interest and, reasoning that sugar would do equally well, he persuaded the Durban firm of Milner and Milner to import a consignment of cane plants from Bourbon. These he

successfully cultivated at Compensation and so, with other farmers emulating him, founded a lucrative South African industry. Morewood's primitive mill, powered by four Zulus and with wooden rollers fashioned from timber from a wrecked ship, produced juice from which the country's first sugar was refined in 1851. He was declared bankrupt the following year, however, and spent the rest of his life as a tutor on sugar estates in Brazil. A replica of his mill, modelled on remnants of the original which were found in 1948, is the focal point of the memorial garden.

Return to the R102 and continue northward, passing Shaka's Kraal after 9 km.

SHAKA'S KRAAL was the name given to the railway station to the south of this village, although none of the great Zulu chief's bases was sited here, some 13 km south of Stanger where he built his last major kraal.

Continue northward for 6,6 km to Groutville.

GROUTVILLE Aldin Grout, after whom this village was named, was a missionary from Massachusetts who was sent to minister to the Zulus in 1835. Under the auspices of the American Board of Commissioners for Foreign Missions he established a mission station here on the banks of the Mvoti River, and also cooperated in the publication of the first Zulu Bible. Shaka is believed to have occasionally reviewed his *impis* from a rock which, until recently, could be seen on a hill east of the road through Groutville, but is now at the Shaka memorial in Stanger.

Continue northward on the R102 for 7,2 km to Stanger.

STANGER was laid out in 1873 on the site of Shaka's last kraal, Dukuza, where he was murdered by his half-brothers. The cattle enclosure in which he was buried became holy ground on which grazing and wood-gathering were taboo. When the Stanger Town Council was established in 1920 and the place was named after the Surveyor-General of Natal, William Stanger, an acre of ground was set aside around Shaka's grave off Couper Street. On this the Zulu people, prompted by their leader, Solomon ka Dinizulu, erected an imposing memorial to the founder of their nation. The rock on which Shaka used to sit when reviewing his *impis* near Groutville is incorporated in the memorial layout, which also includes a huge Zulu hut and other elements of the sort of kraal Dukuza might have been. Stanger is now the rail, magisterial and commercial centre of an important sugar-producing district.

Leave Stanger eastward on the R74 and at the interchange where it meets the N2 continue eastward for 4,2 km to Blythedale Beach.

BLYTHEDALE BEACH Numerous angling spots, protection for sea bathers from sharks and a tidal pool contribute to Blythedale's popularity as a North Coast resort.

Return to the N2, drive southward for 10,7 km, then turn left to Tinley Manor Beach.

TINLEY MANOR BEACH, whose main attraction is its good fishing, is a resort reserved for Indians.

Return to the N2 and continue southward for 7,7 km before turning left (SP Umhlali Beach, Salt Rock) to a series of adjacent resorts. After 700 m fork left to Sheffield Beach.

SHEFFIELD BEACH This is mainly a residential development which affords a delightful coastal run northward along Colwyn Drive, past some beautiful homes.

Return along Colwyn Drive and continue southward as it runs successively into Sheffield Drive, Osborne Drive, Ocean View Drive and Compensation Road through Salt Rock, Shaka's Rock, Willard's Beach and Compensation Beach to Ballito.

SALT ROCK, SHAKA'S ROCK AND WILLARD'S BEACH These adjacent resorts, which as a whole comprise Umhlali Beach, have a number of venues for safe swimming, surfing and angling. Salt Rock has a superb beach and good surfing water, and is said to have been the place to which Shaka sent his subjects to collect salt. Shaka's Rock is believed to have been one of his favourite haunts.

BALLITO AND COMPENSATION BEACH This complex is an inviting, rapidly-developing resort with a tidal pool, anti-shark protection for sea bathers and a pleasant coastal pathway. Compensation Beach takes its name from the farm a few kilometres inland where Edmund Morewood pioneered the sugar industry.

From Ballito return to the N2 by way of Ballito Drive and continue southward for 45 km to the N2/N3 Interchange in Durban.

CHAPTER SIX
The Transvaal Highveld

64

350 km

ROUND THE VAAL DAM

Vital to the existence of the vast urban and industrial complex of the Witwatersrand, the Vaal Dam not only provides an adequate water supply, but also fulfils some recreational needs of the area's citizens.

JOHANNESBURG See Tour 67.

At the Geldenhuis Interchange at the south-eastern corner of Johannesburg take the exit SP Heidelberg on to the N3 and travel 38,8 km before taking the R23/R103 exit to Benoni and Heidelberg. After 500 m turn right (SP Heidelberg) and then left (same SP) 500 m further on. Veer left (SP Heidelberg) after 2,8 km and run into Voortrekker Street, reaching the Dutch Reformed church 1,3 km further on.

HEIDELBERG Situated where Mzilikazi, paramount chief of the

Matabele, is believed to have once had his headquarters, Heidelberg was founded at the instigation of one Heinrich Ueckermann. A German shopkeeper, Ueckermann started business in 1860 on the farm Langlaagte at the intersection of the roads from Durban to Potchefstroom and from Bloemfontein to Pretoria, and before long was joined by other traders. The owners of the farm sought and were granted permission by the Transvaal Volksraad to lay out a town which was named after the German city where Ueckermann had been educated. Like its German

namesake but to a more modest extent, the Heidelberg pleasantly situated at the eastern end of the Suikerbosrand is an important educational centre. It was also the seat of the Triumvirate of Paul Kruger, Marthinus Wessel Pretorius and Piet Joubert, who in 1880 formed a provisional republican government in defiance of the British annexation of the Transvaal three years earlier. To Heidelberg rode Petrus Kilian with news of the victory over the British at Majuba in February 1881, and it was here, too, that the treaty which ended the first Anglo-Boer War was signed by the Triumvirate and General Sir Evelyn Wood three weeks later. A monument to the Triumvirate stands in front of the Heidelberg Town Hall. Of considerable historic delight is the excellent Heidelberg Transport Museum at the old railway station. It displays an extensive collection of animal-drawn vehicles, cycles from the earliest velocipedes, penny-farthings and motor cycles to less dated but still veteran two-wheelers, cars of the oldest vintage and a train of a bygone era drawn up at the now disused platform. Though industries have been established in Heidelberg, its economy is based largely on the surrounding fertile grain-producing district which also supports numerous dairy farms

supplying thousands of litres of milk to Witwatersrand towns every day.

Continue south-eastward from the Heidelberg Dutch Reformed church, turn right into H F Verwoerd Street and after 500 m reach the green open space on the left on which Heidelberg's historic 'bakoond' stands.

HEIDELBERG 'BAKOOND' This stone structure in the form of a large outdoor oven was built over a spring and was intended less for baking bread in the traditional Afrikaner way than to conceal Heidelberg's principal source of water from the British forces fighting the Transvaal Boers in 1880 and 1881.

Drive south-westward along H F Verwoerd Street and 600 m beyond the 'bakoond' turn left on to the R23/R103. After 1,7 km turn right (SP Vaal Dam) on to the R549 to travel through pleasant rolling grassland and maize fields which are beautifully green after summer rain. Cross the R54 39,6 km after turning on to the R549, with the Vaal Dam coming into sight ahead to the left, cross the Vaal River 11,1 km further on and see the Vaal Dam wall a short distance upstream. Turn left into Deneysville 1,4 km after crossing the Vaal River.

VAAL DAM With a capacity of 2 394 million cubic metres, the Vaal Dam was for many years after its completion in 1938 the biggest in the country. Now it ranks as fourth, being just over half the size of the H F Verwoerd Dam. Built across the Vaal River 10 km north-west of the inflowing Wilge River so that the dam extends long distances up both valleys, the wall was raised by 6 m in 1952 to double the dam's capacity. Through the Rand Water Board, the dam supplies the urban, industrial and mining complex of the Witwatersrand, Pretoria and Vereeniging, with its population of more than 4 million. In addition, it and its shores afford almost unlimited opportunities for recreation. Keel yachts of considerable size as well as innumerable sailing dinghies can be seen at moorings on the water, and the dam is also popular with powerboating and boardsailing enthusiasts. There are several resorts around its perimeter, and anglers revel in good catches of yellowfish, carp and barbel.

VAAL DAM NATURE RESERVE From 3 km east of the dam wall this 348-ha nature reserve stretches eastward along the Transvaal shore of the Vaal Dam. Its wildlife comprises many bird species, including the fish eagle, white egret, Egyptian goose, yellow-billed duck and coot. The reserve has camp sites and picnic spots.

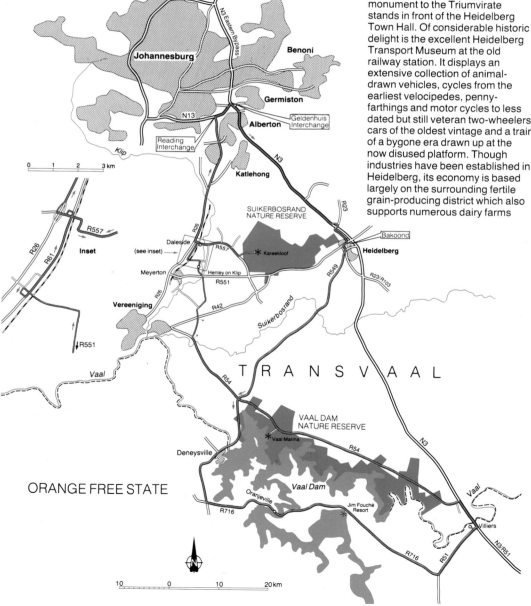

DENEYSVILLE The village and holiday resort of Deneysville was established in 1936 by Dr Hjalmar Reitz and named after his brother, Colonel Denys Reitz, who was Minister of Lands when the Vaal Dam was constructed. In the last days of flying boat travel aircraft visiting the Transvaal landed on and took off from the dam at Deneysville.

Return to the entrance to Deneysville, turn left (SP Oranjeville, Heilbron) on to the R716 and 12,5 km further on turn left again (SP Oranjeville, Jim Fouché Resort). After another 14,5 km turn left into Hans Street in the village of Oranjeville on the Wilge River reach of the Vaal Dam. Then turn right into Malan Street and reach the Dutch Reformed church after 400 m. Turn left into Van Niekerk Street 900 m beyond the church, cross the Wilge River part of the dam by a single-lane bridge 700 m further on and turn right into the Jim Fouché resort 15,6 km from the river.

JIM FOUCHÉ HOLIDAY RESORT Named in honour of the second State President of South Africa, the Jim Fouché Holiday Resort has fully-equipped bungalows for hire, a restaurant and a swimming pool. Its facilities for other sports, particularly water-related ones, include a 32-km stretch of the dam. From the resort there is an uninterrupted view of 24 km of water surface.

Return from the Jim Fouché Resort to the R716, turn right (no SP) and after 23,4 km turn left (SP Villiers) on to the R51. Reach the left turn into Villiers 11,4 km further on.

VILLIERS was laid out in 1882 on two farms, Pearson Valley and Grootdraai, owned by L B de Villiers, after whom the settlement was named. The town boasts a clothing factory, mills and, being on the Vaal River, holiday resort amenities.

At the interchange 1,2 km north-east of the turn-off into Villiers turn left (SP Heidelberg) on to the N3/R51 and cross the Vaal River back into the Transvaal 1,2 km further on. Turn left (SP Vereeniging) on to the R54 after another 5,3 km and right (same SP) 600 m from the N3, remaining on the R54. After 39,7 km pass the left turn to the Vaal Marina and travel another 11,8 km before crossing the R549 to remain on the R54. Cross the Suikerbosrand River 15,2 km from the R549 and turn right (SP Meyerton) 1,1 km from the river. After driving 4,3 km on gravel road cross the R42, pass a left turn to Meyerton 1,9 km further on and a left turn to Riversdale after another 4,7 km, and turn left (SP Witkoppie,

Meyerton) 3,2 km further on. Turn right (SP Henley on Klip) after 500 m and drive into Henley on Klip, passing the right turn to the Henley on Klip Hotel 1 km further on.

HENLEY ON KLIP Nostalgically named after Henley on Thames, this resort on the Klip River has several recreational areas in pleasant surroundings on the river banks, with facilities for camping, picnicking, fishing and boating.

At the stop street 2,3 km beyond the turn-off to the Henley on Klip Hotel turn left (no SP), drive through an avenue of eucalyptus trees and after 2,3 km cross the railway line. Turn left (SP Alberton, Meyerton) 400 m further on, left again (no SP) after another 300 m and left once more (SP Alberton) after 200 m on to the R61. Drive 4,5 km northward before turning left (SP Daleside) off the R61, at the stop street 400 m further on turn left again (SP Daleside), and left once more (SP Witkop) after another 400 m. Cross the R61 400 m still further and 300 m further on cross the road-over-rail bridge at Witkop. At the stop street 300 m from the bridge turn right into Meyerton Road (R557) and 500 m further on turn left (SP Kareekloof), remaining on the R557. Drive 10,3 km before turning left off the R557 and continue another 3,9 km to the Kareekloof Public Resort in the Suikerbosrand Nature Reserve.

SUIKERBOSRAND NATURE RESERVE The 13 337 ha of high ridges and spectacular gorges which comprise the Suikerbosrand Nature Reserve afford some of the urban population of the Witwatersrand an opportunity to get close to nature. Hiking trails through the habitat of eland, red hartebeest, black wildebeest, springbok, blesbok, duiker and cheetah are interspersed with overnight huts. From the visitors' centre at the north of the reserve two-hour bus tours are conducted by information officers who also screen film and slide shows.

Return from Kareekloof to Meyerton Road in Witkop and turn right (SP Walkerville). At the stop street 500 m further on turn left (SP Alberton) and cross the road-over-rail bridge after another 300 m. Turn right (SP Alberton) on to the R26 900 m from the bridge and drive 26,7 km to the Reading Interchange west of Alberton. Take the exit SP Pretoria and follow the N13 and then the N3 8,6 km back to the Geldenhuis Interchange.

186. An 'oven' concealed Heidelberg's water source in the first Boer War

187. A 'medieval castle' on the shore of the Vaal Dam at Deneysville

188. Sunshine through thunderclouds illuminates yachts moored on the Vaal Dam

THE OLD AND THE NEW

On the Highveld between Johannesburg and the Vaal River some towns have been developing since the Transvaal was first settled, while others have been established only recently as bases for new industry.

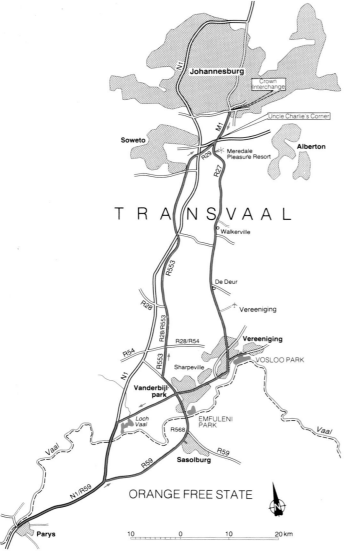

JOHANNESBURG See Tour 67.

At the Crown Interchange south of Johannesburg take the exit SP Orange Free State on to the M1, passing on the right after 800 m a mine dump on which the initials RMP are picked out in white. Cross the railway lines 1 km further on and drive another 5,4 km to Uncle Charlie's Corner. Follow the R27 signs to Vereeniging and turn left (SP Meredale Shopping Centre, Pleasure Resort) 4,3 km from Uncle Charlie's Corner. After 400 m fork left and 300 m further on turn left into Lark Street to drive 400 m to the Meredale Pleasure Resort.

MEREDALE PLEASURE RESORT

Chalets under shady willow trees, picnic spots on extensive lawns, a restaurant, tennis courts, two swimming pools and trampolines are attractions of Meredale Pleasure Resort, which is open from July to May inclusive. A separate caravan park is open throughout the year.

Return to the R27, turn left (SP Vereeniging) and drive 29,2 km through pleasant parkland and farms broken up by thickets of trees and bush to the Dutch Reformed church in the small residential town of De Deur. Continue southward, passing the left turn to the Vereeniging Airport after 5,3 km, and run into Voortrekker Street, reaching the first traffic lights in Vereeniging 11,2 km from the airport turn-off. Turn left into Rhodes Avenue, right into General Hertzog Road after 700 m and take the Golf Road exit from the traffic circle in the Riviera area 300 m further on. Drive along Golf Road past magnificent homes overlooking the golf links and the lawned and well-wooded Vosloo Park on the willow-lined banks of the Vaal River.

VEREENIGING
In 1878 the pioneer South African geologist and ethnologist George Stow discovered coal on the farm Leeuwkuil on the Transvaal bank of the Vaal River. He prompted Samuel Marks and Isaac Lewis to form 'De Zuid Afrikaansche en Oranje Vrijstaatsche Kolen- en Mineralen-Myn Vereeniging', and when a town was established on Leeuwkuil in 1892 it was named after the misspelt 'Vereeniging' in the amalgamation's title. A bare 10 years after Vereeniging came into existence it leapt into world prominence as the place where the peace negotiations were conducted at the end of the Anglo-Boer War, although the Treaty of Vereeniging was actually signed at Lord Kitchener's headquarters, Melrose House in Pretoria. A monument created by the distinguished South African sculptor Coert Steynburg to commemorate the treaty was unveiled in the Vereeniging suburb of Duncanville in 1961. Although the town is pleasantly sited on the banks of the Vaal, has three attractive riverside parks – Dickinson Park, the Van Riebeeck Marina and Vosloo Park – and offers excellent facilities for water sports, its prosperity is based on the extensive coal deposits found in the area by Stow and on industry, particularly heavy engineering. Sharpeville, the black township whose name has been known throughout the world since 67 Africans were killed and 186 wounded in disturbances in 1960, is within the Vereeniging municipality.

Return to Voortrekker Street, turn left and, at the southern end of it, veer right (SP Vanderbijlpark) into Barrage Road (R27/R42). After 10,1 km turn right into Vanderbijlpark.

VANDERBIJLPARK,
the steel town of South Africa, was established on unoccupied land on the north bank of the Vaal River in 1959. It was named in honour of the scientist and industrialist Dr Hendrik Johannes van der Bijl on whose recommendation, as founder and chairman of the South African Iron and Steel Corporation (Iscor), the land was bought for new factories and housing when Iscor's original steel plant in Pretoria outgrew itself. Dr van der Bijl, who was noted for planning on a vast scale, insisted on a model town whose environment would contribute to the happiness of the families of Iscor's personnel, a

189. Angling from the bank of the Vaal at Vosloo Park in Vereeniging

town laid out according to the most modern concepts of urban design. Though within easy access of each other, residential and industrial areas are separated, and double-lane boulevards facilitate the traffic flow. Each residential area has its own shopping centre and there is adequate provision for parks and gardens, the two major parks being the Emfuleni, on the Vaal River, and the Cecil Oldridge Park. The steel works on which the town is based have attracted other industries, particularly in the sphere of heavy engineering.

Return to the R27/R42, turn right and drive 13,2 km to the bridge over the Loch Vaal Creek.

LOCH VAAL, which can be seen to the left of the road from the bridge over the creek, is a delightful stretch of water surrounded by fine homes. It was formed when the Rand Water Board constructed a barrage on the Vaal River about a kilometre below the spot at which it was joined by the creek that now feeds the loch.

Continue 2,1 km south-westward from the bridge, turn left (SP Parys) on to the N1 and cross the Vaal River 2,5 km further on.

VAAL RIVER The Vaal River, principal tributary of the Orange River and, for 800 km of its length, the boundary between the Transvaal and the Orange Free State, was thus named because 'vaal' describes in Afrikaans the muddy colour of its water. The barrage constructed by the Rand Water Board about 2 km upstream of the bridge which carries the N1 over the river was opened by Prince Arthur of Connaught in 1923. It is a concrete structure with 35 sluice gates which, when raised, permit an unrestricted flow of water during floods. Originally the water stored behind the barrage met all the water board's needs but the importance of the structure diminished after the completion in 1938 of the Vaal Dam 84 km upstream. Below the N1 bridge over the Vaal a feature of the river is the large number of islands in it. Between Lindequesdrif, about 16 km downstream of the bridge, and Christiana, more than 350 km still further, nearly 200 of them divide the stream into numerous branches. They became a contentious issue between the republics of the Transvaal and the Orange Free State towards the end of the nineteenth century and, because their ownership was in dispute, there was nothing either republic could do to dislodge miscreants who took refuge on some of them. Both governments accordingly appointed commissions to determine jointly the main current of the river and allocate the islands. It was at Lindequesdrif that the

190. Fun in a public garden at Sasolburg

commissions started their field work in 1877 and, in the resultant Vaal River Island Treaty signed in 1895, the Transvaal was awarded 101 islands with a total area of 280 ha and the Orange Free State 94 with a total area of 200 ha.

Continue 9 km south-westward to the end of the freeway where the road passes under the R59 before joining it. Drive another 18 km on the N1/R59 to the Parys boundary sign and continue into Loop Street.

PARYS About 1 km wide in reaches at Parys, the Vaal River, with its well-wooded island resorts, the camping and caravan sites along its shady, willow-lined banks and the opportunities it affords anglers and watersport enthusiasts, makes the town one of the most popular recreational centres on the Highveld. Parys came into

existence when 113 plots were sold on the farm Klipspruit in 1876, although it was only in 1882 that the Volksraad of the Orange Free State recognised the settlement as a town and made the appropriate proclamation. Of several explanations for the name Parys the one generally accepted is that it was suggested by the surveyor of the layout of the town, a German named Schilbach who had taken part in the siege of Paris in the Franco-Prussian War. It is said that he envisaged a great city spanning the Vaal that would be similar to the French capital on the banks of the Seine. Industries which contribute to the prosperity of Parys include a tobacco-processing factory, two flour mills and light engineering factories.

Return along Loop Street to the Parys boundary sign on the

191. Messing around in a speedboat on the Vaal River

N1/R59, pass the left turn to Johannesburg on the N1 after 18 km and continue 18,7 km on the R59 to the right turn into Sasolburg.

SASOLBURG Until 1950 the site of Sasolburg was featureless veld but its proximity to extensive deposits of the low-grade coal needed for the manufacture of petroleum products, to the adequate water supply of the Vaal River and to the vast petroleum-consuming market of the Witwatersrand led to the establishment of a town there for the South African Coal, Oil and Gas Corporation (Sasol) and its employees. Now the third largest town in the Orange Free State, this model complex has more than 20 residential areas separated by open strips of parkland and is served by shopping centres, thoroughfares radiating from the centre and more than adequate educational, recreational and administrative facilities. The many by-products from the process of converting coal into oil have ensured Sasolburg's status as the centre of the country's petro-chemical industry.

Return from Sasolburg to the R59, turn right and after 2,2 km turn left (SP Vanderbijlpark) on to the R568, passing the interchange exit to Vanderbijlpark South 4,9 km further on. Cross the R27/R42 after another 4 km, turn right (SP Potchefstroom) on to the R553 (Golden Highway) 4,6 km further on and cross the R54 after another 6,6 km. Pass the left turn to Randfontein 8,4 km further on and continue 16,1 km on the R553 before crossing the flyover bridge across the N1. Travel 19 km from the N1 before recrossing it, continue 4 km, now on the R29, to the interchange at Uncle Charlie's Corner and drive the remaining 7,2 km back to the Crown Interchange on the M1.

Potchefstroom, the first capital of the Transvaal Republic, has retained much of the charm of its early years, in contrast to the frenetic bustle of Johannesburg and the brashness of other newer centres.

JOHANNESBURG See Tour 67.

From the Crown Interchange at the southern edge of Johannesburg take the R41 (Main Reef Road) exit and drive 3,5 km to the George Harrison Park on the left.

GEORGE HARRISON PARK See Tour 67.

Continue 20,1 km westward from the George Harrison Park on the R41, which ceases to be the Main Reef Road after 13 km, to reach the left turn (SP Zuurbekom) to the Doornkop Monument.

DOORNKOP MONUMENT About 3,7 km south of the R41, the small Doornkop Monument commemorates the thwarting of the Jameson Raid. At this spot in 1896 the armed invaders whose avowed intention was to redress the grievances of the Uitlanders in the Transvaal capitulated to the republican forces (see Johannesburg, Tour 67).

From the Doornkop turn-off drive 9,5 km westward before turning left (SP Westonaria, Carletonville) to rejoin the Main Reef Road, now the R28, which here is Randfontein's main street.

RANDFONTEIN owes its existence to the cantankerous 'Old Buccaneer' of the pioneering diamond and gold mining days, Joseph Benjamin Robinson. The son of an 1820 Settler, he stood out against the Uitlanders and espoused the cause of the Transvaal Republic in the events that led up to the Anglo-Boer War. Having made a name for himself on the diamond fields, Robinson moved to the Witwatersrand when gold was discovered and went into partnership with Alfred (later Sir Alfred) Beit in the purchase of properties, including a portion of the farm Randfontein, and in the establishment in 1889 of the Randfontein Estates Gold Mining Company, at that time one of the biggest concerns of its kind in the world. The town, which is now a major mining and industrial centre, was laid out the following year. When the Randfontein mining partners separated Beit took control of the interests the company had acquired on the East Rand and Robinson retained the West Rand properties. The controversial magnate, who was created a baronet in 1908, sold his mining interests in 1916 for £4,5 million.

One of the many ways in which Sir Joseph is commemorated is in the name of Robinson Lake, a pleasant resort on Randfontein's northern boundary. Riebeeck Lake with its surroundings, near the centre of the town, is another municipal recreational area.

Continue southward on the R28 from its intersection with Sixth Street and after 15,6 km pass the right turn to Westonaria, a town which owes its existence of a bare half century and its rapid growth to the rich Venterspost and Libanon gold mines as well as others developed more recently. Turn right (SP Potchefstroom) on to the R29 3,1 km from the Westonaria turn-off, right again (SP Carletonville) on to the R501 after another 7,6 km and drive 20,7 km to the right turn into Carletonville. For most of this distance the road lies just outside and for about 6 km actually within the southern boundary of what is known as the Bank Compartment, an area that has been abandoned because of sinkholes.

SINKHOLES While South Africa's biggest sinkhole – 365 m long and 57 m deep – at Doornfontein, near Carletonville, appeared long before the Voortrekkers reached the Transvaal, some of the sudden collapse of the Far West Rand ground has been ascribed to the man-engineered lowering of the water table to avoid flooding of the gold mines in the area. In 1962 the reduction works of the West Driefontein Mine, 5 km west of Carletonville, disappeared into a sinkhole with the loss of 29 lives, and in 1964 five people died when a home on Blyvooruitzicht Mine property, even closer to the town, fell into one of these vast pits. The danger zones have been defined, parts have been evacuated and many millions of rands have been spent on pumping cement, sand and slime into cavities in the underlying dolomite to stabilise weak ground.

192. A sinkhole in the Bank Compartment between Westonaria and Carletonville

CARLETONVILLE is a town that mushroomed after the opening of the Blyvooruitzicht Gold Mine in 1937 and continued to grow rapidly after the subsequent opening of other mines, such as Doornfontein, Western Deep Levels and the richest in the world, West Driefontein. The town was named after Guy Carleton Jones, for 35 years director of Consolidated Gold Fields. Apart from gold mining, Carletonville has numerous business enterprises and a constantly developing industrial economy.

Travel 36,9 km south-westward from the turn-off to Carletonville – the last 10 km or so down the Mooi River valley – before turning right and driving another 1,7 km to the edge of the Boskop Dam. This beautiful stretch of water abounds in waterfowl against which the many anglers attracted by the good fishing and numerous picnic spots provide negligible competition. Return from the dam to the R501, turn right and after 16,3 km cross the Mooi River into Potchefstroom, running straight into Van der Hof Street which becomes Church Street after about 500 m.

POTCHEFSTROOM There are two theories about the name of the oldest town in the Transvaal. One is that it commemorates Andries Potgieter, the Voortrekker 'chef', or leader, who in 1838 established a settlement here on the banks of the stream, known as the Mooi River, where he took his oath of office as first President of the Transvaal Republic. The other suggestion is that the name is a derivative of 'potsherf', since many a potsherd was found alongside the stream at one time. Potchefstroom, where the national flag of the Transvaal Republic, the Vierkleur, was hoisted for the first time, was the first capital of the republic, although Pretoria, as the seat of government, gradually assumed pre-eminence and the town on the Mooi River eventually had to relinquish its status. Among other Transvaal firsts that Potchefstroom could claim were the first Afrikaans and English-medium churches, the first qualified teacher to set up school, the first printing press, the first experimental farm, and the first shot in the war of 1880-1881 between the Transvaal and Britain. After fighting in the streets of Potchefstroom in that war a British garrison under Major R W C Winslow was besieged in the Old Fort (NM) by Boer forces under General Piet Cronjé for about a hundred days. Food became so scarce that the 322 men, women and children in the tiny fort were obliged to eat grass and young maize plants before the siege was lifted at the end of hostilities. In the second

Anglo-Boer War Potchefstroom was occupied by the British and when peace was declared the garrison that remained established a major military base which was used in both world wars and is now the headquarters of the Western Transvaal division of South Africa's armed forces.

Apart from the Old Fort, places of historic interest are the home of President M W Pretorius; the Vyfhoek concentration camp cemetery, which has been converted into a memorial garden; the Kruithuisie, the little stone powder magazine the burghers were authorised to build in 1841; and the Potchefstroom Museum that reflects the cultural history of the region. The Gereformeerde Kerk transferred its theological seminary, established in 1869, from Burgersdorp (see Tour 44) to Potchefstroom in 1905 and the

institution developed into the Potchefstroom University for Christian Higher Education. Lakeside, an attractive resort at the Potchefstroom Dam on the Mooi River, has furnished bungalows, rondavels, a caravan park, a restaurant and facilities for swimming, boating, fishing and other forms of water sport. Grain silos that tower over the town are evidence of the fertility of the surrounding countryside which, in addition to maize, produces other types of grain, groundnuts, fruit, sunflower seed and large quantities of lucerne. The town's industries include South Africa's only chalk factory and one of the largest organ factories in the country.

Continue along Church Street to its intersection with Potgieter Street at the Potchefstroom Town Hall, turn left and drive eastward along

193. Evening near Westonaria

Potgieter Street on to the R29. After 3,2 km pass the right turn to the Modder Dam and turn right to the Danie Theron Monument 44,1 km further on.

DANIE THERON MEMORIAL
Daniel Johannes Stephanus Theron was a man of unrivalled courage, a teacher-turned-lawyer who, when the Anglo-Boer War broke out, formed the 'Wielrijders Rapportgangers Corps', a unit of cycling despatch riders, and later commanded a Boer reconnaissance unit. He was regarded as the finest Boer scout of the war, but before a decision to promote him to the rank of field general could be implemented he was killed in a skirmish he fought single-handed against a British detachment in September 1900. A lofty stylised monument to him pointing skyward from a koppie just to the right of the road indicates the spot where he fell. In 1968 the commando training school at Kimberley was designated the Danie Theron Combat School in his memory.

Continue eastward on the R29 from the Theron Memorial, cross the R28 after about 27 km and turn left on to the N1/R29 29,6 km further on. Take the R29 exit on to the Golden Highway after another 3,3 km, the R29 exit again from the interchange at Uncle Charlie's Corner 4 km further on, and drive 6,5 km back to the Crown Interchange.

194. Like the rest of his modest home in Potchefstroom, this outbuilding was built by President M W Pretorius himself

67

160 km

GOLD – THE METAL THAT STARTED A WAR

Gold is the *raison d'être* of pulsating Johannesburg and its satellite towns. Without it, the Witwatersrand would probably now be like the rest of the Highveld – a region of maize fields and pasture.

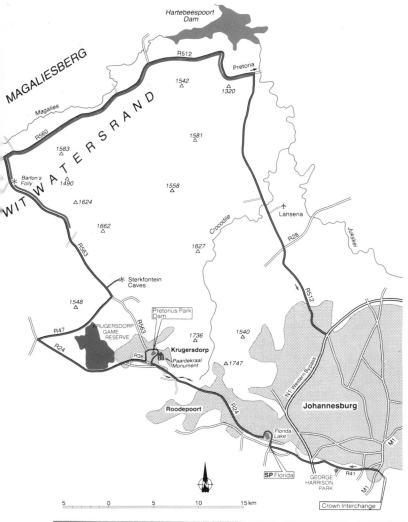

195. An early stamp mill is preserved at the George Harrison Park where the Main Reef was discovered in 1886

JOHANNESBURG There were men and women alive when Johannesburg celebrated its centenary in 1986 who saw what had started as a mining camp of tin shanties and 2 000 souls develop from a town of still no more than 100 000 people at the turn of the century into the second largest metropolis in Africa, with a population of 2 million. The city is focal point of the greatest gold-mining area on earth, one of the world's major market places and centre of the region in which the most sophisticated engineering and manufacturing industries on the African continent are based. Although the gleaming metal had previously been panned elsewhere in the Transvaal, it was the discovery of the main gold-bearing reef on the farm Langlaagte in 1886 that led to the Transvaal Government's proclamation of public diggings on the Witwatersrand and to a stampede of fortune-seekers from all over the world. A dale of small ridges, the government-owned farm Randjeslaagte, was chosen as the site for a town where control could be exercised over the cosmopolitan and potentially unruly throng of diggers. And, taking the Christian names of the men who had proposed the proclamation of public diggings – Johann Rissik of the Surveyor-General's office and Johannes Joubert of the Volksraad – the government called the metropolis-to-be Johannesburg.

The Anglo-Boer War, which broke out a bare 13 years after the town was founded, was precipitated by the political friction that followed the infamous Jameson Raid on the Transvaal in 1896. Although led by Dr Leander Starr Jameson, this abortive armed raid was organised by the Reform Committee that had been elected to redress the grievances against the Transvaal Government of the 'Uitlanders' – the 'foreigners', many of whom were British – among the men digging for gold. In spite of their enormous contribution through burdensome taxation to the hitherto impoverished coffers of the Transvaal, the 'Uitlanders' were accorded no political rights and inadequate public services, and were irked by the government's

arbitrary system of granting monopolies, among other grudges they harboured. When he was appointed Governor of the Cape in 1897 Sir Alfred Milner, an avowed imperialist, seized on their grievances as reason for having British troops sent to South Africa in spite of efforts being made to avert war. The arrival of the troops provoked an ultimatum from the Transvaal Government which Britain rejected and the Anglo-Boer War began on 11 October 1899. Costly and tragic though it was for both victor and vanquished, the conflict did not retard the growth of Johannesburg. Indeed, when the war was over the city boomed to the benefit not only of its own citizens and the Transvaal, but of South Africa as a whole – once the former Boer republics and British colonies had been welded together by the Act of Union in 1910.

Take the R41 (Main Reef Road) exit at the Crown Interchange and drive 3,5 km to the George Harrison Park on the left.

GEORGE HARRISON PARK
George Harrison, one of the discoverers of the Witwatersrand Main Reef, was on his way to Barberton late in 1885 with a friend, George Walker, but tarried to do some building on part of the farm Langlaagte owned by Gerhardus Ooshuizen. When the two men discovered the Main Reef in February 1886, Harrison pegged Claim 19 and Walker Claim 21. Claim 19 was registered as 'een zoekers claim', which has been interpreted as recording that Harrison was the discoverer, and although there is strong evidence to this effect, a Historical Monuments Commission committee of inquiry decided that the find was made by Walker, probably in association with Harrison. The latter sold his claim in November 1886 for the equivalent of R40 and nothing more is known of him. Walker, a former diamond digger and Barberton gold prospector, sold his claim for £350 two months before Harrison sold his, became a mine employee, contracted pneumoconiosis (phthisis) and was reduced to poverty. The George Harrison Park (NM), which was opened in an unprepossessing part of the metropolis in 1949, includes parts of the original claims registered in the names of Harrison and Walker, shafts dug by the early miners and a stamp battery used in those pioneering days.

Continue 8 km westward on the Main Reef Road (R41) and take Exit 7 (SP Florida) to the right into Hebbard Road (R564). Turn left into Kathleen Street (R24/R564) after 1,1 km and reach the south-eastern corner of Florida Lake at the intersection of Kathleen Street and Fourth Avenue 300 m further on. Turn right into Fourth Avenue (R564) to drive around the lake, then turn first left into Swan Green, fourth right into First Avenue, first left into Eeufees Avenue and first left into Westlake Road to reach the entrance to the lake resort on the left 700 m further on.

FLORIDA The settlement of Florida, now a residential area in the Roodepoort-Maraisburg municipality, was established in 1889 by Hendrik van der Hoven on his farm Vogelstruisfontein. Florida Lake, a tree-fringed stretch of water in pleasant parkland at the south-western corner of the town, has picnicking, camping and caravan sites and facilities for swimming, angling and boating. At the lake an exhibit of the Roodepoort Historical Museum that depicts bronze figures surrounding a pond from which a pneumatic drill emerges, commemorates the discovery of gold on the Witwatersrand.

Continue 400 m from the lake resort entrance to the traffic lights at the southern end of Westlake Street, turn right into Hamberg Road (R24) and drive 3,1 km through the suburbs of Hamberg and Georgina to the Roodepoort boundary sign.

ROODEPOORT Its red soil was the reason for naming the farm Roodepoort, on which Jan Bantjies secured prospecting rights in 1885 and discovered gold the following year. The farm was proclaimed a goldfield and one of the owners, J A Nel van Wyk, laid out a town on his portion. The population increased rapidly as mining progressed, and other farms were acquired to establish the settlements of Florida, Hamberg and Maraisburg, which with Roodepoort became a municipality. The Roodepoort Historical Museum near the Town Hall has documents and photographs relating to the West Rand and the Jameson Raid, exhibits connected with the Great Trek, examples of work by Boer prisoners of war on Bermuda, and a number of old vehicles.

As the westbound traffic through Roodepoort separates from the eastbound, follow the R24 signs from Hamberg Road – turning left into Kerkhof Street, right into Olivier Street and right into Dumat Street – to rejoin the Main Reef Road, the designation of which now changes from R41 to R24. Fork right 200 m from Dumat Street and after another 9,4 km turn right across the railway, following the R24/R36 signs. Fork right on to the R36 2,2 km from the railway and, at the Krugersdorp Town Hall 1,4 km further on, turn right into Market (Mark) Street.

196: From a mining camp only a century ago, Johannesburg with its tower-block skyline has grown into the second largest metropolis in Africa

KRUGERSDORP The important gold-mining and industrial centre of Krugersdorp was founded in 1887 by Marthinus Pretorius when he applied to have his farm Paardekraal proclaimed as public diggings and sold part of it to the Transvaal Government for development on condition that it was named Krugersdorp. The attractive Coronation Park at the entrance to the town was laid out on 36 ha of land presented by the British Government in 1902 to mark the coronation of King Edward VII. To the north of it, Pretorius Park incorporates the site presented by Marthinus Pretorius for the Paardekraal Monument (NM) which commemorates the hoisting of the Vierkleur in 1880 to signal the start of the first war between Britain and the Transvaal Boers. When the war broke out about 4 000 burghers gathered at Paardekraal and erected a 3-m cairn of stones as a symbol of faith. A monument, to which an annual pilgrimage is made on the Day of the Covenant, 16 December, was erected over the cairn after the war to commemorate the Boers' victory in that conflict and to reaffirm the covenant taken before the Battle of Blood River. In the Anglo-Boer War the British removed the historic cairn and are believed to have dumped the stones either in the Vaal River at Vereeniging or in the sea at Durban.

From the Krugersdorp Town Hall continue north-eastward in Market Street (R28), passing the Paardekraal Monument on the right after 1,2 km, and turn left round the Pretorius Park Dam into Viljoen Street 900 m further on. Turn left again into Fourth Street (R563) after another 1,8 km and right into Commissioner Street (R36) 1,4 km

still further. At the stop street after 3,3 km turn right on to the R24 to drive 1,6 km to the entrance on the right to the Krugersdorp Game Reserve.

KRUGERSDORP GAME RESERVE White rhino, giraffe, several antelope species and blue wildebeest are among the animals that roam the grassed hills and bushy ravines of the 1 400-ha Krugersdorp Game Reserve, which includes a 200-ha lion enclosure. The reserve has a rest camp with equipped rondavels and chalets, a caravan park, a tearoom and a picnic site.

From the game reserve entrance continue 8,7 km westward before turning right (SP Pretoria) on to the R47. Travel through attractive countryside and after 10,2 km turn left (SP Hekpoort) on to the R563 and then right 1,5 km further on. Drive another 1,6 km to the Sterkfontein Caves.

STERKFONTEIN CAVES It was in the Sterkfontein Caves (NM), opened up in lime-quarry blasting towards the end of the nineteenth century, that the first adult skull of the ape-man *Australopithecus africanus transvaalensis*, 'Mrs Ples', was found in 1936 and identified by Dr Robert Broom. The nickname is short for *Plesianthropus transvaalensis*, as Broom first designated the individual who lived here tens, perhaps hundreds of thousands of years ago. The caves have proved to be one of the most prolific sites of hominid fossils in Africa and have also yielded the petrified remains of several extant and extinct animal species. On their way out of the caves the 50 000 people who annually visit the Sterkfontein site pass a bust of the distinguished anthropologist who identified 'Mrs Ples' and of whom General Smuts wrote: 'Every South African scientist feels prouder because of

Robert Broom. Every South African feels bigger because of him.'

Return from the caves to the R563, turn right and, after driving 16,7 km through a beautiful gateway cutting the Witwatersrand, pass the farm Hekpoort on which stands Barton's Folly.

BARTON'S FOLLY Quite different from other blockhouses built by the British during the Anglo-Boer War, Barton's Folly was a link in a short chain of forts across the valley of the Magalies River between the Witwatersrand and the Magaliesberg range. It was named after Major-General Geoffrey Barton, commander of the Fusilier (6th) Brigade on service in the area. In the design and siting of this blockhouse Barton seems to have been as much of a disappointment as he had been earlier on the Natal battlefields, where he inspired little confidence in Sir Redvers Buller, then Commander-in-Chief of the British Army in South Africa.

Continue 3,5 km northward on the R563, turn right (SP Pretoria) on to the R560 and travel down the fertile Magalies River valley, alternately through bush country and rich agricultural land with fine homesteads. There are numerous picnicking and camping sites along the river and in the kloofs. Turn right (SP Pretoria) on to the R512 21,5 km after joining the R560 and turn right again (SP Lanseria) 15,9 km further on. Reach the left turn to Lanseria after 17,7 km.

LANSERIA AIRPORT See Tour 68.

From the Lanseria turn-off continue 5 km south-eastward on the R512, cross the R28 and drive 11,6 km in Pelindaba Road to the Western Bypass. From there select a route to the desired destination in Johannesburg.

68
120 km
ROUND THE HARTEBEESPOORT DAM

The Hartebeespoort Dam, in the valley between the Witwatersrand and the Magaliesberg range, is surrounded by indigenous vegetation that differs markedly from the grassland of the Highveld.

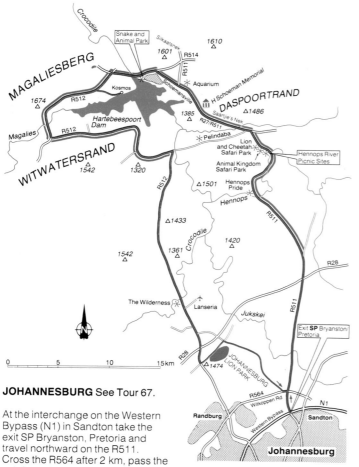

JOHANNESBURG See Tour 67.

At the interchange on the Western Bypass (N1) in Sandton take the exit SP Bryanston, Pretoria and travel northward on the R511. Cross the R564 after 2 km, pass the exit SP Krugersdorp on the R28 11,6 km further on and fork left (SP Pelindaba, Hartebeespoort Dam) after another 2,2 km to remain on the R511. After a pleasant drive through the Hennops River Hills reach Hennops Pride Pleasure Resort on the left, 9 km from the fork.

HENNOPS PRIDE Picnic and camping sites, swimming pools, boats for hire and angling are among the attractions of the Hennops Pride Pleasure Resort on the Hennops River. From the resort the river flows another 5 km westward to become a tributary of the Crocodile River which, in turn, becomes the Limpopo after joining the Groot Marico River more than 200 km to the north-west.

From the entrance to the Hennops Pride Resort continue northward on the R511, cross the Hennops River 4,5 km from the resort and reach the Hennops River picnic sites 1,3 km further on. Although rondavels may be hired here, camping is not allowed. Cross the Hennops River again 200 m from

the picnic sites and after another 200 m pass the Animal Kingdom Safari Park and then the Lion and Cheetah Safari Park. Carry straight on at the intersection 3,5 km from the last crossing of the Hennops River, where the R511 joins the R27. The National Nuclear Research Station at Pelindaba is about 5 km along the road running to the south-west from the intersection.

PELINDABA On part of the farm Pelindaba, bought by the South African Atomic Energy Board, the country's first nuclear research reactor, Safari-1 (South African Fundamental Atomic Reactor Installation 1) was inaugurated in 1965. Within the imposing buildings of the National Nuclear Research Station the vessel containing the core of the reactor is submerged in a pool of water 10 m deep which in turn is surrounded by high-density concrete walls up to 3 m thick. While the reactor was designed primarily for research and as a source of neutron radiation, radioactive isotopes are also produced in ever-increasing quantities.

From the last intersection the R27/R511 runs towards Daspoortrand and cuts through it by way of Saartjie's Nek. On a hilltop to the right of the road 5 km from the intersection there is a

stone cross commemorating General H J Schoeman, a member of the Volksraad of the Transvaal Republic. Another 3,7 km further on, again to the right of the road, is the Hartebeespoort Aquarium, said to be Africa's largest fresh-water aquarium, where in addition to the attraction of exotic as well as indigenous fish, there are crocodiles and performing seals. The R511 – which drivers of vehicles of more than 4,5 tons or 4,57 m in height must take to avoid the Hartebeespoort Dam Tunnel – veers to the right 600 m beyond the aquarium. Continue on the R27 and 2,6 km further on pass a right turn to Pretoria on the R514. Drive into the small town of Schoemansville, a mainly residential area with many fine homes in beautiful settings on the steep, wooded slopes overlooking the Hartebeespoort Dam.

HARTEBEESPOORT DAM The wall of the 1 620-ha Hartebeespoort Dam, completed in 1923, was built in the narrow gorge between Silkaatsnek and Kommandonek where the Magaliesberg range is cut by the Crocodile River just below its confluence with the Magalies River. The top of the wall is 59 m above its lowest foundation level and the main road from Pretoria to Rustenburg runs along its 149,5-m length. Water from the dam is conducted by way of two major canals and a series of minor ones to irrigate more than 13 000 ha of land on which wheat,

197. A single-lane road runs along the top of the Hartebeespoort Dam wall

tobacco, oats, lucerne and vegetables are the principal crops grown. The Hartebeespoort Dam has been a popular recreational stretch of water almost from the outset and there are several angling and boating clubs, including the Transvaal Yacht Club, at the water's edge. Among the fish caught are kurper, yellowfish, carp, barbel and eels.

SCHOEMANSVILLE The village of Schoemansville was founded by Johan Schoeman and named after his father, General Hendrik Jacobus Schoeman, who is commemorated by the stone cross on the hill in Saartjie's Nek. Prominent in public affairs and a member of the Transvaal Volksraad, General Schoeman invaded the Cape Colony at the head of a republican force in the Anglo-Boer War and fought against General John French. He was killed in an accident in Pretoria not long after the end of the war.

The Hartebeespoort Snake and Animal Park is on the left of the R27 2,1 km from the right turn to Pretoria, and 1,1 km further on is the entrance to the tunnel through which the road passes before reaching the wall of the Hartebeespoort Dam. From the north-western end of the 53-m tunnel cross the dam wall and 2 km further on turn left (SP Krugersdorp, Pretoria) off the R27 on to the R512. Take the left turn to Kosmos 1,7 km further on.

KOSMOS is another resort founded by Johan Schoeman. Inspired by the tranquillity of the scene as he rowed towards the hill on which the settlement was to be developed, he chose the Greek word for the universe with which to name it. A profusion of flowering shrubs and trees enhances the scene Schoeman found so enchanting.

Return to the R512, turn left and continue 8 km south-westward before crossing the Magalies River. Turn left (SP Pretoria) 1,2 km from the river, turn right (SP Johannesburg) 16 km further on to remain on the R512 and cross the Crocodile River after another 16,5 km. Reach The Wilderness on the right 500 m from the river.

THE WILDERNESS is a charming resort on the Crocodile River where there are shade trees, lawns, a tearoom and a swimming pool.

The left turn to Lanseria Airport is 300 m south of The Wilderness.

LANSERIA AIRPORT This modern airport – with runways of 2 200 m and 1 500 m built to internationally accepted standards, variable-intensity ground lighting and

198. A picnic spot beside the Crocodile River

199. One of the attractions of the Johannesburg Lion Park is its Ndebele village

24-hour customs and immigration facilities – is privately owned by the Transvaal Board for the Development of Peri-urban Areas, the Roodepoort and Krugersdorp municipalities and the Lanseria Management Company. It is used by the owners of private aircraft and in 1975 was the venue of Air Africa '75 International, the first international air show held in this country.

Continue southward on the R512, crossing the R28 5 km from the Lanseria turn-off. Turn left 1,4 km from the R28 and drive another 1,9 km to the entrance to the Johannesburg Lion Park on the right.

JOHANNESBURG LION PARK
More than 60 lions, which are fed between 09h00 and 09h30 every day, live in an enclosure of the Johannesburg Lion Park. After passing through other parts of the reserve, where there are gemsbok, blesbok, impala, wildebeest and ostrich, a winding, one-way road continues through the enclosure. Also within the boundary of the

park, which is open from 08h00 to 16h30 every day of the year, are an old Ndebele village, a restaurant, tea garden, swimming pool and picnic sites.

From the entrance to the Lion Park turn right and continue 1,5 km north-eastward before turning right again (SP Witkoppen). Turn left into Witkoppen Road 8,8 km further on and right into Fourways after 400 m. Reach the Western Bypass (N1) 2,1 km from the last turn and select a route back to the desired destination in Johannesburg.

69
170 km MAGALIESBERG

A low range of mainly unspoilt beauty, the Magaliesberg has, as well as historic and prehistoric associations, pleasant resorts to which town-dwellers escape for recreation.

200. The Anglican church in Rustenburg was reconstructed in 1967

MAGALIESBERG RANGE The 160-km arc of the Magaliesberg, stretching from a point roughly 30 km north-west of Rustenburg to the north-eastern suburbs of Pretoria, was once known as the Cashan Mountains, a corruption of Khashane, the name of the chief of the people who inhabited the region when the first white men hunted along the range. When the Voortrekkers arrived, however, they named the range after a more

recent black leader, Mohale, whose name they pronounced and spelt Magalie. The range, though rarely much higher than 400 m above the surrounding countryside, has a relatively high rainfall which, with a favourable geological structure, makes it a major watershed, nourishes the vegetation that contributes to the appeal of the region and sustains such of the wildlife as has survived the merciless hunter's gun – the

occasional leopard, antelope species, baboons, monkeys, the peregrine falcon and the Cape vulture. Although peaceful now, the Magaliesberg was once the scene of violent human conflict, at first between the warlike Mzilikazi and the black people he encountered when he arrived here from Natal, and then between white men engaged in the Anglo-Boer War. The remains of many British forts can still be seen on the high ridges.

RUSTENBURG, the third oldest town in the Transvaal, was founded in 1851 by burghers who, with the Voortrekker leader Andries Pretorius, had settled in the area a decade earlier. They were granted permission by the Transvaal Volksraad in Potchefstroom to build the second church in the young republic and to establish a village on the farms Witpensfontein and Kafferskraal. The new settlement's name, which means 'castle of rest', could recall the peace that followed the defeat of the Matabele *impis* under Mzilikazi by the Voortrekkers at Vechtkop in 1836 and at Mosega and Kapain the following year. On the other hand, it may allude to the rest that came to those who had found land suitable for settling and farming at the end of their Great Trek. And there are those who contend that the Reverend Philip Eduard Faure of Wynberg, for many years a member of the Moderamen, or executive body of the synod of the Dutch Reformed Church, wrote to Pretorius suggesting that the town be named after the estate of Rustenburg in the Cape. The future President of the Transvaal, Stephanus Johannes Paulus (Paul) Kruger, who at the age of 11 in 1836

had arrived in the Transvaal with his father, Casper Kruger, was granted a farm near present-day Rustenburg when he was 16. He named it Waterkloof and took his first young bride, Maria du Plessis, to live there the following year. In 1862 he bought the farm Boekenhoutfontein, about 15 km north of the town, and the homestead (NM) he built here became his permanent residence from 1873. His place of prayer on the hill behind the house is enclosed by railings. Even after he became President of the Transvaal Republic in 1883 and moved to Pretoria he retained Boeken-houtfontein, and it remained his property until his death. It is now owned by the Simon van der Stel Foundation. In front of the Rustenburg Town Hall a bronze statue sculpted in 1901 by the French artist Jean Archand commemorates Oom Paul's association with Rustenburg. The work portrays a dejected leader, Archand explaining that the tragic greatness of Kruger was so apparent to him that 'it was for ever chiselled in my mind'. The sculpture was discovered in Paris in 1919, bought for the Union Government by General Louis Botha and General Jan Smuts and, because it was not big enough for Church Square in Pretoria, was donated to Rustenburg. The town has witnessed a number of momentous occasions in South African history. In 1852 it was the scene of the reconciliation between the two former Great Trek leaders Andries Pretorius and Hendrik Potgieter after Pretorius had incurred the displeasure of his political opponents by concluding the Sand River Convention with the British. And under a great syringa tree dissenting religious fundamentalists decided in 1859 to form their own free Gereformeerde Kerk. A granite replica (NM) of the tree stump is preserved in Church Street. Some of the British soldiers who fell in the Anglo-Boer War battles of Buffelspoort, Moedwil, Koster River and Olifantsnek are buried in the old Rustenburg graveyard.

The town, which is a popular health and holiday resort and has several industries, is the centre of a prosperous agricultural district in which beef cattle are raised and tobacco, citrus fruit, maize, wheat, groundnuts and sunflower seeds are produced. The district also has a great variety of minerals, of which the most important to be exploited is platinum. On the south-eastern outskirts of the town the Kwaggapan Game Park has a variety of wildlife, particularly giraffe and kudu, and a lookout tower that affords a panoramic view of the region. Coert Steynberg's famous warthog group 'Punt in die Wind' features in a collection of sculptures in the Paul Bodenstein Nature Park, and in the south-west the Rustenburg Nature Reserve accommodates several antelope and more than 140 bird species. A two-day hiking trail and one which takes only three hours are among this reserve's other attractions.

From the Rustenburg Town Hall in Plein Street turn left into Burger Street and 200 m further on left again into Van Staden Street to leave town south-eastward on the R24/R30. Pass left turns to Kroondal at 6,6 km and 9,2 km from the Town Hall, the left turn to Pretoria at Rex 11,8 km from the same point and reach the top of Olifantsnek 2,2 km further on.

OLIFANTSNEK This gap, worn through the ridge of the Magaliesberg by the Hex River, has been obstructed by the wall of the Olifantsnek Dam since 1928. Water from the dam, of which there is a fine view from the top of the pass, irrigates almost 2 500 ha of agricultural land.

Pass a right turn to Derby 3,7 km from the top of Olifantsnek and continue 8,7 km before crossing the Hex River. Reach Maanhaarrand 18 km further on.

MAANHAARRAND The hamlet of Maanhaarrand is in an important archaeological area which takes its name, meaning 'maned ridge', from dikes of diabase rock which, thrusting up through the floor of the Magalies River valley, resemble the mane of a lion. The weathered boulders of the ridge provided material for the Stone Age artists and Iron Age village builders who once inhabited the region. Prehistoric rock engravings have been found in the area, as have, in big ash heaps among the ruins of villages, the remains of the humans, their pottery and the bones of the animals they had slaughtered for food. The outlines of many Iron Age villages can be clearly seen on aerial photographs of the valley.

201. In the Magaliesberg

Turn left (SP Hekpoort) on to the R560 8,2 km from Maanhaarrand and after about 7 km come abreast of the highest peak of the Magaliesberg range on the left.

BATTLE OF NOOITGEDACHT
It was on the slopes of this 1 851-m mountain in the Magaliesberg range that commandos led by the Boer generals Koos de la Rey, Jan Smuts and Christiaan Beyers scored a signal victory in a surprise attack on a British force commanded by Major-General R A F Clements in December 1900. Clements, trapped in a gorge in which he was encamped below the sheer mountain walls, extricated his force with great skill, but only after 637 men had been killed, wounded or taken prisoner. The dead, wounded and captured of the Transvaalers totalled about 100.

Cross the Magalies River 10,8 km after turning on to the R560 and reach the Hekpoort Picnic and Pleasure Resort on the left 1 km from the river.

HEKPOORT PLEASURE RESORT
About 2 km of shady river bank on which there are picnic spots and a swimming pool are among the amenities of the Hekpoort Pleasure Resort on the Magalies River.

Pass the right turn to Krugersdorp 800 m from the resort and continue down the fertile Magalies River valley on the R560, passing byways to several picnic and camp sites alongside the river and in the kloofs beyond. After 21,5 km join the R512 coming in from Pretoria on the right and travel first northward, recrossing the Magalies River after 1,2 km, and then north-eastward before passing the right turn to Kosmos (see Tour 68) 8 km further on. Turn left (SP Rustenburg, Brits) on to the R27/R512 1,7 km from the Kosmos turn-off, pass right turns to Brits 1,5 km and 8,4 km further on and drive through an enchanting landscape, alternately bush-covered and cultivated, stretching from the Magaliesberg in the south to the hills of southern Bophuthatswana in the north. Pass 1 378-m Wolhuterskop on the right about 3,5 km from the second Brits turn-off, the turn-off to Mooinooi after another 16,3 km, and 7,6 km further on the left turn to the Buffelspoort Dam. Pass a left turn to Maanhaarrand 11,7 km from the Buffelspoort Dam turn-off and enter Kroondal 8,1 km further on.

KROONDAL, situated on a farm originally known as Kronendal, was one of 22 German Lutheran mission congregations established in Natal and the Transvaal. The farm, which was in existence in 1843, was registered in 1858 in the name of Jan Michiel van Helsdingen, formerly of the Hermannsburg Missionary Society. A mission was established here, but when the society could no longer afford to provide maintenance for anyone but the missionaries, the lay workers who had worked at the station settled as independent farmers nearby. The settlement was surveyed and divided into plots in 1889 and a school which acquired a reputation for excellence was founded. Among those of the pupils who were not German-speaking were Louis Botha, who was to become South Africa's first Prime Minister, and the Afrikaans poet Totius, J D du Toit.

Continue on the R27 from the western outskirts of Kroondal and reach the Rustenburg Town Hall in Plein Street after 7,5 km.

202. Church architecture that testifies to the German origins of Kroondal's early settlers

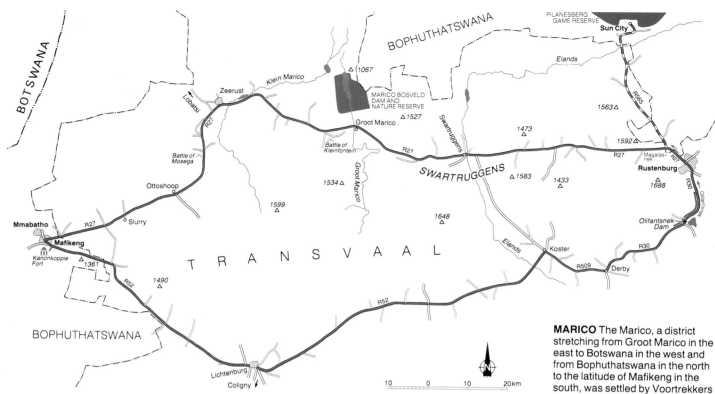

THE WESTERN TRANSVAAL

70
390 km

From horizon to horizon the vast plain of the western Transvaal is planted with maize which, when the summer rainfall has been adequate, forms a great ocean of green.

RUSTENBURG See Tour 69.

Leave Rustenburg north-westward along Van Staden Street from its intersection with Malan Street (SP Zeerust, Swartruggens, Sun City) and follow the R27, entering Bophuthatswana after 5,2 km and leaving it again at the right turn to Sun City and Boshoek 1,2 km further on. To make the detour to

Sun City, turn right off the R27 on to the R565 and keep to the tarred road, turning right again after about 26 km and then left into the resort 5,3 km further on.

SUN CITY In the south of the Pilanesberg range, Sun City is the mecca of many a South African intent on playing the tables of its casino; golfing on its superb 18-hole

course; watching boxing matches in the vast stadium; attending performances by some of the most popular stars of the entertainment world; or simply lazing in the plush modern ambience of the huge complex with its luxury hotels, restaurants and swimming pools. Tours through the surrounding wildlife reserve can be arranged.

From the Sun City turn-off travel westward on the R27 and reach Swartruggens after 50,6 km.

SWARTRUGGENS, the name of which is derived from the series of black ridges in the area, was laid out on the farm Brakfontein in 1875. Most of the surrounding countryside is somewhat featureless bushveld that is noted for cattle ranching but also produces wheat and tobacco under irrigation. Diamonds were discovered at Swartruggens in 1933 and digging continues at the Mallin and a few smaller mines.

Continue westward through Swartruggens on the R27, crossing the Elands River in the town, and 30,7 km from the river turn left into Groot Marico on the eastern boundary of the region known as the Marico.

203. Farmers of the Groot Marico community at a cattle auction

MARICO The Marico, a district stretching from Groot Marico in the east to Botswana in the west and from Bophuthatswana in the north to the latitude of Mafikeng in the south, was settled by Voortrekkers from 1845 onwards. It is an agricultural district, producing tobacco, wheat, citrus fruit and maize, while cattle ranching is conducted on a considerable scale. Fossil animal remains have been found in dolomite caves in the area, but what really gives the Marico distinction is its place in the stories of Herman Charles Bosman, one of South Africa's best-loved literary figures. As a teacher in 1926 at the little Heimweeberg School on the Marico farm Haasbroek, about 1,5 km from what is now the R27, he studied the farmers and villagers of the district with intense discernment and reflected images of them in the mirrors of his inimitably humorous but thought-provoking words. In the Marico he found a 'pattern of life offering infinite riches in literary material' which were to make their way into the conversations between the characters he created – Schalk Lourens, Jurie Steyn, Fritz Pretorius, Gysbert van Tonder, Oom Koos Gerber, Oupa Bekker and so many others.

GROOT MARICO Although many of the citizens of Groot Marico are descendants of the Voortrekkers who started arriving in the district in 1845, the sleepy, one-street village, with many a character who could have inspired a Bosman tale, was laid out as recently as 1948 by A J M van Aardt and others on the farm Wonderfontein. Considerable quantities of air-dried Virginia tobacco are handled at Groot Marico by a branch of the Magaliesberg Cooperative Tobacco Planters' Association.

Return to the R27, turn left, cross the Groot Marico River after 1 km and reach the scene of the Battle of Kleinfontein 6,7 km from the river.

BATTLE OF KLEINFONTEIN
On 24 October 1901 a Boer force led by General Koos de la Rey killed 400 British troops and captured a considerable number of horses, mules and provision wagons in a battle on the farm Kleinfontein. The Boer casualties were limited to 60.

Cross the Klein Marico River 29,3 km west of the Kleinfontein Battlefield and reach Zeerust 1,8 km further on.

ZEERUST
is the major town of the Marico and was laid out by Diederik Coetzee in 1867 on the farm Hazenjacht, originally called Sebatlani, which means 'dusty place'. The founder named the new settlement Coetzee-Rust, which was subsequently shortened to its present form. The Church of St John the Baptist (NM) was the third Anglican church to be built in the Transvaal and is the oldest still standing.

Continue westward on the R27 through Zeerust and after about 17 km reach the point on the road nearest to the Mosega Battlefield.

BATTLE OF MOSEGA
Sendelingspos, about 1,5 km west of what is now the R27, was established as a mission station in the early 1830s by the French Protestant clergymen Jean Louis Lemue, Samuel Rolland and Jean Pierre Pellissier, who built here the first dwelling for whites in the Transvaal. Within a few years the Matabele had ousted the missionaries and Sendelingspos, renamed Mosega, became one of the two kraals in the vicinity of present-day Zeerust occupied by Mzilikazi. It was here, after Voortrekker outposts along the Vaal River had been overwhelmed by one of Mzilikazi's *impis*, that he suffered a serious defeat in 1837 at the hands of a mounted commando which had set out under the leadership of Andries Potgieter and Gerrit Maritz to seek retribution and recover stolen Voortrekker cattle. More than 500 Matabele warriors were slain in the surprise attack.

Pass the left turn into Slurry 44,2 km from the Zeerust Dutch Reformed church and reach Mafikeng 18,9 km further on.

MAFIKENG
After the annexation of the region by the British, Mafikeng was established in 1885 by Sir Charles Warren, leader of a military expedition which built the fort (NM) on Kanonkoppie at the southern outskirts of the town. Some 16 km further south is Rooigrond, the site

204. The statue of General Koos de la Rey in Lichtenburg

of what was once the capital of the Goshen, one of two tiny republics formed in 1881 by settlers outside the jurisdiction of either the Cape or the Transvaal. Goshen and the other republic, Stellaland, near present-day Vryburg, ceased to exist when the British annexed Bechuanaland to the Cape in 1885. 'Mafeking', as the town used to be known, was a corruption of the Tswana term meaning 'place of rocks'. Today the town is the centre of one of the most important beef and milk regions of South Africa and has one of the country's largest creameries. Though outside what used to be Bechuanaland, it was the seat of the protectorate's administration for many years. However, the events that put Mafeking – to use the name then accepted – on the map, were the Jameson Raid (see Johannesburg, Tour 67), launched from here in 1895, and the seven-month siege started by the Boer general Piet Cronjé when the Anglo-Boer War broke out in 1899. Cronjé chose merely to beleaguer rather than attack the British garrison stationed in Mafeking under the command of Colonel Robert Baden-Powell, although a determined assault might have compelled the small force to surrender. As a result, Baden-Powell was able to strengthen his defences sufficiently

to repulse the first and only real attack, which was led by Field-Cornet Sarel Eloff in April 1900. The Kanonkoppie Fort, with its extensive breastworks, communications trench linking it to the town and bunkers covered with corrugated iron and earth, played a prominent part in the siege. As a result of the wild jubilation with which the relief of Mafeking was greeted in London the word 'mafficking' became part of the English vocabulary to describe rejoicing with hysterical boisterousness.

MMABATHO
Contiguous with the north-western boundary of Mafikeng is Mmabatho, the capital created for Bophuthatswana when the homeland was proclaimed in 1977.

Leave Mafikeng by driving south-eastward along Robinson Street (R52) from its intersection with Shippard Street (SP Lichtenburg), after 1,5 km turn right (SP Hospital) off the R52 and follow further signs to the Bopholeng Hospital. Kanonkoppie Fort is 100 m from the hospital gate. From the fort return to the R52, turn right and drive through bushveld and vast tracts of maize fields. After 63 km cross the R505 into Swart Street in Lichtenburg.

LICHTENBURG
Sometimes called Wilgedorp because of the willow trees along the furrows lining the streets, Lichtenburg was established on the farms Middelbosch and Doornfontein which were presented for this purpose to the Transvaal Republic by Commandant Hendrik Greeff in 1866. The town was the focus of diamond fever between 1925 and 1930, and while it lasted there were some 50 000 diggers and 100 000 labourers active in the district. After an estimated £15 million worth of diamonds had been found the source waned and only a few diggers remained to pursue their dreams of fortune. The backbone of Lichtenburg's economy is now agricultural and the maize produced in the district is handled by one of the biggest cooperative companies in the country. Other grains are also produced and cattle ranching is another major agricultural occupation. Hennie Potgieter's massive equestrian statue of the great Boer general Koos de la Rey, who died in Lichtenburg in 1914, was unveiled in the town in 1965.

Leave Lichtenburg driving eastward in Republic Street (R52) from its intersection with Melville Street, pass a right turn to Coligny 2 km from the intersection and continue 83,9 km north-eastward through more expanses of maizeland to Koster.

KOSTER
Named after Bastiaan Hendricus Koster, a native of Rotterdam who in 1860 settled on the farm Kleinfontein on which the town was later established, Koster is a centre of maize production, although other grains, tobacco and citrus fruit are also grown in the district.

Turn right (SP Derby) off the R52 in Koster on to the R509 and drive 16,5 km to the entrance of Derby.

DERBY
Established for the settlement of indigent people, Derby was named after the British Secretary of State for the Colonies in the early 1880s, Lord Derby. The graves of troopers of the Scottish Horse who lost their lives in an Anglo-Boer War battle in the locality are to be seen in Derby's military cemetery.

Turn right (SP Rustenburg) 400 m after entering Derby and then left (SP Rustenburg) on to the R30 300 m further on. After 17 km turn left again (SP Rustenburg) at the south-western corner of the Olifantsnek Dam and the foot of the Olifantsnek Pass (see Tour 69) and drive 15,6 km, still on the R30, back to Rustenburg.

205. Farmland between Lichtenburg and Koster

71
100 km
THE EASTERN MAGALIESBERG

West of Pretoria the Hartebeespoort Dam and the well-vegetated hills and valleys of the Magaliesberg range afford citizens of the executive capital of South Africa almost unlimited scope for open-air recreation.

PRETORIA With a summer garment of blue jacaranda blossom both carpeting the pavements and on some 50 000 trees lining 640 km of streets; with a climate conducive to the luxuriant growth of a wide variety of flowers and trees; and with its stately buildings and pleasant layout in the valleys formed by the eastern spurs of the Magaliesberg, Pretoria is probably South Africa's most attractive inland city. It owes its status as capital of the Transvaal to the desire of the widely separated Voortrekker groups in the mid-nineteenth century to have a central place of assembly for their legislature. The name of the embryo city was chosen to commemorate the great Voortrekker leader Andries Pretorius and his son Marthinus Wessel Pretorius, first President of the Transvaal Republic. As seat of the Volksraad, Pretoria was selected at the time of unification of the four South African provinces in 1910 as one of the three national capitals. With Cape Town chosen for the legislature and Bloemfontein as the seat of the judiciary, Pretoria became the executive capital. So the administrative headquarters of most South African Government departments are here in some of the city's imposing structures, of which the Union Buildings, designed by Sir Herbert Baker, are the most stately. Pretoria's heart is historic Church Square, where ox wagons used to be outspanned, where the city's first shops and church were established, and where in 1857 the symbol of the Transvaal Republic, the Vierkleur, was hoisted for the first time and struck at the end of the Anglo-Boer War. Vigilance by the conservation-minded has saved much of the square from modern development, with the result that buildings of historic and architectural value – not least among them the old Raadzaal

– continue to lend interest to its picturesque appeal. Dominating the centre of Church Square is Anton van Wouw's statue of Paul Kruger, the last President of the Transvaal and most distinguished head of state of all the Boer republics. Kruger House, in Church Street West, was Oom Paul's presidential residence and is now a museum devoted to his life. Another museum is Melrose House in Jacob Maré Street which, while it was occupied

by Lord Milner and Lord Kitchener in 1902, was the venue for the signing of the Treaty of Vereeniging at the end of the Anglo-Boer War. The well-proportioned rooms of this stately building, dating from 1886, house items of rare and beautiful Victoriana.

Defence Headquarters, the State-controlled Iron and Steel Corporation (Iscor), the Council for Scientific and Industrial Research, the South African Bureau of Standards, the Atomic Energy Board, the Weather Bureau and the Human Sciences Research Council are all situated or based in or near Pretoria. The city's major educational institution is the University of Pretoria, the biggest residential university in the country.

Drive 800 m northward in Potgieter Street from its intersection with Church Street (two blocks west of Church Square) and turn right into Boom Street. Turn left (SP Wonderboom) into Paul Kruger Street 700 m further on and, after passing under a railway bridge 2,1 km from Boom Street, cut through Wonderboompoort about 3 km still further.

WONDERBOOMPOORT This gap in the part of the Magaliesberg range called the Wonderboom Ridge, on which some of Pretoria's northern suburbs are situated, conducts the railway line and the old main road from South Africa's administrative capital to the country's northern neighbours. These arteries follow trails blazed more than 50 000 years ago by successions of prehistoric men moving north and south through the defile cut through the Magaliesberg by the Apies River. Just how many successions of people passed this way has been indicated by many thousands of stone implements exposed by a road cutting through a branch of the defile. Archaeologists judge by the type of implement found in numerous layers that Wonderboompoort was a natural game trap where hunters were able to kill animals with relative ease and haul the carcases into a branch of the defile for butchering. A security fence now protects the site.

Drive 1,7 km through Wonderboom-poort, turn right (SP Warmbaths) on to the R55 and after another 400 m turn right again into the Wonderboom Nature Reserve.

WONDERBOOM NATURE RESERVE The 'wonder tree' (NM) alluded to in the names of the Wonderboom Nature Reserve, Wonderboompoort and Fort Wonderboompoort is a fine

206. Pretoria's monument to the doughty folk who took part in the Great Trek

example of the giant wild fig (*Ficus salicifolia*, previously *F. pretoriae*), a spreading evergreen tree which defoliates completely once in a cycle of years. It is remarkable for its method of vegetative reproduction by natural layering. Extending branches sag to the ground, take root and start new subsidiary trunks which continue the process. Ages ago the parent trunk of the Wonderboom, now 3,75 m in diameter and estimated by carbon dating to be a thousand years old, put out a secondary circle of seven daughter stems, two of which then put out a tertiary circle, the whole giving a spread of 50 m and a height of 22 m. That the Wonderboom – so named by the Voortrekkers who found it in 1836 – has for so many centuries survived all but recent vandalism is ascribed to the sanctity with which it was regarded by the indigenous people. As a result of vandalism in modern times the tree has been in peril of dying, but the danger has been averted since the Pretoria City Council bought the land on which it grows and proclaimed it a nature reserve. There are many picnic spots under the wealth of shade trees in this pleasant 90 ha of parkland, which has a nature trail leading to Fort Wonderboompoort, one of three strongholds built in 1897 and 1898 for the protection of the Transvaal Republic's capital. The other two, Fort Klapperkop (NM) and Fort Schanskop (NM) are both south of the central city area. All three were constructed with bomb-proof casemates, telegraph offices, magazines, store-rooms and engine-rooms, but they were unarmed and unmanned during the Anglo-Boer War as all guns and troops had been sent to the front.

Return from the Wonderboom Reserve to the R55, turn left and drive 400 m before turning right (SP Pretoria North). After 900 m bear right (SP Pretoria North, Roslyn) and 400 m further on turn left (SP Brits, Rustenburg) into Rachel de Beer Street (R513). Continue eastward on the R513, cross the R80 6,9 km further on and turn left (SP Brits, Pretoria) 7,5 km from the R80. Turn right (SP Brits) after 400 m and drive another 3,5 km to the Jopie Fourie Monument on the left.

JOPIE FOURIE MONUMENT
Josef Johannes Fourie, who was educated at Grey College, Bloemfontein, and Victoria College, Stellenbosch, joined the Transvaal Republican force which crushed the Jameson Raid in 1896, served in the Transvaal Volunteer Corps operating against Swazi rebels the following year and, when the Anglo-Boer War broke out, became a scout and despatch rider in the republican forces. As a result of

being severely wounded in fighting near Pretoria he was crippled for the rest of his short life, but joined the Active Citizen Force as a captain after the war and supported Louis Botha's party until jingoes broke up a Kruger celebration of 10 October 1914. Incensed, he joined the burgher force ranged behind Christiaan Beyers who had resigned office as Commandant-General of the Union Defence Force in protest against the government's decision to attack the Germans in South West Africa. Fourie and the commando he led were captured on 16 December 1914 on the farm Nooitgedacht in the Rustenburg district. As neither he nor his brother Hannes had resigned their commissions in the Active Citizen Force, they were tried by court martial on a charge of high treason, Jopie being sentenced to death and Hannes to five years' hard labour. Jopie was executed by firing squad on 20 December 1914 while singing the hymn 'Als wij de doodsvallei betreen' ('When we tread the valley of death'). The execution shocked many and was a factor in the rise of the National Party. The obelisk here at his birthplace, Wildebeesthoek, was originally erected at Nooitgedacht in 1934, but was moved to its present site 30 years later.

Continue westward on the R513 and, if it is a Saturday or Sunday, turn right (SP Crocodile Farm) after 6,5 km. Turn right again (same SP) 1,7 km further on and left after another 1,1 km to reach the farm 1,4 km still further.

CROCODILE FARM What is said to be the only true crocodile farm in South Africa is run by Jan Gierd Kuhlmann. About 10 000 young are hatched in incubators annually either for live export to game reserves or as meat for a growing market in Europe where it is regarded as a delicacy. The farm is open to the public only at weekends, when visitors are conducted on tours and given demonstrations.

Return from the crocodile farm to the R513, turn right (no SP) and then left 7,7 km further on to drive 400 m to the Silkaatsnek Nature Reserve entrance on the right.

SILKAATSNEK NATURE RESERVE At the northern end of Silkaatsnek which cuts through the Magaliesberg range, the 400-ha Silkaatsnek Nature Reserve is a sanctuary for kudu, eland and other antelope species, giraffe, wildebeest, zebra, warthog and ostrich.

SILKAATSNEK Silkaatsnek is a pass through the eastern end of the Magaliesberg a few kilometres

207. Part of the Wonderboom, a giant wild fig in Pretoria's northern suburbs

north-east of the Hartebeespoort Dam. The name derives from Mzilikazi, the Matabele chief whom the Voortrekkers called Silkaats. In 1864 two warring factions of Transvaal burghers met here and agreed to bury the hatchet, and in the Anglo-Boer War, on 11 July 1900, the pass was the scene of an important victory by General Koos de la Rey over a British force.

Retrace the 400 m from the reserve entrance to the R513 and continue 1 km north-westward before turning left (SP Rustenburg) to remain on the R513. Cross the Crocodile River after 4,5 km and turn left (SP Pretoria) on to the R27 at the stop street 1,9 km further on. Reach the wall of the Hartebeespoort Dam after 2 km and drive through the tunnel beyond it into Schoemansville (see Tour 68). The Hartebeespoort Snake and Animal Park is 1,1 km from the tunnel. Turn left (SP Pretoria) on to the R514 2,1 km east of the snake park and after another 900 m turn left to the Hartebeespoort Cableway.

HARTEBEESPOORT CABLEWAY
In an exhilarating 6-minute ride the Hartebeespoort Cableway whisks the visitor 378 m upward to the peak above Silkaatsnek, one of the highest points in the eastern section of the Magaliesberg. The view of the dam, of Schoemansville below and of the surrounding countryside is magnificent.

Return from the cableway station to the R514, turn left and after 1,8 km left again (SP Pretoria, Brits) to remain on the R514. Turn right (SP Pretoria) 700 m further on and continue eastward, still on the R514. After another 4,8 km turn left (SP Boekenhoutkloof) and drive 15,4 km along the southern slopes of the Magaliesberg before running into the road from Hornsnek and turning left back on to the R514 1,9 km further on. Turn right on to the Apies River Motorway 6,5 km after rejoining the R514 and return 2,2 km to Church Street in Pretoria, veering left into Lorentz Street for the last 1,2 km.

208. Hartebeespoort Dam as it appears from the top station of the cableway

THE WATERBERG – HEART OF THE BUSHVELD

Wide open spaces where the wildlife was once prolific, low mountain ranges encircling the featureless plains, and towns steeped in the history of the Transvaal pioneers characterise the region south of the Waterberg.

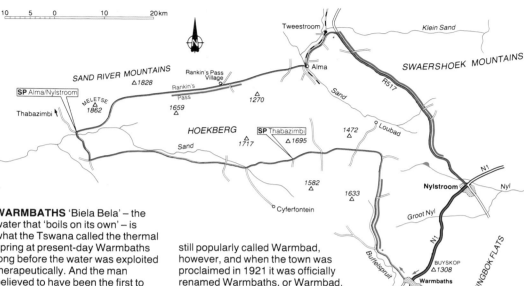

WARMBATHS 'Biela Bela' – the water that 'boils on its own' – is what the Tswana called the thermal spring at present-day Warmbaths long before the water was exploited therapeutically. And the man believed to have been the first to use it for healing was the renegade Coenraad de Buys, after whom the hill 5 km north-east of the town is named (see Buyskop, below). It was the Voortrekker Carl van Heerden, however, who established the first farm at the spring and named it Het Bad, although subsequently it was also variously known as Badplaats and Warmbad. Another name, Hartingsburg, was given the property when the Zuid-Afrikaansche Republiek bought it and in 1882 named it in honour of Pieter Harting, professor of medicine at the University of Utrecht, who championed the cause of the Boers against the British annexation of the Transvaal. It was

still popularly called Warmbad, however, and when the town was proclaimed in 1921 it was officially renamed Warmbaths, or Warmbad. The Transvaal Government started developing Warmbaths by draining the marshes around the spring 10 years after acquiring it, and it has been a popular health and holiday resort ever since. It became a major spa, though, with the opening of the R5 million David Brink Centre in 1979. The centre's 21-m square pool under glass has underwater massage jets and an imposing central fountain, from which the alkaline mineral water at 36 °C flows into an outdoor pool within an enclosed garden. There is also a cooler plunge pool and a pool at 41 °C for the treatment of victims of rheumatic diseases. Other facilities in the attractive complex include

vapour inhalation rooms, electrobaths, carbon dioxide baths, vortex and foot-and-arm baths, mud baths, alternating-temperature massage showers, massage cubicles, a biokinetics clinic, a gymnasium, saunas, a beauty clinic, a hair salon and the services of a qualified physiotherapist and other trained staff. Accommodation in the complex includes 147 chalets built among the surrounding trees.

Warmbaths was one of the places selected by the British for the erection of a blockhouse in the series that protected the railway from Noupoort through the Orange Free State and the Transvaal to Pietersburg. The fortification (NM) is near the railway station. The graves of numerous Voortrekkers are to be found in the old Warmbaths cemetery. Among them is that of Christina Pretorius who, when she became ill here, persuaded her husband, Andries, to leave her behind so that she would not impede the trek party he was leading.

From its intersection with Voortrekker Road (SP Elandsfontein, Alma, Rankin's Pass) drive north-westward along Grobler Avenue, which leads into Robinson Road and out of Warmbaths. Turn right (SP Nooitgedacht) 10 km from Voortrekker Road to travel through the pretty, shallow valley of the Buffelspruit with its grainlands and

citrus groves, passing after 12,2 km the right turn to Donkerpoort and forking left (SP Thabazimbi) 8,4 km further on. Turn right (SP Thabazimbi) after another 20 km, cross one of the two Sand rivers in the area 10,1 km still further and pass a left turn to Cyferfontein 300 m from the river. After travelling 33,1 km through thickly bushed areas and tracts of grassland used for cattle ranching, turn right (SP Thabazimbi), cross the same Sand River after another 6,6 km and turn sharp right (SP Alma, Nylstroom) 500 m from the river. Drive past the 1 862-m Mount Meletse on the left at the western end of the Sand River Mountains, the most westerly range of the Waterberg.

WATERBERG RANGE The Waterberg, so called because of the many streams and swamps in the range, is the collective name for all the mountains in the region, including from the west the Sand River Mountains, the Hoekberg range, the Swaershoek Mountains and the Moepel range. Elevations are limited to about 600 m above the surrounding countryside. This is bushveld, and the names of some of the indigenous vegetation, which includes many aloes and succulents, are expressive of a particular feature of each plant. Thus 'huilbos' is the weeping tree, 'lekkerbreek' breaks easily, 'stamvrug' bears fruit on the trunk and 'raasblaar' has noisy leaves.

The road continues through Rankin's Pass between the Sand River Mountains in the north and the Hoekberg range in the south and reaches the Rankin Pass village 35,3 km from the last crossing of the Sand River. At Alma Station, after another 16,8 km, pass a right turn to Nylstroom and cross the second Sand River in the area for the first time 600 m further on. Continue 10,9 km before turning right (SP Nylstroom) on to the tarred R517. From here the road climbs from the valley of the Klein Sand River up the Swaershoek Mountains and after about 10 km the traveller is confronted by the surprising sight – for this part of the country – of high-trellised grapevines. Cross the second Sand River for the second time 23,6 km after joining the R517 and drive 21,9 km to the intersection of Potgieter and Voortrekker streets in Nylstroom.

NYLSTROOM When the Jerusalemgangers, a Voortrekker party of religious fanatics heading for the Holy Land reached these parts under the leadership of Johan Adam Enslin they spotted in the distance what they thought was a pyramid and verily believed they had arrived in the Middle East. They

209. Hot mineral water fountains into the main indoor pool at the Warmbaths spa

were also convinced that the Mogalakwena River flowing past the 'pyramid' – which is actually the solitary hill now known as Kranskop, 12 km east of present-day Nylstroom – was part of the headwaters of the Nile and named it accordingly. Inspired by their 'prophetess', a widow Gous, the Jerusalemgangers refused to worship with other Voortrekkers in the region, thwarted Dutch Reformed clergymen who came to hold services and became involved in a dispute with Commandant-General Andries Pretorius which led to a lawsuit. Although the sect petered out after Enslin's death in the early 1850s, the name the Jerusalemgangers gave the Mogalakwena River persists. And so does the name of the town founded in a beautiful setting on its southern bank in 1866.

Nylstroom is the principal town of the Waterberg district where excellent crops, including groundnuts, can be grown under irrigation along the rivers. Table grapes have also been produced in recent years and the town promotes the industry with an annual grape festival. This centre has one of the country's largest agricultural cooperative societies, a factory where visitors may observe groundnuts being sorted and another producing peanut butter, about half of which is exported. Nylstroom was the home of Christiaan Beyers, the distinguished Boer general who became Commandant-General of the Union Defence Force but resigned in protest against South Africa's attack on the Germans in South West Africa in World War I. In the early years of this century the poet, journalist, lawyer, naturalist and author Eugène Marais farmed in the Waterberg district and made his great studies of the behaviour of termites and baboons which led to the publication of *The Soul of the*

210. Bontebok in the bushveld of the Waterberg

White Ant and *My Friends the Baboons*. The distinguished architect Gerhard Moerdijk was born in the town. And South Africa's fifth Prime Minister, J G (Hans) Strijdom, practised here as an attorney for many years and represented the Waterberg parliamentary constituency within which Nylstroom falls. The J G Strijdom Park, with its recreational facilities and bird sanctuary, is named after him, and his home, Strijdomhuis, is now a museum. 'Nylstroom', one of the first steam locomotives to haul trains between Pretoria and Nylstroom when the Spoorwegmaatskappij Beperkt line was completed in 1898, is preserved at the railway station.

211. Springbok Flats

Leave Nylstroom on the N1 by driving south-westward along Voortrekker Street (SP Warmbad, Pretoria) from its intersection with Potgieter Street, cross the Groot Nyl River 9,3 km from the intersection and, after breasting a rise about 10,5 km further on, observe the Springbok Flats stretching away to the south-east.

SPRINGBOK FLATS The vast, featureless plain known as the Springbok Flats stretches for about 130 km from west to east and some 100 km from north to south. It is hot, has a rainfall of less than 600 mm a year and, although mainly cattle country, maize, groundnuts and, where irrigation is available, citrus fruit are extensively produced. The name is a forlorn reminder of the great herds of springbok that populated the plain before all the game – apart from what is protected in private reserves – was wiped out by man.

About 13 km from the Groot Nyl River pass Buyskop on the left.

BUYSKOP Among the rebels of Graaff-Reinet who flouted the authority of the Dutch East India Company and established their own 'free republic' in 1798 was Coenraad de Buys, an intelligent giant of a man who was declared an outlaw with a price on his head. He subsequently lived with a number of Xhosa women and then married one with whom, after much roaming in other parts, he lived within the domains of various chiefs in the Transvaal. He founded several coloured communities and eventually trekked to Mozambique in 1821 to start another with a Goanese woman. The sons he sired in the Transvaal were favourably disposed to the Voortrekkers who caught up with them and they rendered the newcomers valuable assistance. Buyskop is named after the notorious renegade because of a ruse he is said to have perpetrated while besieged on the hill by a hostile *impi*. Judging by their own water deprivation in the summer heat, the warriors believed the Buys party must be worse off after days of siege, but Buys tipped the last of the precious contents of a waterskin out over the hill to prove that he had resources not available to ordinary mortals. And the superstitious *impi* withdrew. Buyskop, from which stone was hewn for the construction of the Union Buildings in Pretoria, was the halfway post for the stagecoach between Pretoria and Pietersburg in the days of the Zuid-Afrikaansche Republiek.

Reach the entrance to Warmbaths about 4,5 km south-west of Buyskop.

INTO THE SOUTPANSBERG

Wide plains and high plateaux, majestic mountain ranges and deep valleys, ancient indigenous forests and modern plantations, rivers, waterfalls and dams characterise the northern Transvaal's landscape of contrasts.

212. A boulder-strewn koppie outside Louis Trichardt

LOUIS TRICHARDT, in its beautiful setting on the slopes of the southern foothills of the Soutpansberg range, affords a pleasant stop-over for travellers on the Cape-to-Cairo road or on the way to Punda Milia, or Punda Maria as it is now known, the oldest and most northerly entrance to the Kruger National Park. This picturesque town was established after the Mphephu War of 1889 in which the Commandant-General of the Transvaal, Piet Joubert,

subdued those of the Venda chiefs who, under Mphephu, had defied the authority of the Transvaal Government, refused to pay taxes and terrorised the Shangana-Tsonga people known as the Magwamba who also lived in the Soutpansberg fastnesses. Mphephu, whose tribe had condemned him to death many years previously for an affair with one of his father's wives, had escaped to work on the Kimberley diamond fields and is said to have acquired only the vices of civilisation. In spite of his reputation as a lazy drunkard, he was recalled to the Soutpansberg to succeed his

father as chief of the Bavenda by conspirators antagonistic to the designated new leader, thus causing serious tribal friction. A reminder of the conflict between the early white settlers and the Bavenda is the Geloftekerk, or Church of the Vow, in Krogh Street, that was built in fulfilment of a promise made by Joubert and his commando on the eve of the battle against Mphephu. Once the Venda chief had been dealt with, and in response to requests to the government by farmers in the region, a village was laid out below the Magato Ridge of the Soutpansberg. It was proclaimed in 1899 and named, at the request of his grandson, Colonel Stephanus Trichardt, in honour of the Voortrekker leader whose party had outspanned here for 15 months

before making their disastrous, for many even fatal, expedition to Delagoa Bay more than 60 years previously. In the Anglo-Boer War the women and children of Louis Trichardt were evacuated by the British to Pietersburg and the deserted village was totally destroyed by the Bavenda. It was rebuilt after the war and the town that has developed 45 km north of the Tropic of Capricorn in the warm, sunny Bushveld is now the centre of a region of cattle and game ranching, although its main industry is the processing of timber logged in the extensive surrounding plantations. The value of wood is accorded recognition by the display of 94 different tree species in Louis Trichardt's Indigenous Tree Park next to the municipal caravan park in Messina Road, which links Krogh Street with the N1.

Drive north-eastward in Krogh Street from its intersection with Trichardt Street (SP Messina) on to the N1 and after 3,3 km reach the left turn to the Hanglip Forest Reserve a short distance from the main road.

HANGLIP FOREST RESERVE
With a permit from the forester at the Hanglip Nursery the visitor may picnic at any of the approved sites in the shade of indigenous forest giants, or take any one of a number of delightful walks below the mighty crag of the 1 719-m Hanglip, one of the highest peaks of the Soutpansberg. The sacred burial ground of chiefs such as Magato and Mphephu is on the mountain.

Return to the N1 and turn left, continuing 17,8 km from the Hanglip Forest turn-off through beautiful, densely-wooded defiles to the first of the two Verwoerd Tunnels in Wyllie's Poort, which cuts a way for the Great North Road through the Soutpansberg.

SOUTPANSBERG RANGE The range is thought to have been named by Coenraad de Buys (see Buyskop, Tour 72), who left the eastern Cape in about 1813, trekked northward with a Xhosa wife and their progeny and settled temporarily at a large salt pan at the western end of the Soutpansberg. When he trekked on in 1821 he left his coloured clan at what is now known as Buysdorp, where they were encountered by the first of the Voortrekker arrivals in the region and were subsequently accorded land-ownership rights by President Kruger. The Buys descendants still occupy the land as a self-contained community. The Soutpansberg, running about 150 km east and west, has a high rainfall which, through irrigation systems, promotes the agricultural prosperity of the region and makes extensive

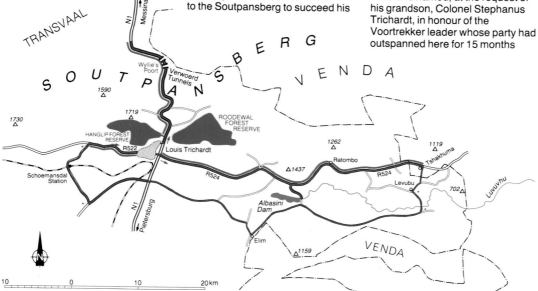

afforestation possible. Like so many other ranges in southern Africa, the Soutpansberg was originally the domain of Bushmen who were eventually driven out by other peoples, in this case the southward-moving Venda tribes from north of the Limpopo River. The Bavenda now occupy most of the plateau from the Soutpansberg to the Limpopo.

WYLLIE'S POORT For scenic splendour Wyllie's Poort, named after Lieutenant C H Wyllie who mapped out the first road through the Soutpansberg in 1904, compares with some of the most famous South African passes. Though parts of it were washed away at times, the road as Wyllie located it was used until 1961, when the two Hendrik Verwoerd Tunnels were driven through spurs in the defile and made possible a new route at a lower level. Of those made for roads in South Africa only the 573-m tunnel through Daspoortrand on the western outskirts of Pretoria is, at present, longer than the Verwoerd Tunnels, the first being 381 m and the second 290 m long.

After driving to the northern end of Wyllie's Poort about 6 km beyond the second tunnel, which is less than 1 km from the first, return by the same route to Louis Trichardt. Set out again east-south-eastward along Trichardt Street (R524) from its intersection with Krogh Street and drive 22,3 km through the beautiful countryside south of the Soutpansberg before turning right to the Albasini Dam, which is 2 km from the R524.

ALBASINI DAM The Albasini Dam, a popular stretch of water with anglers and watersport enthusiasts, perpetuates a name brought to the Soutpansberg by João Albasini, who became an elephant-hunter at the age of 18 when he landed in Mozambique in 1831, and later moved into the Transvaal where he traded with the Voortrekkers. He settled at Schoemansdal (see below) and established Goedgewensch, a model farm run on feudal lines with a fort as his homestead. Appointed by the Portuguese Government as its consul in the Transvaal, he did much to establish trade relations between Delagoa Bay and the republic. The Transvaal Government appointed him superintendent of the Soutpansberg tribes and, although his main function was the collection of taxes, he survived the sacking of Schoemansdal by the Bavenda in 1867 and continued to live in his fort until his death in 1888.

214. Venda women prepare a lunch of mealies

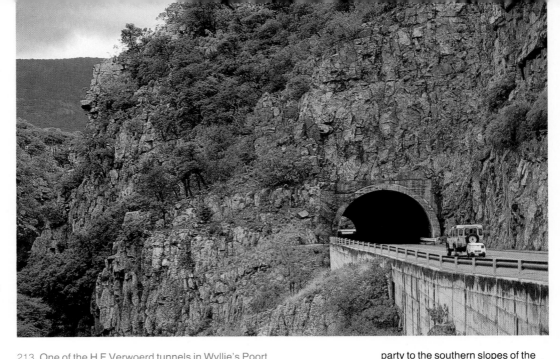

213. One of the H F Verwoerd tunnels in Wyllie's Poort

Return to the R524 from the Albasini Dam, turn right and continue eastward, passing one right turn to Levubu after 14,7 km and another one 3,8 km further on. Travel another 5,1 km to the village of Tshakhuma and turn right (SP Levubu) off the R524 to drive through dense subtropical vegetation, much of which has been cleared for banana groves. At Levubu, 4,4 km from the R524, pass a right turn to Louis Trichardt and after another 3,8 km turn right (SP Elim) to reach the Elim Hospital 28 km further on.

ELIM, where there is now an important tuberculosis hospital in a charming sylvan setting, was founded as a mission station in 1879 by Ernest Creux who, with Paul Berthoud, persuaded the Protestant Free Church in the Swiss canton of Vaud to send them to South Africa to establish the Mission Vaudoise, later to become the Mission Romande. After training at the Basutoland station of the Paris Evangelical Missionary Society they became the first

missionaries to minister to the Magwamba of the Soutpansberg region, who were known to the Voortrekkers as the 'Knopneuse', or 'Knob noses'. The sobriquet was given because of the form of facial tattooing practised by the Magwamba which resulted in big black keloids, fibrous growths associated with pigmented scarring.

From the entrance to the Elim Hospital continue 600 m westward before turning right (SP Louis Trichardt) and cross the N1 18,5 km further on. Cross the main railway line to Zimbabwe after another 2,5 km and turn right (SP Schoemansdal Station) 8,5 km from the railway. Recross the railway at Schoemansdal Station 7,3 km further on.

SCHOEMANSDAL When the ever-restless Hendrik Potgieter became disillusioned with Andries Ohrigstad, the town he had established in 1845, and fell out with the other, more democratically minded Voortrekker leader there, Kootjie Burger, he trekked with his

party to the southern slopes of the Soutpansberg in 1848 and founded a settlement, Zoutpansbergdorp, also known as Oude Dorp. He regarded the territory his company occupied, which became known as the Zoutpansberg Republic, as autonomous and independent of the Transvaal Republic. Trade routes between Zoutpansberg and the Portuguese ports of Delagoa Bay and Inhambane were established, with ivory being the major export. Portuguese merchants, among them João Albasini, opened shops in Zoutpansbergdorp, a church, parsonage and other houses were built and by 1855 the population was reported to number about 1 800. By this time Hendrik Potgieter, who had died in 1852, had been briefly succeeded by his son Piet and when the younger Potgieter was killed in a punitive action against the Ndebele chief Makapan in 1854, the quarrelsome Stephanus Schoeman assumed office as commandant-general, renaming Zoutpansbergdorp after himself the following year. During Schoeman's regime relations between the ivory-hunters based at Schoemansdal and the local black people became so intolerable that the town was evacuated on 15 July 1867. That night the Bavenda destroyed the town by fire – and a ghost town it has remained, with only the name of Schoemansdal Station, the grave of Hendrik Potgieter and the plaque proclaiming the site a national monument to recall the lively community that once existed here.

Continue 4 km north-westward from the railway at Schoemansdal Station, turn right (SP Louis Trichardt) on to the R522 and drive the remaining 15 km back to Krogh Street in Louis Trichardt.

CHAPTER SEVEN

The Eastern Transvaal

74
190 km

MAGOEBASKLOOF AND THE KOEDOES RIVER VALLEY

Primeval forest, the deep green velvet of tea plantations, a pot-pourri of perfumes, and groves of subtropical fruit lend enchantment to a drive starting along the spectacular road up Magoebaskloof from Tzaneen.

TZANEEN See Tour 75.

Leave Tzaneen on the R71, travelling south-westward from the intersection at the northern end of Danie Joubert Street. Turn right (SP Pietersburg, Duiwelskloof) on to the R71/R36 after 3 km and after another 1,2 km cross the bridge over the south-western arm of the Fanie Botha Dam. Turn right to the Fanie Botha Dam Nature Reserve 3,1 km from the bridge.

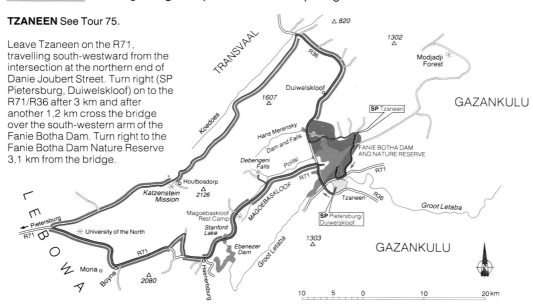

FANIE BOTHA DAM NATURE RESERVE The Fanie Botha Dam and 200 ha of surrounding land have been a nature reserve since 1978, the year after the dam was completed. While it has a limited variety of animal life, more than 150 bird species have been recorded, including the fish eagle. There are facilities, such as launching ramps, for water sports and the reserve, which has a caravan park and picnic sites, is popular with anglers as the dam is stocked with yellowfish, blue kurper, black bass and eels.

215. Magoebaskloof

Return to the R71/R36, turn right and then left (SP Magoebaskloof, Pietersburg) on to the R71 200 m further on. Drive through banana groves among lush subtropical vegetation into Magoebaskloof.

MAGOEBASKLOOF This beautiful mountain pass, which climbs 610 m in only 5,6 km, runs through primeval forest, deep green tea plantations and groves of subtropical fruit with flowering trees on either side of the road. Peaceful though it is now, it was once the scene of bitter conflict. In 1894, when the Transvaal Government sent out a commando to subdue

recalcitrant tribes in the northern Transvaal, all but the Tlou, a Sotho clan under the chieftainship of Makgoba, submitted and moved to the areas allocated to them. Makgoba's people fled into the dense forest of the kloof that bears his name – albeit in corrupted form – to this day, and a punitive force of 800 burghers and 6 000 Swazi auxiliaries under Commandant-General Piet Joubert was sent to flush them out. The Swazis, after killing one of two Tlou women they captured, tortured the other until she disclosed the tribe's stronghold, which they surrounded. Makgoba accepted the Swazi challenge to

man-to-man combat with their own *induna* but was beaten and decapitated, and his head was delivered to Joubert in support of the Swazis' claim for bounty. After their leader's defeat the Tlou tribe dispersed and lost its identity.

Pass the right turn to the Magoebaskloof Dam 7,8 km from the last turn, turn right (SP Debengeni Falls) 1,4 km further on and, after climbing steeply up 3,4 km of winding road carved through jungle-like indigenous forest, reach the gate to the Debengeni Falls area on the right. The waterfall is a short but steep walk down from the gate.

DEBENGENI FALLS In this captivating glen the powerful flow of the Ramadipa River, a tributary of the Politsi, cascades into a deep pot-like pool which accounts for the name Debengeni, 'the place of the big pot'. There are facilities for picnicking and a natural slide into the crystal-clear river.

Return from the falls to the R71, turn right and continue 7,5 km south-westward up Magoebaskloof to the Magoebaskloof Rest Camp. Pass the Magoebaskloof Hotel 4,6 km from the rest camp and after another 3,7 km reach Stanford Lake, where there are chalets for hire in surroundings abounding with flowering shrubs and trees. Haenertsburg is about 6 km south-west of the lake.

HAENERTSBURG The village of Haenertsburg was once the centre of the Woodbush Goldfields and owes its name to the man who started the rush of diggers to the area, C F Haenert. Woodbush itself, now called Houtbosdorp, is about 12 km north of Haenertsburg. Haenert, one of the pioneers of coffee cultivation in the region, started a large plantation of trees on his farm, Last Hope. The extensive timber plantations in the vicinity are served by a sawmill in Haenertsburg.

Soon after passing through Haenertsburg the scenery changes dramatically from dense rain forest to hilly scrubland dotted with thousands of aloes as the road runs through Lebowa. Travel 18,8 km from Haenertsburg to reach the village of Boyne, from which Zion City Moria can be seen on the slopes across the intervening valley.

MORIA The nondescript cluster of buildings which would be passed unnoticed but for the big white star picked out on the hillside with 'Moria City' and the initials 'ZCC' next to it is the headquarters of the church purporting to attract the biggest annual assembly of worshippers in

Christendom. Traffic officials and newspapermen have estimated that the number of pilgrims who travel, mainly by bus, from all over southern Africa to attend the Zion Christian Church's open-air Easter services ranges between 2 and 3 million.

At Turfloop, 9,8 km from Boyne, pass the entrance to the imposing buildings of the University of the North.

UNIVERSITY OF THE NORTH Founded in 1959 as a subsidiary college of the University of South Africa, the University of the North acquired full university status in 1970. Although it is situated in Lebowa, it serves all the Northern and Southern Sotho peoples and the Tsonga, Tswana and Venda, and admits students from other parts of southern Africa too. Fine prehistoric rock art has been found in caves near Turfloop.

Turn right (SP Dap Naudé Dam, Houtbosdorp) off the R71 3,6 km from Turfloop and drive on a fine tarred road through a landscape dotted with hills, many of whose summits are of solid rock. After 20,9 km the tar ends as the road leaves Lebowa at the Katzenstein Mission and, once past Houtbosdorp (formerly Woodbush) about 4 km from the mission, returns to mountainous terrain where it runs along the edge of the high eastern wall of the Koedoes River valley before descending into rich farmland. After summer rain the condition of this stretch of road may be poor but the scenery is so magnificent that the drive is worthwhile. Turn right (SP Duiwelskloof) on to the tarred R36 38 km from the Katzenstein Mission and reach Duiwelskloof 17,7 km further on.

DUIWELSKLOOF The name Duiwelskloof, given to this small town with lovely gardens in a tranquil picturesque setting, sounds like a misnomer. For the transport riders who are believed to have named the gorge, however, its crude, muddy track must have been the very devil to negotiate in the muggy subtropical heat of the rainy season.

Pass the Hans Merensky Dam on the right 6 km after entering Duiwelskloof and the falls of the same name on the left 500 m further on.

HANS MERENSKY After a distinguished career in South Africa as a mining geologist and having amassed a fortune, German-born Hans Merensky turned to farming in the Duiwelskloof area. Here he applied his scientific abilities to such effect in a wide variety of

agricultural spheres that South Africa as a whole derived untold benefit. His many benefactions, which have continued since his death in 1952, have included education endowments and support for hospitals, charitable institutions and cultural enterprises.

Turn left (SP Modjadji) 2,1 km beyond the Hans Merensky Falls and drive through thousands of planted eucalyptus trees before crossing the bridge over the northern arm of the Fanie Botha

Dam 3 km further on. Turn right (SP Tzaneen) 5,5 km from the bridge and right again (SP Tzaneen) after another 2,5 km. The road to the left leads about 31 km to Modjadji.

MODJADJI A magnet for botanists in the tribal area of Modjadji is the Modjadji Forest where the world's largest concentration of a single cycad species grows. These living 'fossils' of *Encephalartos transvenosus*, known as 'Modjadji palms', evolved 50 million years ago and probably formed a major

216. On a bed of solid rock a brook races down to join the Koedoes River

part of the dinosaur's diet. The name of the area derives from the settlement here in the sixteenth century of a tribe from the north led by Princess Modjadji, a reputed rain queen whose descendants have successively inherited her rain-making formula and reputation. It was the legend of Modjadji that inspired Sir Rider Haggard to write *She*.

Turn right (SP Pietersburg) on to the R71 5,2 km from the last turn, cross the Groot Letaba River 800 m further on and turn right again (SP Fanie Botha Dam) 1 km from the river. After 300 m pass the National Institute for Tropical Diseases and the Siegfried Annecke Memorial Garden (see Tzaneen, Tour 75) and reach the wall of the Fanie Botha Dam 1,8 km further on. Return to the R71 and cross it to run into Danie Joubert Street in Tzaneen.

217. Moria, headquarters of the Zion Christian Church

ON THE ZEEDERBERG STAGECOACH RUN

Before the railways expedited communication and travel in the Transvaal passengers and mail were conveyed by a stagecoach service which included a run to the Murchison goldfields.

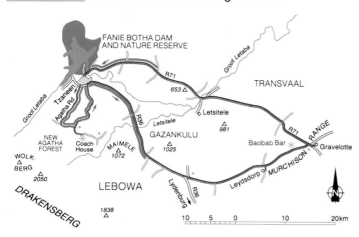

TZANEEN Of all the explanations of the origin of the name Tzaneen the most probable is related to the situation of the town on the banks of the Letaba River in a beautiful basket-like hollow surrounded by forested mountains. The Tsonga word for a basket and the shrub whose bark is used for weaving in these parts is 'tsana'. Other suggestions are that it is derived from 'dzana', a Karanga word meaning 'to dance' and that this was the place for dancing; from 'Tsaneng', the earliest known name for the entire Duiwelskloof area; or from 'batsanene', the 'people of the small villages'. Whatever the derivation, the countryside round Tzaneen – redolent as it is at different times of freshly-picked tea, of orange blossom, pine trees, carnations and luxuriant indigenous subtropical vegetation – could not be sweeter. Here, where plant growth is as luxuriant as in a hothouse, the gardens and flowering trees splash every shade of colour over the predominant green of the town and countryside. The first modern settlement developed when the colonial government of the Transvaal established a research station for tropical and subtropical agriculture in 1903. Abandoned for research by 1916, the land was taken over by the Union Government for settlement, and the town was laid out in 1919. The growth of Tzaneen, where the spectacular road down Magoebaskloof emerges through the Drakensberg foothills, was at first retarded by malaria. Then in 1931 came that pioneer in the study of tropical diseases Dr Siegfried Annecke, a man of determination,

initiative and boundless energy. It was he who established the malaria research station at Tzaneen through which, after painstaking research and exacting field operations, the scourge was brought under control in the Lowveld – the once-dreaded fever belt. He then turned his attention to bilharzia. The research station, named the Siegfried Annecke Research Institute to honour him after his death, continues the campaign against bilharzia. With malaria checked, Tzaneen developed rapidly and now serves extensive tea estates, a major forestry area and a thriving community of farmers producing citrus fruit, tomatoes, subtropical fruit, coffee, tobacco and cut flowers, particularly carnations. It is also a popular tourist centre, and

the surrounding countryside is a paradise of wilderness areas and trails for backpackers. Known as the 'Agatha Road', a splendid 35-km circular drive from Tzaneen affords fine views as it runs through woodland intersected by streams and farmland.

For the Agatha Road drive head south-westward from the fork formed by Peace Street and Agatha Street in Tzaneen, turn left (SP Agatha) after 900 m, left again (SP Letsitele Valley) 10,9 km further on and after another 3,5 km pass a left turn to Tzaneen just before the end of the tar at the New Agatha Forestry Station.

AGATHA was the name of the wife of Christiaan Johannes Joubert, a member of the Transvaal Volksraad and head of the republic's department of mining at the time of the early gold rushes. In response to pleas for a hospital site from the diggers of the Murchison goldfields when he visited them in 1890, Joubert selected a spot on the Thlabina River and named it after his wife. Malaria had such a devastating effect there, however, that the hospital village was moved to a healthier site here in the north-eastern shadow of the Wolkberg – and the name came with it. The Agatha area is now given over to forestry and agriculture.

Continue past the left turn to Tzaneen and reach The Coach House after 2,5 km.

THE COACH HOUSE In 1888, when the Murchison range was the scene of intense gold-mining activity, Heinrich Altenroxel and Conrad Plange built the New Agatha Hotel here where the Zeederberg Stagecoach halted to change mules on its way between Pietersburg and Leydsdorp. The Zeederberg service was launched in 1879 when Christiaan ('Doel') Zeederberg, who had been a transport rider, took his brother Roelof into partnership and operated the first regular mail run between Kimberley and Johannesburg, using coaches built by American firms such as the Abbot-Downing Company of Concord in New Hampshire. In 1890 they started their weekly Kwagga Coach service between Pretoria and Pietersburg – with a 'branch line' to Leydsdorp – and eventually extended it to Rhodesia, continuing their operations for a considerable period even after the railway system became extensive. The Coach House, a modern luxury hotel in some 500 ha of its own farmland and forest, is on the same site as the hotel built by Altenroxel and Plange and overlooks one of the most splendid of the many wonderful panoramas in the Transvaal Drakensberg. In July every year the early days of the post-house are recalled when a full span of oxen hauling a wagon over the old transport riders' route takes a break here.

Backtrack 2,5 km from The Coach House, turn right (SP Tzaneen) and drive through rank indigenous vegetation interrupted by plantations of eucalyptus and groves of macadamia nuts, pecan nuts and kiwi fruit. Vista upon vista opens up as the fine tarred road

218. The Coach House, a luxury hotel on the site of an inn on the Zeederberg Stagecoach run

curves round and climbs up and down hill after hill until, about 13 km from the last turn, it runs into Claude Wheatley Street back in Tzaneen. Leave Tzaneen again, driving 500 m south-eastward along Danie Joubert Street from its intersection with Agatha Street before turning left (SP Nelspruit, Lydenburg, J G Strydom Tunnel) on to the R36, and cross the border into Gazankulu 9,7 km further on. Pass the 1 072-m Mount Maimele on the right after about 15 km and turn left (SP Letsitele) off the R36 22,8 km from the border. Pass the left turn to Letsitele 500 m further on where the tar ends and the signpost indicates Gravelotte ahead. The road now runs through dense bushveld where there is extensive cattle ranching. Pass the left turn to Rubbervale 17,8 km after leaving the R36 and turn right 100 m further on to drive 1 km to Leydsdorp.

LEYDSDORP It would hardly be gratifying for President Paul Kruger's distinguished Secretary of State, Dr Willem Johannes Leyds, if he were alive today to visit the town named in his honour. After gold had been discovered in the Murchison range the settlement started off as a gathering of prospectors round Auguste Robert, or French Bob as this familiar character at several of the early Transvaal diggings was known. French Bob's Camp was renamed Leydsdorp when it was proclaimed a town in 1890. It soon became a bustling community of 5 000 served by stores, a post office, hotel, police station and even a newspaper, *The Leydsdorp*

Leader. The yield of gold in the area was disappointing, however, the diggers gravitated to more profitable fields and Leydsdorp declined. By 1924 it was practically dead and all that is left today is a small cluster of derelict, dilapidated buildings, including the Zeederberg Coach stables, abandoned workings and pieces of rusting machinery in the bush that has reclaimed its own ground. It has been suggested that the ghost town be restored and developed as a tourist attraction.

Backtrack the 1 km from Leydsdorp and turn right to travel through the thickly bushed hills of the Murchison range.

MURCHISON RANGE The Murchison range was named after the prominent Victorian geologist Sir Roderick Murchison who, with Edward Button and James Sutherland, prospected in these parts. Gold was found in 1870 and, although the source was disappointing and soon petered out, mining of other minerals in the region continued, initially at a low tempo and now on an extensive scale.

Turn left (SP Kremetartboom) 6,7 km from the Leydsdorp turn-off and drive 400 m to a noted baobab tree.

BAOBAB BAR This giant baobab is the only one known to have been used as a bar. In the gold fever days up to 30 parched prospectors used to gather round the tree at the end of a hard day's fossicking in the

sunbaked veld to wet their dusty whistles with the tipple that an enterprising bootlegger dispensed from the hollow trunk.

Continue 3,5 km eastward from the baobab turn-off before crossing the railway. Turn right (SP Gravelotte) 100 m further on and enter Gravelotte after another 400 m.

GRAVELOTTE Antimony and emeralds are now mined where once gold was the magnet that drew prospectors to Gravelotte. The little town is thought to have been named by the Reverend Fritz Reuter, an early Transvaal missionary. As a dragoon Reuter had fought at the Battle of Gravelotte in the Franco-Prussian

War and vowed that if he were spared he would dedicate the rest of his life to the cause of Christianity.

Backtrack 400 m to the last turn and continue westward on the R71, passing on the right the Gravelotte and Alpha shafts of the Johannesburg Consolidated Investment Company and then, 26,1 km from Gravelotte, the left turn to Lydenburg and Letsitele. The Groot Letaba River is crossed 200 m further on and, after the left turn to Letaba Station has been passed 11 km still further, the route again becomes scenic. Turn left back into Danie Joubert Street in Tzaneen 16,7 km from the Letaba Station turn-off.

219. Jacarandas make a colourful splash in a tea plantation near Tzaneen

220. Drinks were once dispensed from the baobab bar near Gravelotte

ANCIENT MINING VILLAGE RESURRECTED

One way into the Kruger National Park is through Phalaborwa where rich mineral deposits, from which Stone Age craftsmen obtained their ore, have been rediscovered and exploited by modern mining engineers.

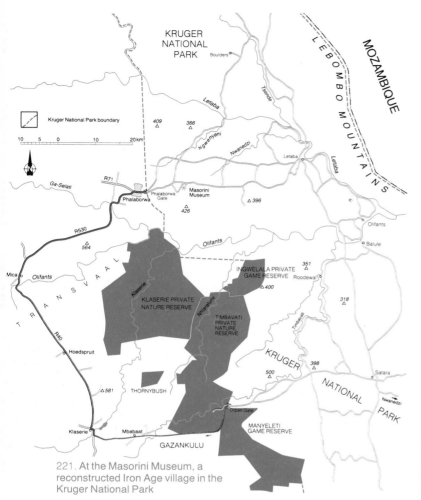

221. At the Masorini Museum, a reconstructed Iron Age village in the Kruger National Park

*The distance given allows approximately 200 km of travelling within the Kruger National Park.

PHALABORWA Many centuries ago, so archaeologists have determined, the Mmakao people of Central Africa, migrating southward, reached the region of the Lowveld below the Drakensberg escarpment where places like Bosbokrand and Acornhoek have since been established. Persecuted by other tribes, they moved on again, this time returning some distance northward to a place they called 'Lule', meaning 'steep hills'. This site was not only more congenial, but turned out to be a rich source of iron and copper for their crafts, for they were metal-workers rather than pastoralists. They were so much more content in their new domain that they came to be known as the 'ba Phalaborwa', the 'people in a place better than the south', and their headquarters assumed the same name. Parts of their ancient workings have been traced deep into the granite hills, two of which, Sealene and Kgopolowe, are in what is now the town of Phalaborwa and have been declared national monuments. Lule – or Loolekop, as the main source of the Mmakaos' raw material came to be known long after their industry came to an end – has now disappeared. In place of the hill there is a vast hole, nearly 1,5 km long and 1 km wide, excavated in the open-cast operations of the Palabora Mining Company which, with a simplified spelling of the name, started one of the world's major copper and metallurgical enterprises here in 1965. This was not the first mining at Phalaborwa in modern times. Prompted by the distinguished geologist Dr Hans Merensky's positive findings on a wealth of minerals in the area, the Transvaal Ore Company opened a vermiculite mine in 1933, while in 1951 the Phosphate Development Corporation (Foskor) was created and now produces all the country's phosphate requirements from a deposit of apatite expected to last several centuries. The founding of Foskor led to the establishment in 1957 of this spacious town which enjoys a year-round summer and almost every conceivable recreational amenity, including an 18-hole golf course on to which antelope, giraffe and even elephant have been known to wander from the adjacent Kruger National Park.

Leave Phalaborwa driving eastward along Palm Avenue from

its intersection with Kiaat Street and crossing straight over (SP Kruger National Park) at the first four-way stop street. Turn left (SP Kruger National Park) 1,7 km from the start right (SP Kruger National Park) on to the R71 300 m further on and reach the Phalaborwa Gate of the Kruger National Park after another 1,4 km.

KRUGER NATIONAL PARK See Tour 78.

From the Phalaborwa Gate any one of various routes – with sidetracks – may be taken to the Orpen Gate via Letaba and Satara, the choice being influenced on any particular day by advice from park officials or reports from other visitors on areas in which game may be concentrated. The route and the time taken over it must be subject to the 40-km/h speed limit in the park, to the opening and closing times of the park gates at the particular time of the year and to the set times between which visitors may travel outside rest camps.

NORTHERN SECTION OF THE KRUGER PARK It is in the mopane vegetation of this the northern section, between the Olifants River in the south and the Limpopo in the north, that most of the Kruger National Park's estimated 7 500 elephant population is concentrated. And it is in this region too that the visitor has a fair chance of spotting some of the rarer species of buck, such as the nyala, tsessebe and eland, as well as roan and sable antelope. Roads that hug the Letaba and Olifants rivers in the south-eastern corner of the zone afford wonderful opportunities for spotting and photographing animals and birds, although the lush vegetation that flourishes along the banks in response to good rain may at times be frustrating. A variation from game-spotting in the south of the northern region is afforded by a visit to the Masorini Museum, a reconstructed Iron Age village 10 km along the road due east of the Phalaborwa Gate. The main rest camp in the southern part of this zone is Letaba, while to the north a small private camp, Boulders, has recently been completed.

LETABA On a bend in the river after which it is named, Letaba is probably the most appealing of all the Kruger National Park's rest camps. At sunset the view of the river from the trees that shade the lawns quite high above the slowly-flowing water is a bonus to add to the 'trophies' the weary visitor may have bagged in a long, tiring and perhaps hot day of concentrated game-spotting. And, with luck, there may be more 'trophies' for the collection when animals come down to the opposite bank for their evening drink. There is also a large pool nearby where hippo and crocodile are regularly seen, and elephant, attracted by the fronds of the ilala palms, have been known to wander into the camp. It is a camp well situated to contrast the northern zone of the park with those of the south. Accommodation for 273 is available at Letaba in 91 rondavels, while there are sites for 20 caravans or tents. It is also a camp that has one of the most attractive restaurants, with a verandah overlooking the river.

BOULDERS The only camp in the park with all buildings on stilts and the only unfenced private camp, Boulders lies about 50 km north-east of the Phalaborwa Gate. Game – especially elephant, buffalo, zebra, impala, giraffe and sable antelope – abounds in the area and may at times be observed at a waterhole about 100 m from the verandah of the main building. The five sleeping huts, with maximum accommodation for 16, are connected to each other and the main building by a covered but open-sided catwalk. Reservations for the camp as a unit can be made no earlier than three months in advance.

CENTRAL SECTION OF THE KRUGER PARK All five of the animals the majority of visitors most wish to see – elephant, lion, rhino, leopard and buffalo – are to be found among the marula, knobthorn and leadwood trees scattered over the grassland of the central section of the Kruger National Park, between the Sabie River in the south and the Olifants River in the north. And, of course, the visitor is likely to see many more of the 122 different mammal, 33 amphibian, 100 reptile and 450 bird species protected in the reserve. The central plains are the habitat of vast herds of antelope, zebra and wildebeest. And where there are zebra and wildebeest there are sure to be lion, this region in fact boasting a greater population of them than any other. The main camps in the central area are Olifants and Satara, and there are smaller ones at Orpen Gate and Balule. Both Nwanedzi and Roodewal, being private camps, have to be reserved as units.

OLIFANTS One of the larger of the park's camps and a recommended base for game-viewing, Olifants is also one of the most beautiful. Situated on a cliff overlooking the Olifants River, it commands a magnificent vista which at times is animated by many species of game that come down to the banks to drink. Amenities include hut accommodation for nearly 300, a filling station and a large central

222. The Olifants River meanders quietly through the Kruger Park

complex housing, among other facilities, the reception office, a shop and a restaurant.

SATARA The lawns and rondavels of Satara, the second biggest camp in the park, are shaded by Natal mahogany and sausage trees as well as the marula and acacia which, with knobthorn, are typical of the trees that dot the surrounding grassland. Birds of many species teem in the vicinity of the camp, and guests are not infrequently excited by animals which arrive to quench their thirst at a waterhole specially dug just outside the fence. A total of 410 visitors can be accommodated here in 158 huts, there is a large self-service restaurant and campers and caravanners have the use of 30 sites.

BALULE For those who prefer to experience the wild in an atmosphere disturbed by no more than the barest facilities for an overnight stay, the small spartan Balule camp, with accommodation for visitors in only five three-bed rustic huts and 10 sites for tents or caravans, is ideal. It has no shop, restaurant, filling station or even reception office, and visitors with reservations check in at Olifants. Situated on the southern bank of the Olifants River, it is reached by a side road off the main route between Letaba and Satara.

ORPEN GATE The Orpen Gate, which has limited accommodation, is named after James Orpen and his wife Eileen who made an invaluable contribution to the cause of wildlife conservation in South Africa. James was involved in the surveying of the Addo Elephant National Park and was at one time a

223. Letaba, one of the most appealing of the Kruger Park's rest camps

member of the National Parks Board, and Eileen presented seven farms totalling 24 338 ha for inclusion in the Kruger Park.

Drive about 7 km southward from the Orpen Gate between the private game reserves of Timbavati on the right and Manyeleti on the left and then about 17 km westward with only Timbavati on the right. Even after passing the Timbavati gate 18,4 km from the Orpen Gate there is still game to be seen. Cross the Timbavati River 26,1 km from the Orpen Gate, pass a left fork to Acornhoek 3,1 km further on and continue another 12 km before turning right on to the R40. After 2 km turn right again (SP Hoedspruit) to remain on the R40 and reach the left turn into Hoedspruit 23,7 km further on.

HOEDSPRUIT Two developments in recent years have made Hoedspruit far more important than it would ever have become as just a railway station whence the subtropical fruit and vegetables grown in the area were despatched along the line between Kaapmuiden and Soekmekaar. One was the completion in 1963 of the branch line to the new mining complex at Phalaborwa, thus turning Hoedspruit into a busy junction, and the other was the selection of a site near the town for the establishment of a major South African Air Force base.

Continue 24 km north-westward from Hoedspruit on the R40 before crossing the Olifants River, pass the left turn to Lydenburg at Mica 3,1 km from the river and after another 5,4 km, where the R40 takes a left turn to Gravelotte, continue straight on to the R530 (SP Phalaborwa). Drive 31 km north-eastward before turning right to remain on the R530 and 2 km further on turn left, still on the R530, to drive another 5 km back into Phalaborwa.

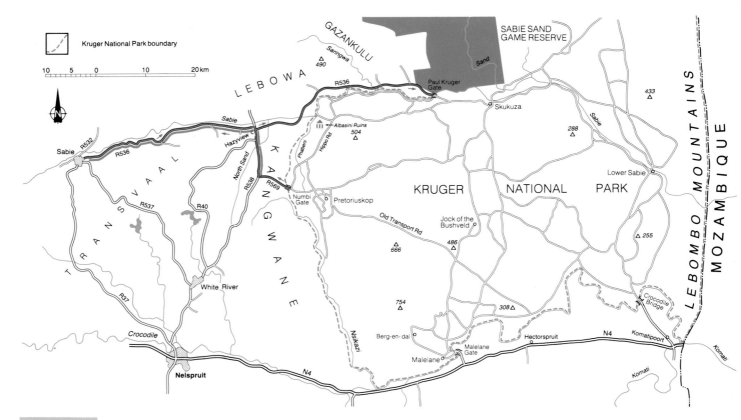

77
350 km*

JOCK'S HAPPY HUNTING GROUND

It was alongside the Old Transport Road in what is now the Kruger National Park that the puppy immortalised by Sir Percy FitzPatrick in *Jock of the Bushveld* was born and had his first hunting lessons.

The distance given allows approximately 200 km of travelling within the Kruger National Park.

SABIE See Tour 82.

Leave Sabie driving eastward on the R536 from the intersection of Market Square and High Street (SP Hazyview). The broad road with an excellent surface runs down the Transvaal Drakensberg escarpment through a soft verdant landscape of ever-changing vistas with oceans of eucalyptus and pine plantations as well as tracts of indigenous vegetation on the mountain slopes. As the road nears the Lowveld the plantations give way to groves of citrus trees, banana palms, other subtropical fruit and fields of tobacco. Turn right (SP White River) on to the R40/R536 44,6 km from the starting point and left (SP Skukuza) on to the R536 at Hazyview 900 m further on. Cross the Sabie River after another 10,8 km and travel for short distances first through KaNgwane and then Gazankulu. Reach the Sabie Crocodile Farm on the left 31,5 km from the Sabie River, recross the river 300 m east of the crocodile farm and drive another 100 m to the Paul Kruger Gate of the Kruger National Park.

KRUGER NATIONAL PARK See Tour 78.

From the Paul Kruger Gate any one of various routes – with sidetracks – may be taken to the Numbi Gate via Skukuza and Pretoriuskop, the choice being influenced on any particular day by advice from park officials or reports from other visitors on areas in which game may be concentrated. The route and the time taken over it must be subject to the 40-km/h speed limit in the park, to the opening and closing times of the park at the particular time of the year and to the set times between which visitors may travel outside rest camps.

SOUTHERN SECTION OF THE KRUGER PARK See Tour 78.

SKUKUZA As the headquarters of the Kruger National Park, Skukuza is fittingly named after Colonel Stevenson-Hamilton, who made it his base from 1902 when he was appointed first warden until he retired in 1946. A variation of uSikhukhuza, meaning 'to scrape clean', it is the name Stevenson-Hamilton was given by his Shangaan workers to describe in a more familiar idiom one 'who sweeps clean'. From a dilapidated blockhouse, built at what was then called Sabie Bridge in the Anglo-Boer War and taken over by the warden, Skukuza has grown into a rest camp of 199 huts with accommodation for 490 visitors, 50 sites for campers and caravanners and, for tours of up to 64 schoolchildren, a four-dormitory complex with its own dining room and separate huts for teachers. Among the amenities at Skukuza

224. An elephant halts the progress of visitors in the Kruger Park

are two restaurants – one of them a former railway dining car on a section of the old Selati line which once ran through Skukuza – and a snack bar, a post office, a bank, a shop with a wide variety of merchandise and curios, an AA repair workshop, a filling station and an airport used daily for flights between the rest camp and Johannesburg. There is also an amphitheatre where wildlife films are screened, but pride of place among Skukuza's amenities is the Stevenson-Hamilton Memorial Library. An imposing gift from the Wildlife Protection Society, the library incorporates reference, museum and photographic sections. As the administrative centre of the park, Skukuza is the base of the park warden, the engineer and the trade manager, and there is housing for many members of the park's staff and their families. For this reason there has been a school at the rest camp for almost 30 years.

Of the drives that can be undertaken from Skukuza into the surrounding bushveld the one most recommended is along the southern bank of the Sabie River to Lower Sabie. The vegetation along the watercourse is the habitat of a wide variety of animals and birds. Hippos and crocodiles may be seen in the water, and more advantageously of course, basking on the sandbanks. This and other drives in the vicinity of Skukuza can result in sightings of lion, elephant, wild dogs, kudu, impala, steenbok, bushbuck, giraffe and occasionally the rare nyala.

PRETORIUSKOP The oldest Kruger National Park rest camp, Pretoriuskop takes its name from the rocky hill to the north-west of it. Here, under a spreading wild fig tree that is still standing, the renowned hunter-turned-conservationist Harry Wolhuter based himself when Major Stevenson-Hamilton appointed him and Gaza Gray assistant game wardens in 1902.

Wolhuter had been making a living as a professional hunter in Swaziland when, with the special assignment of shooting game for the British troops in the Anglo-Boer War, he joined a unit of irregulars designated Steinacker's Horse. Ludwig Steinacker, a cocky, diminutive German who sported a 25-cm waxed handlebar moustache and an extraordinarily dandy uniform of his own design, had come to southern Africa during the European powers' scramble for colonies on the continent. After persuading the British at the outbreak of the war to allow him to raise a small anti-republican force, he recruited 40 swashbucklers who proudly called themselves the Forty Thieves as they galloped through the eastern Transvaal breaking

Boer lines of communication. Though recalcitrant to a degree and scornful of any authority but his own, the little German had been authorised to increase his force to 600 generally less ruffianly men assigned to harass Boer guerillas by the time Wolhuter joined him and to title them respectably Steinacker's Horse. After many squabbles with the authorities Steinacker committed suicide at the outbreak of World War II.

When the Anglo-Boer war was over Wolhuter was faced with the difficult choice between killing or conserving wildlife, but he never regretted accepting Stevenson-Hamilton's invitation to join him as a game ranger – one of the greatest, it has been said. Of the many tales told about him the best known is the one relating how he killed a lion with his knife. He was returning to Pretoriuskop from an anti-poaching patrol near Nwanedzi when his way was barred by two maned lion. There was no time to shoot so he pulled his horse round and put his spurs in, but one of the big cats sprang and the terrified mount, throwing Wolhuter in its efforts to escape the mauling claws and jaws, bolted. The other lion seized the game ranger by his right shoulder and dragged him away on his back with his face buried in the beast's mane and his legs trailing between those of his attacker. Though severely injured and in great pain, he contrived to extricate his knife from a jacket pocket and stabbed the lion fatally, twice in the heart and – as it released him – once in the neck. By the time the first lion returned from its fruitless pursuit of the horse Wolhuter had hauled himself into a tree and belted himself to a branch. The siege was lifted only when the black rangers in Wolhuter's party caught up with him and drove the uninjured lion away. The ranger's survival after having hospital treatment for his dreadful injuries and his return to 43 more years of dedicated duty are regarded as a miracle.

Of great historic interest is the road running south-eastward from Pretoriuskop, known variously as the Oude Wagenweg, Old Transport Road and the Voortrekker Road and pioneered by the transport riders conveying supplies from Delagoa Bay to Barberton or Lydenburg. It was the road on which the young transport rider Percy FitzPatrick was travelling in 1884 when he acquired the puppy that was to become famous as Jock of the Bushveld. Indeed, Jock was born near the hill on the right of the road about 12 km south-east of Pretoriuskop that was known as Ship Mountain, or Skipberg, because it resembles the upturned keel of a ship. And he first showed his mettle both as a devoted companion and as a

225. The caravan site at Skukuza, headquarters of the Kruger National Park

hunting dog as he journeyed with the youthful wagoner who was to become as famous as Jock himself. About 16 km from Ship Mountain and on the left of the road are the Makhuthwanini Hills, which Sir Percy referred to in his book as the Giraffe Kopjes. And it was where the Old Transport Road reached the Crocodile River at Nellmapiusdrif, near Hectorspruit, that the lion-hearted dog and Jim Makokel' had their epic fight with the crocodile. From Pretoriuskop the 20-km Hippo Pool Road runs northward to a pool in the Sabie River to which hippos attract thousands of visitors every year. A 4-km sidetrack to the left of this road leads to the ruins of the homestead built at Makashula's Kraal by the first white man to live in what is now the Kruger National Park, the hunter-trader João Albasini (see Albasini Dam, Tour 73), at a time when he had it in mind to turn all of the Lowveld into a Portuguese colony.

From a ranger's base in 1902 Pretoriuskop has developed into a rest camp with accommodation for 306 in huts and 50 camping and caravan sites. It is an ideal base for visitors in summer when the newborn lambs, foals and calves of the many animal species in the area lend an added dimension to game-spotting. And it is an area crisscrossed by roads from which leopard, cheetah and prides of lion may be seen, as well as elephant, buffalo, giraffe, zebra, wildebeest, several antelope species, including the roan and sable, wild dogs and spotted hyena. White rhino make the Pretoriuskop region of the park

special, however. After hunters had exterminated the species from the park a few specimens obtained from the Umfolozi Game Reserve were quarantined near the camp in 1961 and, with others more recently introduced, have established themselves so well that there are now more than 600 concentrated in the triangle formed by Pretoriuskop, Malelane and Skukuza.

From the Numbi Gate drive 7,2 km westward on the R569 before turning right (SP Hazyview) on to the R538. Pass the left turn to White River on the R40 after 8 km and the right turn to Skukuza 2,5 km further on. Turn left on to the R536 after another 900 m and drive the remaining 44,6 km back to Sabie.

226. One of the plaques that mark the route followed by Jock through the Kruger National Park

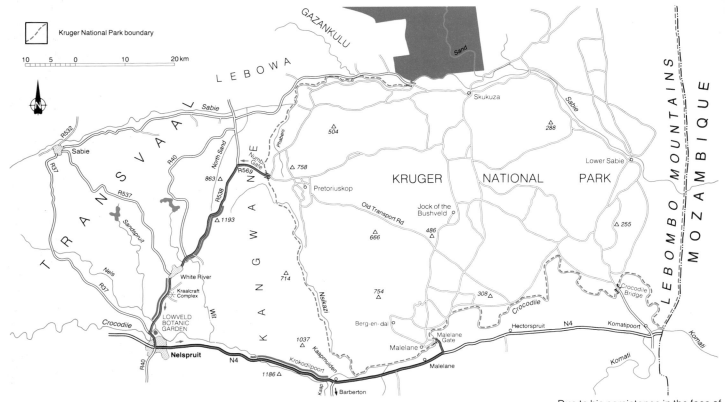

Kruger National Park boundary

78
320 km*

HERITAGE PRESERVED

An hour's drive from Nelspruit is the Kruger National Park, the idea of which was conceived by President Paul Kruger and developed with dedication by James Stevenson-Hamilton.

The distance given allows approximately 200 km of travelling within the Kruger National Park.

NELSPRUIT See Tour 80.

Drive north-eastward along Louis Trichardt Street (N4) from its intersection with Voortrekker Street (SP Komatipoort) and after 500 m fork right (SP Komatipoort) to remain on the N4 and travel past the fascinating humpy mountains and hills of the Krokodilspoort range. The rocky, yet densely vegetated mountains project upwards from the surrounding plain for all the world as though they had simply been dumped there. Running close together, road and rail share with the Crocodile River the beautiful 15-km defile it has worn for itself through the range, starting about 20 km east of Nelspruit. Cross the river 22,4 km from the start of the tour, recross it 14,8 km further on, pass the right turn to Barberton 2 km from the river and reach the left turn into Kaapmuiden after another 300 m.

KAAPMUIDEN The Kaap River, which flows through the broad valley known as De Kaap (see Tour 80), joins the Crocodile River at Kaapmuiden, whose name means 'mouth of the Kaap'. The village is

the centre of a region in which winter vegetables, subtropical fruit and sugar cane are grown on a large scale. British forces blew up the Kaapmuiden bridge on the Boer's important railway link with Delagoa Bay in the Anglo-Boer War, but the burghers were able to put it back into commission before hostilities ended.

Continue 9,5 km eastward on the N4 from Kaapmuiden before crossing one of the colourfully but inexplicably named streams in the area, Jam Tin Creek, into a landscape of cattle ranches and intense agriculture. Pass the left turn into Malelane 9,1 km from Jam Tin Creek.

MALELANE The village on the farm Malelane, which was proclaimed a township as recently as 1949, is another winter vegetable and subtropical fruit centre, and its name is a corruption of 'emlalani', 'the place of the lala palms'.

Turn left (SP Malelane Gate) on to the R570 4,5 km east of the turn-off into Malelane, after 3,2 km reach the bridge over the Crocodile River at a stretch where the reptiles that

227. The rest camp at Berg-en-dal, near the Malelane Gate

account for its name are often seen, and drive another 500 m to the Malelane Gate of the Kruger National Park.

KRUGER NATIONAL PARK In the naming of the most celebrated game reserve in Africa, the authorities were not merely honouring a politician in what has become the customary South African fashion. The reserve in fact owes its existence to the vision of Paul Kruger, President of the Transvaal Republic, and his conviction that a region should be set aside for the conservation of the subcontinent's dwindling wildlife.

Due to his persistence in the face of considerable opposition from his contemporaries, part of the 19 010 sq km which today comprises the Kruger National Park was proclaimed a 'government reserve' in 1898. The Sabie Game Reserve, as the first section of the park was known, lay between the Crocodile and Sabie rivers – a mere quarter of the size of the park in which it is now incorporated – and, as there was no warden, the police at Komatipoort were nominally charged with implementing the law that prohibited the destruction, hunting or wounding of animals in the area. The extermination of wildlife continued, however. It was only in 1902, when it was decided that a strict disciplinarian was needed to halt the destruction, that Major James Stevenson-Hamilton of the 6th (Inniskilling) Dragoon Guards was appointed warden of the Sabie Reserve. But, like Kruger,

he met with bitter hostility. Now it was from men who believed the reserve had been proclaimed to protect its game from black hunters and so ensure more targets for their own weapons. Stevenson-Hamilton's authority was repeatedly flouted until he successfully prosecuted a police officer for poaching. While the conviction demonstrated his resolution and the hunting decreased, antagonism towards him persisted in indirect proportion to his determination, unflagging energy and love of the territory entrusted to him. Part of his struggle was to convince the public of the need for wildlife conservation and of the value of game reserves, a struggle that continued for 24 years. And then, with the support of the Ludorf Commission of 1916; the Transvaal Wildlife Protection Society; the South African Railways administrators who found that passengers regarded the Sabie Reserve as the highlight of tours through the eastern Transvaal; a growing nature-conscious sector of the public; and a sympathetic Press, the concept of a national park was eventually accepted. In 1926 the National Parks Act was passed and the Sabie Game Reserve was renamed, at Stevenson-Hamilton's instigation, the Kruger National Park. The National Parks Board, appointed in terms of the new legislation, immediately initiated plans to open the Kruger Park to the public through the construction of roads, pontoons, bridges and rest camps. In the meantime the park had been augmented in area by the addition of the Shingwedzi region from the Letaba River to the Luvuvhu (Levubu) River, which had been proclaimed a reserve as early as 1904, and by the acquisition in 1925 of the private land between the Sabie and Letaba rivers. It thus stretches 340 km from north to south and an average 60 km from west to east, while a staff of about 3 000 is now employed to see to the welfare of both the wildlife and the visitors. Over the years protection has ensured the balanced proliferation of animal species that had almost been exterminated, while others which had indeed been wiped out have been re-introduced. There are six gates, from Punda Maria in the north to Malelane and Crocodile Bridge in the south; more than 700 km of tarred road and 1 200 km of gravel road from which wildlife may be viewed; and accommodation in 17 rest camps for more than 400 000 visitors a year.

For this tour any one of various routes – with sidetracks – may be taken from the Malelane Gate to the Numbi Gate via Skukuza and Pretoriuskop, the choice being influenced on any particular day by advice from park officials or reports from other visitors on areas in which game may be concentrated. The route and the time taken over it must be subject to the 40-km/h speed limit in the park, to the opening and closing times of the park gates at the particular time of the year and to the set times between which visitors may travel outside rest camps.

SOUTHERN SECTION OF THE KRUGER PARK There are seven rest camps – Berg-en-dal, Crocodile Bridge, Jock of the Bushveld, Lower Sabie, Malelane, Pretoriuskop and Skukuza – between the Crocodile and Sabie rivers, in the southern section of the Kruger Park. Although lion are distributed throughout the park, these magnificent animals are prolific in the area between Crocodile Bridge and Lower Sabie. Wild dogs, which prefer flat country, are often seen north-west of Malelane, and the southern section is also the principal habitat of the square-lipped (white) rhino and the black rhino, although the latter also roam the central region. Apart from these animals, the species as likely to be seen in the south as in the central and northern parts include cheetah, spotted hyena, African buffalo, hippopotamus, impala, bushbuck, nyala, waterbuck, sable antelope, kudu, Burchell's zebra, blue wildebeest, giraffe, warthog and the chacma baboon. And while elephant are most abundant towards the north, a few may also be spotted in the southern region.

BERG-EN-DAL Some 11 km from the Malelane Gate the Berg-en-dal rest camp, though new, is expected to become one of the most popular in the Kruger National Park. One of its principal attractions is the fine view it commands of the Matjulu stream, and of several dams where animals come to drink. In addition to 69 three-bed chalets, 18 family cottages, seven guest houses and 70 sites for tents or caravans, Berg-en-dal has many amenities, including a restaurant, shops, an information bureau and a swimming pool.

CROCODILE BRIDGE There are 20 huts and 12 camping sites at the Crocodile Bridge, in the vicinity of which impala, kudu, giraffe, zebra, wildebeest and warthog abound, although lion, cheetah and buffalo may also be seen.

JOCK OF THE BUSHVELD At the end of a 3-km side road 30 km from the Malelane Gate on the way to Skukuza, the Jock of the Bushveld camp lies in a delightfully tranquil setting at the confluence of the Mitomeni and Mbyamiti rivers. The roaring of lions, which are rarely absent from the area, contributes to the chorus of the wild heard in the

228. Buffalo in the Kruger National Park

229. One of the beasts visitors to the Kruger Park most hope to see

camp after nightfall. When its sponsors – like others who, by virtue of having donated private camps to the National Parks Board, enjoy preferential booking – are not in occupation the public has access to the Jock of the Bushveld camp, but the accommodation for a maximum of 12 people in three cottages can be reserved no earlier than three months in advance.

LOWER SABIE With 96 huts in which 220 people can be accommodated, as well as 27 sites for campers or caravanners, shady Lower Sabie, on the bank of the Sabie River in one of the best game-viewing regions of the park, is among the bigger rest camps.

MALELANE is a private camp which has luxury huts and must be reserved as a whole for parties of up to 19. The animals that may be seen in the vicinity include lion, cheetah, impala, kudu, giraffe, zebra, wildebeest, rhino, buffalo, wild dogs and the ubiquitous warthog.

PRETORIUSKOP See Tour 77.

SKUKUZA See Tour 77.

From the Numbi Gate drive 7,2 km westward on the R569 before turning left (SP White River) on to the R538. Turn left (SP White River) on to the R40 18,1 km further on, cross the Wit River after another 1,1 km and enter Theo Kleynhans Street in White River 1,2 km further still. Turn right into Kruger Park Street (SP Nelspruit) after 300 m.

WHITE RIVER See Tour 82.

Drive southward along Kruger Park Street (R40) from its intersection in White River with Theo Kleynhans Street, pass the right turn to Sabie on the R537 2,6 km from the intersection and the Kraalkraft Curio and Crocodile Ranch complex (see Tour 82) after another 4,1 km. Cross the Nels River 7,6 km further on, the Crocodile River 2,6 km from the Nels and, after another 2,6 km, pass the Andrew Street entrance to Nelspruit at the first traffic lights on the outskirts of the town. Turn left into Nelspruit at the second traffic lights 500 m further on.

PICTURESQUE ENCLAVE

The kingdom of Swaziland, an enclave between South Africa and Mozambique, is one of the world's smallest sovereign states, its colourful, friendly people numbering just over half a million.

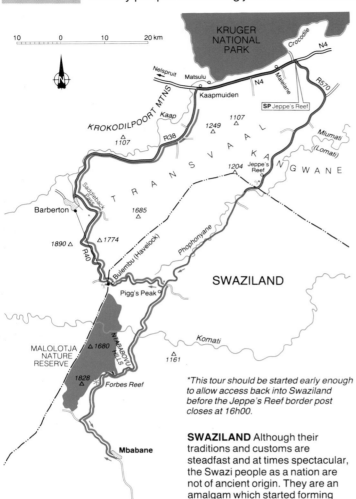

This tour should be started early enough to allow access back into Swaziland before the Jeppe's Reef border post closes at 16h00.

SWAZILAND Although their traditions and customs are steadfast and at times spectacular, the Swazi people as a nation are not of ancient origin. They are an amalgam which started forming towards the end of the eighteenth century around a nucleus of Nguni migrants from Central Africa who had gradually worked their way to Mozambique and then trekked inland to settle in the south of what is now Swaziland. The nucleus was to become the Nkosi-Dlamini, the ruling clan, which absorbed smaller neighbouring groups and extended its domain. Under the wise leadership of Sobhuza I, the third ruler in the new country, the Baka Sobhuza, 'people of Sobhuza', were able to keep the mighty Zulu *impis* of Shaka at bay. But it was his son, Mswazi, who from 1840 built up a mighty army, subjugated yet more clans than his predecessors had done and consolidated the authority of the Dlamini. Territorial boundaries were extended even further under Mswazi's rule and the people now known as the Baka Mswazi he forged into the nation which has retained his name. As Ngwenyama – 'the Lion', to use the name given to the paramount chief – Mswazi was succeeded in 1875 by Mbandzeni. The influx of a cosmopolitan crowd of foreigners in search of trade, grazing, game and gold led to the granting by Mbandzeni of such a multitude of land and mineral rights as well as every conceivable type of monopolistic concession that the Swazis lost much of their own country. After the Transvaal Republic had lost the administrative control it had assumed over Swaziland at the end of the Anglo-Boer War and the country had become a British High Commission territory, it still took years to prise from the concessionaires most of the land that had been 'bartered' away. Swaziland remained a British High Commission territory until independence was achieved in 1967 with the Ngwenyama, Sobhuza II, as king and head of state. One of the most viable territories in southern Africa, Swaziland has fertile land, adequate rainfall, a temperate climate and various mineral resources. Its major agricultural products include sugar, maize, cotton, tobacco, pineapples, groundnuts, vegetables, citrus fruit, rice and subtropical fruit. Southern Africa's biggest recorded bunch of bananas (55 kg) was grown in the Pigg's Peak area in 1973. Dairy farming and cattle ranching are also pursued, while intensive afforestation makes possible the export of timber products, including wood pulp. The minerals exploited include asbestos, iron, coal and tin.

MBABANE Town planning was certainly not a feature of the development of the straggling capital of Swaziland, but this probably contributes to the appeal of busy Mbabane in its delightful hilly setting at the edge of wooded mountains. It was in these mountains that the earliest of the Swazi people settled, and it was on the north bank of the Mbabane River that in 1887 Michael Wells – probably a veteran of some British military campaign, since he is sometimes referred to as Bombardier Wells – opened the store that provided a nucleus for the town. Like most centres in the country, Mbabane has a Swazi market, usually a bustling forum where citizens who are not preoccupied with efforts to sell handcrafted goods and souvenirs to visitors bargain with each other over a variety of wares, particularly fruit and vegetables. For anyone spending time in Mbabane a truly worthwhile experience is a visit to the enchanting Mlilwane Wildlife Sanctuary, one of Swaziland's major tourist assets. It is reached by a sideroad to the right about 16 km south of the capital on the main road to Manzini.

MLILWANE WILDLIFE SANCTUARY The Mlilwane Wildlife Sanctuary is on the slopes of the escarpment overlooking the beautiful valley known as Ezulwini, 'place of heaven'. It was established on his own farm by Ted Reilly, a former game ranger, and opened to the public in 1964 at a time when much of the country's wildlife had disappeared. The species that had survived on the farm have been joined by many others – including white rhino, hippo and giraffe – that have been re-introduced since the farm became a reserve. The area has been increased to more than 4 500 ha and indigenous trees and grass have been allowed to obliterate the unsightly environmental damage caused in the past by the mining of tin. Among the other animals in the park are buffalo, wildebeest, warthog, sable, eland, kudu and impala, but the sanctuary is particularly noted for the variety and abundance of its birdlife. There are chalets and a restaurant in a rustic rest camp overlooking a hippo pool, and horses are provided for those who prefer riding to driving. Of interest to many visitors are a collection of thousands of poachers' snares removed from the sanctuary and another Swazi reserve, and the Gilbert Reynolds Memorial Garden of aloes.

From the fountain at the lower end of Allister Miller Street in Mbabane head westward away from Warner Street and curve southward around the Swazi Market before turning right (SP Ermelo) on to the Mbabane bypass after 300 m. Turn right (SP Pigg's Peak, Bulembu) after 15,7 km and drive 18,1 km to the entrance to the Malolotja Nature Reserve on the left.

MALOLOTJA NATURE RESERVE The magnificent scenery of such regions as the Komati River Gorge,

230. Pots and Swazi hats for sale at the market in Mbabane

the valley of the Mahulungwe River with its waterfalls, potholes and tree ferns, the imposing 1 680-m Silotfwane Mountain and the valley of the Mhlangampepa River is as much of a feature of the Malolotja Nature Reserve as its wide variety of animal species. The reserve, which is administered by the Swaziland National Trust Commission, harbours more than 150 bird species, as well as several species of flora unique to the region, including the Barberton, woolly and Kaapsehoop cycads. It takes its name from one of seven waterfalls within its boundary, the Malolotja Falls which, at 90 m, are the highest in Swaziland. Of historical note are several abandoned mines, such as at Forbes Reef, where gold was found in modern times, and at Mount Ngwenya, where – according to carbon dating – iron ore was mined in the era of Neanderthal Man 42 000 years ago. The Ngwenya mines are indeed the oldest yet discovered in the world and of profound archaeological significance. There is accommodation at Malolotja in attractive log cabins and at camping and caravan sites. The reserve has a limited road system and is geared primarily to walkers and backpackers.

From Malolotja continue north-eastward, at first between rolling green hills with rocky tops and then down through the Ntababovu Hills into the deep Komati River valley, where the scenery is majestic. Cross the Komati River 15,2 km from Malolotja, climb the other side of the valley and reach the Swazi Bank in the main street at Pigg's Peak 16,5 km from the river.

PIGG'S PEAK William Pigg, who discovered the Devil's Reef while prospecting for gold in 1884, gave his name to the little town that developed near his find. Pigg's Peak was a gold-mining centre for some considerable time but, once the reef was exhausted, forestry became of primary importance and the region is blanketed with the plantations of Peak Timbers.

Turn left (SP Havelock, Barberton) 600 m from the Swazi Bank and drive 17,4 km up hill and down dale to Havelock (Bulembu) through vast tracks of Peak Timbers plantations on a gravel road which is fair in fine weather. Here and there openings in the afforestation permit splendid views of the mountainous landscape.

HAVELOCK Though officially now designated Bulembu, this town is still most generally known by its old name, Havelock. The private mining village in its lofty setting of mountain splendour owes its existence to the

discovery of extensive deposits of chrysotile here in the 1920s and the consequent development of one of the world's five biggest asbestos mines. Because the only access was by way of a rough meandering track quite unsuitable for conventional transport, the mining company constructed a spectacular 20,2-km cableway running directly, but for a single 4° deflection at Angle Station, its highest point, over mountains and valleys to Barberton. The cables, which at one place conduct the 224 ore-conveying gondolas at a height of 186 m above the ground and at others so low across the road that it seems as if one could stretch out and touch them, are suspended from 52 pylons and 11 stations, the longest free span being 1 206 m between two mountain ridges. The cableway ascends 473 m from Havelock to its highest point and then descends 634 m to Barberton.

Fork right 1,4 km from the Havelock Mine on an extremely rough gravel road that meanders steeply upwards for 2 km to Swaziland's Bulembu border post. The South African border post 500 m further on is Josefsdal. Fork right (SP Barberton) on the R40 1,9 km from the Josefsdal gate. The pleasure of being permitted to travel at 100 km/h after being limited in Swaziland to 80 km/h is tempered by the condition of the road which in places makes any speed over 30 km/h hazardous. But the scenery, with the imaginatively-named Maid of the Mist peaking at 1 890 m on the left, is wonderful, and there is the added interest of the cable cars crossing and recrossing above the meandering road. The road becomes tarred 29,5 km from Josefsdal and descends through the Saddleback Pass into the Kaap Valley. Turn left (SP Barberton) on to the R38 9,4 km from the beginning of the tar and turn right (SP Nelspruit, Johannesburg) into Bland Street in Barberton 2,1 km further on.

BARBERTON See Tour 80.

Return to the R38/R40 intersection and head northward (SP Kaapmuiden) on the R38 for a scenic drive through typical Bushveld vegetation interspersed with groves of papayas, mangoes and other subtropical fruit. There are none of the ubiquitous 'spruits' along this stretch of road, only 'creeks' and evocative place names like Caledonian, Fig Tree Creek, Joe's Luck, Revolver Creek, Handsup, Honeybird Creek and Sheba which bear testimony to the origins and characters of those who

231. Part of the cableway between Havelock and Barberton

once fossicked around in the area in search of gold. Turn right (SP Malelane) on to the N4 49,8 km from the R38/R40 intersection and pass the left turn to Kaapmuiden 300 m further on.

KAAPMUIDEN See Tour 78.

From the Kaapmuiden turn-off continue on the N4, passing after 18,7 km the left turn to Malelane and after another 4,6 km the left turn to the Malelane Gate of the Kruger National Park. Turn right (SP Jeppe's Reef) on to the R570 100 m further on, cross the KaNgwane border after another 26,9 km and reach the South African side of the Swaziland border at Jeppe's Reef 14,9 km from the KaNgwane border. The Swazi side of the

border post is 300 m ahead. Cross the Lomati River 3 km from the Swazi border post and drive up the beautiful Phophonyane River valley where the Bushveld is patched with maize fields which eventually give way to the vast eucalyptus and pine afforestation that covers many of Swaziland's mountain slopes. Pass the right turn to Havelock and Barberton 36,8 km from the Lomati River, reach the Swazi Bank in Pigg's Peak after another 600 m and continue 16,4 km through magnificent mountain scenery again as the road winds deep down to the Komati River. Climb back up the Ntababovu Hills, turn left (SP Mbabane, Manzini) 33,3 km from the Komati River and left again (SP Town Centre) into Mbabane 15,3 km further on.

232. Mineworkers' dwellings at Havelock

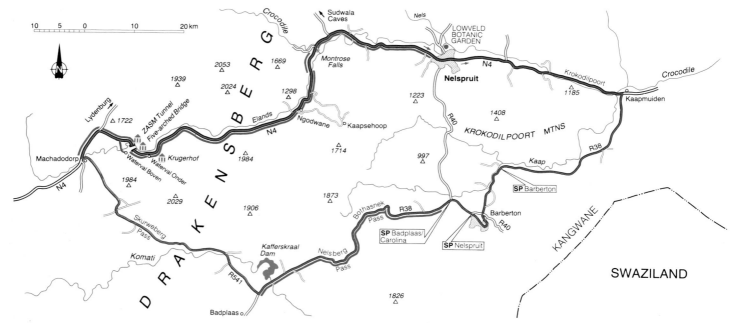

EVOCATIVE AND BEAUTIFUL

80
320 km

The beauty and romance of De Kaap, where South Africa's first significant gold discoveries were made in modern times, and relics of the 'Oosterlyn' between Mozambique and Pretoria are features of a tour from Nelspruit.

233. The facade of the Transvaal's first stock exchange, in Barberton

NELSPRUIT Cascades was its name when Sir Percy FitzPatrick, politician, pioneer of the fruit industry and author of *Jock of the Bushveld*, rented the farm on which Nelspruit developed on the bank of the Crocodile River. And he chose the name because of the Crocodile Falls (Nelspruit Cascades) which are reached at the end of a short walk through the lovely Lowveld Botanic Garden – a regional division of the National Botanic Gardens – on the northern outskirts of the town. The farm was bought in 1890 by the brothers Gert, Andries and Louis Nel and a village came to life here the following year when the

'Oosterlyn' being laid from Delagoa Bay by the Nederlandsche Zuid-Afrikaansche Spoorweg-Maatskappij reached it. The station was named after the Nels, as was the Nels River which flows into the Crocodile River just north of the town. After President Kruger had retreated from Pretoria towards the end of the Anglo-Boer War the village of Nelspruit became the seat of the Transvaal Government for a time. Since then it has developed into an attractive, well-planned town under a cloak of multi-hued bougainvillea, flamboyants, jacarandas and acacias, with wide boulevard-like streets and an imposing Spanish-style town hall. It is the industrial centre of the Lowveld and the hub of a region of

intensive agriculture producing citrus and subtropical fruit, tobacco, vegetables and groundnuts.

Drive north-eastward along Louis Trichardt Street from its intersection with Voortrekker Street (SP Komatipoort) on to the N4 and fork right after 500 m to remain on the N4 for a scenic drive through the Krokodilspoort range. Cross the Crocodile River 22,4 km from the start of the tour, recross it 14,8 km further on and after another 2 km turn right (SP Barberton) on to the R38. The road runs through typical Bushveld vegetation – which in parts has been cleared for groves of subtropical fruit – and into the valley known as De Kaap.

DE KAAP Although the remains of ancient workings bear testimony to the recovery of gold in southern Africa from time immemorial, the first significant mining – as opposed to panning – for the precious metal in recent times was in the valley through which the Kaap River runs. At first it was indeed alluvial gold that was found at the western end of the valley – known as the Duiwelskantoor, or Devil's Office, because of its bizarre rock formations – but with the unwavering optimism of their breed the early prospectors, who were reminded of the Cape of Good Hope by the scenery that surrounded them, named the valley Kaapsche Hoop. Today where once a mining commissioner's office, two banks, other commercial buildings and government offices stood at

what is now Kaapsehoop, there is only a hamlet with a police station, post office, hotel and two shops.

Continue through De Kaap Valley on the R38, passing long-abandoned places with such evocative names as Caledonian, Fig Tree Creek, Eureka (now, with its ruins, the mere ghost of a once prosperous mining town), Joe's Luck, Revolver Creek, Handsup, Honeybird Creek and Sheba. Cross the railway 38,8 km after joining the R38, fork left (SP Barberton) immediately afterwards and drive 14,3 km before forking right into De Villiers Street in Barberton.

BARBERTON Among the early prospectors in De Kaap was Graham Barber who reported a rich gold-bearing reef on 21 June 1884. He and his cousins, Harry and Fred Barber, were visited three days later by the mining commissioner, David Wilson, who proclaimed their camp a township and named it Barberton. New reefs were subsequently reported almost daily and the rush of fortune-seekers from all over the world was given even greater impetus when Edwin Bray found the fabulously rich Sheba Reef in 1885 and started the once-famous Bray's Golden Quarry. Barberton mushroomed as tin shanties, shops and scores of canteens sprang up to meet the diggers' needs. Within two years, when the town's first post office was opened, its first newspaper, *The Barberton Herald*, was launched, and the Transvaal's first stock exchange started dealing here, the population of 20 000 was greater than that of any other Transvaal town. The façade of the Kaap Gold Fields Stock Exchange Ltd is preserved as a national monument, as is the 1887 Globe Tavern, one of Barberton's many early hostelries and a fine example of the type of building erected extensively on the eastern Transvaal goldfields in the late nineteenth century. In Coronation Park, other reminders of the pioneering days are a Class 6 locomotive used on the run between Kaapmuiden and Barberton, and the huge fig tree under which President Kruger conferred with a deputation of miners in 1887 and made his first speech in English. FitzPatrick Park, where there is a statue of Jock of the Bushveld, recalls the role Sir Percy played in the development of what is now an enchanting garden town with only memories of the romance of gold. Once the treasure of the Witwatersrand had been discovered, Barberton represented to most of the miners – in parlance they might have used – no more than a flash in the pan, and within three years of the Barbers' find the exodus to Johannesburg was as frenetic as the influx had been, although a few companies retained their confidence in De Kaap and continued mining successfully for a long time.

From the intersection of De Villiers and General streets, at the Barberton Town Hall, drive northward along General Street, which continues as Voortrekker Street (R38/R40), and 3,5 km after crossing the railway line turn left (SP Nelspruit) to remain on the R38/R40. After another 3,6 km turn left again (SP Badplaas, Carolina) on the R38 where it separates from the R40 and drive through rolling grassland,dotted with trees. Start the ascent of the Bothasnek Pass about 13 km from the division of the R38 and R40 and reach the top about 8 km further on. Eucalyptus plantations tend to obscure the scenery, but a viewpoint over a grand vista to the north is reached about 26 km from the R38/R40 division. About 10 km further on start the descent of the Nelsberg (Nelshoogte) Pass into the valley of the Komati River, where the scenery changes to expanses of grassland with patches of maize and other crops. Cross the Komati River 54 km from the R38/R40 division, turn right (SP Machado-dorp) on to the R541 3,5 km from the river, ascend the scenic Skurweberg Pass and 30,1 km after joining the R541 observe two former South African Railways sleeper cars, now privately owned, in a most improbable mountain setting on the right of the road. Drive another 20,7 km to the entrance to Machadodorp and turn right into Generaal Smit Street 200 m further on.

MACHADODORP, which is noted principally for the reputed therapeutic value of its sulphur springs, takes its name from

Joaquim José Machado who made a major contribution to the construction of the railway between Delagoa Bay and Pretoria. The line was opened in 1894 and, although the village was proclaimed only 10 years later, it was one of the places which became the temporary seat in 1900 of the Transvaal Government after President Kruger retreated from Pretoria. Thanks, so it is said, to a vigilant railway conductor, there is good trout water in the surrounding countryside. Noticing when his train reached Machadodorp on an occasion in 1910 that fingerlings consigned to a more distant destination were about to expire, the railwayman released them into the Elands River which flows past the town. Anglers have been catching the offspring of the fish since 1914.

Turn right (SP Nelspruit) on to the N4 1,2 km from the turn into Generaal Smit Street, pass the left turn to Lydenburg after 6,5 km and turn right off the N4 4,7 km further on. Cross the Elands River into Waterval Boven after 1,3 km.

WATERVAL BOVEN One of the few South African place names that have been permitted to survive in the original Dutch form is Waterval Boven, a name given by the

engineers of the Nederlandsche Zuid-Afrikaansche Spoorweg-Maatsskappij to the station above the waterfall here in the Elands River when the 'Oosterlyn' they were building reached the spot in 1894. Because trains from Mozambique had to negotiate a gradient of 1:20 between Waterval Onder, a few kilometres to the east, and Waterval Boven a rack-railway line was constructed over this sector. It included a steep, curved tunnel, the ZASM Tunnel (NM), and the graceful five-arched bridge known as the Vyfboogbrug (NM) over the Dwaalheuwelspruit. For some time after the railway was diverted over a longer, easier gradient, the ZASM Tunnel carried road traffic, but it is now disused. At the Waterval Boven station a short piece of rack rail and one of the innumerable boulders that had to be manhandled out of the bed of the permanent way serve as a monument to the men who died of fever, drunken fights and accidents during the project – at the rate of one for every sleeper laid, some say.

Return from Waterval Boven to the N4, turn right (SP Nelspruit) and, after driving through a more modern road tunnel, reach the old ZASM Tunnel parking area on the left 4 km further on. Drive 1,2 km

234. The 'Vyfboogbrug' over the Dwaalheuwelspruit

beyond the tunnel parking area to find another place to park and follow a path downward to the tall, dressed-stone Vyfboogbrug over the pretty Dwaalheuwelspruit tumbling to its confluence with the Elands River. Continue on the N4 and turn right into Waterval Onder 3,3 km further on.

WATERVAL ONDER Unlike Waterval Boven, Waterval Onder, an important railhead below the Elands River Falls during the construction of the 'Oosterlyn', has not retained the original Dutch form of its name – Waterval Beneden. Tucked away in a charming glade in the little town is Krugerhof (NM), the last official residence of President Kruger, who stayed there from July to August 1900 before going into exile in Europe.

Return to the N4 from Waterval Onder and turn right (SP Nelspruit) for a scenic drive back to Nelspruit down the Elands River valley, passing several roadside stalls where fresh trout are offered for sale, and a huge paper mill at Ngodwane 34 km from Waterval Onder. The Elands River has to be crossed several times before the Crocodile River is crossed in the Montrose Pass 17,5 km from the paper mill. A short distance from the river a sidetrack leads to an hotel, chalets and camping and caravan sites near the Montrose Falls, a 3-minute walk away through the forest. Pass the left turn to the Sudwala Caves (see Tour 82) 4,7 km after crossing the Crocodile River, recross the river 5,7 km further on, cross the R40 into Nelspruit 20,9 km from the river and turn left into Kruger Street after another 800 m.

235. Krugerhof in Waterval Onder, the last official residence of President Kruger before he went into exile

VOORTREKKER TOWNS AND DRAKENSBERG PASSES

Magnificent scenery, towns that were once Voortrekker outspans, and mountain gateways, including the famous Long Tom Pass, are features of a drive from Nelspruit through the Transvaal Drakensberg.

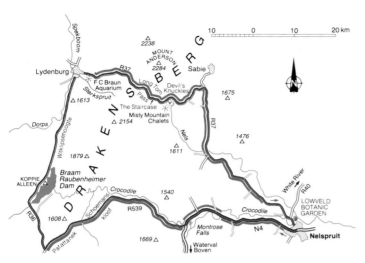

NELSPRUIT See Tour 80.

Drive westward along Voortrekker Street from its intersection with Louis Trichardt Street on to the N4, cross the R40 1,1 km from the intersection and drive between many tidy orchards in the Crocodile River valley. Pass the left turn to Kaapsehoop 19,1 km from the R40, cross the Crocodile River 1,7 km further on and pass the right turn to the Sudwala Caves (see Tour 82) after another 5,8 km. Recross the Crocodile River – where there is an hotel, chalets and camping and caravan sites near the Montrose Falls – 4,6 km further on and turn right (SP Bambi) on to the R539 400 m from the river. The tree-lined route now winds through the splendid scenery of Schoemanskloof.

236. Lydenburg's Voortrekker Church was built in 1853

SCHOEMANSKLOOF This lovely, fertile valley, in which citrus fruit and grain are cultivated, runs through the foothills of the Transvaal Drakensberg for about 30 km and ends in Patattanek (or Skaap-wagters Pass), entailing a 900-m climb into the higher part of the range. The kloof, to which Highveld sheep farmers bring their stock for winter grazing, is named after the Schoeman families who were allocated farms here in 1848.

Turn right (SP Lydenburg) on to the R36 46,8 km after joining the R539, make a short descent through the Chomsehoogte Pass back into the valley of the Crocodile River and pass the right turn to the Braam Raubenheimer Dam 10,4 km after joining the R36. Being relatively new, this dam has yet to acquire a measure of appeal although it is in imposing mountainous surroundings. Cross the Crocodile

River again 2,3 km further on and by way of Witklipsehoogte ascend from the valley to a wide plain of well-husbanded farmland. Reach the intersection of Viljoen and Voortrekker streets in the centre of Lydenburg 37,5 km from the Crocodile River.

LYDENBURG In his determination to distance himself and his followers as far as possible from the sphere of British influence, Andries Hendrik Potgieter left Potchefstroom for the eastern Transvaal in 1845 and founded Andries-Ohrigstad, named after himself and an Amsterdam merchant, Georgius Gerhardus Ohrig, whose sympathies lay with the Voortrekkers. Four years later so many of the settlers had died of malaria that the town was abandoned and the Voortrekkers found a healthier locality higher in the Drakensberg, where the Dorps River and the Sterkspruit join to form the Spekboom River. After all their previous tribulation they named the new settlement Lydenburg, 'town of suffering'. Theirs was the third Dutch Reformed congregation to be formed in the Transvaal, and their first church (NM), built between 1851 and 1853, is the oldest still standing north of the Cape. The restored building, at the corner of Church and Kantoor streets, is now a museum. Across the road is the Voortrekker School (NM), a simple thatched building in the architectural style of the Transvaal pioneers, where the congregation worshipped before the church was complete. It is probably the oldest surviving schoolhouse in the Transvaal. The kiaat pulpit in Lydenburg's second Dutch Reformed church, which was consecrated in 1894, is a replica of the beautiful pulpit in the Stellenbosch Moederkerk. Standing back from Viljoen Street, near its intersection with Voortrekker Street, is the Lydenburg Kruithuis (NM) which recalls two conflicts: the first between the British authorities in the Transvaal and the Bapedi under Chief Sekhukhune; and the second between the British and the Transvaal Republic in 1880. After Sekhukhune was subdued at the end of 1879 the 94th Regiment under Lieutenant-Colonel Philip Anstruther was left in Lydenburg to police the troubled area, and when he and most of his force were summoned to relieve Pretoria the following year 22-year-old Second-Lieutenant W H Long took over the Lydenburg base. Long strengthened his position by

building Fort Mary just outside the town, naming it after his wife. When the war between the British and the Boers ended the fort was abandoned and in 1883 the stone of which it was constructed was used to build this magazine in Viljoen Street. The names of troops of the '94th' are engraved on some of the stone. The town was the capital of 'De Republiek Lijdenburg in Zuid-Afrika', which seceded from the Transvaal in 1856 as a result of the dispute between the then leader of the burghers here, Commandant Stefanus Schoeman, and the President of the Transvaal, Marthinus Wessel Pretorius. The Lydenburg Republic merged with the Republic of Utrecht in 1857 and the combination rejoined the Transvaal Republic in 1860. Alluvial gold was found in the district in 1875 and a short drive out of town northward from Viljoen Street leads to claims that are still being worked as well as the remains of abandoned diggings. Rich platinum deposits in the region have been exploited more recently, but Lydenburg is mainly an agricultural centre, the products of the district being grain, lucerne, wool, tobacco, citrus fruit, cotton, groundnuts, subtropical fruit and more soya beans than are grown in the rest of South Africa.

Drive south-eastward along Voortrekker Street from its intersection with Viljoen Street (SP Sabie, Kruger National Park) on to the R37 and reach the entrance to the F C Braun Aquarium on the right 1,6 km further on.

F C BRAUN AQUARIUM In 1903, on his own initiative, a German-born jeweller of Lydenburg named F C Braun started stocking the swift-flowing mountain streams in the region with trout obtained from hatcheries in the Cape. His ichthyological spadework led to the establishment here alongside the Sterkspruit of the Transvaal Provincial Administration hatchery and aquarium, which in 1961 were named in Braun's honour. There are more than 60 species of indigenous and tropical fish in the aquarium.

From the aquarium the road ascends through magnificent scenery still higher into the Transvaal Drakensberg by way of Masjiennek, the Visierkerf and the Long Tom Pass, the summit of which is reached 18,7 km from the aquarium.

LONG TOM PASS One of the most splendid scenic highways in the country, the Long Tom Pass in the southern shadow of the 2 284-m Mount Anderson, highest peak in the Transvaal Drakensberg, ascends 670 m in 20 km from

The Old Harbour Road can be seen 3,4 km beyond the summit and The Staircase, near which a Long Tom shellhole has been preserved, 100 m further on. Drive 11,4 km beyond the summit of the pass to reach the right turn to the Misty Mountain Chalets on the site of the Old Trading Post. This was one of the links in the chain of stations at which the enterprising João Albasini (see Albasini Dam, Tour 73) bartered beads and cloth for ivory, skins and possibly gold. After another 2,5 km reach the site of the last emplacement, on the Devil's Knuckles, of the Long Toms and 300 m further on reach a viewpoint over a wonderful Lowveld panorama. Turn right (SP Nelspruit), remaining on the R37, 12,5 km from the viewpoint, and cross the Nels River after another 20,3 km. Pass a right turn to Sudwala 300 m from the river, a left turn to White River 12,5 km further on and drive another 17 km – the last 10 of which are along an avenue of African flame trees that are a blaze of colour in summer – before turning right (SP Nelspruit) on to the R37/R40. After 300 m cross the Crocodile River, pass the left turn to the Lowveld regional garden of the National Botanic Gardens 1,4 km further on and pass the first set of traffic lights at Andrews Street on the outskirts of Nelspruit after another 1,1 km. Turn left into Voortrekker Street at the second set 600 m further on.

238. A replica of one of the four Long Toms used against the British in the Anglo-Boer War stands in position in the Long Tom Pass

Lydenburg to its summit at 2 150 m above sea level, one of the highest points reached on a major road in South Africa. The road then drops a spectacular 1 000 m in 18 km towards Sabie. The original transport riders' road through the pass is thought to have been constructed in 1871 by Abraham Espag, and the modern highway with easier gradients follows his route fairly closely over the Visierkerf, which means the notch in the backsight of a rifle; over Blystaanhoogte; then the Devil's Knuckles; and finally Koffiehoogte, where it is believed travellers usually stopped to rest their animals and make coffee for themselves. The route was both difficult and perilous for wagoners who had to coax their spans up or down appalling gradients. They drove them over and round the Devil's Knuckles projecting upwards from the narrow ridge connecting the eastern and western parts of the escarpment; negotiated The Staircase and Die Geut ('gutter'), whose names aptly reflect their nature; and invariably were forced to a standstill at Blystaanhoogte, 'the heights where one is left standing'. At least one wagon and its oxen are known to have thundered to destruction below. At different places off the road there are signs that early Portuguese adventurers prospected for gold up here. Parts of the 'Old Harbour Road', as the transport riders' track to Delagoa Bay was known, can be seen here and there, but particularly well at a point 3,4 km east of the top of the pass. The name of the pass is taken from the two 155-mm Creusot fieldpieces, the well-known 'Long Toms', which went into action against the British for the last time in the Anglo-Boer War at the Devil's

237. A modern road has replaced the arduous route through Long Tom Pass

Knuckles. Although the Transvaal Government had bought four of these siege cannon – each of which was capable of hurling a 42,6 kg shell 9 km – for the defence of Pretoria, the Boer forces used them only in the field. After taking Lydenburg on 7 September 1900 General Redvers Buller pursued the Boers, led by General Louis Botha, eastward over the Drakensberg escarpment. To cover the retreat of his men through the pass Botha used the two 7-ton Long Toms they

had laboriously dragged up the mountain, the last emplacement being at the Devil's Knuckles. A replica of one of them now mounted on the site is aimed at The Staircase down which the Tommies advanced in their pursuit. The British had made every effort in the past to eliminate the formidable Long Toms, and the Boers, equally determined that they should not fall into their enemy's hands, destroyed all four when the last of their ammunition had been used.

GOLD, A CAVERNOUS REFUGE, AND PREHISTORY

The forested Drakensberg slopes where some of South Africa's first profitable gold discoveries were made in modern times, the Sudwala Caves and the Owen Museum's prehistoric replicas ensure a day of variety.

SABIE Long before there was any permanent settlement here on the banks of the Sabie River, and before the discovery of gold had brought a flurry of activity to the area, hunters and explorers used to camp at what was then known as 'Sabielala', meaning 'Sabie, the resting place'. And in its splendid setting at the foot of mighty Mount Anderson it certainly is an idyllic place to rest. The first title deed at Sabielala was granted in 1846 to D J Badenhorst who, with two brothers, established the farm Grootfontijn and later sold it to P de Villiers. In 1871 Tom McLachlan and two other prospectors – some records name James Sutherland and Edward Button while others mention G R Parsons and J L Valentine – found gold on the farm Hendriksdal, south of the 1 675-m Spitskop which, in turn, is 8 km south of present-day Sabie. Their discovery and an even richer source on the slopes of Spitskop itself led to the proclamation of diggings in 1873 and the inevitable gold rush. Thomas Henry Glynn, who came to the area in search of game and gold in 1880, bought Grootfontijn and in 1895 discovered his own reef at the falls on the farm, a deposit that was exploited by the Glynn Lydenburg Mine from 1897 to 1950. Glynn, the 'Squire of Sabie', was the prime mover in having the mining camp that developed proclaimed a town. The demand created by the mines for props led to the forestry which has now superseded the recovery of gold as

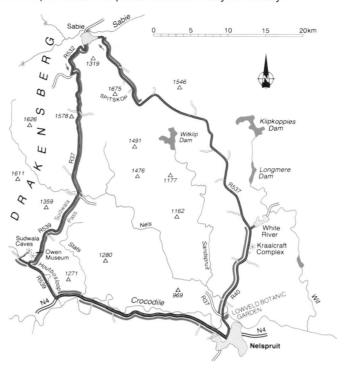

the area's major industry. Joseph Brook Shires established the first eucalyptus plantation in 1876, Transvaal Gold Mining Estates followed in 1904 with 150 ha of *Eucalyptus resinifera* and black wattle, and the vast Graskop Plantation was started by the Department of Forestry two years later. Now the mountain slopes for miles around are covered with plantations as well as large tracts of

indigenous forest. The Sabie Forestry Museum in the centre of town, which houses a fascinating display of exhibits illustrating the development of the industry, is well worth a visit.

Drive southward along High Street from its intersection with Market Square on to the R532 and after 9,1 km turn left (SP Nelspruit) on to the R37. Cross the Nels River

20,3 km further on, turn right (SP Sudwala) on to the R539 300 m from the river and drive through the Sudwala Pass before turning right (SP Sudwala Caves) at a T-junction 16,2 km from the R37. Turn right again (SP Sudwala Caves) 1,2 km further on and drive 2,2 km up a steep concrete road to the entrance to the caves and the adjacent Owen Museum, a park of sculptured prehistoric animals.

SUDWALA CAVES Tucked away in dense vegetation on the slopes of Mankelekele, which forms part of the eastern wall of the Houtbosloop valley, is the entrance to one of the most extensive and fascinating cave complexes in the world. Visitors are conducted on a 600-m tour lasting 90 minutes among wonderful dripstone formations known as speleothems, many of which are illuminated by spotlights. The formations have such fanciful names as the 'Screaming Monster', the 'Devil's Pulpit', 'Lot's Wife', the 'Fairy Glen', 'Little Red Riding Hood and the Wolf', the 'Weeping Madonna', the 'Jeweller's Shop' and the 'Space Rocket', which is more than 11 m tall and 7 m in circumference. A six-hour tour to the Crystal Chamber is conducted by arrangement on Saturdays, but even this does not reach the limit of the cave system, which is believed by some people to be many kilometres away from the entrance. Speleologists have penetrated to a distance of 2 500 m and discovered a chamber 90 m long and 45 m wide which contains magnificent many-hued stalagmites and stalactites. The main chamber, which is included in the tours, is the

239. Forestry workers' cottages in dense vegetation near Sabie

P R Owen Hall, named after the farmer who opened the caves on his property to the public in 1964. This chamber has a dolomite dome 37 m high over an area 67 m in diameter and has such excellent acoustics that it has been used for musical recordings. Natural ventilation in the form of a current of cool, fresh air from some as yet undiscovered source maintains a constant year-round temperature of 17 °C in the caves. From time immemorial men have used the Sudwala Caves as a fastness, the last major group of refugees having been led by Somcuba, brother of Sobhuza I, King of the Swazis. On the death of Sobhuza his wife, LaZidze, assumed the regency and in association with Somcuba and another of the king's brothers, Malambule, ruled the Swazis on behalf of her minor son, Mswazi. Mswazi came of age in 1840 and, having built up a mighty army with the aid of his mother, drove Somcuba and his followers out of his kingdom. Somcuba's people built a 'city' of their own in the Houtbosloop valley and retreated into the caves whenever they were harassed by Mswazi's *impis* attempting to retrieve cattle with which the exiles had decamped. For three weeks on one such occasion the pursuers tried to smoke the fugitives out of their bolt hole and traces of the fire in the entrance to the caves can still be seen. The siege was lifted by the Lydenburg Commando, which was favourably disposed to Somcuba, but in a subsequent surprise attack he and most of his followers were massacred. Leadership of the survivors who stayed on in the vicinity was assumed by one of Somcuba's *indunas*, Sudwala, who gave his name to the caves. The exiled Swazi regent is commemorated by Somcuba's Gong – a formation projecting downward in the entrance to one of the passages – which, when struck, resounds through the caverns.

OWEN MUSEUM The open-air Owen Museum, dedicated to the man who founded it on his farm and opened the Sudwala Caves to the public, is said to be the biggest and most scientifically accurate in the world. The park's lifesize replicas of prehistoric creatures, some of which are enormous, were executed in ferro-asbestos-cement by the distinguished animal sculptor Jan Theron van Zyl, who designed the black wildebeest on the reverse of South Africa's 2-cent piece and the springbok on the R1 coin. His work was based on diligent research in natural history museums all over the world, in which he was assisted by Dr André Keyser, chief of the Palaeontological Division of the Department of Mines. His

240. The Sudwala Caves were once a bolt-hole for Swazi dissidents

accurately-coloured recreations of beasts that held sway over the earth during the 140 million years of the Mesozoic Era, which ended about 65 million years ago, stand in natural surroundings landscaped by Philip Owen. With his brother Theo, Philip took over the management of the caves and the park from their father.

Return 3,4 km to the T-junction mentioned in the last route directions and continue straight over on to the R539. Turn left (SP Nelspruit) on to the N4 after 6,8 km, cross the Crocodile River 5,7 km further on and reach the traffic lights at the intersection of the N4 and the R40 in Nelspruit 20,9 km from the river.

NELSPRUIT See Tour 80.

Leave Nelspruit from the N4/R40 intersection, heading northward (SP White River) on the R37/R40. Pass the right turn to the Lowveld Botanic Garden after 1,2 km, cross the Crocodile River 1,7 km further on and continue on the R40 where the R37 goes left to Sabie. Reach the Kraalcraft Complex, an African handicraft centre and a crocodile ranch, 10,5 km from the river. At the T-junction 4,1 km from the complex carry straight on into White River.

WHITE RIVER The area around the picturesque town of White River – the name deriving from 'emanzimhlope', or 'white waters', as the river flowing by was called – was settled by white farmers in the 1880s and in 1904 became the centre of the White River Settlement, a smallholding scheme initiated by Lord Milner for veterans of the Anglo-Boer War. The settlement failed because the holdings, planted with citrus trees, were too small to be viable. Most of the plots were sold to a private company which rejuvenated the land and made a success of farming with subtropical as well as citrus fruit. The town is a picture in summer when the many flowering trees that line the streets are in blossom.

Return to the last T-junction on the outskirts of White River, turn right (SP Sabie) on to the R537 and after 34 km pass on the left the 1 675-m Spitskop where the first gold discovery in the vicinity of Sabie was made in 1871. Turn left (SP Sabie) 44,5 km after joining the R537 and reach the starting point at Market Square in Sabie 500 m further on.

241. Massospondylus, largest of the life-size replicas at the Owen Museum

83
250 km

PANORAMA ROUTE HIGHLIGHTS

Beautiful waterfalls, the incomparable Blyde River Canyon, caves occupied by men for 50 000 years and a national monument comprising an entire mining village are among the highlights of part of the Panorama Route.

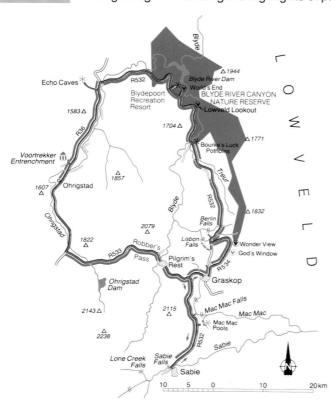

SABIE See Tour 82.

Drive northward along Sabie's Main Street from its intersection with 10th Avenue on to the R532, pass the left turn to Lone Creek Falls after 800 m and cross the Sabie River 200 m further on. After another 200 m pass the left turn to the Sabie Waterfall, which is 100 m off the R532 on the town commonage.

Turn right (SP Mac Mac Pools) 10,1 km further on and drive 1,1 km on gravel to the pools.

MAC MAC POOLS This series of stepped natural swimming pools on a tributary of the Mac Mac River was once the centre of hectic gold-mining activity. In 1873 the prospector Tom McLachlan bought the farm Geelhoutboom through

which the stream flows and immediately found gold on it. Other diggers who started arriving found the metal in all the other streams on the farm and by 1884 it was an important goldfield with more than a thousand fortune-seekers. The gold has long been exhausted at Mac Mac and forestry has become the major local activity.

Return to the R532 and after 1,9 km turn right to the Mac Mac Falls parking area, from which steps lead down to a viewing site.

MAC MAC FALLS The Mac Mac Falls, which present a splendid sight as the Mac Mac River plunges 56 m into a densely-wooded chasm, was divided into two separate streams by diggers in their search for gold. The streams reunite before reaching the pool below.

From the falls continue 4,1 km northward to reach a plaque recording that Jock of the Bushveld, the dog immortalised by Sir Percy FitzPatrick, passed this way in 1885. There is a beautiful glade laid out for picnickers 600 m beyond the plaque. After 7,7 km fork right (SP Graskop) on to the R532, which now runs on to a plateau of rolling grassland, and 3,1 km further on reach a natural bridge where a pretty brook flows under an arch of rock tucked into thick undergrowth. Enter Graskop, 'Window to the Eastern Transvaal', 800 m further on.

GRASKOP, magnificently situated on the Drakensberg escarpment above Kowyn's Pass, was

established in the 1880s on the farm owned by Native Commissioner Abel Erasmus near the kraal of Kowyn, chief of the Bakwena. Erasmus, who was known to the Bakwena as 'Dubula Duze', 'the man who shoots at close range', gave his name to the pass on the road between Ohrigstad and Hoedspruit. Originally a gold-mining settlement, Graskop is now another major forestry centre, although deposits of manganese, asbestos and phosphates also contribute to its economy.

Turn left into High Street (R532) at the stop street 1,1 km from the Graskop boundary sign, right into Louis Trichardt Avenue after another 200 m, left (SP Blyde River Canyon, Blydepoort) 600 m further on, and right (SP God's Window) on to the R534 after 1,8 km. Drive 2,7 km to one of several viewing sites on this section of the Transvaal Drakensberg, the most celebrated of which is God's Window 1,7 km still further.

GOD'S WINDOW, a gap in the Drakensberg escarpment, presents an unforgettable panorama of the Lowveld and the Kruger National Park in the east, the forest-clad mountains in the west and the Blyde River Canyon in the north. From the parking area footpaths lead to several wonderful vantage points.

Continue 1,3 km north-eastward on the R534 to reach Wonder View, a site from which there is another spectacular panorama. Turn right (SP Blyderiviierspoort) back on to the R532 6,9 km further on, left (SP Berlin Waterfall) on to gravel after another 1,2 km and left again (same SP) 1,8 km still further to drive 300 m to the falls. Because the loop on the R534 to the east of the R532 has been taken, the Lisbon Falls, one of the most beautiful of the many cascades in the area, will have been missed. It can still be reached before continuing northward to the Blyde River Canyon by travelling about 2 km south from the Berlin Falls turn-off, turning right and driving another 2 km.

BERLIN FALLS After forcing its way through a narrow gully the Berlin Creek plunges 47,8 m in a lovely fall to a deep dark pool, a spectacle well worth the deviation.

Return from the Berlin Falls to the R532, turn left (SP Bourke's Luck), after 17,6 km pass a memorial to the Voortrekker leaders Louis Trichardt and Hendrik Potgieter who passed this way, and cross the Treur River 3,9 km further on.

242. The view from God's Window at the edge of the Drakensberg escarpment

TREUR RIVER Leaving the main body of his Voortrekker party camped at the river here in 1884, Andries Hendrik Potgieter undertook a journey with a handful of men to Delagoa Bay. After a long wait those left behind assumed the explorers had perished and, in their grief, named the river the Treur ('sorrow') before moving on.

Recross the Treur River 2,7 km further on, pass the South African Defence Force Dog Centre 900 m from the river, and a left turn to Pilgrim's Rest after another 300 m. Cross the Blyde River 500 m still further.

BLYDE RIVER When the Potgieter party of Voortrekkers reached this river they were overtaken by their leader and his companions, all safe though late in their return from Mozambique. To mark their relief they named it the Blyde River ('river of joy').

Turn right (SP Bourke's Luck Potholes) 600 m after crossing the Blyde River and drive 400 m to the visitors' centre at the potholes, where there is a permanent exhibition of the fauna, flora and cultural history of the Blyde River Canyon Nature Reserve.

BOURKE'S LUCK POTHOLES The Bourke's Luck Potholes – optimistically but ironically named after Tom Bourke whose nearby claim was unproductive although he predicted correctly that gold would be found in the vicinity – are situated in a gorge at the confluence of the Treur and Blyde rivers. The deep, cylindrical potholes have been scoured out over millions of years by sand and stones swirled round by the water. From the potholes the Blyde River starts its rapid northerly descent through the mighty canyon it has created.

Continue 9 km on the R532 along the western brink of the Blyde River Canyon to the Lowveld Lookout, another viewing site. Turn right after another 4,7 km and drive 2,9 km to World's End, from which there is a splendid view of the Three Rondavels across the deep, narrow valley.

BLYDE RIVER CANYON Unsurpassed by scenic splendour of its kind anywhere in Africa, the Blyde River Canyon – in places 700 m deep – was formed as the plunging river from which it takes its name gouged its way more than 1 000 m downwards over a distance of only 20 km through the Drakensberg escarpment to the Lowveld. While the Lowveld is hot and dry, precipitation from moisture-laden air blown in from the Indian Ocean ensures cool, misty conditions over the escarpment where the rainfall may be as high as

2 000 mm a year. And the rain nourishes the dense indigenous forest which clads the slopes above the tortuous curves of the river. The canyon is the focal point of the 22 667-ha Blyde River Canyon Nature Reserve with its walks, hiking trails and bridle paths through vegetation that teems with birdlife. Among other amenities, there are chalets, camping sites, restaurants and sporting facilities at the F H Odendaal Camp on the western shore of the Blyde River Dam and at the Sybrand van Niekerk Camp on the northern shore.

From the World's End turn-off continue 2,5 km northward on the R532 to the Blydepoort Recreation Resort on the right. After veering away from the canyon turn left (SP Ohrigstad) on to the R36 21,3 km further on. Turn right (SP Echo Caves) off the R36 1,2 km further on and reach the caves after another 4,3 km.

ECHO CAVES Implement finds have shown that the Echo Caves (NM) were occupied by man from the Middle Stone Age to more recent times. They were opened to the public in 1924 by A J Claasen after he had bought the farm on which they are situated. He also started the Museum of Man, an open-air display of archaeological and palaeontological exhibits near the caves. Six chambers extending over about 200 m of the total series are open to visitors, who will hear the echo effect responsible for the name when tour guides tap certain stalactites.

Return to the R36 from the caves and turn right (SP Ohrigstad). Turn right again (SP Voortrekker Entrenchment) after another 19,2 km and right once more (SP Voortrekker Laager) 200 m further on to drive yet another 200 m to the old fortification.

VOORTREKKER ENTRENCH-MENT A mud-and-stone wall which formed part of fortifications built here by the Ohrigstad Voortrekkers is protected from vandals and the elements by an unprepossessing mesh-wire fence and iron roof. Outside the adjacent Andries Potgieter Hall is a monument commemorating the 'Voortrekkers who lived, laboured and died here', and buried below it is a chest which is to be opened in 2038.

Reach Ohrigstad 3,3 km south of the turn-off to the fortification.

OHRIGSTAD Malaria had caused so many deaths within four years of the founding of Andries-Ohrigstad in 1845 that Andries Potgieter's party abandoned the settlement, moved to a healthier region 40 km

243. Carvings on a rock face near the Echo Caves

to the south and named the new place Lydenburg (see Tour 81). Ohrigstad, which had lost the first part of its name even before it was evacuated, was re-established only in 1923 after considerable control of the malaria-bearing mosquito had been achieved. It is now the centre of an irrigated area producing tobacco, wheat and citrus fruit.

Continue through Ohrigstad on the R36 and after 18,9 km turn left (SP Pilgrim's Rest) on to the R533. Drive through beautiful mountain scenery including Robber's Pass, the summit of which is reached 18,1 km after leaving the R36.

ROBBER'S PASS In spite of all the gold produced, only two robberies occurred in the first 30 years of the history of Pilgrim's Rest. In the first incident two masked and mounted highwaymen held up the bi-weekly Lydenburg-bound coach at what is now called Robber's Pass and made off with £10 000 worth of bullion that was never seen again. The second robbery was a ham-handed operation by the Pilgrim's Rest barber-turned-laundryman, Tommy Dennison, who in 1912 used his own well-known horse to imitate the earlier crime, went straight back to town with his loot, embarked on a spending spree, spent five years in the Pretoria Central Prison for his trouble and returned unrepentant to Pilgrim's Rest to open a business which he had the audacity to call The Highwayman's Garage.

Turn right (SP Pilgrim's Rest) on the R533 8,5 km from the pass summit and cross the Pilgrim's Creek into Pilgrim's Rest by way of the dressed-stone Joubert Bridge (NM) which was built in 1897.

PILGRIM'S REST When the Mac Mac goldfield became too crowded for a loner like Alec Patterson, he packed his few belongings into the vehicle that had earned him the nickname Wheelbarrow Alec and trundled it off over the mountains into the next most westerly valley

where he found his eldorado in September 1873. His isolation was short-lived, however. Along came William Trafford, who struck it rich in the same stream and is fancifully believed to have originated the name of the town that was to develop by yelling: 'The pilgrim is at rest!' More probably, though, the town was named after 'The Pilgrims' from Pietermaritzburg, one of the earliest expeditions to reach the area. While Patterson was determined to keep his find secret as long as possible, Trafford reported his immediately and within days the valley was swarming with diggers – including such characters as The Bosun, French Bob, Sailor Harry, German George, Charlie the Reefer, Wally the Soldier, Black Sam, Spanish Joe, Yorkie, Bismarck, American Knox, Artful Joe and Yankee Dan – who, almost without exception, found not only alluvial gold but nuggets in Pilgrim's Creek. So beset by concession-hunters did the Transvaal Volksraad become that in 1881 the government properties on which the goldfields lay were ceded to London financier David Benjamin in return for £1 000 a year or 2,5 percent on all stones and metal found. The diggers departed and Benjamin floated the Transvaal Gold Exploration Company (TGME), one of the few outside the Witwatersrand whose shareholders were to be satisfied with its output. The Theta, Clewer, Ponieskrantz, Jubilee and Beta mines were opened and produced some £20 million worth of gold before the source petered out. Although the last TGME mine here was closed in 1971, Pilgrim's Rest has not become a ghost town. The entire village has been proclaimed a national monument and restoration of much that survives from the early days is continuing.

Continue south-eastward on the R533 and fork right (SP Sabie) on to the R532 after 8,6 km. Cross the Sabie River into Main Street in Sabie about 24 km further on and drive 1 km to the start of the tour.

244. Mac Mac Falls

INDEX

Page numbers in bold refer to main entries; page numbers in italics indicate illustrations.